History, Biography, and the Genre of Luke-Acts

Biblical Interpretation Series

VOLUME 177

The titles published in this series are listed at *brill.com/bins*

History, Biography, and the Genre of Luke-Acts

An Exploration of Literary Divergence in Greek Narrative Discourse

By

Andrew W. Pitts

BRILL

LEIDEN | BOSTON

Library of Congress Cataloging-in-Publication Data

Names: Pitts, Andrew W., author.
Title: History, biography, and the genre of Luke-Acts : an exploration of literary divergence in Greek narrative discourse / by Andrew W. Pitts.
Description: Leiden ; Boston : Brill, 2019. | Series: Biblical interpretation series, ISSN 0928-0731 ; volume 177 | Includes bibliographical references and index.
Identifiers: LCCN 2019017889 | ISBN 9789004406537 (hardback : alk. paper)
Subjects: LCSH: Bible. Luke—Criticism, interpretation, etc. | Bible. Acts—Criticism, interpretation, etc.
Classification: LCC BS2589 .P58 2019 | DDC 226.4/066—dc23
LC record available at https://lccn.loc.gov/2019017889

Typeface for the Latin, Greek, and Cyrillic scripts: "Brill". See and download: brill.com/brill-typeface.

ISSN 0928-0731
ISBN 978-90-04-40653-7 (hardback)
ISBN 978-90-04-40654-4 (e-book)

This book is printed on acid-free paper and produced in a sustainable manner.

"One who has unreliable friends soon comes to ruin, but there is a friend who sticks closer than a brother."—Proverbs 18:24

To my best friends, Dr. Alexandra Nukta and Dr. Drew Wegner,
both of whom have stood by my side through thick and through thin,
inspiring me to complete this work and many more beyond.

∵

Contents

Acknowledgements

This book is an expansion of ideas that I began to develop in the context of my dissertation, and which first found fruition in a 2015 SBL paper for which I was awarded the Paul J. Achtemeier prize for New Testament scholarship. So, to begin with, I would like to thank the Society of Biblical Literature for the recognition of my work, as it provided the impetus for the current book. The comments of the two respondents to my Achtemeier paper, Richard Burridge and Greg Sterling, were strategic in refining and shaping my argument into a book-length treatment. Burridge's insistence that I look more closely at literary theory, in particular, dramatically influenced the direction that this book would ultimately take. Although I end up ultimately disagreeing with Burridge, he has been a helpful dialogue partner at several turns in my journey with genre. I would also like to thank Arizona Christian University and Ed Clavell for allowing me the time to work on this project. A number of other individuals helped in refining my ideas along the way as well. First, my mentor, Stanley Porter, was extremely influential on many aspects of this work, sharpening it in countless ways. My colleague and friend Sean Adams also provided very helpful feedback on the pre-publication version of the manuscript. Paul Anderson, editor of the Biblical Interpretation Series, improved the quality of the work in many ways through his insightful comments and suggestions on the path to publication. I am grateful not only for Paul's contribution to the book, but also for his gracious decision to publish it in the Biblical Interpretation Series. Finally, I wish to thank Theo Joppe at Brill, for his editorial patience and gracious spirit in the copy editing process.

Tables and Figures

Tables

Figures

Abbreviations

AB Anchor Bible
ABRL The Anchor Bible Reference Library
ACNT Augsburg Commentary on the New Testament
AGAJU Arbeiten zur Geschichte des antiken Judentums und des Urchristentums
AJP *American Journal of Philology*
AJT *American Journal of Theology*
AnBib Analecta biblica
AJSL *American Journal of Semitic Languages and Literature*
AJSR *Association for Jewish Studies Review*
ANRW *Aufstieg und Niedergang der römischen Welt: Geschichte und Kultur Roms im Spiegel der neueren Forschung.* Edited by H. Temporini and W. Haase. Berlin, 1972–
APAMS American Philological Association: Monograph Series
APB *Acta Patristica et Byzantina*
ARCA ARCA, Classical and Medieval Texts, Papers, and Monographs
BBB Bonner biblische Beiträge
BCAW Blackwell Companions to the Ancient World
BCP Biblical and Comparative Perspectives
BECNT Baker Exegetical Commentary on the New Testament
BETL Bibliotheca Ephemeridum theologicarum Lovaniensium
BHT Beiträge zur historischen Theologie
BIAC *Bulletin of the Institute for Antiquity and Christianity*
BIOSCS *Bulletin of the International Organization for Septuagint and Cognate Studies*
BIS Biblical Interpretation Series
BL Biblical Languages
BMI The Bible and its Modern Interpreters
BO Biblica et orientalia
BWA(N)T Beiträge zur Wissenschaft vom Alten (und Neuen) Testament
BZNW Beihefte zur Zeitschrift für die neutestamentliche Wissenschaft
CA *Classical Antiquity*
CBC Cambridge Bible Commentary
CBQ *Catholic Biblical Quarterly*
CBR *Currents in Biblical Research*
CBSC The Cambridge Bible for Schools and Colleges
CDA Collection d'Études Anciennes
CGTSC Cambridge Greek Testament for Schools and Colleges

CILT	Current Issues in Linguistic Theory
CL	*Christianity and Literature*
ClaW	*The Classical World*
CM	Christianity in the Making
COQG	Christian Origins and the Question of God
CP	*Classical Philology*
CQ	*Classical Quarterly*
CRINT	Compendia rerum iudaicarum ad Novum Testamentum
CSCT	Columbia Studies in the Classical Tradition
CW	*The Classical Weekly*
EBib	Etudes bibliques
ECHC	Early Christianity in its Hellenistic Context
ESEC	Emory Studies in Early Christianity
ECSSH	St. Edmund's College Series of Scripture Handbooks
ESHM	European Seminar in Historical Methodology
EvT	*Evangelische Theologie*
GR	Greece and Rome
FF	Foundations and Facets
FRLANT	Forschungen zur Religion und Literatur des Alten und Neuen Testaments
HCS	Hellenistic Culture and Society
HDAC	Histoire des doctrines de L'antiquité classique
HE	Historia, Einzelschriften
Hermeneeia	Hermeneia—A Critical and Historical Commentary on the Bible
Historia	*Historia: Zeitschrift für Alte Geschichte*
HT	*History and Theory*
HTKNT	Herders theologischer Kommentar zum Neuen Testament
HTR	*Harvard Theological Review*
HZ	*Historiche Zeitschrift*
Interp	*Interpretation*
ISBL	Indiana Studies in Biblical Literature
JBL	*Journal of Biblical Literature*
JGRChJ	*Journal of Greco-Roman Christianity and Judaism*
JHS	*Journal of Hellenic Studies*
JJS	*Journal of Jewish Studies*
JLrSM	Junua linguarum Series major
JLSM	Janua linguarum Series minor
JR	*Journal of Religion*
JRS	*Journal of Roman Studies*
JSJSup	Journal for the Study of Judaism Supplement
JSNT	*Journal for the Study of the New Testament*

JSNTSup	Journal for the Study of the New Testament: Supplement Series
JSOTSup	Journal for the Study of the Old Testament: Supplement Series
JSPSup	Journal for the Study of the Pseudepigrapha: Supplement Series
JPTSup	Journal of Pentecostal Theology: Supplement Series
JTS	*Journal of Theological Studies*
JQR	*Jewish Quarterly Review*
KEHNT	Kurzgefasstes exegetisches Handbuch zum Neuen Testament
LBS	Linguistic Biblical Studies
LC	Literature and Culture
LEC	Library of Early Christianity
LHBS	Library of Hebrew Bible/Old Testament Studies
LNTS	Library of New Testament Studies
LSTS	Library of Second Temple Studies
MAARSup	Memoirs of the American Academy in Rome. Supplements
MBCB	Mnemosyne Bibliotheca Classica Batava
MH	*Museum Helveticum*
MHUC	Monographs of the Hebrew Union College
NAC	New American Commentary
Neot	*Neotestamentica*
NICNT	New International Commentary on the New Testament
NIGTC	New International Greek Testament Commentary
NovTSup	Supplements to Novum Testamentum
NTD	Das Neue Testament Deutsch
NTM	New Testament Monographs
NTS	*New Testament Studies*
NTSI	New Testament and the Scriptures of Israel
ÖBS	Österreichische biblische Studien
OCM	Oxford Classical Monographs
OTP	James H. Charlesworth, *The Old Testament Pseudepigrapha*. 2 Vols. ABRL. New Haven: Yale University Press, 1985.
PAST	Pauline Studies
PL	*Philosophy and Literature*
PWRE	August Friedrich von Pauly, *Paulys Realencyclopädie der classichen Altertumswissenschaft*. New Edition begun by Georg Wissowa. Stuttgart: J.B. Metzler, 1890–
RBL	*Review of Biblical Literature*
RevExp	*Review and Expositor*
RNTS	Reading the New Testament Series
RRJ	*Review of Rabbinic Judaism*
RRTCA	*Revista de Retórica y Teoría de la Comunicación Año*

SB	Sources bibliques
SBG	Studies in Biblical Greek
SBLDS	Society of Biblical Literature Dissertation Series
SBLMS	Society of Biblical Literature Monograph Series
SBLSP	*Society of Biblical Literature Seminar Papers*
SBT	Studies in Biblical Theology
Sch	Sources chrétiennes
SCS	Septuagint Commentary Series
SCSt	Septuagint and Cognate Studies
SH	Studia Hellenistica
SJ	Studies in Judaism
SM	Studies and Monographs
SNT	Studien zum Neuen Testament
SNTG	Studies in New Testament Greek
SNTSMS	Society of New Testament Studies Monograph Series
SPhilo	*Studia philonica*
SS	Semeia Studies
SPHS	Scholars Press Homage Series
SSEJC	Studies in Scripture in Early Judaism and Christianity
STDJ	*Studies on the Texts of the Desert of Judah*
STP	Studies in Theoretical Psycholinguistics
StPB	Studia post-biblica
StudNeot	Studia neotestamentica
SUNT	Studien zur Umwelt des Neuen Testaments
SVTP	Studia in Veteris Testamenti pseudepigrapha
SwJT	*Southwestern Journal of Theology*
SymSBL	Symposium series [Society of Biblical Literature]
TAPA	*Transactions of the American Philological Association*
TCSup	Trends in Classics. Supplementary volumes
TENTS	Texts and Editions for New Testament Studies
TL	Trends in Linguistics
TNTC	Tyndale New Testament Commentary
TS	*Theological Studies*
TSAJ	Texte und Studien zum antiken Judentum
TTCABS	T&T Clark Approaches to Biblical Studies
TUGAL	Texte und Untersuchungen zur Geschichte der altchristlichen Literatur
WBC	Word Biblical Commentary
WUNT	Wissenschaftliche Untersuchungen zum Neuen Testament
YCS	*Yale Classical Studies*

CHAPTER 1

Genre and Method in Luke-Acts Research

The question of which genre the author of Luke-Acts selected as the medium for his composition continues to fuel discussion among New Testament scholars. Since the significant work of Henry Cadbury,[1] many scholars have viewed Luke and Acts as a two-volume collection, especially on the basis of the historical profile of the preface form found in the Gospel (Luke 1:1–4) and its recapitulatory link in Acts 1:1. This has become a significant factor for those desiring to affirm Luke as history since it seems more suitable to maintain a unified genre for both volumes.[2] Since scholars often identify Acts as history,[3] they should do so for Luke as well—or, so the argument goes.[4]

This analysis has not gone uncontested, however. In addition to questioning the literary unity of Luke and Acts, contemporary New Testament scholars have now put a range of potential literary antecedents for the genre(s) of Luke-Acts on offer. In the vein of scholars like C.W. Votaw, Charles Talbert, Philip Shuler, Albrecht Dihle, Richard Burridge, and Justin Smith,[5] many adopt a

1 Henry J. Cadbury, *The Making of Luke-Acts* (London: S.P.C.K., 1968).

2 Cf. S.E. Porter, "The Genre of Acts and the Ethics of Discourse," in *Acts and Ethics*, edited by Thomas E. Phillips (NTM 9; Sheffield: Sheffield Phoenix, 2005), 1–15.

3 Thomas E. Phillips, "The Genre of Acts: Moving toward a Consensus?" *CBR* 4 (2006) 365–96 (384–85) argues for consensus that views Acts as some form of history; for a more recent review of Luke-Acts as history, see Sean A. Adams, *The Genre of Acts and Collected Biography* (SNTSMS 156; Cambridge: Cambridge University, 2013), 5–23.

4 David Aune, *The New Testament and its Literary Environment* (LEC 8; Philadelphia, 1987), 77. Charles Talbert, *Literary Patterns, Theological Themes, and the Genre of Luke-Acts* (Missoula: Scholars, 1987), moves in the opposite direction. Committed to the biographical nature of the Third Gospel, Talbert insists that both Luke and Acts are intellectual biography. See also, Loveday Alexander, "Acts and Ancient Intellectual Biography," in *Acts in its Ancient Literary Context: A Classicist Looks at the Acts of the Apostles*, by Loveday Alexander (ECC; LNTS 289; New York: T&T Clark, 2005 [orig. 1993]), 43–68. 31–63. Most recently, Adams, *Genre of Acts*—for similar reasons—identifies Luke-Acts as collected biography.

5 C.W. Votaw, 'The Gospels and Contemporary Biographies', *AJT* 19 (1915): 45–73, 217–49; C.H. Talbert, *What Is a Gospel?: The Genre of the Canonical Gospels* (London: S.P.C.K., 1978); P.L. Shuler, *A Genre for the Gospels: The Biographical Character of Matthew* (Philadelphia: Fortress, 1982); Albrecht Dihle, 'Die Evangelien und die biographischen Traditionen der Antike', *ZTK* 80 (1983): 33–49; R.A. Burridge, *What are the Gospels? A Comparison with Graeco-Roman Biography* (3rd 25th Anniversary Editition; Waco, Tex.: Baylor University Press, 2018 [org. Cambridge, 1992]) (I cite the third edition unless otherwise noted); J.M. Smith, *Why βίος?: On the Relationship between Gospel Genre and Implied Audience* (LNTS 518; London: T&T Clark, 2015).

 | DOI:10.1163/9789004406544_002

biographical thesis for the genre of the Third Gospel. In recent years, Stanley Porter, Burridge, and Sean Adams have enlisted similar arguments for viewing Acts as biographical discourse,[6] though a large contingent still holds out for Luke-Acts (or at least Acts) as history.[7] Some seek to situate one or both volumes among the epics and/or novels of the ancient world[8] while other recent work remains skeptical as to whether meaningful genre distinctions may be drawn between the βίος and other genres.[9] All of these studies seem to proceed from the assumption that genre similarities provide a sound basis for establishing genre identification.

Perhaps this accounts for the current *impasse* in literary analysis of Luke-Acts. If genres are understood mainly in terms of literary similarities, then Burridge only needs to accentuate Lukan commonalities with the βίος to advance his case for a biographical reading of Luke-Acts. Aune only needs to show the inclusion of symposia, genealogy, speeches, travel narratives, first person interjection, letters, identification of sources, historical prefaces, etc., in Luke-Acts can likewise be identified among the historians.[10] And Smith and Kostopoulos can recruit a convincing range of family resemblances shared by the history and the biography to establish their appeal for genre blending.[11]

6 S.E. Porter, 'The Genre of Acts and the Ethics of Discourse', in T.E. Phillips (ed.), *Acts and Ethics* (NTM 9; Sheffield: Sheffield Phoenix, 2005), 1–15; R.A. Burridge, 'The Genre of Acts Revisited', in Steve Walton (ed.), *Reading Acts Today: Essays in Honour of Loveday C.A. Alexander* (LNTS 472; London: T&T Clark, 2011), 3–28; S.A. Adams, *The Genre of Acts and Collected Biography* (SNTSMS 156; Cambridge: Cambridge University Press, 2013).

7 E.g. D.A. Aune, *The New Testament in its Literary Environment* (LEC 8; Philadelphia: Westminster, 1987), 77–115; G.E. Sterling, *Historiography and Self-Definition: Josephos, Luke-Acts, and Apologetic History* (NovTSup 64; Leiden: Brill, 1992); D.P. Moessner, *Luke the Historian of Israel's Legacy, Theologian of Israel's 'Christ'* (BZNW 182; Berlin: De Gruyter, 2016). So also B. Shellard, *New Light on Luke: Its Purpose, Sources, and Literary Context* (JSNTSup 215; London: Sheffield Academic Press, 2002), 18–23 and C.K. Rothschild, *Luke-Acts and the Rhetoric of History: An Investigation of Early Christian Historiography* (WUNT 2.175; Tübingen: Mohr Siebeck, 2004), 16–23, who both view Luke-Acts as a branch of rhetorical history. For a recent review of Luke-Acts as history, see Adams, *Genre*, 5–23; cf. also T.E. Phillips, 'The Genre of Acts: Moving toward a Consensus?' *CBR* 4 (2006): 365–96.

8 E.g. R.I. Pervo, *Profit with Delight* (Philadelphia, Penn.: Fortress, 1987) and D.R. MacDonald, 'The Breasts of Hecuba and Those of the Daughters of Jerusalem: Luke's Transvaluation of a Famous Iliadic Scene', in J.A.A. Brant, et al. (eds.), *Ancient Fiction: The Matrix of Early Christian and Jewish Narrative* (SymSBL 32; Atlanta: Society of Biblical Literature, 2005), 239–54.

9 E.g. D.L. Smith and Z.L. Kostopoulos, 'Biography, History, and the Genre of Luke-Acts', *NTS* 63 (2017): 390–410.

10 Cf. Aune, *New Testament*, 120–31, for a convenient survey.

11 E.g. Smith and Kostopoulos 'Biography', 390–410.

Without considering genre differences (esp. within larger discourse structures), cases for multiple genres may be developed concurrently and defended with equal vigor, not unlike the situation we discover in contemporary studies of the genre of Luke-Acts.

We find ourselves, then, with an enigma in Lukan studies. How do we move beyond the literary ambivalence propelled by Luke's persistent use of features common to several ancient literary genres? Do we give up the search as an ultimately futile quest, as Daniel Smith and Lundin Kostopoulos recommend?[12] I wish to contend that such a concession to the complexities of the discussion, while well-intentioned, seems premature. The problem, though real, is workable. The answer to the Gospels genre enigma is one that has been known to literary critics for many years but which New Testament scholars have not yet fully appreciated. Unlike contemporary literary-linguistic configurations of genre, current methodologies for the study of the Gospel genre are designed *only to target genre similarities not genre differences*. This basic oversight results in the convoluted discussion we witness in genre study today. Each recent treatment of genre represents a distinct effort to draw parallels between Luke-Acts and a specific (or multiple) literary tradition(s). These studies all underestimate the role of *literary divergence* in genre analysis, leveraging much—if not, all—of their case on *literary proximity*.[13] This monograph will show how attention to literary divergence from a number of angles may bring resolution to the increasingly complex discussions of the genre(s) of Luke-Acts.

1 The Origins of a Consensus

The thesis that the Gospels are literary decedents of the Greco-Roman biography is no longer widely contested in contemporary Gospels research. Scholars typically attribute the foundations of this view to Richard Burridge's monograph, *What are the Gospels?*.[14] Two recent article-length studies elucidate the impact of Burridge's work. First, Steve Walton's CBR article, 'What are the Gospels?', argues that 'Burridge's research has been widely accepted and has produced a new consensus, that the Gospels are a species of ancient biography

12 Smith and Kostopoulos 'Biography', 390–410.

13 As A. Collins, 'Genre and the Gospels', *JR* 75 (1995): 239–46 (241), points out: 'Burridge's case for defining the Gospels as bios appears strong in large part because he did not seriously consider any alternative'.

14 Burridge, *What are the Gospels?*

(βίος)', consulting a range of recent monograph and commentary literature on the Gospels to illustrate this point.[15] Walton states,

> [Burridge's] study is significant because it is not given to many to turn round a scholarly consensus in their lifetime, and it is given to even fewer to do that with their PhD work. Yet this is what Burridge's study of the Gospel genre did: scholarship largely adopted his view that the Gospels are a form of Graeco-Roman biography.[16]

Ian Markham has also written on 'Richard Burridge's Achievement'. This article details Burridge's reception of the 'prestigious Ratzinger Prize, set up as a kind of Nobel Prize for Theology'.[17] And Markham argues that it was Burridge's work on the biographical nature of the Gospels that won him this impressive award.

If one scans the literature on the genre of the Gospels, not only will they discover the Gospels-as-biographies thesis as a working assumption, they will constantly find statements like, Burridge's book, '*What are the Gospels?*, has become the definitive treatment on the subject. Today, a growing majority of scholars regard the Gospels as Greco-Roman biography'.[18] And: 'The research of Richard Burridge has been pivotal in this respect, creating what amounts to a new consensus in Gospel studies'.[19] Some go as far as to contend that anyone who views the Gospels (including Luke) as something other than biography registers 'surprisingly inaccurate' opinions[20] while announcing that, 'Richard Burridge is so compelling … that it ought to end any further dissent about the matter'.[21] Burridge is often praised, specifically for his methodological precision. *What are the Gospels?* 'is a masterpiece of thoroughness, clarity of method, and precision in execution', according to David Moessner.[22] Along similar lines, Justin Smith believes that 'Burridge has shown great sensitivity to the matters of genre analysis and theory, as well as to the historical development of βίος as a genre', devoting 'an entire chapter to genre criticism and literary theory'.[23]

15 Steve Walton, 'What Are the Gospels? Richard Burridge's Impact on Scholarly Understanding of the Genre of the Gospels', *CBR* 14 (2015) 81–93 (81).

16 Walton, 'What Are the Gospels?', 82.

17 Ian Markham, 'Richard Burridge's Achievement', *First Things* (2014) 22–24.

18 Licona, *Why are there Differences in the Gospels?*, 3.

19 Adams, *Parallel Lives*, 19.

20 See C. Keener, *Acts* (Grand Rapids, Mich.: Baker, 2012).

21 See Keener, *Acts*, 1:54.

22 Moessner, *Luke*, 64.

23 Smith, *Why βίος?*, 36.

Perhaps Burridge's work did account for a kind of paradigm but there is certainly another possible reading of the story, at least as I see things. It could be that Burridge's study was not, at least initially, accepted for its methodological rigor but as the most ready-made theory available to stand in place of the form-critical view of genre. Thus, form criticism's loss of steam into the 1980s seems to have created somewhat of a vacuum for literary analysis of the Gospels where the biographical thesis was potentially the only viable non-form critical theory of the Gospels genre. Thus, rather than a paradigm shift, we have a movement away from form criticism and its attendant assumptions about the Gospels genre and the biographical thesis functioning to stand in the place of the *sue generis* thesis.

Form criticism meets Thomas Kuhn's well-known criteria for a paradigm (it was practiced for decades and used to solve puzzles as what we might call *normal historical science*).[24] Correspondingly, we may ask whether the *sui generis* theory of the Gospels genre practiced as a global paradigm used for puzzle-solving in *normal historical science* or did it function more like a what Kuhn calls a *rule*—an axiomatic assumption—underlying the broader theoretical framework? In the first part of the twentieth century, critics tended to believe that the Gospels were popular rather than literary documents (*Kleinliteratur gegen Hochliteratur*),[25] equated with "legend-books and folk-books" (*Legendenbüchern und Volksbüchern*)[26] not ancient literature.[27] In this respect, the *su generis* theory seems to be nothing more than a bi-product of this basic axiom in form-critical thought. If one adopted the form-critical paradigm, it suddenly made comparisons between early Christian texts and the literature of antiquity methodologically inappropriate.

The *su genris* theory then seems to function more as an axiomatic assumption connected to the form-critical paradigm rather than a paradigm in itself that the biographical thesis supplanted. Naturally, biblical scholars working within the form-critical model made no attempt to situate the Gospels as documents in relation to surrounding literary culture since this violated a

24 Thomas S. Kuhn, *The Structure of Scientific Revolution* (Chicago, Ill.: The University of Chicago Press, 1964).

25 K.L. Schimdt, "Die Stellung der Evangelien in der allgemeinen Literaturgeschichte," ΕΥΧΑΡΙΣΤΗΡΙΟΝ: Studien zur Religion und Literatur des Alten und Neuen Testaments (FRLANT 36. Göttingen: Vandenhoeck & Ruprecht, 1923), 59–62.

26 Schmidt, "Die Stellung der Evangelien," 61.

27 Franz Overbeck, "Über die Anfänge der patristischen Literatur," HZ 12 (1882) 417–72, had already perpetuated this disconnect with his insistence on viewing the New Testament and the apostolic fathers as *Urliteratur* in contrast to the later Christian fathers who employed secular literary media in their writings.

major rule of form criticism. The Gospels emerged *sui generis* as anthologies of popular tales, not primitive literary compositions shaped by the constraints of Greco-Roman literary standards. To suggest anything contrary would violate one of the basic axioms of the paradigm.

Take, for example, C.H. Dodd's articulation of the gospel-as-*kerygma*. Many view Dodd as the most developed expression of the view that the Gospel tradition was one that was culturally distinct due to its origins in missionary preaching.[28] Yet Dodd's book is not a treatment of genre. It just so happens that the form-critical *su generis* idea fits nicely with his proposal regarding the kerygmatic substructure of New Testament theology, where Gospel forms evolve from this basic message. It is not as though the *su generis* thesis did a great deal of explanatory work for Dodd. As an axiom of his model, it helped substantiate his broader form-critical claim about the unifying message of the New Testament. In other words, the entire discussion of the genre of the Gospels is curtailed in this era by the assumptions of form criticism, as it was for Dodd.[29]

The debate about form criticism—at one level—can be understood as a discussion about the nature of early Christian literature. We might say that the form critics advocated a popular configuration of these texts while a parallel (even if initially marginal) stream ran throughout form criticism's reign that insisted upon a literary configuration of early Christian texts. The form critics sought to show that the literature of the most primitive Christians was unique and cultic whereas as another emerging group of scholars throughout the last century insisted that we situate these texts among literary culture of the Greco-Roman world.

We see the embryonic stages of this latter position in the works of Adolf Deissmann and J.H. Moulton, who both sought to draw literary and linguistic parallels with many of the then recently published non-literary papyri.[30] The beginnings of the biographical thesis emerged around the same time. The several "Lives of Jesus" that Albert Schweitzer documents seem to assume that one can extract a kind of biographical portrait of Jesus from the Gospels.[31] Others,

28 C.H. Dodd, *The Apostolic Preaching and Its Developments: With an Appendix on Eschatology and History* (Grand Rapids, Mich.: Baker Book House, 1983).

29 Rudolf Bultmann, *Theology of the New Testament* (New York: Scribner, 1951), for example, argues that Mark at the very least constitutes its own unique literary genre, given its distinct preliterary development. Dibelius, *Tradition*, 288, notes that the Gospels represent a hybrid type of document, mainly characterized as folk-tale, but distinct even from folk-tale, due to their function as propaganda literature, a role altogether lacking for folk-tale.

30 E.g. Adolf Deissmann, *Light from the Ancient East the New Testament Illustrated by Recently Discovered Texts of the Graeco-Roman World* (London: Hodder & Stoughton, 1910); James Hope Moulton and George Milligan, *The Vocabulary of the Greek Testament* (London: Hodder and Stoughton, 1930).

31 Albert Schweitzer, *The Quest of the Historical Jesus: A Critical Study of Its Progress from Reimarus to Wrede* (trans. W. Montgomery; 2nd ed; London: Adam and Charles Black, 1911).

as early as 1915, marshalled arguments in support of the biographical thesis. Source and form criticism subsequently establish themselves as the prevailing methodology and proposals like Votaw's are quickly discounted as methodological outliers.

By the 1960s and 70s, we discover a growing number of scholars questioning form-critical assumptions, in particular related to the genre of the Gospels. Norman Petersen, for example, argued that while Mark was a Gospel (*sui generis*), John functioned as a type of Greek biography, Luke-Acts as history, and Matthew as an early church manual[32] and similar positions were advanced by Petersen and his colleagues on the SBL *Task Force on Gospel Genre*. Although Albrecht Dihle explicitly denies any point of contact with Greek βίος, he states rather cautiously possible points of contact between the Gospels and Roman biography (*vita*) due to their "historiographic" function.[33] There were also the so-called *theios aner* and related categories (such as aretalogy or holy men), especially in Hellenistic (but also in Rabbinic) Judaism. The function of *theios aner* as antecedents for Gospel christologies in a hand full of studies in the 1970s also generated discussion around possible biographical literary contexts for Gospels as well.

The biographical thesis continues to attract advocates into the 1980s, with challenges to the basic tenants of form criticism now being given more serious attention. Charles Talbert's work provides a milestone for genre studies in this era.[34] Talbert argued extensively against Bultmann's denial of a biographical context for Gospel origins on the basis of their mythical character and cultic function. In response to the first plank of Bultmann's argument, Talbert seeks to demonstrate that many βίοι in the ancient world had "immortals" as their biographical focus (e.g. Hercules, Dionysus, and the Dioscuri), showing that mythological elements were hardly lacking in ancient biographies.[35] Talbert identifies specifically the myth of descending-ascending redeemers as a mythological structure present in Greco-Roman and Jewish biographies, as well as in John's Gospel.[36] As for the second plank, Talbert develops a typology of ancient βίοι and shows that Bultmann's failure to identify analogies between the Gospels and ancient βίοι resulted from an overly circumscribed understanding of the genre.[37]

---

32 Norman Petersen, "So-called Gnostic Type Gospels and the Question of the Genre 'Gospel.'" Unpublished SBL Paper (1970) cited in Charles H. Talbert, *What is a Gospel? The Genre of the Canonical Gospels* (Philadelphia: Fortress, 1977), 20.

33 Albrecht Dihle, "The Gospels and Greek Biography." In *The Gospel and the Gospels*, edited by Peter Stuhlmacher (Grand Rapids: Eerdmans, 1991), 361–86.

34 Talbert, *What is a Gospel?*

35 Talbert, *What is a Gospel?*, 25–52.

36 Talbert, *What is a Gospel?*, 53–89.

37 Talbert, *What is a Gospel?*, 115–31.

Talbert did not immediately convince everyone. Many scholars were extremely critical of his work.[38] He did, however, issue a significant blow to the current form-critical analysis of Gospel genre. Similarly, Martin Hengel had already rejected the *su generis* thesis for all but Luke-Acts[39] but in 1991 includes Luke among the other Gospels as instances of biography. He says that the Gospels should be understood as,

> ... unique 'biographies' which bear witness to the career and teaching of the unique Messiah and Son of God, Jesus of Nazareth. No one in antiquity thought that the Gospels were a literary genre of a quite new and special kind. It was not the literary genre that was unique but the person described in it and his work of salvation.[40]

Yet Hengel had come to this conclusion prior to Burridge's work. In a similar vein, Philip Shuler[41] argued that (esp.) Matthew was an encomium type of biography. Hubert Cancik, likewise, proposed the biography as the most appropriate literary label for at least Mark's Gospel.[42] More wide-reaching (applied to all four Gospels) biographical proposals were advanced, even if cautiously

38 E.g. David Aune, "The Problem of the Genre of the Gospels: A Critique of C.H. Talbert's What is a Gospel?" in *Gospel Perspectives: Studies of History and Tradition in the Four Gospels*, edited by R.T. France and David Wenham (Sheffield: JSOT, 1981), 9–60, concludes his thorough criticism of Talbert's book by claiming that "A careful and critical appraisal, then, of the theses advanced by Professor Talbert must conclude that his arguments are flawed, the evidence adduced is frequently unable to bear the weight given it, and his proposal that the gospels share the genre of Graeco-Roman biography falls embarrassingly short of demonstration"—strong words from a scholar who would later embrace three of the four Gospels as Greco-Roman biography in Aune, *New Testament*, 17–47. And still in 1981, Aune, "Problem," 49, can talk about the "present critical consensus that the gospels constitute a unique genre in the history of literature...." Even within the early 1990s, Guelich, "Gospel Genre," 205, can give a thorough survey of prior genre proposals and hardly engages at all with the notion of biography in this discussion. Instead, he interacts extensively with Dodd's gospel-as-*kerygma* proposal. Guelich eventually adopts the *sui generis* view of Gospel genre and argues that we only remove the term "unique" in the designation of the Gospels as a "unique literary genre."

39 Martin Hengel, *Acts and the History of Earliest Christianity* (Philadelphia: Fortress Press, 1980), 32.

40 Martin Hengel, 'Literary, Theological, and Historical Problems in the Gospel of Mark', in *The Gospel and the Gospels*, edited by Peter Stuhlmacher (Grand Rapids: Eerdmans, 1991), 209–51 (212).

41 Shuler, *Genre*.

42 H. Cancik (ed.), *Markus-Philologie*, WUNT 33 (Tübingen: J. C. B. Mohr, 1984), chapter 1.

stated, in this era by Klaus Berger (1984) and Helmut Koester (1984).[43] And by the end of the 1980s, David Aune (1987) can include an entire chapter, arguing for the "Gospels as Ancient Biography,"[44] followed by an additional article-length defense of the position a year later (1988).[45] Similarly, Graham Stanton incorporates a section on "The Gospels as Biographies," in a book on Jesus[46] and D. Dormeyer and H. Frankemölle attempted to make the same case a year later.[47] By 1989, the theory had made its way into an introduction to the Gospels by E.P. Sanders and Margarete Davies.[48] Therefore, as even Burridge acknowledges, "By the start of the 1980s, there was building up a frequently, if not always cogently, argued case for a biographical genre of the gospels."[49] Burridge even calls the biography thesis the "New Orthodoxy"[50] at the time *he wrote* in 1992. But if Burridge shifted the paradigm, as Walton proposes, how could Burridge already call the biographical thesis the new orthodoxy at the time he wrote?

In 1991, Larry Hurtado states that, 'Similarities to other Greco-Roman narrative genres such as biography reflect the cultural setting in which the Gospels were written'.[51] However, he argues that Matthew and Luke seem more literarily conscientious than Mark or John in this respect so that the former seem to better reflect Greco-Roman literary culture, including biographical literary conventions.[52] One of the virtues of these earlier biographical proposals was the caution with which they are stated. Burridge seems more certain and less

43 Klaus Berger, "Hellenistische Gattungen im Neuen Testament', in ANRW II.25.2 (1984) 1031–432 and 1831–85.

44 Aune, *New Testament*, 47–76.

45 David Aune, 'Greco-Roman Biography', in *Greco-Roman Literature and the New Testament: Selected Forms and Genres*, ed. David E. Aune (Atlanta, Geo.: Scholars, 1988), 107–26.

46 G.N. Stanton, *The Gospels and Jesus* (OUP, 1989), pp. 15–20.

47 D. Dormeyer and H. Frankemölle, 'Evangelium als literarische Gattung und als theologischer Begriff. Tendenzen und Aufgaben der Evangelienforschung im 20. Jahrhundert, mit einer Untersuchung des Markusevangeliums in seinem Verhältnis zur antiken Biographie', ANRW II.25.2, pp. 1543–1704; D. Dormeyer, *Evangelium als literarische und theologische Gattung* (Darmstadt: Wissenschaftliche Buchgesellschaft, 1989); H. Frankemölle, *Evangelium—Begriff und Gattung: ein Forschungsbericht* (Stuttgart: Katholisches Bibelwerk, 1988); *ANRW Aufstieg und Niedergang der römischen Welt*, ed. Wolfgang Haase, Berlin: Walter de Gruyter.

48 E.P. Sanders and Margaret Davies, *Studying the Synoptic Gospels* (London: SCM, 1989), 25–48.

49 Burridge, *What are the Gospels?*, 86.

50 Burridge, *What are the Gospels?*, 92.

51 Larry W. Hurtado, "Gospel (Genre)," in *Dictionary of Jesus and the Gospels*, ed. Joel B., Green, Scot McKnight, and I. Howard Marshall (Downers Grove, IL: InterVarsity Press, 1992), 276–82.

52 Hurtado, "Gospel," 82.

occupied with the many differences between the Gospels and ancient biographies while he never even considers potential other genres. In these ways, it is perhaps a step back relative to prior studies, at least methodologically. Besides perhaps Talbert and a few others, most scholars stated their position somewhat apprehensively prior to Burridge, *due to many clear differences between the canonical Gospels and the biographies of the ancient world*, as reflected in the comments by Dihle or Hurtado above, for example.

By 1992, the Gospels-as-biographies seems to be in the air of New Testament studies, so to speak, if not the new orthodoxy. Form criticism had breathed its dying breath and Richard Burridge publishes his monograph, *What are the Gospels?*, which was essentially a more comprehensive statement of a position that had been maintained as the most viable alternative to the form-critical position for some time. It seems that Burridge's work should be viewed, then, as less of a paradigm-shifting monograph and more as the most sustained representation of the non-form-critical position on genre. Adela Collins is correct.[53] In her review of the original (1992) publication, she is not blown away by the novelty of the proposal. Instead, she aptly observes that Burridge merely attempts 'either to give the biographical hypothesis a scholarly footing or to expose it as a false trial'.[54] Notice, she does not accredit the biographical thesis to Burridge—he merely adds data to an already established position in many circles.

In the decades leading up to 1990s, form criticism had died and, by extension, so had its assumptions about the nature of early Christian literature. In a parallel development, as scholars slowly questioned the validity of the form-critical position, they likewise began to critique the *su generis* view of the Gospels that it assumed. By the 1980s, the biographical thesis had become the dominate genre alternative to form criticism, put forward in a variety of expressions. Burridge's book likely did put the final nail in the form-critical view of the genre of the Gospels, but his book by no means shifted the paradigm in the Kuhnian sense. Perhaps this is not the right way to read the story but it is certainly the most generous to New Testament scholarship because it accounts for why a work like Burridge's (based on a flawed literary method, see below) could emerge—at least in the minds of many—as a kind of consensus-setting book.

53 Adella Y. Collins, *Is Mark's Gospel a Life of Jesus? The Question of Genre*. Père Marquette Lecture in Theology (Milwaukee: Marquette University, 1990), 239.

54 Collins, *Is Mark's Gospel a Life of Jesus?*, 239.

2 What Went Wrong?

Stressing parallels or similarities with other ancient texts has played a significant role in the storied history of New Testament interpretation. It had gotten to the point in the 1960s that Samuel Sandmel felt the need to censor our discipline for its proclivities toward what he famously termed paralellomania.[55] In concert with many streams of New Testament study, literary resonances in the Gospels with the Greco-Roman biographical tradition had been exploited for several years before Burridge in attempts to better understand the Gospels genre. We think immediately of the contributions of Votaw, Talbert, David Aune, Shuler, and Dihle—all of which recruit a range of shared formal features as a basis for establishing a literary connection between the Gospels and the Greco-Roman biography.[56]

Burridge did not establish this model, but he did enshrine it methodologically, so that most recent treatments of genre defer to him on questions of literary method.[57] Burridge's *What are the Gospels?* continues the trend of former studies in correlating a list—albeit a more comprehensive one—of features present in both ancient biographical and Gospel literature. Burridge also expands the theoretical basis of this method by introducing Alistair Fowler to the discussion. In his *Kinds of Literature*, published in 1982, Fowler recruited Ludwig Wittgenstein's family resemblance model in an effort to construct a robust theory of literary genre.[58] Burridge is convinced and insists with Fowler that the 'Family resemblance theory seems to hold out the best hope to the genre critic'.[59] He defines the focus of his investigation as an attempt to 'identify … "generic features" as a list against which we can compare the

55 S. Sandmel, 'Parallelomania', *JBL* 81 (1962): 1–13.

56 The recent argument of S. Walton, 'What Are the Gospels? Richard Burridge's Impact on Scholarly Understanding of the Genre of the Gospels', *CBR* 14 (2015): 81–93, that Burridge's work established the current consensus on the Gospels genre is likely overstated in this respect.

57 E.g. Adams, *Genre*, 58; Smith, *Why βίος?*, 36; M.R. Licona, *Why Are There Differences in the Gospels?: What We Can Learn from Ancient Biography* (New York: Oxford, 2017), 3.

58 Burridge, *What are the Gospels?*, 38: 'The attraction of "family resemblance" is that it is sufficiently vague to cope with the blurred edges of genre (unlike "class"), yet still sharp enough to have some meaning'.

59 Burridge, *What are the Gospels?*, 38. Many of Burridge's followers likewise uncritically adopt Fowler's family resemblance paradigm. See, e.g., J.M. Smith, 'Genre, Sub-Genre, and Questions of Audience: A Proposed Typology for Greco-Roman Biography', *JGChJ* 4 (2007): 184–216 (191).

gospels and Graeco-Roman βίοι, to see whether they exhibit the same pattern and *family resemblance*' (emphasis mine).[60]

Though initially appealing to some, the family resemblance method—at least, as a stand-alone model—was short lived in literary theory due to significant deficiencies exposed early on in its development. Earl Miner states the problem this way:

> The logical difficulty with the principle of family resemblance is that it posits likeness for admissibility to a set and minimizes differences to exclude from a set. In other words, how is one to decide family resemblance does *not* exist? ... In short, we need grounds for postulating that a work's assignment to a given family is more explanatory than its assignment to other families. Perhaps we have not achieved the means of making these distinctions. Perhaps we never shall. But family resemblance, as useful as it is, does not fill these needs.[61]

As John Frow notices, using likeness as the basis of similarity raises the problem of how dissimilarity may be drawn from.[62] For this and related reasons, the family resemblance model proved to be problematic shortly after its inception.[63] Under the collective force of these criticisms, even Fowler eventually (in 1993) came to reject his notion of family resemblances, confessing that it 'represented an unsatisfactory amalgam of Wittgenstein, Carnap and the

60 Burridge, *What are the Gospels?*, 105.

61 E. Miner, 'Some Issues of "Literary Species, or Distinct Kind"', in B.K. Lewalski (ed.), *Renaissance Genres: Essays on Theory, History, and Interpretation* (HES 14; Cambridge, Mass.: Harvard University Press, 1986), 24.

62 J. Frow, Genre (New Critical Idiom; London: Routledge, 2015), 54.

63 These are representative samples of a much broader stream of critique in literary theory. J. Swales, *Genre Analysis: English in Academic and Research Settings* (Cambridge: Cambridge University Press, 1991), 51, for example, raises similar problems: 'Family resemblance theory can make anything resemble anything' and, therefore, 'the definitional approach is much better established'. C.A. Newsome, 'Spying out the Land: A Report from a Genealogy', in Roland Boer (ed.), *Bakhtin and Genre Theory in Biblical* Studies (SS 63; Atlanta: Society of Biblical Literature, 2010), 19–30 (23), helpfully frames the break down. On the family resemblance theory, '[T]exts in group A might exhibit features a, b, c, group B might exhibit features b, c, d, and group c might exhibit features c, d, e, and so forth. One is left with the uncomfortable conclusion that the family resemblance model could produce a genre in which two exemplars in fact shared no traits in common!' Cf. also T. Sawaki, *Analysing Structure in Academic Writing* (Postdisciplinary Studies in Discourse; London: Palgrave Macmillan, 2016), 56, for different version of this objection. For a rejection of family resemblances in biblical studies in favor of more recent trends, see J.J. Collins, 'The Genre of Jubilees', in Eric F. Mason (ed.), *A Teacher for All Generations: Essays in Honor of James C. VanderKam* (SJSJSup 153; Leiden: Brill, 2011), 737–55 (739).

non-structuralist element in Saussure; and ... overestimated the part played in interpretation by coding'.[64]

Although contemporary theorists continue to acknowledge the importance of proximity features of genre (something like family resemblances), these are typically assessed in the context of a wider *genre agnation* or genre relations framework. These new genre agnation models, arising partially in response to the failure of family resemblance are, by definition, designed to plot genre relations in terms of *both genre similarity and divergence*. For example, genre agnation models not only ask how a document like Luke-Acts might be similar to ancient biographies but also how it may be different. Genre agnation then describes a methodological principle used in modern literary and linguistic study to model genre relations in terms of both similarity *and* difference. To put the matter more precisely: the family resemblance model based as it is on generic similarity fails as *an exclusive model* for genre identification. This does not entail the stronger claim that the kinds of features that the family resemblance model has typically focused upon should be curtailed or in some way mitigated by newer models. Rather, newer models tend to incorporate something at least very akin to family resemblance criticism in the context of their wider models, which also assess literary-linguistic divergence.[65]

The problems introduced by Burridge *via* Fowler are not merely theoretical. They surface directly in his analysis. Greek history and biography share many things in common as instances of related but distinct Greek narrative discourse, a point where the Fowler-Burridge family resemblance model struggles to make convincing distinctions. The problem materializes most directly in the feature categories Burridge uses to construct his family resemblances.

For example, Burridge's 'mode of representation',[66] where βίοι are composed in (for the most part third person) prose narrative, is applicable to many instances of Greek narrative, not exclusively to biographies. Similarly, 'Length and size' may be a helpful feature to consider but it too detects several groups of works not just biographical texts. As instances of narrative, Greco-Roman histories, monographs of various sorts, biographies, and many more, are composed in the same prose meter so this provides another feature common to

64 A. Fowler, 'Genre', in M. Coyle, et al. (eds.), *Encyclopedia of Literature and Criticism* (Routledge Companion Encyclopedias; New York: Routledge, 1993), 151–63 (158).

65 It should be noted that much of this discussion had gone on prior to Burridge's original publication in 1992 and the family resemblance model had long fallen out of fashion by the time of Burridge's 2004 revision of his dissertation, despite his insistence on utilizing the latest and best in literary theory.

66 Burridge, *What are the Gospels?*, chapter 5, provides a list of Burridge's criteria, referred to here.

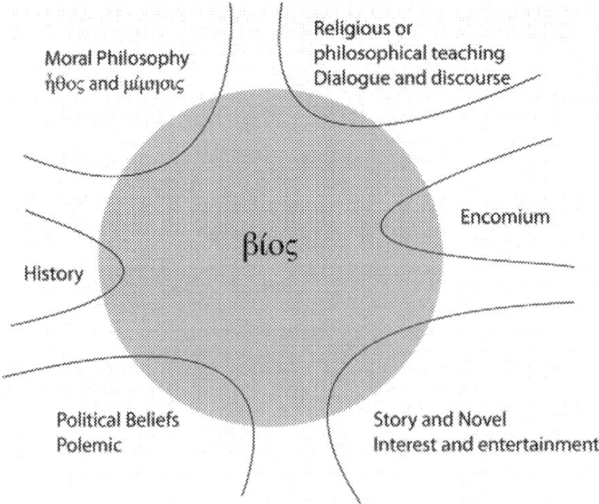

FIGURE 1.1 Burridge's model of the Greek βίος based on family resemblances

multiple genres (cf. Dionysius of Halicarnassus, *Comp.* 3[67]). Burridge recognizes the literary overlap of the βίος with several other genres in the ancient world. He represents this visually with a helpful display of the literary relation of βίοι to other Greco-Roman literary forms in the ancient world:[68]

The grey circle (which I have darkened from the original) highlights all of the material that Burridge's criteria catch. As it stands, most of Burridge's criteria not only detect βίοι, but also features found in both the βίος and overlapping genres.

Burridge confronts here a problem that has traditionally faced the family resemblance model for genre study. Genre detection criteria (family resemblances) help isolate the group of related genres that includes the βίος, but we need more rigorous genre disambiguation criteria to complement this analysis by further distinguishing the βίος from within this larger group of related genres.[69] Sustained genre analysis must emphasize[70] both features for genre detection

67 Dionysius here divides genres into metered (poetry) and non-metered (narrative).

68 I have adapted this figure from Burridge, *What are the Gospels?*, 64.

69 For example, one immediately thinks of the model of prototypicality used by Swales, *Genre Analysis, passim* and others. The model, in other words, should be constructed not (as Burridge does) around family resemblances but on a model designed to calibrate both resemblances and divergences from a given (genre) prototype.

70 I say 'emphasize' because Burridge does propose at least one genre agnation criteria (verbal subjects), which I examine in chapter 2, but it seems insufficient, for reasons I will mention.

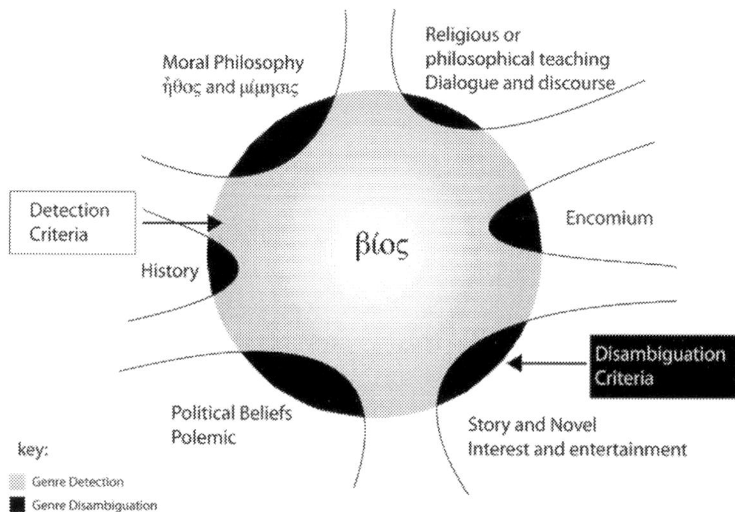

FIGURE 1.2 Detection (topological) and disambiguation (typological) criteria
Note: In response to Burridge's critique (*What are the Gospels?*, 1.76–77) that I do not define genre disambiguation or detection sufficiently, it should be noted that I use these terms as descriptions for the two sides of modern genre study which focuses on genre agnation or, in other words, genre relations, i.e. how genres differ (disambiguation) and how they are similar (detection criteria). The terms are meant as descriptive components of a wider theory of genre agnation, a prevalent concept in modern genre criticism. I talk in more detail below about genre agnation. In contemporary genre agnation analysis, genres are detected in terms of similarities by topological criteria and related by differences in terms of typological criteria. See below.

and genre disambiguation (as contemporary genre agnation models do), especially with closely intersecting genres, such as the βίος and the Greek history.

It may be beneficial to study proximity features or 'family resemblances' in our efforts to understand genre. But overlapping features require a further set of criteria designed to push beyond family resemblances and disambiguate the literary environment of texts with overlapping formal characteristics (as in Fig. 1.2). This has been the traditional critique of the family resemblances model and Burridge's use of it does little to avoid it.[71]

71 Smith and Kostopoulos, 'Biography', 394, claim that the position of those like Burridge, which assumes the ability to distinguish between ancient genres, fails 'to take advantage of the best in contemporary genre theory, which has moved away from the *pigeonholing*

3 What is the Solution? 'New' Genre Studies as a Way Forward

While many New Testament scholars were preoccupied with family resemblance criticism and related methods, a new movement in genre studies was emerging in the interdisciplinary context of literary, linguistic, and rhetorical criticism. This new view sought to restore the sociolinguistic context to genre that structuralism had displaced.

Most connect this new interpretation of genre primarily with the seminal article by Carolyn Miller in 1984, 'Genre as Social Action'. Miller contends that traditional genre criticism 'invites reductionism, rules, formalism', creating a 'critical-determinism of the worst sort' leading to 'useless and tiresome taxonomies'.[72] Instead, for Miller, 'a rhetorically sound definition of genre must be centered not on the substance or form of discourse but on the action it is used to accomplish'.[73] As Miller understands things, genre functions within a layered hierarchy of language with the widest levels incorporating features of the social context. 'Since context itself is hierarchical', she reasons, 'we can think of form, substance, and context as relative not absolute, they occur at many levels on a hierarchy of meaning'.[74] John Swales then helped solidify the movement, outlining a sustained sociological theory of genre in his *Genre Analysis* in 1990.

Many of these developments, however, were anticipated much earlier by M.A.K. Halliday, upon whom both Miller and Swales depend. Although current approaches to genre pull partially from work in literary theory, they draw more so from linguistic, rhetorical, and sociological traditions.[75] Especially

---

activity endorsed by modern scholars and ancient critics' (emphasis mine). Ironically, as it turns out, neither study appears to draw significantly upon contemporary genre study and they both end up failing for precisely this reason. The reference to 'pigeonholing' by Smith and Kostopoulos refers to Fowler's distinction between genre as pigeon and genre as pigeonhole. But Fowler only deploys this distinction as a metaphor for the flexibility of family resemblances (they form classifications more like pigeons than pigeonholes). Smith and Kostopoulos's argument boils down to noting a range of similarities (i.e. overlap in formal features) between ancient biographical and historical genres, contending that genre similarities undermine genre boundaries. And this is precisely where Burridge went wrong. Genre similarities do not establish genre boundaries. This occurs *via* genre divergence, which Smith and Kostopoulos fail to consider because they too proceed from Fowler's flawed family resemblance theory.

72 Miller, 'Genre', 151.

73 Miller, 'Genre', 151.

74 Miller, 'Genre', 159.

75 A.S. Bawarshi and M.J. Reiff, *Genre: An Introduction to History, Theory, Research, and Pedagogy* (Reference Guides to Rhetoric and Composition; West Lafayette, Ind.: Parlor Press, 2010), 29.

compelling for genre studies will be models that successfully fuse all three orientations (the social, rhetorical, and linguistic) into a coherent framework. Halliday's work in register and genre analysis (now thoroughly developed by J.R. Martin) represents one such model. According to Halliday, a discourse is composed of *contextual* and *co-textual* components. *Context* refers to the social environments that provide the setting for the production of the discourse and are, therefore, extralinguistic. *Co-textual* components are intralinguistic. Halliday organizes these components according to a hierarchical rank scale (word, word group, clause, clause complex, etc.). This hierarchal view of language enables the interpreter to conceive of linguistic structures and analysis in terms of distinct levels of linguistic meaning, as Miller recommends.

These and other studies provide a distinct movement away from the formalist-structuralist project toward an entirely new way of thinking about genre. Whereas formalism privileged technique over context, 'New genre study', seeks to assess technique or text alongside content as comprising action in context.[76] Bawarshi and Reiff layout the landscape of the field in this way:

> Over the past thirty years, researchers working across a range of disciplines and contexts have revolutionized the way we think of genre, challenging the idea that genres are simple categorizations of text types and offering instead an understanding of genre that connects kinds of texts to kinds of social actions. As a result, genres have become increasingly defined as ways of recognizing, responding to, acting meaningfully and consequentially within, and helping to reproduce recurrent situations.[77]

Already by the late 1980s and early 1990s, social interpretations of genre had replaced structuralist notions of a tightly reader- or author-bound expectation framework[78] in favor of what had become the new paradigm in genre studies.

76 A.J. Devitt, 'Re-fusing Form in Genre Study', in J. Giltrow and D. Stein (eds.), *Genres in the Internet: Issues in the Theory of Genre* (Amsterdam: John Benjamins, 2009), 27–47 (34). I follow Devitt here in referring to the group of theories discussed in this section as the 'new' genre theory. I am hesitant to refer to any modern theory as 'new'—since there will soon come a time when it will no longer be new, e.g., the *New* Criticism—but we will refer to this group of theories in this way to remain as consistent as possible with the field of literary studies.

77 Bawarshi and Reiff, *Genre*, 1. Similarly, as A.J. Devitt, *Writing Genres*, 1–2, points out, 'Scholars have studied genres for centuries; neither is it a new topic in English studies'. 'In recent years, however, views of genre have changed, shifting from a formalistic study of critics' classifications to a rhetorical study of the generic actions of everyday readers and writers'.

78 Note Burridge's heavy dependence upon Jonathan Culler, *Structuralist Poetics*, in his theory of genre. Burridge's theory of *construction of meaning*, for example, is developed from

We see the persistence of this older model for genre study in contemporary understandings of Luke-Acts, most of which follow Burridge in reducing genre to a list of formal features that form the basis of a family resemblance. As in prior models, the role of social context is displaced in favor of a focus on the internal features of a text.[79] When the wider sociological context is considered (e.g. other genres), it is mostly in the service of demonstrating genre blending or overlap through literary commonality. Little attention is given to the divergent relations of these genres—only their relative proximities. New Genre study insists on restoring the role of context minimized by older models through—among other things—situating the discussion of genre sociologically in the context of genres at various levels of proximity *and divergence*. Genres function in relation to one another as distinct social vehicles. The success of their social goals depends upon the ability of authors to create distinct literary mediums. In the context of Luke-Acts, this means not only comparing common features between Luke-Acts, biographies, histories, and/or novels, it must also plot divergences between the traditions that form literary boundaries. Luke deploys genre to accomplish a social purpose, the success of which will depend upon his ability not only to relate his work to a particular tradition, but also his aptitude in demarcating it from others.

4 Genre Agnation and the 'New' Genre Studies[80]

'Genre agnation'[81] refers to how genres relate to one another, both in terms of their *similarity and difference from one another*. In contemporary theory, genre likeness is assessed through genre topology and genre differences are assessed through genre typologies. In this context, therefore, *genre agnation means*

'the structuralist observation' that, in agreement with Culler, we are '*homo significans*: a creature who gives sense to things'. Culler in Burridge, *What are the Gospels?*, 48.

79 I grant that Burridge discusses so-called 'external features'.

80 My attention to current or new genre studies was inspired in large part by Richard Burridge's comments on my Achtemeier paper given at SBL 2015, at which he was a respondent. The initial idea for this book came from that paper and one of Burridge's biggest critiques was that I did not pay enough attention to genre theory. My work in this book has sought to make up for that shortcoming in the embryonic forms of this work. See Richard Burridge, *What are the Gospels?*, 1.77–79.

81 J.R. Martin, 'Analysing Genre: Functional Parameters', in F. Christie and J.R. Martin (eds.), *Genre and Institutions: Social Processes in the Workplace and School* (London: Cassell, 1997), 3–39 (13).

genre relatedness.[82] Buying a cup of coffee and getting a haircut will likely be characterized by similar language, at least at the beginning and end of the encounter. Why? Because both involve the social exchange of supplying a service of some sort to a customer. But the middle portion of the communication will likely be quite different. For example, the exchange during the haircut will be longer and likely more personal, etc. Through genre agnation models, we can see both how these two interactions are similar and how they differ in terms of their social purpose and linguistic structure. According to this approach, genre features are set up as categorical oppositions (e.g. event- vs. participant-oriented discourse) and compared in order to factor out similarities and differences between various genres.[83]

The study of genre agnation embodies one of the most significant theoretical advancements in new genre study for Lukan scholars. Several theories attempt to address the weaknesses of older family resemblance models by deploying more comprehensive genre agnation frameworks as the basis for their analysis. In other words, rather than focusing upon family *resemblances*, these models encourage focus upon family *relations* both in terms of proximity *and* divergence.[84] And, therefore, this issue of genre relatedness in terms of literary similarities and divergence between genres—or in other words, *genre agnation*—is the key difference between newer approaches to genre and more antiquated methods based on family resemblance. To put it concisely: *genre agnation focuses upon family relations rather than family resemblance.*

I find the most promising development in these approaches for the study of Luke-Acts in the work of J.R. Martin. Martin defines genre as *a staged, goal-oriented social process*, preferring the 'traditional SFL approach to genre

82 Tuomo Hiippala, *The Structure of Multimodal Documents: An Empirical Approach* (New York: Routledge, 2016), 71.

83 Martin, 'Analysing Genre', 13.

84 For example, Halliday and Hasan argue that each genre constitutes a combination of optional and obligatory (macro)structural elements that will fall in a particular order, but it is the obligatory elements that enable the interpreter to isolate one genre from another. M.A.K. Halliday and R. Hasan, *Language, Context, and Text: Aspects of Language in a Social-Semiotic Perspective* (Oxford: Oxford University Press, 1989), 63. Similarly, John Swales, *Genre Analysis*, 86, borrows the concept of prototypicality from cognitive semantics as a basis for assessing genre relations. Within genre prototypes, prior knowledge provides the basis for the 'image', and in this way contributes 'to a recognition of genre and so guides the production of exemplars'. So instead of a list of features that form family resemblances, Swales suggests that we establish genre relations in terms of proximity to or divergence from a genre prototype. For a comparison of the SFL approaches to genre in Halliday and Martin, see B. Yang and R. Wang, *Language Policy: A Systemic Functional Linguistic Approach* (China Perspectives Series; New York: Routledge, 2017), 42–88.

agnation, via **typology**' (emphasis his) over other models. SFL stands for Systemic Functional Linguistics, which will provide the methodological foundation for this study. The *systemic element* of SFL should not be confused with *systematic*. The term is used to signify that the fundamental concept in language is that of system. What is a system? An SFL system is nothing more than a set of linguistic options, classified typologically by opposition relations.[85] Take the Greek verb system, for example. When a Greek author chooses the aorist tense (perfective aspect), they select against other possible forms (i.e. non-aorist or non-perfective forms, such as the present or imperfect tense). To choose a perfective (aorist) verb is to choose not to select non-perfective (non-aorist) verbs. The *functional element* of SFL has to do with the impact that the use of language in society has had upon its evolution. As Halliday puts it, "The social functions of language clearly determine the pattern of language varieties, ... or linguistic repertoire, of a community or of an individual, is derived from the range of uses that language is put to in that particular culture or sub-culture."[86]

A conversation about the weather (intra-linguistic), for example, may take place while buying a coffee (extra-linguistic). The extra-linguistic events which surround the communicative act (functional) (obviously more difficult to determine for ancient discourse than for modern), then, would be purchasing a coffee while the subject matter, indicated by inter-linguistic phenomenon (systemic), would be the weather. The social context for an instance of language usage will limit the linguistic choices that a user can make. While a conversation about the weather may be appropriate to discuss with a barista, a conversation about the size of blue jeans that she wears may not be. Such a remark will be considered awkward or possibly even offensive, because of the social context. However, at a department store, this question may feel totally appropriate between two strangers. So, when dealing with SFL, we are essentially looking at two things. First, the choices a language user makes in terms of relatedness to other choices and second, how those choices are constrained by social factors.

Martin sets up categorical oppositions that he uses to factor out similarities and differences among genres.[87] To model a very simple typology, we could employ a systemic paradigm, such as this one.[88]

85 Halliday, *Halliday*, 4.
86 Halliday, *Explorations*, 14.
87 Martin, 'Analyzing Genre', 13.
88 Reproduced from Martin, 'Analyzing Genre', 13.

	Particular	Generalized
activity focused	*procedural recount* [1]	*historical recount* [2]
entity focused	*description* [3]	*descriptive report* [4]

FIGURE 1.3 Paradigm model for genre typology

Martin also uses *procedures* as immediately agnate in historical recounts that share in common a generalized focus on activity. Martin suggests that whereas 'historical recounts make a statement about the past, procedures direct activity which has yet to be undertaken'.[89] For Martin, 'Typological description of this kind and its formalization in system networks is ... the cornerstone of SFL Theory and description'.[90] However, typological analysis on its own remains inadequate since these binary networks cannot account for genre blurring. At this point, Martin draws an analogy with M.A.K. Halliday's treatment of intersecting vertical and horizontal descriptions of process types. When Halliday models process types systemically (i.e. vertically), each process type opposes another. But when modeled on a related intersecting (horizontal) cline, we see that there are intervening processes, creating soft boundaries for process types. Therefore,

> process types can also be interpreted as blending into one another as one colour to another in a rainbow. Behaving (*laughing, pondering, looking*) is between acting (material processing) and sensing (mental processing) just as purple can be read as a cline between red and blue.[91]

This suggests the importance not only of typological genre agnation but also *topological perspective*, according to Martin. 'A topology, in mathematical terms, is a set of criteria for establishing degrees of nearness or proximity among the members of some category'.[92] As an example, he models a set of

89 Martin, 'Analyzing Genre', 14.

90 Martin, 'Analyzing Genre', 14.

91 Martin, 'Analyzing Genre', 14.

92 Martin, 'Analyzing Genre', 14. He leans heavily here upon the paper by J.L. Lemke, 'Typology, Topology, Topography: Genre Semantics', Unpublished Paper (1987, rev. 1999), who suggests that 'There are units, and probably sub-units in some constituency hierarchy, that are unique to a genre. But obviously, in a realization hierarchy, eventually some genre-specific units must be realized by sequences of lexical items and grammatical structures which are not unique to the genre. The highest-ranking non-genre-specific

secondary school history genres using pedagogical development as a cline for measuring genres, where the cline increasingly assumes a greater competence level for the student (and correspondingly, lesser competence, at the other end of the cline).[93]

Having outlined Martin's genre agnation model, we may now note a few specific virtues that commend it as a compelling option for the study of the genre(s) of Luke-Acts. To begin with, Martin and Rose emphasize the agnation of 'historical genres' (including biography, autobiography, and history proper) in their research, genres of particular relevance for the study of Luke-Acts. SFL models are also among the oldest and most developed within the tradition of modern genre studies, going back to Halliday. In contemporary research, therefore, Systemic Functional theories of genre often take center stage: 'the *functional* turn of the last two decades ... fundamentally shaped the discipline, so that the vast majority of genre studies have a strong *functional* bias' (emphasis mine).[94] So in contrast to much recent work in New Testament studies,

units in terms of which the lowest-ranking genre-specific units are realized form a useful starting-point for considering similarities and differences between genres. For texts and topographic text formations like genre (i.e. those with essential structural-textural properties), similarity and difference need not be limited to paradigmatic, system-like agnation relations: typology can be extended toward a topology of genres as well (cf. Lemke 1987). A topology, in mathematical terms, is a set of criteria for establishing degrees of nearness or proximity among the members of some category. It turns a 'collection' or set of objects into a space defined by the relations of those objects. Objects which are more alike by the criteria are represented in this space as being closer together; those which are less alike are further apart. There can be multiple criteria, which may be more or less independent of one another, so that two texts, for instance, may be closer together in one dimension (say horizontal distance), but further apart in another (vertical distance). What is essential, obviously, is our choice of the criteria, the parameters, that define similarity and difference on each dimension. These parameters must be chosen so that any two texts for which the criteria are relevant can be represented as more or less alike. The same set of parameters allows us to describe both the similarities and the differences among texts, or genres. Ideal genres can be represented by definite points in such a topological space, marking the centers of clusters of other points representing actual texts. Those clusters ("fuzzy sets" or distributions) may overlap, representing ambiguity (or "multiple inheritance" cf. Stillar 1992) in the genre classification of texts. Texts of different genres may be very much alike by some criteria, even though along other dimensions they are different enough that there is no doubt about assigning them to different ideal genres. It now becomes possible to define possible genres that would be in a definite sense intermediate between actual genres, and to describe the evolution of genres in terms of changing distributions of actual texts over time'.

93 Martin, 'Analyzing Genre', 14.

94 T. Hyde, 'A Model for Describing New and Old Properties of CMC Genres', in J. Giltrow and D. Stein (eds.), *Genres in the Internet: Issues in the Theory of Genre* (PB 188; Amsterdam: John Benjamins, 2009), 239–61 (243).

in SFL genre analysis we deploy one of the most up-to-date, widely tested research models in the field today. Finally, the fruitfulness of several other recent applications of SFL to the Greek of the New Testament (often involving register and discourse analysis) suggests its potential utility in other domains of New Testament study as well.[95]

5 Typological Agnation Analysis: Assessing Genre Differences

Martin and Rose provide a powerful resource for the study of genre(s) in the Gospels and Luke-Acts in their SFL account of historical genres (among others). According to Martin and Rose, classifying genres as a taxonomy in

95 The systemic functional method is positioned in C.R. Campbell's recent survey, *Advances in the Study of Greek: New Insights for Reading the New Testament* (Grand Rapids: Zondervan, 2015), chapter 7, as one of the two major methods operative in Greek linguistic study today, especially in discourse analysis. He mentions Levisohn and Runge as the other (chapter 8). Those interested in the Greek of the New Testament have been working with SFL models for decades now. See, for example, J.T. Reed, *A Discourse Analysis of Philippians: Method and Rhetoric in the Debate Over Literary Integrity* (JSNTSup 136; Sheffield: Sheffield Academic Press, 1997); G. Martín-Asensio, *Transitivity-Based Foregrounding in the Acts of the Apostles: A Functional-Grammatical Approach to the Lukan Perspective* (JSNTSup 202; Sheffield: Sheffield Academic Press, 2000); S.L. Black, *Sentence Conjunction in the Gospel of Matthew: Kai, De, Tote, Gar, Syn and Asyndeton in Narrative Discourse* (JSNTSup 216. Sheffield: Sheffield Academic Press, 2002); M.B. O'Donnell, *Corpus Linguistics and the Greek of the New Testament* (NTM 6; Sheffield: Sheffield Phoenix Press, 2005); C.L. Westfall, *A Discourse Analysis of the Letter to the Hebrews: The Relationship between Form and Meaning* (LNTS 297; SNTG 11; London: T&T Clark, 2005); J.H. Lee, *Paul's Gospel in Romans A Discourse Analysis of Rom. 1:16–8:39* (LBS 3; Leiden: Brill, 2010); C.D. Land, The Integrity of 2 Corinthians and Paul's Aggravating Absence (NTM 36; Sheffield: Sheffield Phoenix Press, 2015); H.T. Ong, *The Multilingual Jesus and the Sociolinguistic World of the New Testament* (LBS 12; Leiden: Brill, 2016); F.G.H. Pang, *Revisiting Aspect and Aktionsart A Corpus Approach to Koine Greek Event Typology* (LBS 14; Leiden: Brill, 2016). This provides a representative selection of the work that has been done over the last several years applying SFL linguistic models to the Greek of the New Testament from a variety of angles and often with quite fruitful results. Much of the work in SFL New Testament studies has been initiated around the methodologies or under the supervision of Stanley Porter. For a summary of the impact of Porter and the SFL school in New Testament studies, see A.W. Pitts, 'Interdisciplinary New Testament Scholarship: An Introduction to the Research of Stanley E. Porter', in L.F. Dow, C.A. Evans, and A.W. Pitts (eds.), *The Language and Literature of the New Testament: Essays in Honor of Stanley E. Porter's 60th Birthday* (BINS 150; Leiden: Brill, 2016), 1–70 (11, 57–58) and for a broader treatment of the SFL school in discourse analysis (in addition to Campbell, *Advances*, noted above), see S.E. Porter and A.W. Pitts, 'New Testament Greek Language and Linguistics in Recent Research', *CBR* 6 (2008): 214–55 (234, 237–38).

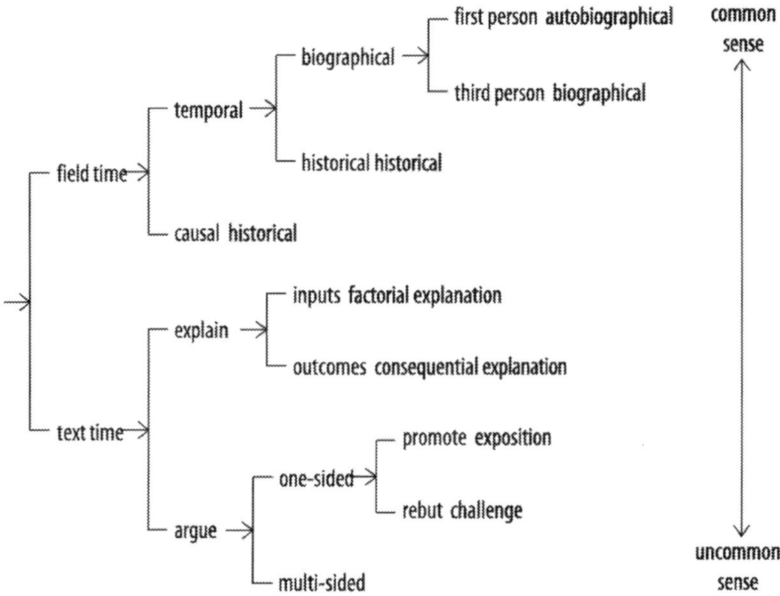

FIGURE 1.4 A typological perspective on relations between history genres
Note: Taken from Martin and Rose, *Genre Relations*, 130.

a system network means 'privileging one dimension of texture over another as more or less critical for categorization'.[96] For example, in historical genres, Martin and Rose privilege the opposition of *field time* (texts that unfold around a particular field, e.g. a participant) to *text time* (texts that unfold rhetorically), meaning it is the first or least delicate choice within the system network.

The next move is the choice between *temporal* (recounts) and *causal* (accounts) connections. A recount may focus on *individuals* (autobiography, biography) or *groups* (historical recounts). Biographies, furthermore, can be characterized by *first person* (autobiographical) or *third person* (biographical) *discourse*. These networks all emerge from the first choice of field time rather than text time. But rhetorically organized or text time genres have subnetworks as well. A rhetorically organized genre may be organized around external causation (explanations) or internal causation (arguments). Arguments have a further subnetwork in that they can be one-sided or multi-sided, and one-sided arguments can promote exposition or rebut challenges. More complicated typologies like this one may be displayed as a system network rather than a paradigm (see Tab. 1.1) as shown above (see fig. 1.4).

96 J.R. Martin and David Rose, *Genre Relations: Mapping Culture* (Equinox Publishing, 2008), 130.

Martin and Rose explain: the above typology models relations 'from discourse patterns of autobiographical accounts that most resemble those of everyday common sense to those of written argument genres that are most remote from the unfolding event time of everyday experience'.[97]

6 Topological Agnation Analysis: Proximating Genre Likeness

In their work on genres, Martin and Rose note that 'The alternative to taxonomising ... is topology, which allows us to relate genres as more or less like one another, from as many angles as we wish'.[98] Clines or scales may also be employed to assess levels of proximity. For topological analysis, Martin and Rose assess history genres from the perspective of pedagogic discourse. Based on prior field work, they view the 'personal recount' as the closest 'domestic genre for secondary schools'. They propose participant identification and time management as the sample variables in their topological landscape. In terms of *participant identification*: histories 'foreground groups of people over individuals' while autobiographies/biographies exhibit the opposite trend, but neither manifests these identification strategies exclusively.[99] And in order to produce personal recounts, students must learn time management strategies, specifically *episodic time* vs. *field time*:

> And this means organising texts around phases of activity scaffolded by clause initial circumstances of location in time—the move from 'and then' to 'later on in another period of time' (from 'sequence in time' to 'setting in time' in Gleason's terms).[100]

Narrative deploying *serial* or *field time* organizes text in a sequence from each significant *temporal phase* to each significant *temporal phase* (e.g., the successive development of the character of one person, presumably telling the story from a lifetime of experience) while *episodic* or *text* time jumps *quickly through time* (episodically), treating instead each significant activity or event.[101] While history genres do employ field time where necessary, it happens less often here than in biography or autobiography.

97 Martin and Rose, *Genre Relations*, 131.
98 Martin and Rose, *Genre Relations*, 131.
99 Martin and Rose, *Genre Relations*, 131.
100 Martin and Rose, *Genre Relations*, 131.
101 See Martin and Rose, *Genre Relations*, 103–105.

Instead, historical reports tend to lean more on episodic time and tend to prefer third person discourse as a default. And biography utilizes field time less than autobiography.[102] So we find a cline of time management organized around episodes or around temporal phases connected to a single field (i.e. person or thing, usually the former) by which we can gage degrees of proximity. We see then the importance of a topological landscape because it plays 'these vectors off against one another to create a space', where for example, 'recounts can be mapped as more or less focused on individuals or groups'.[103] Again, these all work on a cline in historical genres and, therefore, should not be confused with family resemblance or strict categorical genre analysis:

> *Once again these are not categorical distinctions.* Personal and autobiographical reports do feature 1st person reference, especially as Theme; but the narrator interacts with other participants as the texts unfold. Similarly, personal, autobiographical and biographical recounts feature individuals, although reference is made to groups of people as well; historical recounts on the other hand foreground groups of people over individuals, although the 'grand narratives' of modernist history include specific reference to great men (*sic.*) by way of enacting their patriarchal reading of the past. (emphasis mine, *sic.* his)[104]

These are not categorical features but cline features, Martin emphasizes. Clines are multivariate and scaled and thus are able not only to list features (cf. the family resemblance model) but to model their relationship to one another on a number of scaled dimensions (criteria/linguistic features). This will help assess not only genre overlap, but more importantly: degrees of genre proximity relative to any scaled sociolinguistic feature or set of scaled sociolinguistic features, e.g. the field time / episodic time cline. However, even here we are limited—since it would be hard to imagine how to model more than two dimensions topologically—so Martin and Rose propose dual axis topological perspective models, even though the model posits a range of interacting scaled dimensions.

102 Martin and Rose, *Genre Relations*, 131, propose that the differing densities here could be due to the autobiographer's greater access to details and the same could probably be said of the variation in densities between histories and biographies. But it also has to do with the focus of historical reports compared to biographies or autobiographies (e.g. activity focused or entity focused).

103 Martin and Rose, *Genre Relations*, 133.

104 Martin and Rose, *Genre Relations*, 132.

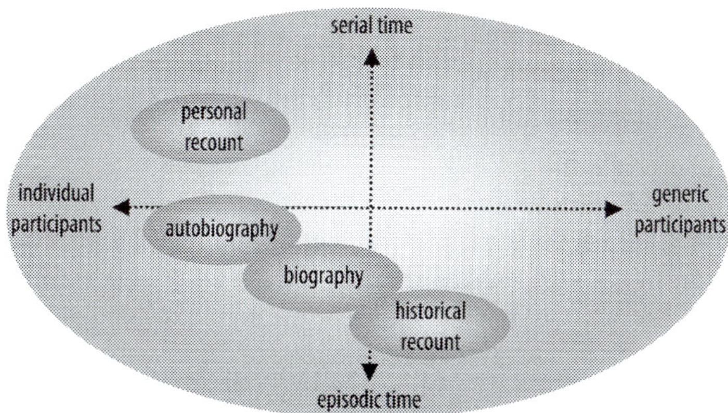

FIGURE 1.5 A topological perspective on recount genres

One can imagine how a number of further dimensions could be plotted in the above manner. The point to note here is the ability of topological perspective to take into account a document's proximity to related documents relative to any specific sociolinguistic feature.

7 Conceptions of History and Biography in Antiquity

Up to this point, we have been concerned primarily with genre theory. In the remainder of this chapter, we will turn to consider several important implications of this theoretical for assessing ancient Greek historical and biographical genres. To begin with, we will want to answer a set of related questions: How did the ancients understand the literary designations, ἱστορίας and βίος? Did they even make such distinctions? And if so: how did the two genres relate to one another, formally and in terms of their evolutionary development leading into the first century and beyond?

The Greeks did not seem to have a single genre for history. Felix Jacoby classically delineated a typology of historical genres and their development that included five components: (1) mythography or genealogy, (2) ethnography, (3) chronography, (4) contemporary history (*Zeitgeschichte*), and (5) local history or horography.[105] Several accept this basic framework, with a few caveats. Many protest Jacoby's replacing of the Greek genre 'history' with 'contemporary

105 F. Jacoby, 'Über die Entwicklung der griechischen Historiographie und den Plan einer neuen Sammlung der griechischen Historikerfragmente', *Klio* 9 (1909) 80–123.

history'.[106] We also must be careful not to rigidly apply or force ancient writings into one of the genres since many writings exhibit a combination of the historical genres and we must also account for innovation.[107] Another persistent problem with Jacoby's taxonomy involves his explanation of the βίος and horography, both of which he saw as inferior decedents of narrative, in relation to Greek history.[108] Most now accept instead Arnaldo Momigliano's reconstruction of its origins, going back far earlier (even if not in a very developed form) than Jacoby allowed.[109] Momigliano showed that the βίος likely developed out of the tendency of the ancients to collect sayings, antidotes, traditions about a person, autobiographical notes used as the raw data of historians as well as the practice in ancient rhetoric of eulogizing or criticizing another person.[110] The narrative and sequential organization of this material seems to have then developed later in relation to the Greek history. As D.S. Potter observes, 'The authors of the lives of great men (always men, it seems) found themselves increasingly drawn to the methods of narrative historians, creating a quite independent genre in its own right'.[111]

This results in a situation by the first century in which the Greek history and the βίος remain notoriously difficult to distinguish formally—even to the point that many ancients and moderns view the βίος as a form of historiography.[112] Burridge, David Balch, Stanley Porter, and Smith and Kostopoulos caution against drawing a hard and fast distinction between the two genres since both make use of so many of the same literary forms.[113] Balch's remarks appear

106 See C.W. Fornara, *The Nature of History in Ancient Greece and Rome* (Berkeley: University of California Press, 1983), 2.

107 See T.J. Luce, *The Greek Historians* (London: Routledge, 1997), 78; J. Marincola, 'Genre, Convention, and Innovation in Greco-Roman Historiography', in C.S. Kraus (ed.), *The Limits of Historiography: Genre and Narrative in Ancient Texts* (MBCB 191; Leiden: Brill, 1999), 281–324; D.S. Potter, *Literary Texts and the Roman Historian* (London: Routledge, 1999), 63–71.

108 See A. Momigliano, *The Development of Greek Biography* (Carl Newell Jackson Lectures 143; Cambridge, Mass.: Harvard University Press, 1993), 25.

109 E.g. Potter, *Literary Texts*, 68.

110 Momigliano, *Development*, 38.

111 Potter, *Literary Texts*, 68.

112 E.g. R. Syme, 'History or Biography. The Case of Tiberius Caesar', *Historia* 23 (1974): 481–96 (481).

113 D.L. Balch, 'ΜΕΤΑΒΟΛΗ ΠΟΛΙΤΕΙΩΝ—Jesus as Founder of the Church in Luke-Acts: Form and Function', in T. Penner and C.V. Stichele (eds.), *Contextualizing Acts* (Atlanta: Society of Biblical Literature, 2003), 139–88 (143); Burridge, *What are the Gospels?*, 275–79; S.E. Porter, 'The Use of Authoritative Citations in Mark's Gospel and Ancient Biography: A Study of P.Oxy. 1176', in T.R. Hatina (ed.), *Biblical Interpretation in Early Christian Gospels.*

appropriate, at this stage: 'the line between history and βίος is not so easily drawn, as the overlap in material is not always statistically evident'.[114]

Although the evidence is sketchy and often complicated by interpretive issues, a number of ancient authors discuss or seem to hint at contemporary conceptions of history and βίος, including what seemed to characterize and distinguish each. In a much-debated passage in the preface to his parallel life of *Alexander-Caesar*, Plutarch insisted that he wrote βίοι, not history: 'For it is not Histories that we are writing, but Lives' (οὔτε γὰρ ἱστορίας γράφομεν, ἀλλὰ βίους) (Plutarch, *Alex.* 1.2). There are issues especially connected with what Plutarch means here by ἱστορίας, and we will attend to these issues below,[115] but we note for now that for Plutarch, history (whatever that means) involved a comprehensive account of peoples' actions (πράξεων) (Plutarch, *Alex.* 1.1). It detailed the 'battles where thousands fall, or the greatest armaments, or sieges of cities' whereas a βίος limited material to what yielded 'greater revelation of the character' of an individual (Plutarch, *Alex.* 1.2). In his βίος of *Niceas*, Plutarch refuses to list all of the events and actions of Niceas's life and restricts his βίος instead to only those details that support the 'appreciation of character and temperament' (Plutarch, *Nic.* 1.5). He makes the same argument for including lengthy discussions about Cato's personal affairs (*C.min.* 37.5). Nepos confirms this distinction when he urges that 'if I start to give a full account of [Pelopidas'] actions (*de virtutibus*), I may seem, not to be documenting his life (*vitam*), but to be writing a history (*historiam*)' (Nepos, *Pel.* 1.1). Similarly, Tacitus speaks of a βίος as 'a record of the deeds and characters of distinguished men' (*Agr.* 1.1).

The historians stress similar distinctions. They define their agendas more broadly in terms of events and groups of participants rather than along the more individualized trajectory of the βίος. Herodotus proclaims that he will write of 'great and marvelous deeds, some displayed by the Hellenes, some by the barbarians' (1.1.1). Polybius draws a clear line between 'panegyric' (a literary predecessor to the βίος) and his own historical work (ἱστορία), and therefore, refuses to focus on issues of character related to the praise or blameworthiness of Philopoemen (a person for whom he provides a biographical description). Instead, he limits himself only to true statements and 'the policy which dictated the several actions' (Polybius 10.21.8; cf. also Lucian, *Hist.* 7 for the distinction between history and encomium). Diodorus Siculus, in the preface to his

Volume 1: *The Gospel of Mark* (LNTS 304; London: T&T Clark, 2006), 79–96 (118); Smith and Kostopoulos, 'Biography', 390–410.

114 Balch, "ΜΕΤΑΒΟΛΗ," 143.

115 E.g. T. Duff, *Plutarch's Lives: Exploring Virtue and Vice* (Oxford: Oxford University Press, 2005), 15–19, cautions here about over-pressing Plutarch's use of the language.

Library, can describe the entire enterprise of universal history as the 'presentation of events with the most excellent kind of experience' (τῆς πραγματείας ταύτης περιποιοῦσι τοῖς ἀναγινώσκουσιν) (Diodorus Siculus 1.1.1).[116] And Cassius Dio thus refers to a history Nero was composing as the 'deeds of the Romans' (τῶν Ῥωμαίων πράξεις) (Cassius Dio 62b.29.2); for as Herodian puts it, history is 'the memory of past events'(Herodian 1.1). Naturally, then, Xenophon can describe the future of Greek history as τὰ … μετὰ ταῦτα when he ends his *Hellenica* by saying 'Thus far be it written by me; the events after these will perhaps be the concern of another' (ἐμοὶ μὲν δὴ μέχρι τούτου γραφέσθω· τὰ δὲ μετὰ ταῦτα ἴσως ἄλλῳ μελήσει) (Xenophon, *Hell.* 7.5.27). And Lucian directs the historian to 'give a fine arrangement to events [εἰς καλάν διαθέσυαι τὰ πεπραγμένα] and illuminate them as vividly as possible' (Lucian, *Hist.* 52). Similarly, according to Dionysius of Halicarnassus, 'a good historian not only narrated historical events, but could assess their causes [ἀφανεῖς αἰτίας], as Theopompus could' (*Ep. Pomp.* 6.7 = T 20). So, according to Christopher Pelling, 'Thucydides shapes his narrative' so that 'selection, emphasis, articulation, temporal dislocation come together to impose a particular reading of events'.[117]

So while the Plutarch passage (*Alex.* 1.1–2) may be in question from certain angles, several ancients still seem to suggest or perhaps assume a formal distinction between the Greek history and the βίος.[118] Clearly, a great deal of overlap exists between the two genres. History may exhibit biographical interest or intent, resulting in greater levels of participant orientation, for example. But this must be distinguished from the βίος as an independent literary form structured around a singular participant.[119] Such a relationship is best modeled topologically along a set of clines.

8 Evolutionary Topology and Genre Proximity

In approaching the literary landscape that incorporates the Greek history and the βίος, we notice several influences upon the two genres in the early stages of

116 For similar statements regarding ancient history, see Diodorus Siculus 1.1.2, 3; 2.1. Adams, *Genre*, 122, thus rightly notes 'Individual biographies, in contrast to histories, begin with reference and focus on an individual'.

117 C.B.R. Pelling, *Literary Texts and the Greek Historian* (London: Routledge, 2000), 4.

118 *Contra* Smith and Kostopoulos, 'Biography', 390–410.

119 Cf. P. Stadter, 'Biography and History', in J. Marincola (ed.), *A Companion to Greek and Roman Historiography* (BCAW; Malden: Blackwell, 2007), 528–40 (528); *Contra*, Smith and Kostopoulos, 'Biography', 390–410.

their development.[120] As observed above, the βίος would eventually borrow the narrative form of Greek historical discourse, even though it otherwise developed independently of it in the context of moral discourse, rhetoric, and especially encomium. I will attempt to track here the development of both genres, noting points of common influence that may contribute to literary overlap but also places where the genres seem to have evolved somewhat independently of one another.

Prior to the fairly quick development of history within Hecataeus, Herodotus, and Thucydides, ancient rhetoric (esp. the *epitaphios* or Greek funeral oration) was the primary vehicle for transmitting Greek history, especially the history of Athens.[121] Juridical, deliberative, and epideictic rhetoric all functioned as mechanisms for the traditioning process in ancient Athens.[122] Funeral orations were particularly well suited for this purpose. Nicole Loraux insists that as one of their fundamental functions, they convey 'The Athenian History of Athens'.[123] Various individuals and their fate emerge from these settings. Demosthenes (19.273) tells of the punishment of Callias, for example. The orators also document the relation of various democratic heroes. Although the sources remain

120 Others have adopted the label 'general history' to describe the genre of Luke-Acts. For example, Aune, *New Testament*, 88, states that general history narrates '... the important historical experiences of a single national group from their origin to the recent past'. He is followed by J.B. Green, *The Gospel of Luke* (NICNT; Grand Rapids: Eerdmans, 1997), 3.

121 R. Thomas, *Literacy and Orality in Ancient Greece* (Cambridge: Cambridge University, 1992), 199.

122 J. Grethlein, *The Greeks and Their Past: Poetry, Oratory and History in the Fifth Century BCE* (Cambridge: Cambridge University, 2010), 106, acknowledges, 'The past comes into play in all three types of oratory, but ... in judicial speeches the focus is mostly on the case under discussion and references to the past are limited.... Owing to the difference in function and setting [between deliberative and epideictic oratory], they draw on the past in different ways. The use of the past in the same narrative form, albeit in different settings, is particularly interesting for a study that examines the ways in which ideas of history are shaped by narrative form and communicative context'. He points to Lysias as an example of epideictic oratory and Andocides as an example of deliberative.

123 N. Loraux, *The Invention of Athens: The Funeral Oration in the Classical City* (Cambridge, Mass.: Harvard University Press, 1986), 132–71. She (132) summarizes the basic historical function of the funeral oration as follows: 'Whatever the real power of Athens may have been in the Greek and Mediterranean world, and whether the dead were victors or vanquished, the funeral oration was responsible for reminding Athenians that, in its many acts, diversity of situations, and vicissitudes of change, the city remained one and the same. It is not, therefore, strictly speaking, a history in the sense that a "historical account" of events leads from the city's origins to the last year of war, the direct cause of present ceremony. But we still have to examine, in the rhetorical, pre-established form of the narrative itself, the techniques that make it possible for the oration to present always the same satisfying version, effacing the problems that a critical study reveals'.

somewhat bleak, both Demosthenes (23.205) and Andocides (3.3) relate traditions about Cimon and his role in the formation and history of Athens in their speeches. Rosalind Thomas insists that among these speeches, the *epitaphios* was put to frequent use in the transmission of oral tradition about the city. She examines several funeral orations including those of Pericles' Samian oration in Thucydides (2.35; although perhaps the most famous, it is somewhat atypical), Lysias' *epitaphios* on the Corinthian War (Lysias 2),[124] Plato's *epitaphios* in the *Menexenus*, and the Phliasian oration in Xenophon (*Hell.* 6.5.38).[125] Thucydides (1.73.2l; 11.36.4) shows knowledge of the general format of these speeches, which, following the *prooimion*, included a *epainos* or section of praise. But rhetorical theory influenced the development of the ancient βίος so that it serves as an influence upon both genres, especially the rhetorical use of the *encomium*. Written mechanisms for gathering historical data also seem to have served an important function. The collection of annals, for example, apparently had a central role to play in the early formations of both genres (see Cicero, *De orat.* 2.52–53).[126]

Hecataeus's *Genealogies* (500 BCE) provides the most well-known sample of the first historical genre identified by Jacoby and others.[127] Hecataeus and other genealogists, as the name indicates, sought to establish family relationships between the heroes of historical and mythical eras. Later historians continue to draw upon the genealogical tradition of history writing, showing a distinct interest in genealogical information within their histories, and drawing upon or competing with the work of the genealogical historians (e.g. Herodotus, 2.143.1–4; 5.36.2; 6.137.1; Josephus, *Ant.* 1.108, 159). However, genealo-

124 On the transmission of history in Lysias, see Grethlein, *Greeks*, 105–25 (109), who contends 'Lysias presents Athenian history from the beginning to the present in chronological order. Needless to say, the narrative has a strong patriotic bent, and of course, only few selected events are mentioned. Whole periods are skipped; for example, the Archaic Age is left out completely and the Peloponnesian War is only touched upon most perfunctorily. Yet, despite this patriotic cherry-picking, Lysias' account somehow looks like an uninterrupted sequence, since temporal markers link the single events to each other and transform the 'best-of' collection into a coherent succession'.

125 Thomas, *Orality*, 206–13.

126 Cicero states: 'For *historia* began as a mere compilation of annals, on which account, and in order to preserve the general traditions, from the earliest period of the City down to the pontificate of Publius Mucius, each High Priest used to commit to writing all the events of his year of office, and record them on a white surface, and post up the tablet at his house, that all men might have liberty to acquaint themselves therewith, and to this day those records are known as the Pontifical Chronicles' (*De orat.* 2.52–53; Sutton). On the role of written sources in the biographical tradition, see Momigliano, *Development*, 38.

127 On the treatment of these historical genres, see esp. Fornara, *Nature*, 12. My treatment below draws extensively from his work.

gy as a distinct historical genre seems to be replaced by (or rather incorporated in) within later historiography.

Ethnography, by contrast, continued into the late Roman empire. It involved documenting the 'self-conscious study of non-Greek peoples' in prose form,[128] designated later by an adjective that identified the object of the people group under investigation (e.g. *Persika, Lydiaka*). Herodotus's history is deeply indebted, therefore, to the Greek ethnographic tradition. Horography or local history recorded a city's history year by year or centered upon some aspect of a city, for example its local cult (sacred history).[129] Jacoby identified Hellanicus of Lesbos (*FrGrH* 323[a]) (fifth century BCE) as the first local historian; however, Dionysius of Halicarnassus (*De Thuc.* 5) seems to contradict this, placing horography even earlier.[130] In any case, local histories were apparently being produced by at least the fifth century BCE, Cicero describes chronography as *annals* (*De Rep.* 2.10, 18). This became the 'backbone' of Greek historiography.[131] Most date chronography to the fifth century BCE, originating with the organization of historical events into chronological lists (e.g. Hippias's *List of Olympic Victors*; the *Athenian Archon List*).[132]

What the Greeks call 'history' (ἱστορία) goes back to Hecataeus (550–476 BCE) and is then continued by Herodotus (484–425 BCE) and later Thucydides (460–395 BCE), being embodied in the historical war monograph and later in histories ranging from histories of nations to local histories. These works can be broadly defined as focusing on the actions of groups of men and nations (cf. the βίος, which focused on the character of a man).[133] As Momigliano asserts: 'The relation between biography and history is ... Greek historians were concerned with political and military *events*. Their subject matter was states, *not individuals*' (emphasis mine).[134] These works often identify themselves through a focus on πράξεις (Thucydides 1.1.2; Polybius 1.1.1; 9.1.5–6; Diodorus Siculus 1.1.1; 4.1.3 = T 9; cf. the *res gestae* in Quintilian, *Inst.* 2.4.2).[135]

128 J.E. Skinner, *Invention of Greek Ethnography* (Oxford: Oxford University Press, 2016), 3.

129 See J. Dillery, 'Greek Sacred History', *AJP* 126 (2005): 505–26.

130 Fornara, *Nature*, 17; Dillery, "Greek Sacred History," 505–07; R.L. Fowler, *Early Greek Mythography* (2 vols.; Oxford: Oxford University Press, 2000–2013), 65–66.

131 Fornara, *Nature*, 28.

132 Cf. J. Mansfeld, *Studies in the Historiography of Greek Philosophy* (Assen: Van Gorcum, 1990), 314–16.

133 But cf. Aune, *New Testament*, 78, on the πράξεις of a single man, especially in the Roman empire where the Latin *res gestae* is used instead of πράξεις to describe the 'acts' of a man (e.g. *Res Gestae Devi Augusti*).

134 Momigliano, *Development*, 39.

135 Biographies also use πράξεις but tend to apply in individualized rather than generic (i.e. group) participants. As Adams, *Genre*, 99, notes: 'Though Plutarch examines the *actions* of

Similarly, Diogenes Laërtius mentions a historian named Strabo who documented the πράξεις of Philip and Perseus' war against the Romans (Diogenes Laërtius, *Vit. phil.* 5.61; cf. also 4.5)—βίοι sometimes use similar language but in much more individualized ways.[136]

The issues become more complex when we turn to the origins of the development of the Greek βίος. For the vast majority of potentially early βίοι (usually fourth and fifth centuries BCE), we only possess fragments or references from other writers including, for example, Skylax of Caryanda, *The Story of the Tyrant (or king) Heraclides of Mylasa*; Xanthos of Lydia, *On Empedocles*; and Stesimbrotos of Thasos, *On Themistocles, Thucydides, and Pericles*. However, there is debate on whether these really represented an early form of the βίος or functioned more like precursors to the genre.[137] Perhaps the earliest widely regarded biographical document is Satyrus' *Euripides* (3rd century BCE), but only portions of it survive. Therefore, many see Plutarch in the first century CE as one of the first complete formal representations of the genre (see chapter 2 for discussion), with a great degree of formalization in Plutarch, further crystalizing in those who wrote in the biographical tradition after him (e.g. Diogenes Laërtius; Philostratus).

9 Genre Elasticity and Blurring

With genre proximity comes genre blurring where the formal boundaries of a genre may not always be clear or maintained by its sample texts. Most recent treatments of genre note the phenomenon of genre blending, bending, or blurring, including those among New Testament scholars. As Martin and Rose indicate, 'The elasticity of discourse and the attendant facility with which texts adapt to their context means that now and again we'll come across texts which are difficult to categorise as one genre or another (i.e. texts that "blend" genres)'.[138] However, hope is not lost, since, 'At the same time, the metastability of culture as a predictable system of genres means that we regularly recognise

his subjects, it is with the intention of delineating *their virtues and vices* in order to elicit (positive) change within the reader' (emphasis mine). But Adams mentions only sparse evidence in the biographical tradition for reference to biographies as πράξεις. When they do, however, they are highly individualized portraits. See Eunapius, *Vit. phil.* 453–54 and Diogenes Laërtius, *Vit. phil.* 7.175, noted in Adams, *Genre*, 119.

136 See Adams, *Genre*, 118.

137 On these early nonextant (potentially) biographical works, see Adams, *Genre*, 71–73.

138 Martin and Rose, *Genre Relations*, 133.

and participate in texts as enacting one genre or another'.[139] Additionally, Systemic Functional Linguistics (SFL) builds topological clines into its model in large part to account for genre blending.

While several ancients (noted above) appear to proceed from what seems to be a fairly clear distinction between ancient βίοι and history, some classicists have recently noted the inherent ambiguity of some of these distinctions. Plutarch's differentiation of history and the βίος in *Alex* 1.1–2 (noted above) has come under a great deal of scrutiny. Tim Duff famously points, for example, to several other places where Plutarch seems to be using the two almost interchangeably or using history in contrast to myth, not to other genres (See, e.g., Plutarch, *Nic.* 1 and *Aem.* 1.1).[140] Or consider this passage from Dionysius of Halicarnassus.

> ἀνάγκη δ' ἴσως πρῶτον, ὡς παρέλαβον ἐκ τῶν κοινῶν ἱστοριῶν, ἃ κατέλιπον ἡμῖν οἱ τοὺς βίους.
>
> And I ought to mention first, that I have taken from the current **histories**, which the **biographers** left behind for us.
>
> *Amm.* 3.15

Here, it seems that the biographers are the historians that Dionysius uses for his sources. Or perhaps the biographers left the histories that Dionysius used (i.e. they were the biographers' sources). Interpretation here depends upon the meaning of κατέλιπον. It could have a more general meaning but it could mean 'bequeathed', so that the biographies are passing down the history. The active voice and focus on sources probably tip the scales in favor of the biographers as the historians but the more general view cannot be ruled out. This kind of ambiguity pervades the classical literature when βιός and ἱστορία occur as collocates.[141] So at least in certain instances, it seems that the ancients may

139 Martin and Rose, *Genre Relations*, 133.

140 Duff, *Plutarch's Lives*, 15–19. See also C.B.R. Pelling, 'Plutarch's Method of Work in the Roman Lives', *JHS* 99 (1979): 74–96; C.B.R. Pelling, 'Plutarch's Adaptation of His Source Material', *JHS* 100 (1980): 127–40; D.L. Balch, *Contested Ethnicities and Images Studies in Acts and Arts* (WUNT 345; Tübingen: Mohr Siebeck, 2015), 200–203; J. Grethlein, *Experience and Teleology in Ancient Historiography Futures Past from Herodotus to Augustine* (Cambridge: Cambridge University, 2016), 92.

141 On these blurred distinctions, see also esp. B. Gentili and G. Cerri, *History and Biography in Ancient Thought* (Amsterdam: J.C. Gieben, 1988), *passim*.

not have maintained as clear a literary distinction between history and the βιός as we would like. Such passages punctuate the problem of genre blurring.[142]

Genre blurring occurs as a result of genre proximity and generic elasticity. Prior studies of the Gospels genre allow for overlapping genre categories but do not provide us with *scaled* (only category) features for the βίος genre. But given the elasticity of genre, some features manifest more strongly and consistently than others (they have stronger *generic codification*),[143] a phenomenon not easily modeled through feature categories. Clines handle these difficulties quite capably. A βίος might fall on the far end of a cline with respect to one feature, for example, but in the middle of the cline with respect to another. Clines allow us in this way to move beyond the simple observation that genre boundaries blur, enabling us to also explore *how, in what directions, and to what degrees, they blur—and relative to what features.*

10 Typological Analysis of Greek Historical Genres

Typological analysis assesses genre differences. We will begin by considering the role of feature clusters in genre agnation. After highlighting some of the salient limitations of feature cluster analysis in the treatments of genre by Burridge and Adams, we turn to the role of SFL genre agnation scales for further theoretical assistance in assessing genre divergence. From here, we will provide the methodological outline that will drive our analysis in the subsequent chapters.

10.1 *Feature Clusters in Genre Agnation*

Burridge provides parameters for defining genre, when he urges that the 'temptation to think of genre as defined by one particular feature, or even a couple, should be avoided because any one feature can appear in a number of different sorts of works'. Therefore, he concludes, 'one should look for many features; it is the combination of them which constitutes the genre'.[144] Adams has recently endorsed this basic assessment.[145] The family resemblance model of contemporary (New Testament) genre critics essentially locates clusters of features in what many identify as instances of the Greek βίος. It then seeks to

142 This problem leads Smith and Kostopoulos, 'Biography', 390–411, to question our ability to distinguish certain ancient genres at all.

143 On linguistic codification of formal features, see P.H. Matthews, *Syntax* (CTL; Cambridge: Cambridge University Press, 1981), 20–21.

144 Burridge, *What are the Gospels?*, 41.

145 Adams, *Genre*, 58–59.

show that Luke-Acts or the Gospels manifest parallel clusters of features. *But this does not demonstrate that Luke-Acts or the Gospels are βίοι.* It only shows that *they share a set of features that Burridge and others have identified in several βίοι.* After all, could not one of these feature clusters occur in other genres as well? Since Burridge's model admittedly does not provide sustained comparison of the βίος with the related set of genres that his criteria identify, we are left without an answer to that question.

10.2 *Feature Clusters in Burridge's Model of Genre*

It is important to zero in on the precise function of feature clusters in modern genre study, as represented most thoroughly in Burridge's analysis.[146] It must be stressed that the major (containing) cluster (with all of the features one investigates) seldom appears as a whole in any one document. In practice, then, it is a smaller cluster that includes features from the larger cluster that becomes the focus of analysis. In other words, most biographical sample texts *do not exhibit all the features* Burridge and others name, just sectors of the major cluster found in the biographical corpus. Since the features are not scaled or weighted in anyway, features with low levels of realization (e.g. a feature present in 20% of the biographical corpus) are attributed the same evidentiary status as features with highly persistent realization (e.g. a feature present in 80% of the biographical corpus).

For example, βίοι are quite varied in terms of length so that many of the sample texts Burridge provides fail to meet the minimum (10,000 words) (e.g. Isocrates, *Evagoras*; Satyrus, *Euripides*; Nepos, *Atticus*) or exceed (25,000 words) (Philo, *Moses*; Suetonius, *Lives*; Philostratus, *Apollonius of Tyana*) the maximum length range for biographical documents (see Tab. 1.1).[147] How does he account for this? He notes that the *Euripides* text is fragmentary. Although we do not know the length of the biography Satyrus wrote, Burridge follows Hunt in providing an estimate of 3,600 words for the Euripides portion of the fragmentary document.[148] Burridge slips Isocrates into the medium length range by an approximation but technically[149] this document fails to meet the lower end of Burridge's length range as well.[150]

146 Burridge, *What are the Gospels?*; Adams, *Genre*.

147 Burridge, *What are the Gospels?*, 114.

148 Burridge, *What are the Gospels?*, 134.

149 My computer count of Isocrates' *Evagoras* indicates that it contains 4,682 words, which actually fails the minimum word length diagnostic by a few hundred words. We see here the problem of category features since a cline would more helpful here, modeling borderline cases.

150 Burridge, *What are the Gospels?*, 134.

TABLE 1.1 Length ranges for Burridge's corpus of early Greco-Roman βίοι

Ancient work	**Word count (Burridge)**
Biographical Length Range:	**5,000–10,00 words**[a]
Isocrates' *Evagoras*:	about 5,000 words
Xenophon's *Agesilaus*:	7,558 words (computer count)
Nepos' *Atticus*:	about 3,500 words
Philo's *Moses*:	about 32,000 words

a Burridge, *What are the Gospels?*, 113.

That only leaves Xenophon's *Agesilaus* as falling within the biographical length range in the 'early' Greco-Roman βίοι. Burridge suggests that Philo is a two-scroll work but note this is not a collected biography but two volumes on one person, Moses. The total length of the document is relevant, therefore, which comes in at 32,636 words. That means only 1 out of 5 of these documents manifest the appropriate length range for Greco-Roman βίοι proposed by Burridge.

This observation carries over to the 'later' βίοι. Burridge recognizes the extraordinary length of Philostratus's biography but simply concedes that 'Once again, there is a problem in describing the *Apollonius of Tyana* as a βίος'.[151] Yet this text functions as one of his biographical samples. He does not comment on the length of Suetonius' work but this is noteworthy at over 70k words. And he treats the entire 12 lives as a group, rather than singling out one life from a set of parallel lives, as he did with Plutarch's *Cato Minor*, so the size of the entire document seems pertinent. He claims that the tendency of political biographies to exceed the length of intellectual biographies accounts the brevity of the biographies by Nepos and Lucian.[152] But it seems unclear to me at least how this distinction in sub-genre softens the fact these two sample texts fall outside of the established ranges. Among the later Greco-Roman βίοι, only the biography by Tacitus is in range, so 1 out of 5 again, or 2 out of 10, total—essentially, a 20% realization across the corpus. This raises the question of how useful a feature cluster including length may really be or at least how it should be weighted in relation to other features in a cluster, if it is used.

151 Burridge, *What are the Gospels?*, 165.

152 Burridge, *What are the Gospels?*, 164.

10.3 *Feature Clusters in Adams' Model of Genre*

Adams adopts the essential structure of Burridge's methodology (down to the use of his exact criteria), where the quest for genre is guided by assessing groupings of formal features common to the biographical genre:

> The formal features identified by the ancients and discussed above (metre, style, subject, length, opening sentence, preface, structure, and purpose) all assist in genre delineation. Note that for the ancients these components were not used discretely or in isolation, but often worked together, each bringing its own voice to provide clarity to the question of genre.[153]

Adams insists that in addition to these clusters of features—which he acknowledges often occur in many genres—we may look to two additional criteria in order to distinguish the Greco-Roman history from the collected biographies of the ancient world. Adams abandons Burridge's verbal subjects criterion[154] and points instead to the individualized focus and the distinctive organizational paradigm of the collected biographies as potential disambiguating structures.[155] Although Adams' two criteria seem promising—they certainly mark an advancement beyond Burridge—I will argue in subsequent chapters that a further refinement of these criteria ultimately undermines the conclusions Adams draws.

10.4 *The Contribution of Feature Cluster Analysis to Genre Study*

What role do these feature clusters serve then? Intuitively, they do seem important. And they are. Some interesting work has been done lately in web-based genre studies and corpus linguistics utilizing the concept of *cluster analysis* (and related modeling strategies), which is essentially the kind of (though non-digitized) textual phenomena that Burridge and others emphasize.[156] In an ideal world, with richly annotated texts fueling the compilation of immense bodies of ancient linguistic data, we could use feature clusters, as many modern genre theorists do, to create the base categories rather than constructing the categories *a priori* and bringing those categories to the text in question. For example, one could use the 20 features out of 1,000 that tend to cluster

153 Cf. Adams, *Genre*, 49.
154 Adams, *Genre*, 129.
155 Adams, *Genre*, 114.
156 See esp. H. Moisl, *Cluster Analysis for Corpus Linguistics* (QL 66; Berlin: De Gruyter Mouton, 2015).

together in a corpus-wide search of multiple genres. But in biblical studies, due to the primitive nature of the texts we are working with, we do not always live in an ideal world, with richly annotated corpora and software tools designed to search them.

Instead, we will have to limit ourselves to *a priori* categories and features for now but category features can still serve an important proximating function. Feature clusters, in particular, help us identify first and foremost, sets of features potentially common to one or more genres, and second, they raise the question as to whether this cluster(s) (or portions of it) surfaces in other genres and all that this may entail for genre relationships and cross-pollination. In relation to this first role, *feature clusters proximate likeness* (i.e. that a set of documents have a 'likeness' or share similarities in common) *but they do not establish the degree or significance of that likeness because other genres are not considered as part of the model, at least not in any systematic way.*[157] At this point the modern genre critic may protest: yes, many genres share some of these features but they only seem to cluster tightly together (as a kind of constellation) in the Greco-Roman βίοι.[158] Perhaps. But how would they know this since their model does not *systematically* (of course, Burridge and especially Adams do make reference to many other genres) calibrate the role of their feature clusters relative to any other genre but the βίος? In fact, as I noted earlier in this chapter, the feature clusters Burridge identifies (and Adams later adopts) for the Greek βίος *do* tend to be the same ones that we find in the Greek history, despite Burridge's insistence to the contrary.

11 Feature Clines and Genre Analysis: a Methodological Outline

This book and the criteria that it delineates are an expansion of the basic methodology that I outlined in my 2015 SBL Paper, "The Genre of the Third Gospel and Greco-Roman Historiography," which initially plotted out six criteria for distinguishing the Greek βίος from the Greek history (the current project expands this number to nine). The paper won the 2015 Achtemeier award for New Testament scholarship and I presented the paper with Richard Burridge as a respondent. Burridge had many thoughtful and productive responses to

157 A lucid illustration of this point is found in the fact that Burridge only employs a 'control group' corpus for one of his criteria—verbal subjects—and this control group only consists of two authors, two books from one (Homer) and a passage from another (Herodotus). See Chapter 2 for discussion.

158 See Burridge, *What are the Gospels?*, 41; Adams, *Genre*, 49.

the paper and he has now published those responses in his 25th-Anniversary edition of his *What are the Gospels?* (2018). When I decided to expand the paper into the current book, I sought to take Burridge's criticisms of my Achtemeier paper into account at every turn of the project. His biggest critique was that my criteria were not based in modern genre theory, a weakness in my model that I have gone to great lengths to correct. His critiques were not published at the time I wrote this book, so I did not cite them but did take them into account so that many of the points he makes in response to my Achtemeier paper are (hopefully) irrelevant for this new, repackaged version of the argument. Nevertheless, I have included footnotes where he has responsed to the Achtemeier-version of my argument so that the reader can discern whether I have fully addressed his concerns.

We will take as our starting point both the Greek history and the βίος as related instances of Greek prose discourse. As Momigliano and Potter suggest, although the βίος likely developed independently of Greek historiography, it was later influenced by it, especially in terms of its narrative form. So by the first century, instead of a definitive distinction between the Greek history and the βίος, we may imagine a spectrum of Greek prose (historical and biographical) writings that we may differentiate on the basis of several clines, suggested by Martin and Rose.

Martin concludes that histories seem characterized by more generalized narrative whereas biographies tend to be more specified in their orientation.[159] From this basic choice between more general and specified narratives, in fact, seem to flow two further distinctive features for both genres. One of the primary differences between histories and biographies is their *aboutness* or *topic*. Histories tend to discuss several related topics whereas biographies tend toward have more specific topicality, realized around the story of one person. Martin, for example, provides a network 'that shows procedures to be immediately agnate to historical recounts with genres they share a *generalized* focus on *activity*' (emphasis mine). That is, histories tend to be 'activity focused', dealing with large activity sequences,[160] whereas biographies tends to be 'entity focused', dealing with specific people.[161] As Martin and Rose note, 'discourse patterns of texts vary in the degree to which they are organised as activity sequences, and whether they are about specific people and things, or about general classes of phenomena and their features'.[162] Historical and biographical

159 Martin, 'Analyzing Genre', 13.

160 On this terminology, see Martin and Rose, *Genre*, 14.

161 Martin, 'Analysing Genre', 13–14.

162 Martin and Rose, *Genre Relations*, 14.

genres also diverge *via* their *participant identification strategies*.[163] Biographies tend to realize *individualized* participant structures whereas histories tend to be more *generic*, often foregrounding groups rather than individuals as major participants in the narrative.

The organizational architecture of a text provides the most significant and consistent point of realization for formal generic features. Formally, three categories are relevant when discussing the literary-rhetorical organization of Greek historical and biographical discourse: (1) *frames*, (2) *time management*, and (3) *authentication strategy*.

Frames refer to macro-level structures that help 'frame' or stage the narrative.[164] Due to their high-level functionality, these frames often provide insight into the question of genre. The first frame we shall consider is the *initiation*. This functional category allows us to discuss documents both with and without a formal preface since all texts must *initiate* their discourse in some way, with the preface being the most typical formal realization in Greek histories and βίοι. Histories tend to construct more concise, *panoramic* initiations whereas βίοι seem to deploy more detailed, *focalized* initiations. After the initiation, the narrative body commences. *Commencements* may be *event-driven*, as in histories, or *participant-driven*, as in biographies. Another method of literary framing recurs through genre *self-identification*. Most ancient biographies identify themselves as such whereas some genres, such as history, do not employ consistent self-identifications. Finally, I propose that histories and βίοι position their genealogical information at distinct locations in the narrative. Histories tend to *embed* their genealogies more deeply within the narrative body while βίοι *stage* this information, usually on the opening lines of the body of the work.

In addition to various frames, *time management* and *authentication strategies* can provide insight into questions of genre through literary structuring. In terms of *time management*, Martin and Rose proposed the distinction between *episodic time* and *field time*, which has been briefly introduced already. Histories tend to use *episodic time*, moving quickly from sequence of events to sequence of events, whereas biographies tend to progress more slowly, frequently organizing the text through *field time*—the gradual unfolding of time from the perspective of a single field (the subject of the βίος). A final consideration involves *authentication strategy*. One of the primary means of authorization in the

163 Martin and Rose, *Genre Relations*, 131.

164 See J.E. Grimes, *The Thread of Discourse* (JLSM 207; The Hague: Mouton, 1975), 323–36.

ancient world was the authoritative citation of sources.[165] Histories tend to exhibit far lower densities for authoritative citation (i.e. formula citations) than ancient βίοι. In this way, the biographical tradition seems to reflect *unbounded* authentication strategies whereas histories seem to assume more *bounded* environments. At this point, we may summarize the following proposed clines for examining Greek historical and biographical genres:

Cline	The Greek history	The βίος
FOCUS	*Activity Focused*	*Entity Focused*
PARTICIPANT IDENTIFICATION	*Generic Participants*	*Individual Participant(s)*
FRAMES		
INITIATION	*Panoramic*	*Focalized*
COMMENCEMENT	*Event-Driven*	*Participant-Driven*
SELF-IDENTIFICATION	*Nonbiographical*	*Biographical*
GENEALOGIES	*Embedded*	*Staged*
TIME MANAGEMENT	*Episodic Time*	*Field Time*
AUTHENTICATION STRATEGY	*Bounded*	*Unbounded*

FIGURE 1.6 Typological agnation features for the Greek history and βίος genres

In terms of topology, we can locate any given document on a cline relative to their degree of realization (*codification*, i.e. how strongly a feature is codified)[166] for any given feature or set of features above. This allows us not only to proximate genres but also specific documents relative to one another. These features can be configured in binary opposition as well, for typological purposes. If a document in question is *more* episodically driven *than not* (even if less so than most other histories), in binary or typological perspective, we still consider it organized by episodic time. These SFL feature scales, then, allow us to nuance the degree of similarity or divergence while binary typology enables genre agnation.

165 J. Marincola, *Authority and Tradition in Ancient Historiography* (Cambridge: Cambridge University Press, 1997), 243.

166 See Matthews, *Syntax*, 20–21.

12 Linguistic Hierarchy, Macrostructural Analysis, and Macrogenre

Halliday, Hasan, and Martin all view genre as that element of the cultural configuration that determines the *macrostructure* of texts.[167] For Martin, macrostructures bridge the ever-elusive gap between social context (register) and form. Since generically guided macrostructures realize different textual elements (i.e. formal features), we have a direct top-down sociolinguistic hierarchy, from register to form, meeting the modern demands for a sociologically constrained account of genre.

The concept of macrostructural analysis draws from Halliday's distinction between macro- and micro-level discourse structures. *Macrostructures* refer to higher-level (i.e. global) discourse elements (discourse, episode and paragraph level/rank) in contrast to *microstructures* which refer to lower-level (i.e. local) discourse elements (clause complexes or sentences, clauses, word groups, etc.). Halliday envisions these relationships in terms of a *rank scale* or leveled hierarchy of language. As Liesbet Heyvaert notes,

> The levels of analysis that are needed for description of constructions reflect a kind of hierarchy among the symbolic units of language: symbolic units seem to be situated among layers of 'lower' and 'higher' levels of organization, whereby the lower levels define the construction analytically or internally and higher levels situate the construction externally or synthetically. To account for this hierarchy, Halliday (1961) introduced the construct of the *rank scale*. In his original interpretation of the notion of 'rank'—which is very much based on a constituency-oriented model of language—a rank grammar is said to be 'one which specifies and labels a fixed number of layers in the hierarchy of constituents such that any constituent may be assigned to one or other of the specified layers, or ranks' (Halliday 1966b:111). The various levels of organization that may thus be distinguished correspond to specific determinate stretches of structure, characterized by a distinction in 'size', i.e. the *sentence, clause, phrase, word, morpheme* (Halliday 1961) (emphasis his).[168]

Each rank or level can then be assigned formal feature realizations relevant for understanding genre. Macro and microstructures distinguish themselves

167 Halliday and Hasan, *Language*, 63; J.R. Martin, *English Text: System and Structure* (Philadelphia: John Benjamins, 1992), 500–502.

168 L. Heyvaert, *A Cognitive Functional Approach to Nominalization in English* (Cognitive Linguistics Research 26; Berlin: Mouton de Gruyter, 2003), 21–22.

Rank scale		Formal generic features
Macrostructure & Macrogenre	Discourse	narrative initiations (prefaces) narrative terminations (closings)
	Episode	narrative commencements book-level transitions
	Paragraph	embedded genealogies paragraph staging
Microstructure & Microgenre	*Clause Complex*	literary *topoi*
	Clause	
	Word Group	
	Word	

FIGURE 1.7 Formal macro- and micro-structural units relevant for genre agnation

formally in the way they are constructed. Lower-level elements such as the clause complex, clause, and the word group form through syntactic relations. Higher-level elements emerge in connection with a range of discourse structures (e.g. cohesive devices, conjunction usage, etc.) and framing devices.

Much of the ambivalence that persists in modern studies of the genre of Luke-Acts likely results from the focus on micro rather than macrostructures. *Microstructures are important for analyzing microgenres but macrostructure seems more significant when analyzing macrogenre.*[169] Literary *topoi* usually occur at lower levels of the discourse, often introducing ambiguity as they recur across multiple genres, and so we have followed Martin in focusing our analysis instead on the macrostructures of a discourse as the places where genre-specific features will most likely consistently surface. This will include examining the preface and its contents (initiations) from a variety of angles. It will also involve consideration of narrative closings in the wider discussion of field vs. episodic time in ancient historical and biographical discourse. Commencements into the narrative body and transitions from one book to another both provide macrostructures poised for potential generic encoding as well. We also explore paragraph-level *embedded* genealogies in ancient history but these are

169 On microgenre, see Kasper Bro Larsen, *Recognizing the Stranger: Recognition Scenes in the Gospel of John* (Brill's Paperback Collection; Leiden: Brill, 2012), 219–20; Anders K. Peterson, "Generic Docetism: From the Synoptic Narrative Gospels to the Johannine Discursive Gospel," in Kasper Bro Larsen (ed.), *The Gospel of John as Genre Mosaic* (Studia Aarhusiana Neotestamentica 3; Leiden: Brill, 2015), 99–124.

contrasted to the staged higher-level genealogical structures we find in Greco-Roman biographical texts so that higher-level observations still drive the analysis. We will also look at the way paragraphs are 'staged' as supporting evidence for conclusions we draw regarding topicality. And from time to time, we will discuss the paragraph in relation to larger episodic or discourse structures as well.

To illustrate the importance of investigating macrostructure in genre analysis take, for example, epistolary analysis of Pauline literature. Epistolary categories form the basic macrostructural backbone of the Pauline letter. The papyri tend to employ the following discourse- and episode-level macrostructure, which Paul imitates:

(1) letter-opening;
(2) thanksgiving;
(3) letter-body (including body-opening; body-middle; and body-closing) (some debate whether there is a expositional and paraenetic division within the body as well); and
(4) letter-closing.[170]

In fact, we may use epistolary analysis derived from these papryological categories to assess the basic macrostructure of the Pauline letter, and this has been done several times with quite consistent results.[171] But beyond this, epistolary analysis does not provide much help in, for example, determining paragraph divisions. Genre seems to be less determinative (even if its presence is still felt) in the microstructures or at more local levels of the discourse. For example, we do find many epistolary *topoi* (e.g. epistolary formulas) at lower levels of the discourse (usually at the clause or clause complex levels)[172] but these often occur in a variety of other genres as well.[173] It is the configuration of epistolary macro-level components that provides the primary diagnostic for

170 For discussion, see A.W. Pitts, 'Philosophical and Epistolary Contexts for Pauline Paraenesis', in S.E. Porter and S.A. Adams (eds.), *Paul and the Ancient Letter Form* (PAST 6; Leiden: Brill, 2010), 269–306.

171 See recently, e.g., R.E. Richards, *Paul and First-Century Letter Writing: Secretaries, Composition and Collection* (Downers Grove: InterVarsity, 2004); S.E. Porter and S.A. Adams (eds.), *Paul and the Ancient Letter Form* (PAST 6; Leiden: Brill, 2010); J.A.D. Weima, *Paul the Ancient Letter Writer: An Introduction to Epistolary Analysis* (Grand Rapids: Baker Academic, 2016).

172 See S.E. Porter and A.W. Pitts, 'The Disclosure Formula in the Epistolary Papyri and in the New Testament: Development, Form, Function and Syntax', in S.E. Porter and A.W. Pitts, *The Language of the New Testament: Context, History, and Development* (LBS 6; ECH 3; Leiden: Brill, 2013), 432–38, on the various lower levels at which the disclosure formula operates in the epistolary papyri and the New Testament letters.

173 For discussion, see Pitts, 'Philosophical and Epistolary Contexts', 269–306.

identifying this genre in the papyri and in Paul. Then, more local-level features seem to perform a confirmatory function to be interpreted in light of wider literary framing. So, in investigating Greek historical and biographical genres, we will want to pay close attention to macrostructural discourse components as potential locations for generic coding. In particular, we will focus especially on features that tend to occur at the episode levels and higher in the sample texts that we eventually adopt.

13 Conclusions

We opened our brief tour of contemporary genre methodology by drawing attention to New Testament scholarship's neglect of *literary divergence* in genre analysis. The problem surfaces in an especially enigmatic way in the study of Luke-Acts. The author clearly deploys a number of features common to (perhaps) multiple genres. With new or nuanced proposals surfacing all the time, this leaves an important methodological question still unanswered: How do we determine the genre of Luke-Acts, given its resemblance to so many genres? Modern genre theory has an answer to this problem but it is not in the antiquated structuralist account of genre driven by family resemblance criticism, popular among New Testament scholars today. Though they often cast their methods in terms of the newest and best in literary theory, recent studies of the Gospels and/or Luke-Acts fail to engage with recent trends in genre study and so remain unviable for the reasons the prior models on which they are based did. Structuralism is unable to calibrate the role of context sufficiently and family resemblance theory only targets genre similarities, not genre differences.

New genre study, therefore, builds models for agnation into their broader accounts of genre. J.R. Martin and David Rose provide a sophisticated agnation (i.e. genre relations) model in their typology of historical genres, including history, biography, and autobiography. In place of the category features so popular in the structuralist era and among New Testament scholars today, Martin and Rose suggest the use of agnating scales of variation and proximity as the basis for forming genre typologies. But they also stress the role of topological perspective in understanding genre proximity, allowing us to treat issues like genre development, elasticity, and blurring.

Despite frequent formal overlap, SFL genre agnation scales allow us to identify genre boundaries for the Greek history and the βίος (even if these are at times flexible relative to certain sociolinguistic features). We proposed eight scales in particular, either derived from or inspired by Martin and Rose's SFL genre agnation model: (1) focus, (2) participant identification, (3) initiations, (4) commencements, (5) self-identification, (6) genealogies, (7) time management, and (8) authentication strategy. We also emphasized the role of macrostructures in Systemic Functional Linguistic (SFL) genre analysis. These methodological principles will guide our study of Greek historical and biographical texts in subsequent chapters. But first, in the next chapter, I will seek to establish just which texts those should be.

CHAPTER 2

Identifying Greek History and Biography

How do we identify the most representative samples for the Greek historical and biographical genres? The answer to this question is complicated by debates revolving around serval (especially) early biographical writings. I will argue, however, that careful attention to diachronic issues may help better situate this discussion. I also insist upon the importance of corpus design criteria in the process of corpus compilation. Corpus linguistics provides a powerful resource to the contemporary genre critic. But if neglected, it leaves the interpreter vulnerable to compromised data and, by extension, unstable conclusions. After briefly outlining some of the salient principles of corpus linguistics and their application to New Testament genre study, this chapter will identify a corpus of Greek historical and biographical texts that will provide a basis for typological comparisons with Luke-Acts. In this way, the present chapter sets up the remainder of the book, which will compare the Greek history and the βίος to Luke-Acts *via* the eight genre agnation scales developed in the prior chapter.

1 What is a 'Representative' Corpus and Why is it Important?

A great deal of attention is given in contemporary genre study to corpus compilation. Graeme Kennedy urges that the 'purpose of sampling adequately' is 'so that generalizations can be made readily and validly about the whole'.[1] Or as Matthew Brook O'Donnell, in his work on *Corpus Linguistics and the Greek of the New Testament*, insists: when compiling Hellenistic texts in order to make comparative assessments relative to the New Testament on issues like genre,

> The Hellenistic Greek linguist must work primarily with the extant body of documents from the Hellenistic period ... The limited and accidental nature of the extant Hellenistic literature ... requires the careful attention to sampling and compilation criteria that built earlier corpora ... In order to make generalizations and test theories concerning the nature of

1 G.D. Kennedy, *An Introduction to Corpus Linguistics* (New York: Routledge, 2016), 74.

 DOI:10.1163/9789004406544_003

> language, these texts must be classified and grouped in a manner that allows for representative statements to be made.[2]

In other words, a carefully constructed (i.e. representative) corpus is more likely to yield reliable results, and vice versa.

In one recent treatment, exploring the relationship of corpus linguistics to genre theory, Chengyu Fang and Jing Cao note, 'By and large in the past 50 years, the representative function of the corpus has been thoroughly understood and appreciated' in genre studies.[3] When creating a representative corpus, two theoretical issues confront the interpreter of ancient genres: corpus design and compilation.[4] As Kennedy puts it, 'Issues in corpus design and compilation are fundamentally concerned with validity and reliability of research, based on a particular corpus, including whether that corpus can serve the purpose for which it was intended'.[5] And this raises a range of further issues: (1) static vs. dynamic corpora; (2) the degree to which the corpus is representative of a language or genre; and (3) corpus and sample text size.[6] These criteria assess or provide diagnostics for corpus design in terms of both corpus *quality* and *quantity*.

Corpus Quality

1. *Static vs. Dynamic Corpora*. Static corpora seek to establish a very tight group of related texts as a kind of snapshot of the language. These are synchronic in nature. Dynamic or monitor corpora, are so called because they monitor changes in a genre over time. These corpora, then, are diachronic in nature.
2. *Representativeness and Balance*. Kennedy raises the question: representative of what? This depends upon the research focus. If one seeks to investigate grammatical features in Greek, they will need a representative corpus of the Greek language, including its many genres.[7] When analyzing a more specific structure such as genre, one must ensure that the corpus is as 'thoroughly representative' of 'a particular genre, subject field or topic' as possible.[8] 'The particular year or years from which

2 M.B. O'Donnell, *Corpus Linguistics and the Greek of the New Testament* (NTM 6; Sheffield: Sheffield Phoenix Press, 2005), 137.

3 C. Fang and J. Cao, *Text Genres and Registers: The Computation of Linguistic Features* (Berlin: Springer, 2015), 6.

4 Kennedy, *Introduction*, 60.

5 Kennedy, *Introduction*, 60.

6 Kennedy, *Introduction*, 60–69.

7 See O'Donnell, *Corpus Linguistics*, 135–38.

8 Kennedy, *Introduction*, 62.

texts are selected are significant too'.[9] Further issues arise when—as Burridge does—compiling a *comparative corpus*: 'What are the criteria for inclusion?'[10] This also raises the issue of *balance*. With comparative corpora, the two corpora should exhibit balance in quality (see above) and quantity (see below).

Corpus Quantity

3. *Size*. This concerns not only the raw word count for the corpus but also 'how many categories the corpus should contain, how many samples the corpus should contain in each category, and how many words there should be in each sample'.[11]

These principles of corpus design and compilation will guide our selection of Greek historical and biographical texts later in this chapter.

2 Toward a Representative Corpus of the Greek History Genre

In order to apply our SFL feature clines to Greek historical and biographical discourse in order to ultimately see how Luke-Acts fares in comparison, we will need to develop a representative corpus of writings from both genres. We will use history as the genre for forming the base corpus. The nine histories I have chosen are Herodotus (484–425 BCE), Thucydides (460–395 BCE), two works from Xenophon (430–354 BCE) (*Anabasis* and *Hellenica*), Polybius (200–118 BCE), Diodorus Siculus' (90–30 BCE) *Library of History*, Dionysius of Halicarnassus' (60s BCE–after 7 CE) *Roman Antiquities*, Josephus' (CE 37–100) *Antiquities*, and Appian's (CE 95–165) *Civil Wars*. This gives us a wide-ranging chronological sample, with the tightest cluster of histories around the first century, representing very different styles of writing and topic matter and these historians (with the exception of Josephus, who adds Jewish variety, and maybe Appian) are among the most hailed expressions of the Greek historical genre from the ancient world. I limited my selection to only those histories in Greek (excluding the several Latin historians) to create linguistic balance with the comparative corpus of biographical texts (also, all in Greek) and with the Greek text of Luke-Acts. But Latin historians will be cross-referenced (mainly in the footnotes) throughout.

9 Kennedy, *Introduction*, 64.
10 Kennedy, *Introduction*, 64.
11 Kennedy, *Introduction*, 66.

As the first to attempt at a serious history beyond the mythographic epic-writing of his day, many in the ancient world consider Herodotus (484–425 BCE) the father of Greek historiography. Herodotus took over the basic themes (e.g. war) and format (narrative poetry) of the *Iliad* and *Odyssey*, but sought to impute to his work a greater sense of veracity.[12] Herodotus appears unable to fully dislodge himself from the tradition of his mythical predecessors, including many fantastic stories and incredible traditions within the flow of his historical narrative.[13] Thucydides (460–395 BCE) marks the next major development in Greek historiography. Yet, Dionysius of Halicarnassus found him inadequate as a writer, seeking to edit out Thucydides' famous *Archaeology* due to its supposedly poorly formed role in the narrative (Dionysius of Halicarnassus, *Thucy.* 19–20). I think we are all glad Dionysius did not have his way, since the *Archaeology* is, according to Hans van Wess, 'now universally regarded as a landmark of historical analysis'.[14] Picking up where Thucydides left off, Xenophon (430–354 BCE) clearly functions as an eyewitness to many of the events he records. Unlike Herodotus and Thucydides, Xenophon abstains from discussion of his sources. Various friends may also have been involved as sources in Xenophon's historical investigations.[15] Arnaldo Momigliano and John Dillery note that only he is able to rival Tacitus among the historians of antiquity in 'the range of writing that came from his pen'.[16] So it is no wonder that Xenophon counts among M.I. Finley's 'four fathers of history'.[17]

Finley also points to Polybius (200–118 BCE) as one of the founding fathers of Greek history.[18] Only part of Polybius's history survives in full (Books 1–5). The portions that do remain, however, are significant, weighing in at over 300,000 words—the most substantial work preserved from ancient history, even in its fragmentary state.[19] Dionysius accused Polybius—and 'countless

12 Cf. T.J. Luce, *The Greek Historians* (London: Routledge, 1997), 2.

13 Cf. J. Marincola, *Greek Historians* (GR 31; Oxford: Oxford University Press, 2001), 19.

14 H. van Wess, 'Thucydides on Early Greek History', in S. Forsdyke, E. Foster, and R.K. Balot (eds.), *The Oxford Handbook of Thucydides* (Oxford: Oxford University Press, 2017), 39–62 (39).

15 Some propose that he drew upon three of his friends, whom he thanks in the narrative, for information: Pasimelos of Corinth (*Hell.* 4.4.4–12), Prokles of Phleious (*Hell.* 7.3.2), and Euryptolemos (*Hell.* 1.3.33). See D. Thomas, 'Introduction', in *The Landmark Xenophon's Hellenika* (trans. J. Marincola; New York: Anchor Books, 2009), ix–lxvi (lx).

16 J. Dillery, *Xenophon and the History of His Times* (London: Routledge, 2012), 8.

17 M.I. Finley, *The Greek Historians: The Essence of Herodotus, Thucydides, Xenophon, Polybius* (Harmondsworth, Eng.: Penguin, 1977).

18 Finley, *Portable Greek Historians*.

19 Due to its incomplete condition, we will have to state our results cautiously since we do not possess the entire discourse, but it seems that we have enough data still to come to

others' (ἄλλους μυρίους)—of being so long and unornate that it was unreadable (Dionysius of Halicarnassus, *Comp.* 4.110).[20] Debate continues over why polemic against Polybius's historical predecessors occupies such a central role in his history.[21] Many accredit it to jealously, especially of Timaeus.[22] Others point to rhetorical flourish and pedagogy.[23] And still others to a confluence of social, political, literary, and historical motivations.[24] Polybian scholars tend to agree, however, that one of Polybius' primary narrative goals in writing his history was to supplant prior histories by modeling a *truly* universal history (see Polybius 5.33).[25]

Diodorus Siculus (90 BCE–30 BCE) wrote his universal history (*Bibliotheke Historica* or *Library of History*) in the last years of the Republic in the first century. Unfortunately, only 15 of the *Library's* original 40 books survive in their entirety today. Charles Muntz emphasizes the importance of this work in the development of the Greek historiographic tradition when he says that Diodorus 'is the first known author to attempt to comprehensively encompass all of time and space in history, and in particular the first universal historian to integrate the history of the non-Greeks into his work'.[26] Therefore, Kenneth

some important conclusions. Cf. C.B. Champion, *Cultural Politics in Polybius's Histories* (HCS 41; Berkeley: University of California, 2004), 9–10.

20 Cf. F.W. Walbank, *Polybius* (Sather Classical Lectures 42; Berkeley: University of California Press, 1990), 34; Marincola, *Greek Historians*, 36–37; F.W. Walbank, *Polybius, Rome, and the Hellenistic World: Essays and Reflections* (New York: Cambridge University, 2002), 54; McGing, *Polybius' Histories*, 14–15.

21 On polemic in Greek historiography, see Marincola, *Authority*, 218–24.

22 E.g. P. Pédech, *Histories French & Greek 1961–95* (Paris: Belles, 1961), xxxi–xxxiii and P. Pédech, *La méthode historique de Polybe* (Collection d'études anciennes; Paris: Société d'édition Les Belles, 1964), 496–514, argues that, when Polybius visited Alexandria, he discovered that, even though he had visited the Alps, Timaeus was still hailed as the best historian by the scholars there.

23 Marincola, *Greek Historians*, 134.

24 F.W. Walbank, 'Polemic in Polybius', *JRS* 52 (1962): 1–12. Reprinted in F.W. Walbank (ed.), *Selected Papers: Studies in Greek and Roman History and Historiography* (Cambridge: Cambridge University Press, 2010), 262–79. Walbank (278) states: 'Nearly always, Polybius's motives are mixed; and his attitude towards earlier historians can usually be seen to reflect personal or political considerations no less those of literary or historical merit'. Cf. also J. Bollansée, 'Historians of Agathocles of Samus: Polybius on Writers of Historical Monographs', in G. Schepens and J. Bollansée (eds.), *The Shadow of Polybius: Intertextuality as a Research Tool in Greek Historiography: Proceedings of the International Colloquium, Leuven, 21–22 September 2001* (SH 42; Leuven: Peeters, 2005), 237–53 (253); Luce, *Greek Historians*, 92–94.

25 Cf. Marincola, *Greek Historians*, 134.

26 C.E. Muntz, *Diodorus Siculus and the World of the Late Roman Republic* (Oxford: Oxford University Press, 2017), 28.

Sacks suggests that the *Library's* 'claim to universality is established by its range, both geographic and chronological …, provid[ing] important testimony for substantial portions of antiquity'.[27]

Dionysius of Halicarnassus (60s BCE–after 7 CE) represents another key link in the Greek historiographic tradition. Dionysius composed his Roman history for Greek-speaking people. As with Polybius and Diodorus, we only possess parts of this work. From the parts that remain, there is a *Chronicle*, which cross-references dates in Greek history with dates in Roman history, in addition to the 21-volume *Romaïké Archaiologia*. Dionysius depends heavily upon Plutarch as both a source and as a model for his history.[28]

In Josephus (CE 37–100) we witness undoubtedly the greatest influence of Hellenism upon Jewish historiography to date. A number of important Hellenistic Jewish literary predecessors led up to the full-blown Hellenistic Jewish history that we find in Josephus. These predecessors include especially several Hellenistic Jewish historians (dated prior to the first century CE) that have come down to us through the writings of Eusebius (*PE* 9.17–39), Josephus (*Ant.* 1.240), and Clement (*Storm.* 1.21.130; 1.21.144; 123.153–56) (e.g. Demetrius, Eupolemus, pseudo-Eupolemus, Artapanus, Cleodemus)[29]—and these derivative of Alexander Polyhistor. The Maccabean history (esp. 1 Maccabees) as well as the rewritten Jewish histories, *Jubilees* (150 BCE) and 1 Esdras (mid second century to early first century BCE),[30] provide important historical antecedents

---

27 K. Sacks, *Diodorus Siculus and the First Century* (Princeton Legacy Library; Princeton: Princeton University, 1990), 3.

28 A. Mehl, *Roman Historiography: An Introduction to Its Basic Aspects and Development* (Malden, Mass.: Wiley-Blackwell, 2011), 114.

29 On these writings, see G.E. Sterling, *Historiography and Self-Definition: Josephos, Luke-Acts, and Apologetic History* (NovTSup 64; Leiden: Brill, 1992), 137–225; *OTP* 2: 855–887.

30 The date of 1 Esdras is debated. Beginning especially with the seminal work of Pohlmann, some have argued for the so-called *Fragmenthypothese*: that 1 Esdras constitutes a Greek translation of a fragment of a larger work that included 1–2 Chronicles. But before Pohlmann, note the similar views and foundational work of H. Howorth, 'Some Unconventional Views on the Text of the Bible. I: The Apocryphal Book of Esdras A and the Septuagint,' *Proceedings of the Society of Biblical Archaeology* 23 (1901): 147–59; H. Howorth, 'Some Unconventional Views on the Text of the Bible. II: The Chronology and Order of Events in Esdras A, Compared with and Preferred to those in the Canonical Ezra', *Proceedings of the Society of Biblical Archaeology* 24 (1902): 147–72; C.S. Torrey, 'The Nature and Origin of "First Esdras"', *AJSL* 23 (1907): 116–41; R.H. Pfeiffer, *History of New Testament Times with an Introduction to Apocrypha* (New York: Harper and Brothers, 1949), 243; cf. also A.E. Gardner, 'The Purpose and Date of 1 Esdras', *JJS* 37 (1986): 18–27 (18). For a summary of the salient problems with the *Fragmenthypothese*, see M.F. Bird, *1 Esdras: Introduction and Commentary on the Greek Text in Codex Vaticanus* (SPS; Leiden: Brill, 2012), 9–16. Several others have substantiated points of correlation that strongly suggest literary dependence upon the parallel canonical accounts. See, e.g., O. Eissfeld, *The Old*

to Josephus' history as well. Josephus adopts his historiographic framework explicitly from the Greek historians. Josephus knew and used 1 Esdras as well as 1 Maccabees and both provided literary models for him at some level. It appears that when Josephus does not have a Greek source to verify Israel's history, where doubt may potentially be introduced, he cites their sacred Scriptures instead as a source.[31]

Appian's *Civil Wars* (CE 95–165) offers a final history worth considering and provides a chronological anchor extending just beyond the first century, creating a chronological range leading up to the time of and just beyond the composition of Luke-Acts. Although not as advanced or original as Thucydides' history, Appian's *Civil Wars* nevertheless offers an excellent specimen of early second-century CE Greek history. Much of his larger *Roman History*, which he organized geographically rather than chronologically, is unfortunately fragmentary. I have opted therefore to restrict analysis to his *Civil Wars* so we can study a complete discourse with an intact preface and narrative design. Appian organizes the *Civil Wars* around the several generals involved in the wars that he documents. Most Appian scholars think that he has implemented his source material into the narrative often very abruptly,[32] a view especially perpetuated in the influential work of Emilio Gabba.[33] This intrusive use of source material has a dramatic impact on Appian's style.[34] Often, Appian uses overly simplistic or repetitive vocabulary, to the point that many classicists view him as not much more than an editor or compiler of tradition. But this seems like an important sample to include, for precisely these reasons—many view the Gospel writers in quite the same way.

3 Toward a Representative Corpus of the βίος Genre

The selection of βίοι gets a bit more complicated. Friedrich Leo famously traced the origins of Greek βίος to two trajectories. The first he related to the

Testament, An Introduction (Oxford: Blackwell, 1966), 574; T.C. Eskenazi, 'The Chronicler and the Composition of 1 Esdras', *CBQ* 48 (1986): 39–61; T.C. Eskenazi, *In an Age of Prose: A Literary Approach to Ezra-Nehemiah*; SBLMS 36; (Atlanta: Scholars Press, 1988), 155–74.

31 For further on this, see A.W. Pitts, 'The Use and Non-Use of Prophetic Literature in Hellenistic Jewish Historiography', in M.J. Boda and L.W. Beal (eds.), *Prophets and Prophecy in Ancient Israelite Historiography* (BCP; Winona Lake, Ind.: Eisenbrauns, 2012), 229–52.

32 Cf. B.C. McGing, 'Appian's "Mithridatios"', *ANRW* II.34.1 (1993): 496–522 (498–99).

33 E. Gabba, *Appiano e la storia delle guerre civili* (Florence: La Nuova Italia, 1956).

34 F.J.G. Espelosín, '"Appian's Iberiké". Aims and Attitudes of a Greek Historian', *ANRW* II.34.1 (1993): 403–27 (406–13).

Peripatetics, going back to Aristotle and ultimately connected with Socrates. The second, which he referred to as the Alexandrian school or the grammarians, was reflected in the later members of the Mouseion.[35] Leo's division, however, could not account for the immense diversity within the Greco-Roman biographical tradition.

This led others to attempt to construct more flexible typologies. First in classics, Fritz Wehrli extends Leo's two categories to three: (1) lives of philosophers/ poets, (2) encomia, (3) lives of literary characters.[36] Then in New Testament studies, Klaus Berger proposes a fourfold typology: (1) the *Encomium* type (Isocrates, Xenophon, Philo, Tacitus, and Lucian); (2) the *Peripatetic* type (Plutarch); (3) the *popular-novelistic* type (*Vita Aesop; Vit. Sec.*); and (4) the *Alexandrian* type (Suetonius).[37] Also in the context of Gospel studies, Charles Talbert proposes a slightly different set of categories.[38] At the widest level, he discusses *didactic* (biographies concerned with moral example) and *non-didactic* lives (biographies not concerned with moral example, e.g. the Alexandrian type). Didactic biographies have five further sub-types, organized around the author's strategy of achieving the moral emulation of their subject. Most recently, Justin Smith delineates a four-fold typology: (1) non-contemporary-focused (e.g. Satyrus, *Euripides*; Philo, *Moses*); (2) non-contemporary-open (e.g. Philostratus, *Apollonius*); (3) contemporary-focused (e.g. Isocrates, *Evagoras*; Tacitus, *Agricola*); (4) contemporary-open (e.g. Lucian, *Demonax*).[39] The first description has to do with the relation of the author to the time of the events/ participant(s). The second concerns what we know about the audience.

These typologies provide a helpful synchronic perspective on what seems to be a diachronically related group of texts. Leo's original taxonomy was developmental, though limited, but more recent synchronic attempts to classify the data seem to me to fail to maintain important diachronic distinctions. For

35 F. Leo, *Die griechisch-römische Biographie nach ihrer litterarischen Form* (Leipzig: B.G. Teubner, 1901), *passim*.

36 F. Wehrli, 'Gnome, Anecdote and Biography', *MH* 30 (1973): 193–208 (193). For another older typology derived from classical studies, see A.S. Osley, 'Greek Biography before Plutarch', *GR* 43 (1946): 7–20. The remaining references in this paragraph to secondary literature draw from the excellent summary in J.M. Smith, 'Genre, Sub-Genre, and Questions of Audience: A Proposed Typology for Greco-Roman Biography', *JGRChJ* 4 (2007): 193–200 and J.M. Smith, *Why βίος?: On the Relationship between Gospel Genre and Implied Audience* (LNTS 518; London: T&T Clark, 2015), 30–59.

37 K. Berger, 'Hellenistische Gattungen im Neuen Testament', in *ANRW* II.25.2 (1984): 1031–432 and 1831–85.

38 C.H. Talbert, *What Is a Gospel?: The Genre of the Canonical Gospels* (London: S.P.C.K., 1978), 92–93.

39 Smith, *Why βίος?*, 219.

example, are what several label the 'encomium' type of biography really instances of the biographical genre or a sub-genre of it? Is *Evagoras* really a type or sub-genre of the Greek βίος or another genre that exhibits some of the same formal features as the Greek βίος—perhaps a predecessor to the genre? These kinds of questions illuminate the need for diachronic situating before the kind of flat analysis of the Greek biographical genre that Smith and others attempt can be undertaken.

It is interesting that the most recent of these typologies that Smith points to have arisen in biblical not classical studies. The newest study in classics is Wehrli (1974). The others come from Berger, Talbert, and Burridge, all in the context of Gospel studies.[40] Perhaps scolded from the negative response to Leo's typology, classicists tend to avoid these neatly organized schemas for describing the Greek βίος in favor of numerous antecedents to the genre, beginning in the fifth century until reaching its final highly formalized expression in Plutarch and his successors in the first century CE.[41] I realize that a synchronic analysis like the one Smith provides may have its place, but since the available typologies all seem to me (and most classists) to include pre-biographical texts under the sub-genres or types of biography (see below), this leads me at this stage to prefer the antecedent-based approaches utilized by many classicists today over the typologies more popular in Gospel studies.[42]

40 Burridge does not offer a typology in the same way as the others but his developmental scheme is considered by Smith in this connection.

41 The reasons for this involve the recognition that the close associations with the Peripatetic school among the earliest βίοι that Leo imagined can hardly be sustained and the claim that the development of a genre itself had its own external rules governing the process appeared reductionistic. See A. Momigliano, *The Development of Greek Biography* (Carl Newell Jackson Lectures 143; Cambridge, Mass.: Harvard University Press, 1993), 74–76; T. Hägg, *The Art of Biography in Antiquity* (Cambridge: Cambridge University Press, 2012), 67–69, 79.

42 S.A. Adams, *The Genre of Acts and Collected Biography* (SNTSMS 156; Cambridge: Cambridge University Press, 2013), 78, notes further problems with Smith's configuration: 'First, it is problematic to assume that the author has only one audience in mind, and that the audience(s) functions on only one level. Second, it is not possible to identify definitively the relationship between the subject and author as to whether or not they are contemporary or ancient. It is somewhat presumptuous, moreover, to assume that one can know the relationship between the writer and audience, with or without explicit or implied references in the text. Additionally, to create a full-blown typology of this sort involves being selective and requires omitting works that are fragmentary or that do not explicitly outline the author—subject or author—audience relationship(s)'.

3.1 *Biographical Predecessors*

The primary predecessors to the formation of Greek βίος seem to be the various encomia and embedded biographical sketches in various other genres, such as poetry, history, and rhetoric in the fourth century BCE.[43] For example, some trace the origins of the biographical genre back to Homer's *Odyssey*, centered around the adventures of Odysseus.[44] While writers of full βίοι apparently existed in the fourth century and those leading up to the first century CE (e.g. Antisthenes or Aristoxenus),[45] we unfortunately do not possess full copies of their works.

Ronald Mellor is careful to calibrate the role of 'antecedents' to the Greco-Roman βίος before we see the full emergence of the form (especially) in the first century:

> By the fifth century BCE the eulogistic songs sung at banquets and funerals in praise of aristocratic achievements were given a literary form by Pindar and other poets who sketched the lives of mythical or historical personalities in their victory odes. At the same time, Herodotus and Thucydides provide brief portraits of Croesus, Themistocles, and Pericles. It was in the fourth century BCE that the biographical writing burst forth in monographs, dialogues, and what we might call today historical novels.[46]

---

43 Smith, 'Genre', 190, speculates: 'However, as biography developed and took up the function of disseminating biographical information, encomium did not disappear per se, but became subsumed under the new genre of biography and thus became a "type" of biography. It may be the case then that, though the encomium genre survived, in that there were still encomia texts being written, the genre at this point no longer served a biographical purpose but one primarily of acclamation'. But what evidence is there of this having taken place? I cannot see any that seems obvious and Smith does not attempt to provide us with any, other than a footnote on the flexibility of genre boundaries and the freedom to use what would later become biographical *topoi* in non-biographical genres.

44 R. Mellor, *The Roman Historians* (London: Routledge, 2003), 133.

45 See D.R. Stuart, *Epochs of Greek and Roman Biography* (New York: Biblo and Tannen, 1928), 119–54. Other nonextant fourth- and fifth-century BCE (potentially) biographical texts may include Skylax of Caryanda, *The Story of the Tyrant* (*or king*) *Heraclides of Mylasa*; Xanthos of Lydia, *On Empedocles*; and Stesimbrotos of Thasos, *On Themistocles, Thucydides, and Pericles*. For discussion of these texts and their potential role in the formation of the Greek βίος, see Adams, *Genre*, 71–73. Berger, 'Hellenistische Gattungen', 1232–36, also mentions from this era, Plato's *Apology* (as a biography of Socrates); the biographies of the Ptolemies in P.Graec.Hauniensis 6; Antagonus of Carystus' *Successions of the Philosophers*; and Hermippus of Smyrna's *Lives*, among others.

46 Mellor, *Roman Historians*, 133.

From there, he claims, 'Monographs by Xenophon (*Agesilaus*) and the orator Isocrates (*Evagoras*) are prose encomia detailing the achievements and virtues of their subjects, modeled perhaps on the poems of Pindar'.[47]

Isocrates' (436–338 BCE) *Evagoras* marks what many view as one of the earliest antecedents to the biographical genre that we possess.[48] In form, as an epideictic speech that eulogizes a king, *Evagoras* remains exceedingly short compared to later biographical treatments (which were not speeches). The speech has remarkable similarities with Pindar's (and other Greek poets') praises of athletic victors.[49] But the biographical portion of the speech itself, beginning with Evagoras' birth, does not initiate until well into the discourse (*Evag.* 12). Nor does the speech terminate with the death of its subject, a frequent characteristic of later βίοι—the discourse frame, in other words, does not seem to be fundamentally biographical, and most classify it as an encomium not a βίος (*contra* Burridge and those who follow him).[50] The work nevertheless remains significant for the development of the Greek biographical tradition since Xenophon would use *Evagoras* as his model for at least *Agesilaus* but perhaps others as well.

Tomas Hägg claims that ancient biography begins with Xenophon's memoirs, encomia, and romances.[51] D.R. Stuart echoes similar sentiments.[52] In Xenophon (430–354 BCE), we discover a highly underdeveloped beginning to the trajectory toward the formalization of the Greek biographical genre. We

47 Mellor, *Roman Historians*, 133. Similarly, Osely, 'Greek Biography', 9 notes, 'The earliest specimens of Greek biographical writing (if you except the caricatures of men in public life so mercilessly drawn in Aristophanes and the playwrights of the Old Comedy) are contained in Isocrates and Xenophon. Both authors are of the "encomiastic" type'.

48 Adams, *Genre*, 74 contends, 'Arguably the most important work for the development of a discrete Greek biography genre is Isocrates' *Evagoras*. It is not accurate, however, to state that *Evagoras* is a full biography; rather, it is a prose narrative in an encomiastic manner focused on a particular person who has recently died and who is not divine or mythological'.

49 M.E. Gordley, *Teaching Through Song in Antiquity: Didactic Hymnody Among Greeks, Romans, Jews, and Christians* (WUNT 2.302; Tübingen: Mohr Siebeck, 2011), 111.

50 E.g. W.H. Race, 'Pindaric Encomium and Isocrates' Evagoras', *TAPhA* 117 (1987): 131–55; R.L. Hunter, *Encomium of Ptolemy Philadelphus: Text and Translation with Introduction and Commentary* (Berkeley: University of California, 2003), 13; Gordley, *Teaching*, 111; Hägg, *Art*, 30; R. Rees, *Latin Panegyric* (New York: Oxford, 2012), 89; S.B. Ferrario, *Historical Agency and the 'Great man' in Classical Greece* (Cambridge: Cambridge University Press, 2014), 254; H. Lu, *Xenophon's Theory of Moral Education* (Newcastle upon Tyne, UK: Cambridge Scholars Press, 2015), 184; Adams, *Genre*, 74; S. Nevin, *Military Leaders and Sacred Space in Classical Greek Warfare: Temples, Sanctuaries and Conflict in Antiquity* (Library of Classical Studies; London: Tauris, 2017), chapter 4.

51 Hägg, *Art*, 10–66.

52 Stuart, *Epochs*, 31.

begin to observe the biographical genre's initial underpinnings in some of his characterizations in *Anabasis* and later in *Agesilaus* (only the latter of which was an imitation of Isocrates' *Evagoras*).[53] And since he imitates *Evagoras*, it 'follows the tradition of prose encomium'.[54] But his *Cyropaedia* comes closest to the form that we would later identify as the βίος. Momigliano calls it Xenophon's 'greatest contribution to biography ... indeed the most accomplished biography we have in classical Greek literature'.[55] But we may note in *Cyropaedia* the highly sketchy nature of the literary form.[56] Jakub Pigon laments: 'The problem of *Cyropaedia's* genre is notorious'.[57] And Mellor observes that in *Cyropaedia* we do not yet have a biographical text but 'a novelistic treatment of the training of a Persian Prince intended to provide a model for aristocratic education'.[58] Nevertheless, Albrecht Dihle's contention seems likely: that in the combined emergence of these works (esp. also *Agesilaus* and *Evagoras*) we find the beginnings of a formal crystallization of the biographical genre.[59]

Philo's *Life of Moses* (15–10 BCE–45–50 BCE) provides another paradoxical text for considerations of genre, developing in the context of Hellenistic Judaism in Alexandria rather than from a primarily Greek background. Some consider it rewritten Bible,[60] others a biographically oriented encomium like

53 Momigliano, *Development*, 52.

54 Lu, *Xenophon's Moral Theory*, 177. See also A. Dihle, *Studien zur Griechischen Biographie* (Abhandlungen der Akademie der Wissenschaften in Göttingen. Philologische-Historische Klasse 37; Göttingen: Vandenhoeck & Ruprecht, 1970), 27; D.L. Gera, *Xenophon's "Cyropaedia": Style, Genre and Literary Technique* (OCM; Oxford: Clarendon Press, 1993), 120; M. Tamiolaki, 'Xenophon's Cyropaedia: Tentative Answers to an Enigma', in Michael A. Flower (ed.), *The Cambridge Companion to Xenophon* (Cambridge Companions to Literature; Cambridge: Cambridge University Press, 2017), 174–94 (181).

55 Momigliano, *Development*, 54–55.

56 According to Gera, *Xenophon's "Cyropaedia"*, 1, the *Cyropaedia* 'can be described as a biography of Cyrus the Great, a history of the beginnings of the Persian empire, a romance, an encomium, a military handbook, a guide to the political administration of the empire, a didactic work on ethics, morals, and education, etc.; it is, in fact, all of these things'.

57 J. Pigon, *The Children of Herodotus: Greek and Roman Historiography and Related Genres* (Newcastle: Cambridge Scholars Press, 2008), 71.

58 Mellor, *Roman Historians*, 134. Similarly, B. Gentili and G. Cerri, *History and Biography in Ancient Thought* (Amsterdam: J.C. Gieben, 1988), 84, recognize: '*Cyropaedia* is notoriously difficult to classify as several 'generic' features of the history, the eulogy and the pedagogic treatise seem to converge'.

59 Dihle, *Studien*, 28.

60 E.g. F. Damgaard, 'Philo's Life of Moses as Rewritten Bible', in József Zsengellér (ed.), *Rewritten Bible After Fifty Years: A Last Dialogue with Geza Vermes* (JSJSup 166; Leiden: Brill, 2014), 233–48.

Isocrates' *Evagoras*[61] or a Greek βίος.[62] In many ways, Philo's *Life of Moses* does reflect the form of rewritten Bible (perhaps a Jewish form of Greek *mimesis*/imitation) since it retells much of the Torah. However, Philo chooses to do so in a kind of biographical form, telling the story of the Torah through the story of Moses. So, B.C. McGing asks: does all of this preclude Philo's *Life of Moses* 'as a work of biography'? Based on classical scholarship's disregard for the contribution of Philo to the discussion of the Greek βίος, he answers, 'yes', it does preclude Philo's *Life of Moses* from the Greek biographical genre. He emphasizes,

> There is not a single mention of Philo in Leo; nothing in Stuart, nothing in Momigliano; nothing in Dihle. He just does not feature in the classical analyses of the development of the Graeco-Roman biography. And yet as long ago as 1929, Pressing identified the literary form of Philo's biographies as Greek. Pressing was still under the influence of Leo's very rigid categorization of Greek biography, but his argument was persuasive.[63]

Regardless of whether McGing is right or wrong, I do not think anyone can deny that this document has been a hotly contested sample. Part of its anomalous nature could be connected to its emergence during the period slightly before the full formalization of the genre.[64] So though Philo would not be an antecedent to the formation of the βίος genre, his work does fall chronologically within this time period. For this reason, we may conveniently group Philo with the biographical predecessors, adding some Jewish variety to the corpus—a helpful addition for the study of early Christian texts such as Luke-Acts. And this will be a useful exercise, regardless of what one thinks about the genre of the *Life of Moses* since our SFL genre agnation model develops a number of scales

61 L.H. Feldman, Christianity and Judaism in Antiquity: Philo's Portrayal of Moses in the Context of Ancient Judaism (Notre Dame: University of Notre Dame Press, 2008), Chapter 4: 'Philo's Life of Moses as an Aretalogy and as Encomium'.

62 E.g. Burridge, *What are the Gospels?*, 128.

63 B.C. McGing, 'Philo's Adaptation of the Bible in his Life of Moses', in B.C. McGing and J. Mossman (eds.), *The Limits of Ancient Biography* (Swansea: Classical Press of Wales, 2006), 113–40 (118). For this same position, see also M.J. Edwards, 'Biography and Biographic', in M.J. Edwards and S. Swain (eds.), *Portraits: Biographical Representation in the Greek and Latin Literature of the Roman Empire* (Oxford: Clarendon Press, 1997), 228–34 (229–30).

64 As Adams, *Genre*, 72 rightly cautions, 'Although some scholars have used extant titles and citations to claim an early date for the genesis of *bios*, it is important to note that biography did not emerge fully formed, but that it was likely influenced by contemporary historical writers'.

designed to gage how biographical (or not) Philo's work turns out to be relative to other proposed biographical texts in the comparative corpus.

Burridge was sharply criticized by the classical scholar M.J. Edwards for including works too early to represent the biographical genre (e.g. Isocrates' *Evagoras* and Xenophon's *Agesilaus*, which are properly panegyrics, not biography).[65] According to Edwards, Philo's *Life of Moses* never purports to be a βίος and Xenophon's *Memorabilia* exceeds length standards for the ancient βίος,[66] one of Burridge's own criteria.[67] While all of Edwards' criticisms may not be equally valid;[68] in general, Burridge does seem out of step with the consensus views in classics in designating these earlier writings as βίοι and he does not seek to offer any justification for his inclusion of these texts within his sample group, regarded by many as at best earlier historical precedents for the genre or even potentially unrelated to the development of ancient βίος at all (e.g. Philo's *Life of Moses*).

Satyrus's *Life of Euripides*, though fragmentary, counts as evidence of earlier βίοι, even if we do not have them in their complete state. The author, Satyrus (P.Oxy. 1176 fr. 39.23.1)—about whom we know relatively little—originally

65 Edwards, 'Biography', 229–30. Momigliano, *Development*, 49, agrees: 'The encomium is organized in chronological order but cannot properly be described as a biography of Euagoras from birth to death'.

66 Momigliano, *Development*, 53, insists that Xenophon's *Memorabilia* potentially represents a unique genre of its own and, in any case, is not a biography. Gentili and Cerri, *History*, 84, register similar remarks: 'The discussion of biography should be inserted into the wider discussion of literary genres of ancient Greece ... An incontrovertible fact where ancient Greece is concerned, is that we cannot speak of a systematic theory of literary genres before the classification effected by Hellenistic philology in the 2nd–3rd century BC'.

67 Edwards, 'Biography', 229–30. Burridge, *What are the Gospels?*, 266, attempts to answer these criticisms in the second edition of his book by picking apart a few (rightly) incorrect details in Edwards's largely negative appraisal. For example, Edwards seems to think that Burridge only covers these earlier writings when in reality Burridge treats both earlier and later instances of what he considers proper representations of the form. But I think Edwards would say that the early literature Burridge includes should not be weighed at all. So picking apart these incidental details will not blunt the sting of Edwards's main criticism, that the works Burridge considers do not reflect an unambiguous form of ancient biography. Burridge does not directly address this issue and still has not provided adequate justification for using these earlier works, not widely acknowledged to represent the Greek biographical form, other than to simply state that the genre includes a wider range of works than instances of later self-attesting βίοι.

68 E.g. Edward's claim Philo's *Life of Moses* never purports to be a βίος is simply false. Philo, *Mos.* 1.1 states: Μωυσέως τοῦ κατὰ μέν τινας νομοθέτου τῶν Ἰουδαίων, κατὰ δέ τινας ἑρμηνέως νόμων ἱερῶν, τὸν βίον ἀναγράψαι διενοήθην, ἀνδρὸς τὰ πάντα μεγίστου καὶ τελειοτάτου, καὶ γνώριμον τοῖς ἀξίοις μὴ ἀγνοεῖν αὐτὸν ἀποφῆναι.

composed this text as a collection of βίοι on three significant tragedians. Satyrus chose Euripides as the subject of one of the βίοι at the end of the collection and this is the portion of the manuscript that has been preserved. Although the copy of the text we possess dates to the second century CE, the document itself was likely composed in the third century BCE. But even here, we do not have a complete biographical text so it is difficult to require too much from this document.

Dihle goes as far as to assert that in terms of the genre label Greek 'biography', where someone assigns the term 'on conceptual and formal grounds, one can only gain an impression from the parallel "*Lives*" of Plutarch. The genre present here clearly possessed enough vitality to affect regions beyond the literature of the Greeks'.[69] Similarly, while recognizing earlier antecedents during the Hellenistic empire, Momigliano identifies Plutarch as the first person to acknowledge their writing as βίος and insists that the only works of biography which we have direct acquaintance with are the ones from the Roman Empire.[70] So to borrow a category from John Swales, we might say that Plutarch's *Parallel Lives* provides a kind of *prototype* for the Greek biographical genre.

When examining the Gospels, however, consideration for the appropriate historical precedents for the genre will be important since most date the

69 A. Dihle, 'The Gospels and Greek Biography', in Peter Stuhlmacher (ed.), *The Gospel and the Gospels* (Grand Rapids: Eerdmans, 1991), 361–86 (378). In his significant study, Dihle argues (371) that 'All one can say without fear of contradiction is that the *Lives* of Plutarch possess a highly developed literary form and hence that they distinguish themselves from all other extant biographical accounts in Greek literature; further, that this form is inseparably bound up with a conception of ethics'. He goes on: constantly in Hellenistic times, authors 'like Satyrus, who made a name for themselves *inter alia* by writing βίοι, were called Peripatetics in our tradition, although in their case no closer connection with the school of Aristotle can be demonstrated … and the close and very specific link between the literary form and the ethical-anthropological conception of Peripateticism which gives the Lives their distinctive stamp belongs to the tradition of this literary genre and must not just be regarded as the possession of the author'. He notes difficulties with classifying various other sources, therefore, as biography. While the biography of Augustus by Nicolas of Damascus, from about 100 years before Plutarch, is among the only ones that parallels Plutarch, Dihle remains skeptical due to its fragmentary condition. Dihle is more hopeful for the βίοι after Plutarch's *Lives*, especially the *Demonax, Peregrinus Proteus* and *Alexander*, referred to by Lucian (377). He also raises the possibility of Philostratus's *Life of Apollonius* but dismisses it (378) 'because of the religiously motivated miracle-and-travel stories completely overshadow the overall structure of the work'. While most of us probably will not find ourselves quite as skeptical as Dihle he, at the very least, makes a good case for Plutarch as the best representative sample of the βίος genre.

70 Momigliano, *Development*, 9. In Gospels criticism, see also P. Vielhauer, *Geschichte der urchristlichen Literatur* (Berlin: de Gruyter, 1975), 330, 350, citing Shultz, for criticism of the view that the Gospels align with the βίος form.

Gospels either slightly earlier or right around the time when some of the first extant self-identified expressions of the genre begin to emerge in Plutarch's *Lives*, even if there were a small number of proper βίοι in circulation prior to this. Chronologically, then, we find the Gospels not located firmly within the midst of a developed literary tradition but only surfacing at the dawn of the formalization of the Greco-Roman βίος, probably to the degree that not even Philo had perfected the art. While Edwards and others rightly criticize Burridge for his imprecision in identifying the biographical genre, some of the documents (though not all) seem relevant as predecessors or antecedents rather than specimens for consideration due to their chronological relation to the Gospels and formative roles in setting literary trajectories that would carry over into the development of the βίος. We shall explore, then, the following biographical predecessors:

(1) Isocrates, *Evagoras* (436–338 BCE)
(2) Xenophon, *Cyropaedia* (430–354 BCE)
(3) Satyrus, *Life of Euripides* (late 3rd century BCE)
(4) Philo, *Life of Moses* (around 15 BCE–around 50 CE)

3.2 *The Collected Greek βίοι*

Often, when we discuss the βίοι of the ancient world (e.g. Plutarch's *Life of Alexander*), it must be kept in mind that these individual biographical texts are often one of many books in a much larger collection of lives. Besides the four unpaired lives (*Artaxerxes, Aratus, Galba*, and *Otho*), each βίος in Plutarch (often in the range of 6,000–11,000 words) is part of a two-volume set of 'parallel' βίοι. And these sets are themselves part of the much larger collection (totaling 507,184 words). So, Plutarch's Roman life of *Cato Minor* is paired with the Greek life of *Phocion*. The same is true of the biographies by Nepos, Suetonius, and Jerome in Latin. And in the case of Plutarch, most parallel lives comprise three total volumes, the third volume being a comparison of the pair of lives. These levels of discourse differentiation are significant considerations if genre is assessed through macrostructures. Whether a book is a singular, self-standing work or intended to be read in the context of a collection will affect how macrostructures are aligned. In light of recent proposals that Luke-Acts most closely resembles the collected Greek βίοι, it will be important to weigh the evidence from these higher levels of structuring as well as lower level structures (the individual lives contained in the larger collection).

Diogenes Laërtius (3rd century CE) provides another sample of the Greek collected biography to consider. His *Lives of the Eminent Philosophers* totals in at 109,777, divided into ten books, with each book containing several lives. It represents one of many succession works in antiquity, organized around four major founder-successors of philosophical schools.[71] Therefore, Diogenes is not only writing philosophical biography but biographical philosophy. As James Warren puts it, 'he does not limit himself to telling the life-stories of the philosophers; he also wishes to construct from these philosophers' lives the life-story of philosophy itself'.[72] If we maintain Joseph Geiger's strong distinction between intellectual and political biography, the origins of the latter going back to Nepos,[73] then our corpus includes a set of collected biographies from both the political (Plutarch) and intellectual (Diogenes Laërtius) sub-genres of the βίος, but Geiger's classifications have often been viewed as too rigid.[74]

These two large texts can be approached from a number of angles. First, we can—as Burridge and others have done—consider several of Plutarch's individual and/or sets of lives. But we will also want to consider Plutarch's larger *Parallel Lives* as a still wider level of context (for, e.g., Plutarch's *Cato Minor*) relevant for genre investigations. In order to achieve as much linguistic balance as possible, I have chosen only Greek biographical samples. This will also entail limiting our investigation to early biographical texts, since the Latin *Vita* emerged in the fourth century and beyond. Further, these Greek texts together 'represent a cohesive group' over against the fourth-century Latin lives, according to Miller and so should be considered together.[75] And if Luke-Acts is a collected biography, it would fall within the Greek rather than the Latin tradition of biography writing. For the collected βίοι, then, we will use the collected Greek lives of Plutarch and Diogenes Laërtius—two of the three extant collected Greek βίοι (the other being Philostratus, *Lives of the Sophists*). But again, Latin biographical texts (and other supplementary Greek texts, including Philostratus' *Lives*) will be heavily cross-referenced, mainly in the footnotes. Consequently, the selection of collected Greek βίοι will include,

71 Adams, *Genre*, 105.

72 J. Warren, 'Diogenes Laërtius, Biography of History', in J. König (ed.), *Ordering Knowledge in the Roman Empire* (Cambridge: Cambridge University Press, 2011), 133–49 (134).

73 J. Geiger, *Cornelius Nepos and Ancient Political Biography* (Stuttgart: Franz Steiner, 1985); cf. also S.R. Stem, *The Political Biographies of Cornelius Nepos* (Ann Arbor: University of Michigan Press, 2012), 209.

74 E.g. Gentili and Cerri, *History*, 68–85; P. Stadter, 'Biography and History', in John Marincola (ed.), *A Companion to Greek and Roman Historiography* (BCAW; Malden: Blackwell, 2007), 528–40 (531); Hägg, *Art*, 68–69.

75 P.C. Miller, 'Strategies of Representation in Collected Biography: Constructing the Subject as Holy', in T. Hägg, P. Rousseau, and C. Høgel (eds.), *Greek Biography and Panegyric in Late Antiquity* (Berkeley: University of California, 2000), 209–54 (215).

(1) Plutarch, *Parallel Lives* (early second century CE) (as a collection)
  a) *Alexander-Caesar* (Parallel Life 1)
  b) *Demosthenes-Cicero* (Parallel Life 2)
  c) *Theseus-Romulus* (Parallel Life 3)
  d) *Artaxerxes* (Unpaired Life 1)
  e) *Otho* (Unpaired Life 2)

(2) Diogenes Laërtius, *Lives of the Imminent Philosophers* (third century CE) (as a collection)
  a) *Pythagoras* (Life 1)
  b) *Epicurus* (Life 2)

We will emphasize Plutarch here as a potential prototypical case of ancient βίος and will consider several of his parallel *Lives*, both as individual documents, and as sets. I will also use Pythagoras, Epicurus, and a number of other lives from Diogenes to fill out the analysis and add variety from his very large work.

3.3 *The Individual Greek βίος*

Lucian's *Demonax* (125 CE–after 180 CE) provides an (potentially) individual biographical text for consideration. Although Burridge includes this text among his samples, Momigliano refers to it as a document that sits on the boarders of Peripatetic biographies and the *apophthegmata*, collections of antidotes that the *Demonax* resembles structurally.[76] In one of the most recent treatments of this text, Karin Schlapbach is careful to state that Lucian's *Demonax* is not 'a typical biography'.[77] '*The Life of Demonax* is … unusual in that around two thirds of the text are occupied by sayings of the philosopher, so that in addition to the biographical genre, the work is very much in line with gnomologia and apophthegmata-literature'.[78] Nevertheless, as Mark Beck notes, 'Modern questions of genre aside, there seems to be little doubt that Lucian himself considered his work to be a commemorative biography of a man who he claims to have known personally'.[79]

76 Momigliano, *Development*, 73.

77 K. Schlapbach, 'The Spectacle of a Life: Biography as Philosophy in Lucian', in M.B. Diatribai and S. Schorn (eds.), *Bios Philosophos: Philosophy in Ancient Greek Biography* (Turnhout: Brepols, 2016), 127–55 (131).

78 Schlapbach, 'Spectacle', 133–34.

79 M. Beck, 'Lucian's Life of Demonax: The Socratic Paradigm, Individuality, and Personality', in K. de Temmerman and K. Demoen (eds.), *Writing Biography in Greece and Rome: Narrative Technique and Fictionalization* (Cambridge: Cambridge University Press, 2016), 80–96 (80).

In Philostratus' (170–250 CE) massive *Life of Apollonius of Tyana*, we discover another potential sample of the individual Greek βίος. However, controversy rages over the issue of genre here as well. Though Burridge includes Philostratus' *Life* among his samples, he acknowledges that this has been a point of contention.[80] For example, Ewen Lyall Bowie claims that the Latin title of the work (*Vita Apollonii*) is misleading since 'the work is not properly a Vita'.[81] Though contested,[82] if the Gospels are instances of the Greek βίος then these two independent βίοι would be some of their closet antecedents in the Greek biographical tradition, circulating as independent publications rather than as portions of larger works—at least in the case of Matthew, Mark, and John. Luke-Acts would provide a potential exception as a possible case of collected Greek βίοι, so publication format will factor in as an important consideration when we turn to the question of the genre(s) of Luke-Acts.

So as examples of the individual Greek βίος—though sometimes contested—we will examine:

(1) Lucian, *Demonax* (125–after 180 CE)
(2) Philostratus, *Life of Apollonius of Tyana* (170–250 CE)

4 Corpus Linguistics, Gospel Studies, and Richard Burridge

Corpus linguistic research on genre provides an important avenue of recent genre study that New Testament scholarship can profit from. For example, I acknowledged in the previous chapter that Richard Burridge does propose the verbal subjects criterion as a means of differentiating between the βίος and

80 Burridge, *What are the Gospels?*, 156.

81 E.L. Bowie, 'Apollonius of Tyana: Tradition and Reality', in *ANRW* II.16.2 (1978): 1652–99 (1652 n1).

82 Tacitus' *Agricola* (though in Latin, not Greek) (98 CE), another of Burridge's samples, could count as an individual biography text, but as J. Yoder, *Representatives of Roman Rule Roman Provincial Governors in Luke-Acts* (BZNW 209; Berlin: Gruyter, 2014), 68, notes, 'the genre of the *Agricola* has been the subject of debate among classicists'. He says, in addition to biographical features, 'the work contains elements more typical to other genres, including history (the digression on genealogy, ethnology, and history of Britain; the annalistic arrangement of its narrative of Agricola's governship; the speeches prior to the final battle and the detailed description of it) and the *laudatio funebris*, the funeral oration (the unflagging praise of its subject ending in *consolatio*). The "*monumental preface*" is unmatched in extant Roman biography, though contemporary analogues to *Agricola* such as the biographies of Thrasea Paetus and Helvidius Priscus are not available for comparison. It has been suggested that Tacitus' work bears some relation to the martyrologies (*exitus illustrium virorum*) popular in Roman literary circles in Tacitus' time. Although the work qualifies as a biography, it is composite in its contents and interests'.

other ancient genres. Burridge concedes, that for all his features, only 'subject' criteria (where the biographical subject frequently functions as the grammatical subject of a work) are 'determinative for βίοι'.[83] But the validity of this argument depends upon the quality of the 'control group' corpus that Burridge constructs. The corpus consists of Homer's two epics, the *Iliad* and the *Odyssey*, and two books from Herodotus' *Histories*. This might seem like a fairly basic methodological move and exactly what Burridge needs to make his case that verbal subjects—as he calls them—exhibit higher densities in the βίος than in other genres. But such things are not as simple as Burridge and his followers seem to assume. Besides a few scattered references to primary sources in the context of other features he explores, we should note that *Burridge only offers a 'control group' for the verbal subjects criterion*. This confirms prior suspicions that Burridge really is leveraging his entire case for genre disambiguation on this one criterion.[84]

What should we make of the control group that Burridge builds in light of the canons of corpus design and compilation outlined above? First, Burridge's corpus is a dynamic (or at least, diachronic) corpus, incorporating many centuries, but one that attempts to track somewhat stable features—one of the unfortunate limitations of dealing with ancient texts.[85] Nevertheless, the selection of texts Burridge chooses introduces diachronic problems that he fails to attend to. For example, if Herodotus is a history sample (prose) and Homer a poetry sample (verse) then we would need a better sample of history than just books 6–7 of Herodotus, and probably a better sampling of poetry too. And what about all of the other genres of the ancient world?

Second, is this corpus *representativeness and balanced*? As Kennedy asks, 'Representative of what?' All of the nonbiographical Greco-Roman genres? Burridge's description of his corpus as a 'control group' (of both prose and verse) for assessing the 'determinative' feature(s) of the Greco-Roman biography would seem to suggest this much. Kennedy insists, 'The particular year or years from which texts are selected are significant too'.[86] Yet all three texts from the control group predate any of those considered by Burridge as βίοι, with Homer being older by several centuries! This is why Kennedy urges those undertaking *corpus compilation* to consider questions of *corpus design*, such as:

83 R.A. Burridge, *What are the Gospels? A Comparison with Graeco-Roman Biography* (2nd ed.; Grand Rapids: Eerdmans, 2004; org. 1992), 107.

84 See A. Collins, 'Genre and the Gospels', *JR* 75 (1995): 239–46 (241).

85 Cf. Kennedy, *Introduction*, 13–18.

86 Kennedy, *Introduction*, 64.

'What [were] the criteria for [the] inclusion'[87] of these three specific samples in this comparative corpus?

Finally, this brings us to *corpus size*. At the level of raw word counts the two corpora seem fairly balanced (biographical corpus: 231,168 / nonbiographical corpus: 244,004 words). However, many other things relate to the size of a corpus. *Corpus and text-sample size* also addresses how many categories the corpus should contain. For example, if we consider authors as categories, the base corpus ends up with 10 different authors and the comparative corpus only 2. We may also talk about the number of sample texts in each category. We notice imbalance here as well. Burridge's base corpus includes 10 samples, and the control corpus only 3. And so on.

These methodological problems surface directly in Burridge's analysis. When he applies his verbal subjects criterion to his control corpus, the results are, in Burridge's words, 'varied'.[88] For the control corpus to provide a representative sample of nonbiographical literature for analysis of verbal subjects, it must showcase a range of Greek genres where the density levels of verbal subjects *consistently* turn out to be much lower than the densities of this feature in the base corpus (Greco-Roman biographies).

Burridge's results (admittedly) run in the opposite direction. Whereas the *Iliad* deploys fewer proper names in the subject slot of its syntax (i.e. verbal subjects), the *Odyssey* actually features grammaticalized subjects as proper names quite often in a 'pseudo-biographical' way, as Burridge calls it.[89] He later adds Xenophon's *Cyropaedia* and the *Memorabilia* to the control group, both of which he acknowledges likewise behave in a pseudo-biographical way.[90] Further, Burridge only provides a manual clausal analysis or a computer-based morphology search for 7 of the 10 samples in the base corpus. Nowhere that I can find in his book does he provide counts for the verbal subjects in the Isocrates, Philo, or Philostratus samples. And Philo at least turns out to defy the trend, grouping closely with Burridge's non-biographical sample, Homer's *Iliad*.

87 Kennedy, *Introduction*, 64.

88 Burridge, *What are the Gospels?*, 131: 'If we compare these figures with the "control" results from Homer and Herodotus in the previous chapter, the point is clear. In other forms of literature, the subjects of the verbs are wide and varied'.

89 Burridge, *What are the Gospels?*, 112.

90 Burridge, *What are the Gospels?*, 131.

TABLE 2.1 Verbal subjects in Philo's *Moses* and Homer's *Iliad*[a]

Verbal Subjects in Philo's Moses and Homer's Iliad	Nominatives	Achilles (Nom.)	Achilles (all)	Moses (Nom.)	Moses (all)
Total:	*Iliad*: 7,723 *Moses*: 1,326	206	367	36	44
% Against Total Nominatives:	≠	2.66%	4.7%	2.7%	3.3%
Burridge's Number:	≠	2.0%	4.3%	≠	≠

a The data from this chart was collected from Webster, "Architecture of Sentences," 387.

We see here the problem of corpus size—Burridge's only potential criterion for detecting literary divergence between the βίοι and the non-biographical genres is *present in half of the genres of the control group* that Burridge establishes or much more than that when Xenophon's works are also included (i.e. occurring more often than not). But if high densities of verbal subjects is the only form 'determinative of βίοι', why does it show up just as frequently in half or more of the 'control' genres as in the Greco-Roman biographies Burridge considers? Burridge's inability to answer these corpus-related questions not only undermines the viability of the singular criterion in his method designed to assess genre differences (verbal subjects), it reinforces the fact that the Burridge's feature-cluster method may just assess genre similarities, likely targeting text type not genre at all. All of this accentuates the need for carefully compiled corpora in genre discussion and, by extension, justifies the depth of treatment provided for this topic within this chapter.

5 Conclusions and Implications

We began this chapter by stressing the importance of constructing a representative corpus of historical and biographical genres with reference to principles of corpus design and compilation. These principles led us to select 9 histories and a range of biographical texts grouped according to biographical predecessors, collected, and individual βίοι. It seems that the first truly prototypical βίοι (in John Swales' terminology) emerge in Plutarch's multi-volume collection, in the form of parallel lives. We know of at least two potentially individual Greek βίοι, Lucan's *Demonax* and Philostratus' *Life of Apollonius*, but the genres of both documents are contested. Philo could provide another sample but is probably best viewed as a predecessor to the βίος, emerging prior to its most formalized expressions in Plutarch and beyond. Perhaps one could refer to others, such as Polybius' *Life of Philopeomen* but most, including Polybius himself, seems to consider it a rhetorical encomium.[91] Examples could, of course, be multiplied but the point is that we have no *complete uncontestable* examples of the Greek βίος prior to the first century.

The implications of this diachronic assessment, if sound, are nothing short of staggering. It would mean that the Gospels would be literary innovations that were quite ahead of their time. Astonishingly, *if the Gospels are Greek βίοι then they are individual Greek βίοι and in them, we would possess more complete, extant samples of the biographical genre in the New Testament than in any other place in classical literature leading up to the first century.* The Third Gospel could, of course, provide an exception, if viewed in connection with Acts. In this case, Luke-Acts can be identified—as in some recent studies (including Porter, Burridge and esp. Adams)—as part of the collected biographical tradition. This would certainly situate at least Luke-Acts within the broader spectrum of Greco-Roman biography writing, so this is where we will want to devote our attention (among other issues) in the remaining chapters.

Second, it shows that the foundation of the current biographical paradigm in Gospel studies, based in large part upon Burridge' and his work, is far from stable. In fact, the only mechanism for showing that ancient βίος is different from non-biographical genres is the verbal subjects criterion, which—among other ways—fails for the corpus linguistic reasons.

91 Mellor, *Roman Historians*, 133.

CHAPTER 3

Topical Focus and Participant Identification

Proceeding from contemporary Systemic Functional Linguistic (SFL) approaches to genre, we now turn to our first two agnation scales: topical focus and participant identification. These scales function together to support the thematic development of the narrative by identifying what is going on and who is involved. Both clines agnate in opposing directions relative to considerations of genre, at least for Martin and Rose's analysis of modern history and biography. The goal of this chapter is to assess the realization of these clines in our representative corpus of Greek historical and biographical texts in an effort to configure Luke-Acts' potential relationship to these respective literary traditions.

1 Topical Focus: Activity vs. Entity

Histories deploy an activity-focused topical framework that tends to allow for more flexibility and generalized patterns of topicality, united by *general activity sequences* rather than a *specified entity sequence*. This phenomenon may be observed at the discourse level through indications of topical focus in the preface or at the episode level through *staging*. According to Joseph Grimes, 'Every clause, sentence, paragraph, episode, and discourse is organized around a particular element that is taken as its point of departure'.[1] He refers to this point of departure as the 'stage' of a linguistic unit, occurring at thc initial position of its interior structure. Βίοι also stage a very specified thematic framework, almost always (esp. in the later tradition) adopting a sustained topical focus on a singular entity (i.e. the biographical subject), usually from birth to death.

1.1 *Activity Focus in the Greek History*

Notice how Herodotus opens his history: 'This is the display of the inquiry [ἱστορίης] of Herodotus of Halicarnassus, so that things done by humankind [τὰ γενόμενα ἐξ ἀνθρώπων] not be forgotten in time, and that great and marvelous deeds [ἔργα μεγάλα τε καὶ θωμαστά]... may not lose their glory ...' (1.1.0). Herodotus not only claims to write history but also equates this task with

1 J.E. Grimes, *The Thread of Discourse* (JLSM 207; The Hague: Mouton, 1975), 323; cf. G. Brown and G. Yule, *Discourse Analysis* (CTL; Cambridge: Cambridge University Press, 1983), 134.

 | DOI:10.1163/9789004406544_004

chronicling the actions of people (ἀνθρώπων), especially the deeds (ἔργα) of Greeks and foreigners as well as the 'cause of their wars against each other' (Herodotus 1.1.1). This event or activity focus continues at the episode level with the transition from the preface into the narrative body in the discussion of how the Phoenicians journeyed to Egypt and how this was the first of many causal factors that would lead to war (1.1–2.1). Herodotus also maintains a generalized focus on activity at the transitions into a number of other books. The transition into book 2 introduces the preparations of Cambyses' expedition into Egypt. The next major episode(book)-level transition provides the cause for Cambyses' war against Amasis (3.1). Then its Darius' war against the Scythians (4.1), the brutal handling of the Perinthians by Megabazus (5.1), the Ionian revolt (6.1), and 'the message concerning the fight at Marathon' (7.1). Book 8 transitions by introducing 'The Greeks appointed to serve in the fleet' (8.1), and Book 9 details Mardonius' army (9.1). We notice then a very general topical infrastructure where a wide variety of events and activities drive the thematic development of the narrative. Herodotus' focus seems quite generalized to include a wide range of participants, groups, events, and activities.

Thucydides, Polybius, Herodian, Xenophon, Appian, and Josephus all seem event or activity focused in their topical development as well. In his preface, Thucydides proclaims that he will document the 'history [ἱστορία] of the war between the Peloponnesians and the Athenians, beginning at the moment that it broke out'. And Thucydides constantly maintains this generalized activity focus to orient his narrative topically. For example, he describes the prior narrative in book 7 as he transitions into book 8 in the following way: 'Such were the events in Sicily' (ταῦτα μὲν τὰ περὶ Σικελίαν γενόμενα) (8.1). For the purpose of education in 'political acts' (τὰς πολιτικὰς πράξεις), Polybius relates 'the catastrophes of others' (1.1.2) in his history. He acknowledges that he writes about surprising events (αὐτὸ γὰρ τὸ παράδοξον τῶν πράξεων, ὑπὲρ ὧν προῃρήμεθα γράφειν) (1.1.4). And he employs a historical narrative that leaves him 'resolved to confine [himself] to chronicling actions [τὰς πράξεις]' (Polybius 9.1), as does Herodian, who defines his history as 'reviving the memory of past events' (Herodian 1.1). Xenophon's *Hellenica* begins with the formula μετὰ δὲ ταῦτα ('after these things'), indicating a continuation of Thucydides' *Peloponnesian War*, which was—as we have seen—activity focused. Appian uses a similar formula in his preface. After providing an overview of the Roman political climate, he will show 'how these things came to be' (ταῦτα δ' ὅπως ἐγένετο) (*Bel. civ.* 1.6).[2] Josephus records the history of the 'war which we Jews

2 Attestation to an event or activity focus appears to be a quite persistent feature within Greek historiography. Dio Cassius, in a fragment from book 1, says that his history emerges out of a

had with the Romans, and knew myself its particular *actions*' (emphasis mine) as well as to explain the origins and nature of the Jewish people and their governments (Josephus, *Ant.* 1.1.4–5). Although Xenophon's *Anabasis* does not include a preface or statement of intention, several places in his narrative attest to the generalized activity focus of the history (e.g. Xenophon, *Anab.* 2.1; 3.1.13; 4.8.27; 7.1.76).

Dionysius of Halicarnassus and Diodorus Siculus reflect these patterns as well. Dionysius discusses many prior 'historical works' based 'upon deeds inglorious or evil or unworthy of serious study' (*Ant.* 1.1.3). Dionysius seems to summarize the prior historical enterprise here—for better or worse—as accounts of 'deeds' or 'activities'[3] (πραγματείας). He also censors prior historians

desire to write 'a history of all the memorable achievements [μνήμης ἐπράχθη] of the Romans' (Dio Cassius Frag. 1.1 B p. 25; LCL). Diodorus Siculus not only describes universal history as the 'a presentation of events, with a most excellent kind of experience' (1.1.1) but also indicates that 'the failures and successes of other men, which is acquired by the study of history' (Diodorus Siculus 1.1.2) helps educate others—again, the focus remains upon the actions and events of men, rather than their character. For Diodorus, 'the historians, in recording the common affairs of the inhabited world as though they were those of a single state, have made of their treatises a single reckoning of past events [πραγματείας] and a common clearing-house of knowledge concerning them' (1.1.3). He conceives of history as the 'commemoration' (μνήμην) of the 'good deeds' (ἀγαθῷ) of men (1.2.1). History is the guardian of the high achievements of illustrious men, the witness which testifies to the evil deeds of the wicked, and the benefactor of the entire human race' (1.2.3). And Diodorus marks the chronological framework for his historical narrative as covering the activities that transpired between two events: 'from the Trojan War we follow Apollodorus of Athens'(1.5.1). The event or activity focused theory of history apparently assumed by Diodorus in these (and other) passages may go back as far as Ephorus or, possibly the Stoic, Posidonius. Jacoby, *FGrH* 70, F 7–9 Com., thought it derived from Ephorus. So does G.L. Barber, *The Historian Ephorus* (Cambridge: Cambridge University Press, 1935), 70. A. Burton, *Diodorus Siculus: Book I: A Commentary* (Études préliminaires aux religions orientales dans l'empire romain 29; Leiden: Brill, 1972), 36, however, locates the tradition in Posidonius. But even if we cannot link Diodorus' model back to Ephorus, Ephorus still seems to have conceived of the narrative frame of his history in terms of an event or activity focus, with a very generalized orientation. This can be derived from the fragments that indicate his avoidance of the 'mythological period', preferring instead to document the 'events that took place after the Return of the Heracleidae' (Ἔφορος μὲν γὰρ ὁ Κυμαῖος, Ἰσοκράτους ὢν μαθητής, ὑποστησάμενος γράφειν τὰς κοινὰς πράξεις, τὰς μὲν παλαιὰς μυθολογίας ὑπερέβη, τὰ δ' ἀπὸ τῆς Ἡρακλειδῶν καθόδου πραχθέντα συνταξάμενος ταύτην ἀρχὴν ἐποιήσατο τῆς ἱστορίας) (Diodorus Siculus 4.1.3 = T 8). Similarly, Dionysius of Halicarnassus, in his *Epistula ad Pompeium Geminum*, commends the ability of Theopompus (= T 20) to get behind the causes of the actions of men and those that do them (τῶν πράξεων καὶ τῶν πραξάντων) (*Ep. Pomp.* 6.7). A good historian not only narrated historical events, but could assess their causes (τὰς ἀφανεῖς αἰτίας), as Theopompus could (*Ep. Pomp.* 6.7 = T 20). We can see evidence, then, even in several fragmentary historians (for which the preface has not been preserved) of the fundamental event or activity focus of ancient history.

3 BDAG, 859.

for failing to produce an adequate history of Rome. Dionysius, therefore, takes it upon himself to detail, 'through what turns of fortune' (i.e. activities) the founders of Rome 'left their native countries' (another activity sequence) and came together to establish the city (a final activity sequence) (*Ant.* 1.5.1). Diodorus' universal history will naturally be quite general in nature. In fact, he calls history the 'commemoration of goodly deeds' (1.2.1) and, in his own history, he seeks to narrate 'the affairs of the entire world down to his own day' (1.3.6). His tripartite outline of his history likewise reflects generalized action sequences as an organizing principle for the narrative:

(1) first six Books embrace the events and legends previous to the Trojan War,
(2) in the following eleven we have written a universal history of events from the Trojan War to the death of Alexander and
(3) in the succeeding twenty-three Books we have given an orderly account of all subsequent events down to the beginning of the war between the Romans and the Celts (Diodorus, *Lib.* 1.4.6–7)

Several historians provide event-focused perspectives on their work within the flow of their narrative or describe prior historical tradition along these lines (e.g. Polybius 9.1.5–6; Josephus, *Ant.* 2.338;[4] 8.314;[5] Diodorus Siculus 4.1.3; 17.1.1–2;[6] Dionysius of Halicarnassus, *Ep. Pomp.* 6.7).[7]

1.2 *Entity Focus in the βίος*

In contrast to histories, βίοι focus their narratives on a specific *entity* and this entity tends to form the topical backbone of the narrative. The predecessors to ancient βίοι, if they have any introductory material, tend to begin by

4 Josephus ends book 2 here with a reflection of what he has narrated so far concerning the 'actions of Alexander' (τὰς Ἀλεξάνδρου πράξεις) and 'these events/things' (τούτων) that he has documented (cf. Arrian, *Anab.* 1.26; Callisthenes frag. 25). It is thus clear that for Josephus, an activity focus often frames his narrative. He conceives of it as fundamentally structured by a narration of things/activities rather than the character of an individual.

5 As with *Ant.* 2.348, here Josephus cataphorically describes his prior narrative in terms of a litany of 'things' (ἐκ τούτων) that he has recorded.

6 Here Diodorus transitions into book 17, where the narrative frame seems governed fundamentally by an activity rather than a participant. Although Diodorus states that book 16 concerned Philip the son of Amyntas and his career, this merely seems to set a timeline for 'those events connected with other kings, peoples and cities which occurred in the years of his reign' (Diodorus Siculus 17.1.1).

7 Josephus' *Against Apian* is, likewise, activity focused. As a continuation of his *Antiquities of the Jews* (*Ag. Ap.* 1.1–3), Josephus writes about 'the history of five thousand years, and are taken out of our sacred books; but are translated by me into the Greek tongue' (*Ag. Ap.* 1.1) and in this second volume answers criticisms against the events narrated in the *Antiquities* (*Ag. Ap.* 1.2–5).

talking about their subjects (indicating a participant- or entity-focused narrative) immediately after the preface but often provide only limited information. Isocrates's *Evagoras* sustains King Evagoras as the central focus of the speech and his comments on the purpose of the speech to 'honor' the King by recounting 'his principles in life and his more perilous deeds than to all other men' (Isocrates, *Evag.* 2) seem to corroborate this observation. We notice also that the recounting of the 'deeds' of Evagoras serves the much greater end of illustrating his 'virtues' (Isocrates, *Evag.* 4). Though 'deeds' are mentioned, a specified entity (Evagoras) drives the topical development of the narrative (i.e. Evagoras' deeds are only mentioned to illustrate the character of the man). Xenophon's *Cyropaedia* exhibits entity-focused topicality as well. He says regarding Cyrus, the subject of his work: 'Believing this man to be deserving of all admiration, we have therefore investigated who he was in his origin, what natural endowments he possessed, and what sort of education he had enjoyed, that he so greatly excelled in governing men' (Xenophon, *Cyr.* 1.6). Then in 2.1, Xenophon opens with 'The father of Cyrus is said to have been Cambyses'. And subsequently, the topic of Cyrus occupies most macrostructural transitions (e.g. Xenophon, *Cyr.* 3.1.1; 4.1.1; 5.1.1; 6.1.1; 7.1.1; 8.1.1). Philo's *Life of Moses* codifies this pattern strongly as well, beginning his narrative with the birth of Moses and following this through all the way to the death of his subject, where the narrative ends. Satyrus' *Euripides* lacks a preface, so we do not have a self-attestation regarding orientation from that document; however, the portion that remains centers heavily upon Euripides.

The later βίοι employ an entity focus for their narratives as well. Plutarch begins his *Alexander* by stating: 'It is the life of Alexander the king, and of Caesar, who overthrew Pompey, that I am writing in this book' (*Alex.* 1.1). In Plutarch's *Caesar*, a self-attestation of any kind is missing, but classicists almost universally accept that the original beginning of this document is now lost.[8] Plutarch begins his comparison of Demosthenes and Cicero by stating: 'Therefore, in this fifth book of my Parallel Lives, where I write about Demosthenes and Cicero, I shall examine their actions and their political careers to see how their natures and dispositions compare with one another' (*Dem.* 3.1). Again, although actions and events are chronicled, they seem to serve the ulterior purpose of displaying the nature and disposition of the individual. The topical framework assumed by Plutarch, therefore, seems more entity than activity focused. Similarly, in his *Parallel Lives of Theseus and Romulus*, Plutarch states: 'It seemed to me, then, that many resemblances made Theseus a fit parallel

8 See C.B.R. Pelling, *Plutarch and History: Eighteen Studies* (Swansea: Classical Press of Wales, 2011), 129–30, for discussion.

to Romulus. For both were of uncertain and obscure parentage, and got the reputation of descent from gods' (*Thes.* 2.1). Likewise, in his *Demonax*, Lucian immediately focuses his narrative περὶ … Δημώνακτος (*Dem.* 2) and then finally concludes with a death and burial narrative (63–67). Diogenes Laërtius' lives of *Pythagoras* (*Vit. phil.* 8.1) and *Epicurus* (*Vit. phil.* 10.1) both immediately begin their narrative with a focus on their subjects. Diogenes' life of *Pythagoras* ends with his death, followed by a succession list (*Vit. phil.* 8.45), and Diogenes ends his 'entire work *as well as on this philosopher's life* [Epicurus] [καὶ τοῦ βίου τοῦ φιλοσόφου] by citing his Sovran Maxims' (*Vit. phil.* 10.138). The macro-level topical structure encoded in the narrative openings and closing seem to indicate a specified entity focus for both of Diogenes' biographical subjects. Similarly, Philostratus begins with his *Apollonius* with a focus on Apollonius (*Vit. Apoll.* 1.2) and ends with Apollonius preaching after his death and then finally with details concerning his burial (*Vit. Apoll.* 8.31).

1.3 *Focus in the Gospels with Special Reference to Luke*

Histories tend to have a more generalized activity focus driving their topical development within the macrostructures of their discourse. By contrast, βίοι tend to exhibit a more specified, entity focus. Their topical framework is specified to a singular entity's story, usually from birth to death or some other conclusive life-event/accomplishment (e.g. a philosopher's maxims) but *the subject's life supplies the basis for the topical sequence.* Once the biographer chooses their subject, it seems that the interior topical infrastructure is pretty well laid out (i.e. specified) for them. Histories differ from βίοι in this way. Instead of operating from a specified topical framework, where the same individualized entity or participant is distributed across the narrative from beginning to end, histories deploy a more generalized framework. Histories seem to encode topicality through *general activity sequences* rather than a *specified entity sequence*, as in biographies. So where does Luke-Acts fall on this cline? First, we turn to Luke's Gospel.

Luke frames his narrative as an account of contemporary (ἐν ἡμῖν) 'deeds' or 'actions' (πράγματα) (Luke 1:1) not an individualized account of a specific participant[9]—employing language that resembles the historians' frequent self-descriptions of their activity-focused narratives (Thucydides 1.1.2; Polybius

9 R.A. Burridge, *What are the Gospels? A Comparison with Graeco-Roman Biography* (2nd ed. Grand Rapids: Eerdmans, 2004; org. 1992), 196, briefly comments on the 'scale' of Luke as follows: 'This is true of the whole narrative; a wider scale comes in Luke's second volume, Acts—although even here, the focus is still upon certain key individuals, especially Peter and Paul, rather than attempting a comprehensive history of the early church. However, the gospels themselves all restrict their scale to the person of Jesus in a manner typical of βίος

1.4; 9.1.5–6; Diodorus Siculus 1.1.1; 4.1.3; Cassius Dio 62b.29.2; cf. also Josephus, *Ag. Ap.* 1.47–48; Dionysius of Halicarnassus, *Ep. Pomp.* 6.7).[10] As Samuel Byrskog puts it, 'The use of the plural πράγματα would be an odd way of referring simply to the life-story of one person'.[11] In a contemporary history, *autopsy* or first-hand witness of *the events* or *activities* that the historian documents played a crucial role in navigating authority.[12] A focus upon *autopsy*, therefore, often implies an orientation toward activities, especially when used in connection with language for events such as πράγματα. Luke creates this authority *via* autopsy by emphasizing that the events he records happened 'among us' (ἐν ἡμῖν) and that he constructs his account according to (καθώς) eyewitness traditions (αὐτόπται). The terminology διήγησιν helps further establish this activity

literature'. But note that Burridge does not explicate any specific formal features that reveal this entity focus.

10 As H. Cancik, 'The History of Culture, Religion, and Institutions in Ancient Historiography: Philological Observations Concerning Luke's History', *JBL* 116 (1997): 673–94 (675), asserts, 'This historical work (διήγησις) runs "from the beginning" (ἀπ' ἀρχῆς; ἄνωθεν); it is complete (πάντα), exact (ἀκριβῶς), and in order (καθεξῆς). It has many good sources, even eyewitnesses (πολλοί; αὐτόπται). The goal of the work is certainty, knowledge (ἀσφάλεια; ἐπιγιγνώσκειν). Luke's preface corresponds to the topics of prefaces in ancient Western historiography. Strikingly, the theme of the work is characterized by the most general of all possible expressions: Luke will write about "deeds" (πράγματα), and contemporary ones (ἐν ἡμῖν). The expressions that one would expect in light of the ancient historiography of philosophy—βίος of the founder, his teachings (δόξαι, γνῶμαι, αἵρεσις), his successors (διαδοχαί)—do not occur in the prologue of the first logos, which may be the prologue for the whole work'.

11 S. Byrskog, *Story as History—History as Story: The Gospel Tradition in the Context of Ancient Oral History* (WUNT 123; Tübingen: Mohr Siebeck, 2000), 229. In support of this point he observes further that 'Already in 1:1 the author places himself in the midst of the events, they have been fulfilled "among us", evidently regarding his own present time as part of what other authors had dealt with. Not only the past history of Jesus is his concern in the prologue of the gospel, but also the present time of the spirit's continuos [*sic.*] manifestation of Jesus' ministry in deed and word'. Others have recognized the distinct activity focus of this language as well, some even drawing out the connection that this focus moves the reader expectations away from a biographical reading of the Gospel. See I.H. Marshall, *The Gospel of Luke: A Commentary on the Greek Text* (NIGTC; Grand Rapids, Mich.: Eerdmans, 1978), 41; J.A. Fitzmyer, *The Gospel According to Luke I–IX* (AB 28; Garden City: Doubleday, 1981), 293; J.B. Green, *The Gospel of Luke* (NICNT; Grand Rapids: Eerdmans, 1997), 39; W.S. Kurz, 'Promise and Fulfillment in Hellenistic Jewish Narratives and in Luke-Acts', in David P. Moessner (ed.), *Jesus and the Heritage of Israel: Luke's Narrative Claim Upon Israel's Legacy* (Harrisburg: Trinity International, 1999), 147–70 (151); Green, *Gospel of Luke*, 38–39.

12 See J. Marincola, *Authority and Tradition in Ancient Historiography* (Cambridge: Cambridge University Press, 1997), 63–86.

focus,[13] since it was used in a variety of ancient contexts to refer to the assemblage of events into a single narrative and frequently to describe histories, used in conjunction with language for deeds (Diodorus Siculus 11.20.1; Lucian, *Hist.* 55; see also Dionysius of Halicarnassus, *Rom. ant.* 4.7.5). Luke's statement of his intentions resembles Lucian's charge to the historian: εἰς καλὰν διαθέσυαι τὰ πεπραγμένα (Lucian, *Hist.* 52). On its own, the term is not a decisive indicator of genre but in the context of other event/activity language,[14] it helps establish the focus of Luke's narrative toward an activity- rather than an entity-based topical sequence.

Jesus, the main participant on a biographical reading of the Gospel, is not mentioned in the preface. Instead, Luke composes a narrative of activities accomplished among 'us' based on eyewitness testimony of these *events*.[15] And while Luke's Gospel ends—as the other Gospels—with the death and resurrection of Jesus,[16] his Gospel delays its discussion of the birth and life of Jesus (see below). Further, if Luke is understood as part of a two-volume project, together with Acts, then Jesus' death roughly half way through the narrative but at a book-level transition fits well within the pattern of Greek histories for such transitions (e.g. Diodorus, *Lib.* 1.4.6–7; 17.118–18.1; see also below).[17] *At the level of microgenre*, then, Luke does seem to reflect certain biographical components but when the macrostructures are considered, Luke's topical sequence seems to reflect historiographical conventions. Beginning with the circumstances of Elizabeth's barrenness and ending with Paul's trial, Luke-Acts aligns very nicely with the generalized, activity-focused topical sequences of the ancient histories.

---

13 BDAG 245 defines διήγησις as 'an orderly description of facts, events, actions, or words'. Byrskog, *History*, 230, states that it is 'a term describing an account composed of a number of events, without narrow generic implications'. Green, *Gospel of Luke*, 38–39, views the terminology among Luke's special vocabulary for describing the 'mighty deeds of God' (cf. Acts 9:27).

14 This terminology is used to describe several non-historical writings, e.g. Plato, *Rep.* 3.392D; Aristotle, *Rhet.* 2.8.13; 3.16.1; Strabo 8.3.5; Plutarch, *Art.* 11.1.

15 Cf. T. Callan, 'The Preface of Luke-Acts and Historiography', *NTS* 31 (1985): 576–81 (578), for another argument that the lack of the mention of Jesus indicates that Luke records history not βίος.

16 Death of a significant figure often provides a key transitional narrative element in ancient histories. See Herodotus 2.1.1; 6.1; Dionysius of Halicarnassus, *Rom. Ant.* 3.1.1; 4.1.1; Diodorus Siculus, *Lib.* 17.118–18.1.6.

17 This is a point overlooked by Burridge, *What are the Gospels?*, 1.79, in his critique of my Achtemeier paper, where he claims that this criterion is not borne out by Luke's concentration of verbal subjects. This assumes the validity of the verbal subjects criterion (see Chapter 2) and ignores the possible continuity of Luke-Acts as a two-volume work.

Luke is distinct in these ways from the other Gospels. Mark attests to being an εὐαγγελίου Ἰησοῦ Χριστοῦ (Mark 1:1), focused specifically upon its 'beginning' (ἀρχή). While this stops short of calling the work a 'life' (which was uncommon in any case in βίοι without a preface) it certainly—from its opening line—indicates that the document will have a specified focus upon a single participant, Ἰησοῦ Χριστοῦ. Matthew opens in a similar fashion, with Βίβλος γενέσεως Ἰησοῦ Χριστοῦ υἱοῦ Δαυὶδ υἱοῦ Ἀβραάμ (Matt 1:1). Again, this signals a highly entity-driven narrative, with the opening line of the Gospel introducing the participant that will occupy the central focus of the narrative. Burridge thus rightly notices that 'like most Graeco-Roman βίοι, Mark and Matthew include the name of their subject at the very start'.[18] Similarly, in John, Jesus, who is referred to as ὁ λόγος (cf. John 1:17), takes center stage in the opening and occupies the focus of John 1:1–5,[19] again indicating a participant orientation in the programmatic introductory material of the narrative.

So, it seems, with Mark, Matthew, and John, that we have strong indication of a specified entity- or participant-focused narrative. Luke's opening lines do not mention Jesus' name, by contrast (the first occurrence is in Luke 1:31). They remain focused on the events Luke plans to narrate. Burridge seeks to escape the force of this evident difference between Luke and the other Gospels by drawing attention to the fact that some βίοι have a preface.[20] However, the existence of a preface is a feature shared between histories and βίοι, often with many of the same preface features. So that Luke contains a preface does not, on its own, indicate a biographical over against a historical genre.[21]

18 Burridge, *What are the Gospels?*, 189.

19 Cf. Burridge, *What are the Gospels?*, 216.

20 Burridge, *What are the Gospels?*, 189. He mentions Lucian and Philo (having a shorter preface) as well as Isocrates, Tacitus, and Philostratus (having a longer prologue). A. Köstenberger, 'The Genre of the Fourth Gospel and Greco-Roman Literary Conventions', in S.E. Porter and A.W. Pitts (eds.), *Christian Origins and Greco-Roman Culture: Social and Literary Contexts for the New Testament* (TENTS 8; ECHC 1; Leiden: Brill, 2013), 435–62 (439), misses this point when he says, in a list of 'differences between the Gospels and Greco-Roman biographies' that 'First, of the four Gospels, only Luke has a formal literary preface (Luke 1:1–4; cf. Acts 1:1–2)'. Many βίοι, of course, did have a formal literary preface that would exhibit several similarities to Luke, as they would to ancient histories, so this feature cannot count as a difference, on its own.

21 This applies to the kind of evidence assembled, for example, in J.M. Smith, *Why βίος?: On the Relationship between Gospel Genre and Implied Audience* (LNTS 518; London: T&T Clark, 2015), 221–29.

1.4 *Focus in Acts*

Though Burridge views it as a biographical text, he correctly stresses the focus in Acts on 'the happening of the *activity* of God'[22] (emphasis mine).[23] John Squires argues extensively through an assortment of lexical and grammatical features that the theme of the 'plan of God', including 'the actions of God extend[ed] throughout the span of history, from creation to judgement', undergirds the thematic structure of Luke-Acts.[24] Many interpreters note the role of the parting words of Jesus in Acts 1:8 in indicating topicality. Readers of Acts tend to agree that the passage anticipates the coming narrative in some major structural/thematic way. Most view it as a geographical or perhaps salvation-historical[25] outline of the subsequent discourse.[26] Regardless of its precise thematic function, all seem to concur regarding its 'programmatic'[27] significance for understanding its global focus. Acts 1:8 centers upon the missional activity of the apostles and the movement of the kingdom message through specific geographic regions. Luke projects two actions, in particular, onto the foreground of the narrative—one with God as the actor, the other with the apostles: (1) God's outpouring of the Holy Spirt (λήμψεσθε δύναμιν) and (2) the apostles' witness (ἔσεσθέ μου μάρτυρες) to the resurrected Lord Jesus. Regardless of the debate over 'the ends of the earth' as a reference to Rome,[28] Acts does seem mapped on the basic progression outlined in Acts 1:8. As Bruce

22 R.A. Burridge, 'The Genre of Acts Revisited', in Steve Walton (ed.), *Reading Acts Today: Essays in Honour of Loveday C.A. Alexander* (LNTS 472; London: T&T Clark, 2011), 3–28 (15).

23 The reception history for the title of 'the Book of Acts' (ΠΡΑΞΕΙΣ ΑΠΟΣΤΟΛΩΝ), with ℵ and B being the earliest evidence, reveals a tendency among at least some fourth-century Christians to read the document as activity focused.

24 J.T. Squires, *The Plan of God in Luke-Acts* (SNTSMS 76; Cambridge: Cambridge University Press, 1993), 2.

25 R.I. Pervo, *Acts: A Commentary on the Book of Acts* (Hermeneia; Minneapolis: Fortress Press, 2009), 43.

26 E.g. Fitzmyer, *Acts*, 119; Marshall, *Acts*, 66; W.G. Kümmel, *Introduction to the New Testament* (trans. Howard Clark Kee; Nashville: Abingdon, 1975), 155; H. Conzelmann, *Acts of the Apostles: A Commentary on the Acts of the Apostles* (Hermeneia; Philadelphia: Fortress, 1987), 7; F.F. Bruce, *The Book of the Acts* (NCNT; Grand Rapids, Mich.: Eerdmans, 1988), 36–37; J.B. Polhill, *Acts* (NAC 26; Nashville: Broadman & Holman Publishers, 1992), 82; B.W. Witherington, *The Acts of the Apostles: A Socio-Rhetorical Commentary* (Grand Rapids, Mich.: Eerdmans, 1998), 118; C.K. Barrett, *A Critical and Exegetical Commentary on the Acts of the Apostles. International Critical Commentary* (ICC; 2 vols.; Edinburgh: T&T Clark, 2004), 1:79. Cf. also D.L. Bock, *Acts* (Grand Rapids, Mich.: Baker Academic, 2010), 64.

27 Cf. Pervo, *Acts*, 43.

28 See D.R. Schwartz, 'The End of the ΓΗ (Acts 1:8): Beginning or End of the Christian Vision?' *JBL* 105 (1986): 669–76, for discussion.

summarizes it: '"in Jerusalem" covers the first seven chapters, "in all Judaea and Samaria" covers 8:1 to 11:18, and the remainder of the book traces the progress of the gospel outside the frontiers of the Holy Land until at last it reaches Rome'.[29] The activity of the progress of the Gospel, then, seems to provide a (the?) major topical focus in Acts.

Both Burridge and Adams emphasize the importance of the 'subject' of Acts for determining its genre. Burridge applies his verbal subjects analysis to Acts, assuming the theoretical foundation outlined in *What are the Gospels?*[30] Through analysis of verbal subjects, Burridge claims, Acts 'depicts its key actors, namely Peter, Stephen, Paul and the other disciples, interpreting the happening of the activity of God'.[31] But unlike Luke and the other Gospels, Acts is not dominated by a single subject (Jesus), but by the working of God through the early church. Since '*just over 57% of the verbs are devoted to the deeds and words of the first Christians*', Burridge argues, 'this is a group subject rather than an individual', eventually concluding that Acts most closely resembles 'a biographical monograph'.[32]

Having noted several problems with Burridge's verbal subjects criterion already (see Chapter 2), and seeing no major improvements in the methodology at this point, we may move on to consider the potential viability of the proposal put forward by Adams. I take Adams' argument to be that both collected biographies and Acts exhibit similar distributions of narrative space to individual characters (e.g. philosophers in the case of Diogenes; the early disciples in the case of Acts).

Adams points to several collected biographies that formally divide their larger sets of lives according to the specific subjects treated in the collection. Adams argues that since collected biographies 'delineate and segment their work based on individual characters', 'the optimal way of determining the main subject(s) of collected biographies is to look at the amount of narrative given to each character's section'.[33] He elucidates this pattern in several collected biographies, including (1) Suetonius's *Lives of the Caesars*; (2) Nepos's *Lives of the Eminent Commanders*; (3) Philostratus's *Lives of the Sophists*; (4) Eunapius's *Lives of the Philosophers*; and (5) Diogenes Laërtius's *Lives of the Eminent Philosophers*. Adams notices in these works a wide range of space allocation for the subjects treated in the collections. 'In book 2', of Diogenes

---

29 Bruce, *Acts*, 36–37.

30 Burridge, *What are the Gospels?*, 110–112; Burridge, 'Genre', 11.

31 Burridge, 'Genre', 15.

32 Burridge, 'Genre', 28.

33 S.A. Adams, *The Genre of Acts and Collected Biography* (SNTSMS 156; Cambridge: Cambridge University Press, 2013), 126.

Laërtius' *Lives*, 'there are nine characters who each receive less than 2% of the book, and four subjects in book 7'.[34] Yet in 'in books 6, 7, and 8 there is one philosopher that takes up more than 50% of the word count: book 6—Diogenes, 5,526 (59.9%); book 7—Zeno, 15,121 (79.2%); book 8—Pythagoras, 4,509 (56.5%)',[35] noting similar distributions in Acts as well.[36]

The data sets from Acts and the collected biographies differ, however, in important ways. While Adams begins by examining the formal divisions in collected biographies as the basis for topicalization, he then turns and compares those units to the (non-formally segmented) units that he identifies in Acts. Since the author of Acts 'did not formally segment his text as is the case with the collected biographies above', he must depend upon his own analysis of the 'narrative pattern of focusing on characters in series'.[37] In this way, he compares the topicalization strategies of the collected biographies and Acts.

This all raises the question: if *narrative segmentation* drives topical encoding (it tells us what a unit is about) in collected biographies but *non-segmented narrative patterning* drives it for Acts, then is the method transferable to Acts, either in terms of narrative structuring or topicalization? Since Acts does not formally segment the text into book-level episodes around a participant, Adams often ends up examining paragraph-level transitions in Acts but episode-level transitions in the collected biographies so that the levels of analysis are not always aligned. Adams confronts the same problem that Charles Talbert faced many years before him: the collected biographies divide their narratives quite differently than Acts, in virtually all known cases. Gregory Sterling's response to Talbert is still relevant: 'the narrative unity of Luke-Acts is far greater than the sequential lives of the individual figures of the philosophic schools of Diogenes'.[38]

This may be noted by comparing the character introductions in the narrative units Adams proposes for Acts with the beginnings of two sequential lives from Adams' sample corpus, Suetonius' *Lives of the Caesars* and Diogenes Laërtius' *Lives of the Imminent Philosophers*. We begin with Acts. The first unit where Peter becomes the main narrative character (with the other apostles) is Acts 1:15–20 (a paragraph-level unit), according to Adams.[39] After Peter is

34 Adams, *Genre*, 128.

35 Adams, *Genre*, 128.

36 Adams, *Genre*, 130–31.

37 Adams, *Genre*, 129.

38 G.E. Sterling, *Historiography and Self-Definition: Josephos, Luke-Acts, and Apologetic History* (NovTSup 64; Leiden: Brill, 1992), 319.

39 Adams, *Genre*, 130.

mentioned among those in the upper room (his first mention in the narrative, Acts 1:13), he becomes the active subject and speaker in the narrative in Acts 1:15: Καὶ ἐν ταῖς ἡμέραις ταύταις ἀναστὰς Πέτρος ἐν μέσῳ τῶν ἀδελφῶν εἶπεν. Following this transitional formula, the author records Peter's first speech. The author of Acts introduces Saul for the first time as a major character, according to Adams, in Acts 9:1–9 (a paragraph-level unit): Ὁ δὲ Σαῦλος ἔτι ἐμπνέων ἀπειλῆς καὶ φόνου εἰς τοὺς μαθητὰς τοῦ κυρίου, προσελθὼν τῷ ἀρχιερεῖ. Anticipating in some ways our analysis below, first, note that there is no uniform way of introducing these key characters. Second, no titles are employed containing the subject's name. Third, the author does not introduce characters with an origins formula or statement of family tradition for the most significant characters in his narrative.

All of these features, however, consistently dominate the structural transitions of the collected biographies. These large works apply a quite standardized method of segmentation that sharply distinguishes them from the interrelated sets of characters introduced in the non-segmented narrative sequence of Acts. The collected biographies deploy hard formal (typically, episode-level) transitions, including most consistently a title of the life containing the subject's name (titles are in some cases lacking, though not in the cases below) and a statement of their origins or family tradition in the opening line of the life. This set of devices provides a highly formalized sequence followed by virtually all collected biographers. Consider two of the collected biographies that Adams points to as literary models for Acts. Each set below runs in sequence (i.e. two lives in a row) with the formal descriptions (title; origins / family information [in **bold**]) and bracketed text not in the original.

Suetonius, *Lives*

[*Augustus*]

Title: DIVUS AUGUSTUS

Origins / Family Information: *Aug.* 1: **Gentem** Octauiam Velitris praecipuam olim fuisse multa declarant

[… continuous narrative about August …]

[*Tiberius*]

Title: DIVUS IULIUS

Origins / Family Information: *Tib.* 1: Patricia **gens** Claudia—fuit enim et alia plebeia, nec potentia minor nec dignitate—orta est ex Regillis oppido Sabinorum

[… continuous narrative about Tiberius …]

Diogenes Laërtius, *Lives*

[*Thales*]

Title: ΚΕΦ. Α'. ΘΑΛΗΣ

Origins / Family Information: *Vit. Phil.* 1:22: Ἦν τοίνυν ὁ Θαλῆς, ὡς μὲν Ἡρόδοτος καὶ Δοῦρις καὶ Δημόκριτός φασι, πατρὸς μὲν Ἐξαμύου, μητρὸς δὲ Κλεοβουλίνης, ἐκ τῶν Θηλιδῶν

[... continuous narrative about Thales ...]

[*Solon*]

Title: ΚΕΦ. Β'. ΣΟΛΩΝ

Origins / Family Information: *Vit. Phil.* 1:22: Σόλων Ἐξηκεστίδου Σαλαμίνιος

The same pattern can be almost invariably demonstrated throughout the biographical tradition, when the subject of a life is introduced.[40] Therefore, the methodology used by Adams for deriving topicality in Acts based on narrative patterning seems far different formally and structurally than the life-module segments assessed for topicality in the collected biographies.

Acts organizes its topical sequence not as the collected biographies but as Lucian recommends for the good historian. In *How to Write History* 55, Lucian says that good history writing should be evaluated,

> ... partly by the diction, and partly by the treatment of connected events. For, though all parts must be independently perfected, when the first is complete the second will be brought into essential connection with it, and attached like one link of a chain to another; there must be no possibility of separating them; no mere bundle of parallel threads; the first is not simply to be next to the second, but part of it, their extremities intermingling.

40 Major subjects are consistently introduced through an origins formula (and often a title) in both collected and individual biographies, though not in Acts. See, e.g., Plutarch, *Alex.* 2.1; *Cae.* 1.1; *Dem.* 4. 1; *Cic.* 1.1; *Thes.* 3.1; *Rom.* 4.1; *Artex.* 2.1; *Oth.* 2.1; Lucian, *Dem.* 3; Philostratus, *Life* 1.5; *Vit. Aes.* 1; *Vit. Arist.* 1; *Vit. Eur.* 1–2; *Vit. Pind.* 1; *Vit. Soph.* 1; Athanasius, *Vit. Ant.* 1; Diogenes Laërtius, *Vit. Phil.* 1.22, 68, 74, 82, 89, 94, 101, 106, 109, 116; 2.1, 3, 6, 16, 18, 48, 60, 65, 105, 125; 3.1; 4.1, 6, 16, 21, 28, 46, 62; 5.1, 36, 58, 65, 75, 86; 6.1, 20, 85, 94; 7.1, 167, 168, 179; 8.1, 51–53, 78, 79, 86; 9.1, 18, 21, 24, 25, 34, 50, 57, 61; 10.1; Iamblichus, *Pyth.* 2.1; Plutarch, *Lyc.* 1.1–2.1; *Num.* 1.1–4; *Pub.* 1.1–3; Ps.-Herodotus, *Vit. Hom.* 1; Porphyry, *Vit. Pyth.* 1–2; Soranus, *Vit. Hip.* 1; Tacitus, *Agr.* 4; Suetonius, *Aug.* 1–5; *Tib.* 1–5; *Cal.* 1–7; *Cla.* 1.1–6; *Ner.* 1–5; *Gal.* 1–3; *Oth.* 1.1–3; *Vit.* 1.1–3.1; *Ves.* 1.1–4; *Tit.* 1.1; *Dom.* 1.1; Nepos, *Mel.* 1.1; *Them.* 1.1; *Aris.* 1.1; *Paus.* 1; *Cim.* 1.1; *Alc.* 1.1; *Thr.* 1.1; *Dio.* 1.1, and so on; Jerome, *Vir. ill.* 1.1; 2.1; 4.1; 5.1; 7.1; 8.1; and so on.

In relation to the 'treatment of connected events' (τῇ συμπεριπλοκῇ τῶν πραγμάτων) in Acts, one thinks here of the intertwining portraits of Peter, Stephen, Barnabas, and Paul with none of them introduced in the formalized ways of the collected biographies. While formal segmentation allows for effortless structural and topical identification in these texts, as Joseph Fitzmyer observes, 'The structure of Acts is not easy to determine, and there are almost as many suggestions for its outline as there are heads that think about it'.[41]

2 Participant Identification: Generic vs. Individualized

Martin and Rose point to participant identification strategies as another genre agnation scale for biographical and historical discourse.[42] They refer to generic vs. individualized strategies for participant identification.[43] In histories, participant identification tends to be more *generic*, mentioning participants in connection with larger events and/or identifying groups or agencies as the major participants at the macrostructural levels of the discourse. Biographical texts, by contrast, realize *individualized* participant identification where a singular participant tends to be consistently identified throughout higher-level structures, from beginning to end.

2.1 *Generic Participant Identification in Histories*

Histories frequently deploy generic participant identification at the discourse level of their narratives. Martin and Rose discuss the identification of groups or sets of individuals (in the same narrative, i.e. unlike a parallel life) as the major participants involved in the discourse as one means formally encoding of participant identification linguistically.[44] We may examine the preface and major episode level transitions for reference to individuals or groups at these major macrostructural locations. Herodotus writes his history to record the most important movements known in history 'for both Greeks and foreigners' (1.1.2). He documents the great works done 'by the Hellenes, and some by the barbarians' (1.1.0). His entire universal history publishes his investigation the history of *nations* and their wars (e.g. Herodotus, 1.1.1; 3.1.1, 5; 4.1.1; 5.1.1).

41 Fitzmyer, *Acts*, 119.

42 In the historical recounts that they examine, J.R. Martin and D. Rose, *Genre Relations: Mapping Culture* (London: Equinox, 2008), 108, discover that 'Alongside [the] layered phasing of events, historical recounts are also organized by agencies and groups participating in the events'.

43 Martin and Rose, *Genre Relations*, 134.

44 Martin and Rose, *Genre Relations*, 108.

Similarly, because it 'was a great war', Thucydides devotes a substantial amount of space to situating the entire 'Hellenic race' (Thucydides, 1.1) in relation to the 'Barbarian world' (1.2) in his coverage of the Peloponnesian war.

Xenophon begins his narrative with the war of 'the Lacedaemonians and the Athenians', again identifying his major participants as groups rather than individuals in the preface. As the narrative quickly develops in book 1, Xenophon discusses several participants, but only in service of detailing Dorieus' invasion of Athens (e.g. *Hell.* 1.1.2–10). And the major transitions seem to be driven by groups (e.g. *Hell.* 1.1.11, 18; 2.1.1; *Anab.* 2.1.1) or sets of individuals connected with groups (e.g. *Hell.* 1.1.32; 4.1.1; *Anab.* 7.1.2) in Xenophon's histories, usually linked to the wider context of the events being narrated. In *Hell.* 1.1.32, for example, Xenophon transitions in the following way:

> At about this time a revolution took place in Thasos, and the partisans of Lacedaemon and the Laconian governor Eteonicus were driven out of the island. And Pasippidas the Laconian, who was accused of having managed this intrigue, in collusion with Tissaphernes, was banished from Sparta, while Cratesippidas was sent out to the fleet which Pasippidas had collected from the allies, and assumed command of it at Chios.

This passage illustrates an important tendency noted by Martin and Rose in generic identification strategies to isolate *agencies* as the major participants in the discourse.[45] At least two (possibly three, depending upon how the 'revolution' is taken) agencies are identified here—the partisans of Lacedaemon and the Laconian governor, Eteonicus. But these and others mentioned seem to be identified only in connection with the larger activity sequence (i.e. the revolution) that Xenophon references. Even in his somewhat biographically oriented history, *Anabasis*, Xenophon tends to identify groups as the major participants within the macrostructures of the discourse (e.g. generals: 3.1.2, cf. also 2.1.2; the Greeks: 4.1.2; a council: 5.1.2; the people: 6.1.2) rather than any one individual, including Cyrus.[46] And Polybius' stated goal is to chronicle 'the most famous Empires' which have been among the 'favorite themes of historians', 'measuring [their greatness] with the superior greatness of Rome' (1.2.1). And he says he will focus on three empires, in particular—the Persians, Macedonians, and

45 Martin and Rose, *Genre Relations*, 108.

46 *Anab.* 2.1.2 is a possible exception but it is the general and Cyrus that are in view here. And *Anab.* 7.1.2 identifies Pharnabazus and Anaxibius, the admiral, who summons the generals and captains to Byzantium. So here we have agencies at work again as well as sets of significant individuals introduced in the context of the escalating battle.

Romans (1.2). Again, both authors tend toward a more generic form of participant identification.

After an account of the origins of the universe, Diodorus' *Library* introduces his initial participants—'the first men to be born' (1.8.1). He then transitions to the first kings (1.9.1), focusing especially upon Egyptian kings (1.10.1–1.11.2). Beyond this, the entire *Library* is mapped on a generic or group participant identification structure. Most books predominately discuss a different nation or set of nations: e.g. *Book 1*: Egypt; *Book 2*: Mesopotamia, India, Scythia, Arabia, and the islands of the Ocean; *Book 4*: The Greeks; Theseus, the Seven against Thebes. Along the same lines, Dionysius of Halicarnassus describes the historical enterprise as a record of 'the successive supremacies both of cities and of nations' (Dionysius, *Ant.* 1.2.1). His history compares the Assyrians, Medes, and Persians to the greatness of the Roman empire, for example (Dionysius, *Ant.* 1.2.2–4). Among other things, he seeks to fill the lacuna in his day for an excellent treatment of the history for Rome (esp. its early formations). One of his fundamental purposes for writing the *Antiquities* was to 'show who the founders of [Rome] were, at what periods the various groups came together and through what turns of fortune they left their native countries' (*Ant.* 1.5.1). Josephus, by contrast, details the history of one nation and does so from the perspective of the group not any one individual involved.[47] Appian opens his *Civil Wars* with two agency groups—'The plebeians and Senate of Rome' and his history will detail their decisions (*Bel. civ.* 1.1.1).

2.2 *Individualized Participant Identification in the βίος*

We notice a tendency in the opposite direction in the Greek βίοι. Among the biographical predecessors, Isocrates' *Evagoras* discusses the ancestry and birth of Evagoras but fairly deeply into the speech relative to its size (*Evag.* 12). And while Isocrates consistently identifies Evagoras as the subject of praise at significant transitions in the speech (e.g. *Evag.* 19, 22, 33, 35, 40, etc.), he does not end the with the death of the subject (cf. *Evag.* 70–77), as in most later βίοι. Xenophon's *Cyropaedia* also features mixed elements. In some ways, the document is more about ancient education than Cyrus. For example, after a small narrative on the ancestry and outward appearance of Cyrus (Xenophon, *Cyr.* 1.2.1), Xenophon goes into a detailed exposition of the early phases of Persian education. This impacts participant identification since large stretches of narrative discuss the roles of a variety of figures in the training process, without

47 Josephus, *Ant.* 1.2.5: 'Now I have undertaken the present work, as thinking it will appear to all the Greeks worthy of their study; for it will contain all our antiquities, and the constitution of our government, as interpreted out of the Hebrew Scriptures'.

much mention of Cyrus at all (e.g. 1.2.2–16). The *Cyropaedia* does not end with the death of Cyrus but does include this material near the beginning of the last book (*Cry.* 8.6.23). In the fragmentary remains we have of Satyrus' biography, Euripides heavily dominates the narrative but it remains difficult to make discourse-level assessments in this way due to the condition of the text.

But by the time of Philo's *Life of Moses*, individualized participant identification seems more strongly codified. Philo opens his work by indicating that he is going 'to write the life of Moses' (Μωυσέως … τὸν βίον ἀναγράψαι) (Philo, *Mos.* 1.1). The second and final volume begins with a recapitulation of volume one, revealing a high degree of individualized participant identification. He says:

> The first volume of this treatise relates to the subject of the birth and bringing up of Moses, and also of his education and of his government of his people, which he governed not merely irreproachably, but in so exceedingly praiseworthy a manner; and also of all the affairs, which took place in Egypt, and in the travels and journeyings of the nation, and of the events which happened with respect to their crossing the Red Sea and in the desert, which surpass all power of description; and, moreover, of all the labours which he conducted to a successful issue, and of the inheritances which he distributed in portions to his soldiers.
>
> PHILO, *Mos.* 2.1

According to Philo, Moses is the unifying singular participant identified across all major structural divisions suggested by Philo for book 1. And book 2 ends with: 'Such was the life and such was the death of the king, and lawgiver, and high priest, and prophet, Moses, as it is recorded in the sacred scriptures' (Philo, *Mos.* 2.292).

In fact, Philo represents what would become a somewhat invariable feature for later βίοι—an individualized (singular) participant identified across the span of the entire discourse, from the narrative initiation (usually involving a formal preface) to its termination (formal ending). We see this in Plutarch's *Alexander* (1.1; 77.3), *Caesar* (1.1; 69.1), *Demosthenes* (4.1; 31.4[48]), *Cicero* (1.1; 48.1–49.3), *Theseus* (3.1; 35.4–36.4), *Romulus* (2.1–4; 29.7), *Artaxerxes* (1.1; 30.5), and *Otho* (1.1–2; 18.2–4). Diogenes Laërtius follows the same participant

48 The death narrative runs from 29.1–30.4; however, Demosthenes is mentioned in the last line of the work, indicating discourse level individualized participant identification—even though the narrative does not end immediately with his death. Cf. also Plutarch, *Cic.* 49.3.

identification strategy in his lives of *Democrates* (*Vit. Phil.* 9.34, 43), *Zeno* (7.1, 157–160), *Pythagoras* (8.1–2, 45), *Epictetus* (10.1, 138–39), and *Thales* (1.22, 39).[49] We note this in the individual βίοι of Lucian (*Dem.* 1, 65–67) and Philostratus (*Vit. Apol.* 1.1–2; 8.31) as well.

As with the Greek history, however, the βίος may use a range of participant identification strategies at the episode level and below, making reference to both groups and individuals. The two genres remain quite distinct at the discourse level, however, with histories deploying quite generic (usually group-based) participant identification strategies and the βίοι utilizing very individualized participant identification, where the same person is identified at the initiation and termination of the narrative. And even though the Greek βίοι vary in terms of how they identify participants at their major book transitions, it is the singular person rather than a group or set of groups (as in histories) that forms the basis for the participant structure of the narrative, from beginning to end (as evidenced by the above macrostructural phenomena).

2.3 *Participant Identification in the Gospels with Special Reference to Luke*

The Third Gospel provides an interesting case in terms of participant identification. Taken on its own, a number of factors merit consideration. First, the preface seems to focus on several groups—unlike the other Gospels and ancient βίοι, not mentioning the (would-be) subject, Jesus—including (note the plurals) ἐν ἡμῖν (1:1), αὐτόπται (1:2), οἱ ἀπ' ἀρχῆς (1:2), ὑπηρέται γενόμενοι τοῦ λόγου (1:3). The content of the eyewitness testimony, according to Luke, is 'events' (πραγμάτων, 1:1; λόγων, 1:4), apparently not the story of an individual. We may conclude, then, that at least the preface of the Third Gospel, arguably the most significant macro-level structure in the discourse, 'foregrounds groups'[50] in its participant identification strategy not an individual. Further, since the preface potentially provides a discourse-level frame for the entire two-volume set, we may read Luke's introductory comments in 1:1–4 as applicable to the entire narrative structure of the Gospel and its companion volume, Acts, including the participant identification strategies deployed. The participant(s) foregrounded at the discourse level are groups in Luke-Acts, not a single participant or set of participants.

---

49 Though *Pyrrho* provides an exception in that it discusses Pyrrhonian philosophy more than the life of Pyrrho, who is almost never mentioned the last half of the life. And documents in Diogenes such as *Cebes* are too short to assess.

50 Martin and Rose, *Genre Relations*, 108.

Second, while it must be conceded that a substantial portion of Luke's first volume identifies Jesus as the central participant quite consistently across the discourse, the narrative introduction of Jesus in Luke does seem somewhat delayed. Jesus appears on the first lines of Matthew, Mark, and John, but is not even featured in the preface of the Third Gospel. And one of the most persistent features of ancient biographical discourse involves the staging of the subject on the opening lines of the narrative body. Nor does the author mention Jesus at the transition into the narrative body but instead foregrounds (again) a group of individuals. After the temporal marker (Ἐγένετο ἐν ταῖς ἡμέραις Ἡρῴδου), the Gospel highlights both Zechariah and Elizabeth as the major participants. But in cases where a βίος includes a preface, as would be the case with Luke, the biographer almost invariably foregrounds the biographical subject on the opening lines of the body, not an outlying group of participants (see above). Jesus is not identified as the primary participant in Luke until chapter 3, with his baptism (3:21). After this, Jesus does occupy much of the participant space *for the remainder of the first volume*. But if we view the Gospel in unity with Acts then the clear implementation of a 'group subject, rather than an individual'[51] in Acts widens the participant range so that Jesus becomes one major actor of several in the plot of the two-volume narrative. Therefore, the Third Gospel—at least at the macrostructural level—seems to identify its several major participants in light of the larger activity sequence of 'the events fulfilled among us' (πεπληροφορημένων ἐν ἡμῖν πραγμάτων) (Luke 1:1) rather than along the participant axis of a singular life or set of lives. And while the focus for much of the narrative of the Third Gospel does seem to reflect biographical tendencies, since its introduction of Jesus is so delayed, this is likely the biproduct of a microgenre rather than a macrogenre feature of the Gospel.

2.4 *Participant Identification in Acts*

Burridge has already acknowledged that in Acts, we find 'a group subject rather than an individual'.[52] Ironically—in that Burridge attempts here to make a case for Acts as a biographical text—this description of the participant structure of Acts fits nicely with Martin and Rose's criterion for generic or group participant identification strategies, exhibited in both modern and ancient history.

In addition to the preface in Luke (discussed above), several further examples of generic participant identification in Acts recommend themselves as we examine the 'stages' (i.e. opening lines) of its paragraphs.[53] We have discussed

51 Burridge, 'Genre', 16.
52 Burridge, 'Genre', 16.
53 On this terminology, see Grimes, *Thread*, 323–36.

episode- or discourse-level staging through the tendency in biography to open the narrative with genealogical information. In his classic work, *The Thread of Discourse*, Joseph Grimes notes that at the paragraph level, 'a change of theme' is often introduced in 'the first sentence of a new paragraph'.[54] And such staging typically occurs with the introduction of new participants. We will seek, then, to discover whether Luke's participant-staging strategy is more generic (identifying groups) or individualized (identifying individuals) in its structure.

In the portions often said by advocates of the biography thesis for Acts to be about Peter, the episodes typically transition with Peter *and* John (Acts 3:1, 11; 4:1), not just Peter, then it turns to groups (persecuted believers in 4:23; the group [πλήθους] that believed in 4:32). The author skips then to Ananias *and* Sapphira as the group of participants for the paragraph beginning in 5:1. The apostles are the participants identified as the subjects of the next two paragraphs (5:12, 17), then the disciples in the paragraph beginning at 6:1. It is not until the arrest narrative for Stephen, starting in 6:8, that a singular participant is identified as the subject of focus on what Grimes refers to as the 'stage' of the paragraph.

For Saul/Paul, the conversion narrative is fairly individualized but beyond this, Luke tends toward more group-based identification strategies. When Luke narrates his sermon in Damascus, he portrays Paul as proclaiming Jesus *with the disciples in Damascus* (Acts 9:19). The Jews then seek to kill Paul but he escapes to Jerusalem, where only Barnabas is able to provide him with a hearing from the disciples (Acts 9:23–31). The narrative shifts back to Peter for the vast majority of Acts 9:32–12:25 in the kind of interlaced way recommended by Lucian—constructing the portraits of Paul and Peter in Acts not as a 'mere bundle of parallel threads' but with 'their extremities intermingling' (*How to Write History* 55). It finally returns to Paul, but not Paul alone. At his next appearance, Paul is grouped with several other teachers and prophets at Antioch (13:1). Then Paul *and* his companions are introduced as the participants on the stage (i.e. opening lines) of the paragraph beginning at 13:13. And the author continues to carry the narrative shifts with both Paul *and* Barnabas as the participants on the stage of the paragraph at the transitions in Acts 14:1 15:1–2, 22, and 36. Then 'Paul and us' (τῷ Παύλῳ καὶ ἡμῖν) in Acts 16:1 and Paul *and* Silas are coupled as the major participants projected onto the stage of the paragraph in Acts 16:19, 25, 29; 17:1, 4–5, and 10. Interestingly, at around this point Luke-Acts shifts into the travel narrative (Acts 16–28) based on the so-called we-source, often contrasted with a potential Antiochian source for earlier material on

54 Grimes, *Thread*, 335.

the Jerusalem church (Acts 6–12; 15).[55] Regardless of its origins, Luke weaves this material into the narrative so that the pronominal and verbal structures (whether they are from a source or not) constantly group him with Paul for the last phases of his ministry. And Luke continues this theme of generic participant identification through to the end of the narrative (esp. Acts 27–28).

At this stage, we may note two features of the participant structure that seems to underlie the narrative in Acts. First, it is quite generic in its identification strategies. Acts far more frequently identifies groups or pairs of individuals on the stages of its major paragraphs. Both Paul and Peter are paired with other people more often than not but not in the highly structured method of Plutarch's *Parallel Lives* but as groups of interwoven narrative characters, introduced without formal segmentation. And often, Acts uses even larger groups to shift the narrative (e.g. apostles, disciples, etc.). This points to a quite generic participant structure, certainly more generic than the collected biographies of the ancient world. Second, Acts flows in an uninterrupted sequence, introducing characters in the middle of their lives in the context of events and activities. These characters seem tightly interlaced again, as seemingly suggested by Lucian, and it remains quite difficult to divide the narrative based on the treatment of any *single* individual at one time.

Some have argued that the coupling of participants in this (non-segmented) way may still reflect the structure of the collected biographies. Adams, for example, recognizes participant identification in the preface as a potential agnation criterion for histories and collected biographies, noting that the latter begin by identifying individuals or sets of individuals while histories identify ethnic groups or nations, often in connection with a war.[56] Adams makes a methodological advancement here, in that he is the first in the discussion to propose a serious (i.e. viable) genre agnation criterion for history and the Greco-Roman biography.

But Adams goes too far in claiming that Acts resembles the participant identification strategies of the Greco-Roman collected biographers more than those of the historians. He argues that 'Acts, like biographies, *begins* by referencing an individual rather than a national or ethnic group or a war' (emphasis mine).[57] In support of this claim, he points to individualized participant reference in the preface or opening lines of several Greco-Roman biographies, concluding, therefore, that 'Acts opens in a manner more similar to biographies

55 See Helmut Koester, *Introduction to the New Testament, vol. 2*: History and Literature of Early Christianity (Berlin: DeGruyter, 2012), 2:30.

56 Adams, *Genre*, 125.

57 Adams, *Genre*, 123.

than to history'.[58] He suggests further, that 'The use of connective openings', as we find in Acts 1:1–2, 'is much more frequent in biographies in which the author also references the individual in focus'.[59] As I see it, Adams puts forward two arguments here: (1) both biographies and Acts *begin* or *open* by referencing an individual rather than an ethnic group or nation; (2) the recapitulation in Acts 1:1–2 should be understood as a biographical connective formula, linking Acts (book 2) to Luke's Gospel (book 1). Adams seems to assume Burridge's biographical analysis for Luke's Gospel (with its preface) and so *only assesses the recapitulatory link in Acts*, providing very limited discussion of its potential relationship to the Gospel preface in Luke 1:1–4.[60]

I agree with Adams that the recapitulation in Acts 1:1–2 is quite individualized and in this limited way does resemble participant identification strategies in *biographical prefaces*. But this argument only works *if Acts provides the introductory preface for the entire work*. That Acts and biographies both 'begin by referencing an individual' is only a significant and relevant observation if Acts does indeed begin in Acts 1:1–2. But clearly, at least for Adams, it does not—and this assumption is built into the structure of his argument. Argument (2) depends upon the biographical nature of *connective* formulas, assuming a connection with the Gospel (book 1). Adams' argument, stated simply, is that Luke-Acts resembles a biographical succession history, with Jesus (the founder) described in book 1 and his disciples/followers in book 2. But this introduces inconsistency to the analysis. If Acts 1:1–2 merely provides a connective link to book 1, not a preface to the entire work or even its opening line, why should we expect it to function as formal prefaces or initiations more broadly? In other words, Adams' argument seems to equivocate discourse levels, comparing episode-level phenomena in Luke-Acts (a book-level transition) with discourse-level phenomena in the biographical tradition (introductory prefaces).

The importance of precision in analysis at these levels is seen in the fact that when the data is realigned relative to the appropriate discourse levels, Adams' conclusions are reversed. Histories begin in the preface with generic or group participant identification but often use more individualized book-level transitions. For example, we noted the very generic participant structure employed in the Herodotean preface. But in book 2, he transitions with 'After the death of Cyrus ...' (τελευτήσαντος δὲ Κύρου) (2.1.1), a more individualized structure. We

58 Adams, *Genre*, 123.

59 Adams, *Genre*, 124.

60 Adams, *Genre*, 120–25.

note here too the anaphoric function of the individualized transition, referring back to the prior book's narrative (as in Acts) of Cyrus, including his death.

In spite of the generic preface, Diodorus Siculus marks the major episode-level transition at *Lib.* 17.118 into book 18 (and vol. 9) with Alexander's death. And as in Luke-Acts, Diodorus includes a recapitulatory link that sets up his intention to chronicle Alexander's successors after his death: 'The preceding Book included all the acts of Alexander up to his death; this one, containing the deeds of those who succeeded to his kingdom, ends with the year before the tyranny of Agathocles and includes seven years' (*Lib.* 18.1.6). There seems to be no problem with individualized episode-level transitions in Greek history—these structures only seem constrained at the discourse level.

Similarly, though the preface remains quite generic in its participant reference, at the transition from book 2 into book 3 of his *Civil Wars*, Appian refers to the prior narrative *via* an individualized transition by stating, 'Thus was Gaius Caesar, who had been foremost in extending the Roman sway, slain by his enemies and buried by the people' (Appian, *Bel. Civ.* 3.1.1). Again, as in Acts, we have an anaphoric individualized book-level transition referring back to the prior book's narrative of Caesar, including his deeds and death. Or take Josephus' transition into book 2 of *Against Apian*. After reference to book 1, Josephus transitions with individualized reference to Apian in book 2 (Josephus, *Ag. Ap.* 2.1–7).

These all seem quite similar to the structure of Luke-Acts, with book 1 (Luke's Gospel) utilizing generic/group participant reference in the preface for the entire work and at the transition into book 2 (Acts 1:1–4), deploying individualized reference to refer back to the prior narrative's account of a key participant, including (as in the first three examples) his deeds and death (Jesus).[61] The various histories considered as well as Luke-Acts all seem to deploy a kind of localized or microgenre biographical structure for a large portion of a book before transitioning back to the structures of the macrogenre (history). So when Adams concludes that, 'Acts' clear reference to an individual, Jesus, further emphasises th[e] connection with biography and distances it from history', he seems to overlook the fact that though histories *focus on groups in*

61 Adams (cf. *Genre*, 155–56) or others may respond that even the preface in Luke's Gospel does not match participant identification strategies in historical prefaces since Luke does not reference nations or ethnic groups or wars. Granted. But while Luke's preface may not resemble those precise formal categories (i.e. nations or ethnic groups), it does use parallel functional categories proposed by Martin and Rose, with both Luke and ancient histories referencing groups rather than individuals. We also note the heavy orientation toward geography and 'nations' in the book of Acts, as the Gospel spreads from Judea throughout the Roman empire (Acts 1:8).

their prefaces, they often implement *individualized book-level transitions*, as we seem to find in Acts 1:1–2.

Adams claims further that not only the participant identification strategies but the use of connective openings is feature of Greco-Roman biographies, not histories. He insists that 'Each book in the histories by Herodotus, Thucydides, Dionysius of Halicarnassus, Appian, Quintus Curtius, and Xenophon continues the narrative from the preceding book without any authorial insertion'.[62] In the biographical literature, he points to Philo's *Life of Moses*, which references the 'former treatise' (προτέρα σύνταξίς) or book 1 (Philo, *Mos.* 2.1). Likewise, 'Plutarch's *Aem* 1.1 explicitly references previous *Parallel Lives* and links the *Lives of Aemilius and Timoleon* to the larger set'.[63] Finally, Adams mentions, 'Diogenes Laertius' opening of book 4, which connects the lives of Plato's disciples with the previous work on Plato (book 3)'.[64] Based upon these three texts, Adams concludes, 'That Acts commences with a connective opening forms a strong connection with the biography genre, since histories did not make wide use of this literary feature.'[65]

But we do find these kinds of book-level recapitulatory links widely used in ancient histories. Though Acts 1:1–2 resembles Philo's two-volume *Life of Moses*, with the recapitulation referencing back to book 1, it also bears close similarity to book 2 of Josephus' two-volume project, *Against Apian*. In fact, that Josephus' transition not only refers back to the prior book but also, as in Acts, includes an honoree: 'In the former book, most honored Epaphroditus …' (Διὰ μὲν οὖν τοῦ προτέρου βιβλίου, τιμιώτατέ μοι Ἐπαφρόδιτε) (Josephus, *Ag. Ap.* 2.1). At the transitions into both books 2 and 3, Polybius employs a recapitulation referencing the prior book(s) in his history as well. In book 2, he says, 'In the previous book ['Eν μὲν τῇ πρὸ ταύτης βύβλῳ] I have described how the Romans, having subdued all Italy, began to aim at foreign dominion …' (Polybius, 2.1.1) and in book 3: 'I state in my first book that my work was to start from the Social war …' ("Οτι μὲν ἀρχὰς ὑποτιθέμεθα τῆς αὑτῶν πραγματείας τόν τε συμμαχικὸν) (Polybius, 3.1.1). And Herodian's *History of the Empire* transitions into book 2 with a recapitulation referencing book 1 (2.1), just as in Acts, which Adams recognizes.[66] Distinct but in some ways related to this latter point, we find the tendency among some historians to use the end of one book to

62 Adams, *Genre*, 124.
63 Adams, *Genre*, 124.
64 Adams, *Genre*, 125.
65 Adams, *Genre*, 125.
66 Adams, *Genre*, 124.

anticipate themes in the next book, as in book 1 of Luke-Acts (Luke 24:47–53) and books 19 and 20 of Diodorus Siculus (19.110.5; 20.113.5).[67]

Additional evidence for recapitulatory book-level transitions surfaces in connection with the historical tradition conveyed through the summaries at the beginnings of several books in Xenophon's *Anabasis*. In books 2–5 and 7, a transitional unit begins the narrative with the formula ὅσα μὲν δὴ ἐν τῇ ἀναβάσει ('The previous narrative has described …'; Xenophon, *Anab.* 2.1, 3.1; 4.1; 5.1; 7.1) or some variation of it. Though most have understood these units as interpolations,[68] they still seem to reflect a trend in the historical tradition of employing such recapitulatory transitions. Gareth Schmeling proposes that these transitional summaries were added early on in an effort 'to offer orientation to readers who only had access to the roll or rolls which began with that book-opening and not to earlier scrolls'[69] and this may have motivated authorial recapitulations as well. And recapitulations or references to prior works were common not only in biographies and histories but in other ancient genres as well (e.g. Chariton 5.1.1–2; 8.1.1;[70] Josephus, *Life* 412–13; Philo, *Good Person* 1 [LCL, 9.11][71]).

While Acts does provide historical portraits for key figures in its narrative, the structure does not suggest a wider collected biographical framework for the interpretation of these figures. Participant identification in the narrative seems more oriented toward documenting a movement (i.e. 'the way') through numerous references to groups rather than sets of individually segmented lives. The lack of formal segmenting in Acts at the very least reveals a more generic participant identification strategy than what we find in the collected biographies. As Keener contends,

> Ancient historians such as Livy might follow the lives of a famous general or other hero (often interspersing other information where relevant chronologically), but such biographic elements did not change the genre from history to biography. Dionysius of Halicarnassus has biographic

67 Cf. Keener, *Acts*, 651.

68 As far back as 1889, see F.W. Kelsey and A.C. Zenos, *Xenophon's Anabasis: Books I–IV* (Boston: Allyn and Bacon, 1942; orig. 1889), 265, who note the major motivations for viewing the passage at 2.1 as an interpolation: '1. it may be omitted without interrupting the progress of the narrative. 2. The words ἅμα δὲ τῇ ἡμέρᾳ at the beginning of 1.7 follow naturally after ταύτην μὲν οὖν τὴν νύκτα οὕτω διεγένοντο, the closing sentence of Book 1. 3. Unless the summary be rejected, the μὲν in the last sentence of Book 1 has no correlative δὲ'. They apply similar logic to argue for the interpolation of the other transitions as well.

69 G.L. Schmeling, *The Novel in the Ancient World* (MBCB 159; Leiden: Brill, 1996), 98.

70 See Schmeling, *Novel*, 97–100.

71 See Keener, *Acts*, 651.

> sections in his larger history, such as that about Tarquin (*Rom. Ant.* 4.41–85), but his work remains a multivolume history.[72]

Similarly, it seems that Acts—due to the lack formal segmenting—includes biographically oriented (i.e. perhaps the biographic *mode* or *text type*) sections in the context of broader more generic participant identification strategies.

3 Conclusions

Together, topical focus and participant identification support the thematic development of the narrative through identifying what is going and who is involved in the discourse. Both clines agnate in opposing directions within our representative corpus of Greek historical and biographical texts. On the whole, the Greek history tends to construct its narrative around activity-focused topical macrostructures and generic participant identification. The βίος moves in the opposite direction on our scales, toward more entity-focused, individualized narrative. I have argued that the Third Gospel seems more activity- than entity-focused in its macrostructures. The non-Lukan Gospels exhibit the opposite tendency. The most obvious connection to recall here is Luke's failure to mention Jesus in the opening lines of the work, a feature virtually unprecedented in the Greek βίος. And although the Gospel does clearly maintain a focus on Jesus throughout most of its narrative, when considered in conjunction with Acts we may point to a number of histories that follow a similar structure, with special participants occupying a large amount of narrative space (without formal segmentation). Acts likewise reflects a more activity-focused narrative and implements generic or group participant structures at its major macrostructural transitions. Relative to the genre agnation clines—focus and participant identification—I conclude that both Luke and Acts, especially when read together, seem to function more like the Greek history than the βίος.

72 Keener, *Acts*, 60.

CHAPTER 4

Frames I: Initiations and Commencements

One of the primary ways of organizing narrative is through what discourse analysts refer to as *framing*. 'Frames are conceptual knowledge units that linguistic expressions evoke'.[1] According to Alexander Ziem and Catherine Schwerin, 'language users call up these frames from memories to grasp the meaning of linguistic expression'.[2] But framing is used in many different ways in many different disciplines. So to be clear: I do not wish to take on the baggage associated with such terminology due to its background in cognitive theory, case frame semantics, psycholinguistics, or any other field. Instead, I only use frames as an analogy for macrostructural devices in language that help *frame* meaning for large units of text. We can draw this framing metaphor just as easily from cinematography as from cognitive theory. As Halliday notes, 'In cinema, the frame is important because it actively *defines* the image for us'.[3] In the same way, *literary-linguistic frames* actively define the meaning of the narrative for us, especially in terms of its genre. Readers become familiar with the macrostructural location of certain conventionalized features (usually) early on in the discourse and this helps them know what to expect (generically) in the coming narrative. This all transpires via *framing*. A number of textual frames warrant consideration for genre agnation within Greek historical and biographical discourse: (1) narrative initiations (panoramic vs. focalized), (2) narrative commencements (activity- vs. entity-driven), (3) self-identification (biographical vs. non-biographical), and (4) genealogies (staged vs. embedded).

In this chapter, we will examine the first two (initiations and commencements) of these four scales in the Greek history, the βίος, Luke, and Acts. These two clines function together within the interior architecture of the narratives as the first two global fames that the reader will encounter, one at the discourse and one at the episode level.

1 A. Ziem and C. Schwerin, *Frames of Understanding in Text and Discourse: Theoretical Foundations and Descriptive Applications* (Human Cognitive Processing 48; Amsterdam: John Benjamins, 2014), 2.

2 Ziem and Schwerin, *Frames*, 2.

3 M.A.K. Halliday, *Bloomsbury Companion to M. A. K. Halliday* (ed. Jonathan Webster; New York: Continuum, 2015), 391.

 | DOI:10.1163/9789004406544_005

1 Initiation: Panoramic vs. Focalized

Every complete narrative initiates in some way—by virtue of necessity; it has to, ranging from basic introductory remarks to a fully formalized preface. While the majority of interpreters acknowledge that Luke's preface fits most comfortably within the Greek historical tradition,[4] most do not find this consideration alone decisive for aligning Luke with Greek history. Burridge, in particular, is able to use the preface as the basis for a family resemblance that identifies Luke, along with the other Gospels, with the biographical tradition on the basis of a parallel 'opening formulae/prologue/preface' features, defined broadly as 'a formal preface by the author, in the first person, explaining his reason and purpose in writing and giving a clear indication of the genre ...'.[5] On this broad definition, both biographical and historical prefaces can be included. In the case of Luke, then, (at least for Burridge) we have a preface that may create expectations for reading the Gospel as history, but these are corrected by the pervasive biographical features that emerge as the Third Gospel continues to unfold.

The ancients recognize the potential role of the preface/opening features in distinguishing genres. Horace emphasizes the importance of introductory forms within a particular genre (Horace, *Ars* 136–52). Within history, specifically, Lucian appears to view features of the preface as a criterion for agnating history from rhetoric. He says: 'whenever [the historian] does use a preface, he will make two points only, not three like the orators. He will omit the appeal for

4 H.J. Cadbury, 'Commentary on the Preface of Luke', in F.J. Foakes-Jackson and Kirsopp Lake (eds.), *The Beginnings of Christianity* (5 vols.; London: Macmillan, 1922–1933), 1:489–510; W.C. van Unnik, 'Remarks on the Purpose of Luke's Historical Writing (Luke 1.1–4)', in W.C. van Unnik, *Sparsa Collecta: The Collected Essays of W.C. van Unnik* (Leiden: Brill, 1973), 6–15; J.A. Fitzmyer, *The Gosple of Luke I–IX* (AB 28; Garden City: Doubleday, 1981), 287–301; D.L. Balch, 'ἀκριβῶς ... γράψαι (Luke 1:3): To Write the Full History of God's Receiving All Nations', in D.P. Moessner (ed.), *Jesus and the Heritage of Israel* (Philadelphia: Trinity, 1999), 84–123; D.P. Moessner, 'The Appeal and Power of Poetics (Luke 1:1–4)', in D.P. Moessner (ed.), *Jesus and the Heritage of Israel* (Philadelphia: Trinity, 1999), 84–123; D.P. Moessner, 'The Lukan Prologues in the Light of Ancient Narrative Hermeneutics', in J. Verheyden (ed.), *The Unity of Luke-Acts* (Leuven: Leuven University, 1999), 399–417; D.A. Aune, 'Luke 1.1–4: Historical or Scientific *Prooimon?*', in Alf Christophersen, et al. (eds.), *Paul, Luke and the Graeco-Roman World: Essays in Honour of Alexander J.M. Wedderburn* (JSNTSup 217; London: T&T Clark, 2002), 138–48; S.A. Adams, 'Luke's Preface and its Relationship to Greek Historiography: A Response to Loveday Alexander', *JGRChJ* 3 (2006): 177–191.

5 R.A. Burridge, *What are the Gospels? A Comparison with Graeco-Roman Biography* (2nd ed.; Grand Rapids: Eerdmans, 2004; org. 1992), 109.

a favorable hearing and give his audience what will interest and instruct them' (Lucian, *Hist.* 53). The historical preface thus functions to open the minds of the readers to the body of the work which is 'facilitated by a preliminary view of the causes in operation and a precise summary of events' (Lucian, *Hist.* 55). Lucian (*Hist.* 55) insists that there is a proper length for the historical preface, and that it should be neither too long nor too short, relative to the length of the entire history—although he does not indicate what that proportion should be.

Prefaces provide a global or discourse-level (i.e. macrostructural) perspective on a work. One angle from which to examine biographical and historical prefaces (and narrative initiations more broadly) is in terms of panoramic vs. focalized perspectives. Historical prefaces (relative to their length) tend to be more concise and *panoramic* in nature with a view to several related events or incidents (i.e. activity sequences), soon to come in the historical narrative. Biographical prefaces, by contrast, seem more *focalized*—longer (relative to the length of the book), more detailed introductions focalized around one person, often including any processes involved in gathering information concerning this person. Therefore, to investigate the perspective of an initiation (esp. the formal preface) we will look at initiation *length* and *scope* in our sample texts.

Taking our cue from Lucian, that historical prefaces should exhibit a proper length relative to the subject and body of the work (Lucian, *Hist.* 55), we may note the following length ranges for the Greek historical and biographical texts adopted in chapter 2:

TABLE 4.1 Preface length ratio in the Greek history and the βίος[a]

Ancient work	Word length	Initiation/Preface length	% Against entire work
Histories			
Herodotus, *Histories*	184,947	675	.036
Thucydides, *Peloponnesian War*	150,173	3,498	2.32
Xenophon, *Hellenica*	66,514	8	.01
Xenophon, *Anabasis*	57,174	≠	≠
Polybius, *Histories*	311,667	429	0.13
Diodorus Siculus, *Bibliotheca*	200,861	1,833	0.91
Dionysius, *Antiquities*	284,417	2,642	0.92
Josephus, *Antiquities*	305,870	1,086	0.35
Appian, *Civil Wars*	116,927	1,108	0.94

TABLE 4.1 Preface length ratio in the Greek history and the βίος (*cont.*)

Ancient work	Word length	Initiation/Preface length	% Against entire work
Biographical Predecessors			
Isocrates, *Evagoras*	4,682	624 (*prooimion*)	13.32
Xenophon, *Cyropaedia*	79,283	607	0.76
Satyrus, *Euripides*	1,321	≠	≠
Philo, *Life of Moses*	32,636	266	0.81
Collected βίοι			
Plutarch, *Parallel Lives*	507,184	≠	≠
Alexander-Caesar	36,237	138	0.03
Demosthenes-Cicero	19,169	590	3.07
Theseus-Romulus	17,042	285	1.67
Artaxerxes (unpaired)	7,360	127	1.7
Otho (unpaired)	4,159	159	3.8
Diogenes Laërtius, *Lives*	109,777	1,796	1.63
Pyrrho	4,431	≠	≠
Democrates	1,524	≠	≠
Cebes	14	≠	≠
The Individual Greek βίος			
Lucian, *Demonax*	3,172	171	5.39
Philostratus, *Apollonius*	82,000	1,128	1.37

a Burridge, *What are the Gospels?*, 1.78–79, insists that length of the preface is not relevant because histories are much longer. However, the length ratios are relativized according to the length of each work respectively so that the comparison does seem valid. Biographical prefaces are much longer *relative to the entire length of the work than historical prefaces.*

From Tab. 4.1, we note that the panoramic perspective of historical prefaces *via* the formal diagnostic of relative preface length. Historical prefaces tend to present shorter, more concise, *panoramic* perspectives on the subsequent narrative and what went into composing them. Most of the Greek biographical texts, by contrast, deploy longer, more detailed, *focalized* portraits of the coming narrative and any introductory matters connected to it.

Length of historical initiations may vary from as short as 0.01% (Xenophon's *Hellenica*) to 2.32% (Thucydides), with most falling within the range of 0.36–0.94%. Thucydides is atypical when compared to other histories[6] (e.g. Plutarch, *Rise and Fall of Athens*, 0.23%). But his preface length was considered atypical, even by ancient standards (e.g. Dionysius of Halicarnassus, *De Thuc.* 19–20). Βίοι on the whole tend to have larger prefaces relative to the overall size of the work. The preface to each of Plutarch's parallel lives exhibits this feature, as do the prefaces to the larger collections in both Plutarch and Diogenes. This seems to be true of the (though debatable) individual Greek βίοι as well. Lucian's (120–180 CE) *Demonax*, for example, is 3,172 words with a preface length of 171 words (*Dem.* 1–2) constituting 5.39% of the entire work. The same is true of several Latin works. Tacitus's *Life of Agricola* (98 CE), for example, is 6,789 words long with a preface of 387 words (*Agr.* 1–3) which means that the preface accounts for 5.7% of the total length of the book.

Of the samples considered, Plutarch's *Alexander-Caesar* provides the only exception. All other βίοι tend to have prefaces several times larger than historical prefaces relative to their size. This seems true whether we are dealing with the preface to an entire massive collection of βίοι, the preface to a set of parallel lives, or the prefaces to the (potentially) individual Greek βίοι that we've considered. In other words, *initiations*—no matter their macrostructural location—tend to be more expanded in the Greek βίος and more abbreviated in Greek histories. Adams' study of several later collected (mostly) Latin βίοι seems to confirm this assessment in the Roman tradition as well. According to his analysis, the preface of Jerome's *On Illustrious Men* consists of 2.6% of the entire work and the preface of Eunapius, *Vitae Philosophorum*, occupies 4.6% of the entire writing. Similarly, Philostratus, *Vitae Sophistarum* (Greek), has a preface with a length of 836, which accounts for 2.87% of the entire work.[7]

Length ratio does not provide an absolutely determinative criterion since we have at least one exception within each genre—Thucydides and Plutarch's *Alexander-Cicero*—but it does seem quite strongly codified. The broad and quite consistent tendency indicates that on the whole histories utilize much shorter and biographies longer prefaces relative to the length of the entire work. Length ratio, then, represents one formal diagnostic that enables assessment of panoramic versus focalized perspectives for narrative initiations.

---

6 See Adams, 'Luke's Preface', 177–191.

7 S.A. Adams, *The Genre of Acts and Collected Biography* (SNTSMS 156; Cambridge: Cambridge University Press, 2013), 273–78.

The *scope* of the initiation provides another. As a universal history, Herodotus takes on a very wide scope, covering the great and mighty things of all people (of both Hellenes and Barbarians) so that they might not be forgotten with the passage of time (Herodotus, 1.1.0). Thucydides covers an entire war (1.1.1), as does Xenophon's *Hellenica* (1.1). Polybius intends to treat the 'most famous Empires which preceded, and which have been the favorite themes of historians, and measuring them with the superior greatness of Rome' (1.2.1) and Diodorus ambitiously sets out to cover all of space and time in his history, emphasizing the greatness of scale for the events that his history endeavors to relate (*Bib.* 1.1–5). Dionysius prefaces his history by registering his intention to begin with the most ancient legends and then bring the narrative from there all the way up to the First Punic War (*Ant.* 1.8.1). Likewise, in the preface to the *Antiquities*, Josephus reveals his intention to begin with Moses before working up to his own time, with the wars between Rome and the Jews (*Ant.* 1.1–17) in the first century. And Appian's preface declares that the ensuing narrative will give an account of the time of Sempronius Gracchus all the way to the battle of Actium, fought by Octavius Caesar against Antony and Cleopatra (*Bel. Civ.* 1.6). Historical prefaces project a telescopic or *panoramic perspective* on the subsequent discourse, seeking to capture several large-scale events into a single narrative. The only exception from the historical base corpus is Xenophon's *Anabasis*, which begins with information on the life of Cyrus (but cf. *Anab.* 2.1).

We may contrast this to biographical prefaces that tend to be more focalized in their *scope*, introducing a number of topics in connection with one individual. One could certainly make the case the Isocrates' *Evagoras* exhibits a focalized scope in recounting to Nicolas that which would most honor the late King Evagoras (1–4). Philo's preface to the *Life of Moses* is highly focalized, encapsulating Philo's hope to detail all 'that the greatest and most perfect man that ever lived [Moses]' did, 'having a desire to make his character fully known to those who ought not to remain in ignorance respecting him' (*Mos.* 1.1). Likewise, the prefaces for Plutarch's paired lives (*Alex.* 1.1–3; *Dem.* 3.1–3;[8] *Thes.* 1.1–2.2[9]) are focalized around their respective subjects. As for Plutarch's unpaired lives, *Artaxerxes* focalizes its narrative by initiating with the genealogy of Artaxerxes (1.1–3). Similarly, *Otho* (1.1) begins by discussing a speech of the 'new Emperor' and the details several of Otho's political actions (1.2–3). Diogenes Laërtius' *Lives* is a bit different. His individual biographical texts do not include

8 The preface to the fifth book of the parallel lives begins after a short autobiographical digression transitioning between books 4 and 5.

9 Though the initial details may seem a bit more panoramic in scope, as the narrative progresses, we see that it all leads up to how Plutarch decided to write a history of Romulus (*Thes.* 1.2).

a preface. And his preface to the collection centers much of its discussion on the debate over the Greek versus the Barbarian origins of philosophy. But this discussion ultimately ends up providing the basis for his succession history. So in this sense, the story-line of philosophy provides the organizational paradigm for telling the story of Diogenes' many philosophers. Still, topologically, we would say that on a scale of more or less focalized, Diogenes seems less focalized than most biographical works in its preface but still more focalized than most ancient history. The preface to *Demonax*, however, is uncontestably focalized on the author's relationship to Demonax and why Demonax is worthy of imitation (Lucian, *Dem.* 1–2). Philostratus begins his *Life of Apollonius* with a digression on Pythagoras (1.1) but only in the service of comparing him with Apollonius (1.2), so that his preface too remains quite focalized in scope.

1.1 *The Initiation in the Gospels with Special Reference to Luke*

Most scholars now generally grant that Luke's preface aligns with the tradition of Greek historiography[10] but tend to assume that its similarity to the other Gospels (and their notable parallel to the βίος) circumvents the initial historical expectations of the audience toward reading Luke as a βίος rather than a history. However, the role of preface should not be minimized in genre agnation due its strategic macrostructural role in the narrative.

Perhaps the most often discussed indicator of the historical status of the Lukan tradition has been the style of the preface (Luke 1:1–4). Loveday Alexander suggests that the preface aligns with the scientific history preface form in antiquity.[11] However, David Balch, David Moessner, David Aune, and, most recently, Sean Adams, have convincingly shown that Alexander's arguments for making this correlation place too much emphasis upon the normative status of the Thucydidean preface, which was atypical in many respects.[12] Adams demonstrates, 'there are many parallels between Luke's preface and the prefaces of the Greek historians and Luke falls well within the accepted spectrums of style and content for Greek prefaces'.[13] Still, Alexander, George

10 E.g. Cadbury, 'Commentary', 489–510; van Unnik, 'Remarks', 6–15; Fitzmyer, *Luke I–IX*, 287–301; Marshall, *Luke*, 37–41; Balch, 'ἀκριβῶς', 84–123; Aune, 'Luke 1.1–4', 138–48; Moessner, 'Appeal', 84–123; Adams, 'Luke's Preface', 177–191.

11 D. Earl, 'Prologue-Form in Ancient Historiography', in *ANRW* 1.2 (1972): 842–56; L. Alexander, *The Preface to Luke's Gospel* (SNTSMS 79; Cambridge: Cambridge University Press, 1993), 21–42; L. Alexander, 'The Preface to Acts and the Historians', in Ben Witherington (ed.), *History, Literature and Society in the Book of Acts* (Cambridge: Cambridge University Press, 1996), 73–103.

12 Balch, 'ἀκριβῶς', 229–50; Moessner, 'Appeal', 84–123; Moessner, 'Lukan Prologues', 399–417; Aune, 'Luke 1.1–4', 138–48; Adams, 'Luke's Preface', 177–91.

13 Adams, 'Luke's Preface', 191.

Kennedy, and Burridge underplay the significance of historical features in the Lukan preface for genre agnation. They contend that the evidentially historical character of the preface is not inconsistent with the biographical content of the Gospel.[14] The data seems to me to suggest otherwise.

Luke's preface consists of 42 words. The Gospel of Luke is 19,482 words whereas Luke-Acts is 37,982 words, meaning that the preface to the Gospel accounts for 0.21% of the entire book (book 1, if we assume unity) or 0.11% of the two-volume work. Either way—if we position Xenophon's *Hellenica* (0.01) or Polybius' *Histories* (0.13) on the low end and Appian's *Civil Wars* (0.94) on the high end (excluding Thucydides as atypical), Luke-Acts fits comfortably within the preface length ratio range of ancient histories, a feature likewise observed by Adams.[15] And—again noting Plutarch's *Alexander-Caesar* as a potential exception—Luke's preface is far outside of the typical biographical range with Diogenes providing the low end at 1.67 and Lucian's *Demonax*, the high end, at 5.39.

Luke's preface also seems panoramic rather than focalized in scope. First, note Luke's apparent resistance to focalization, with his failure to mention Jesus at an early (macrostructural) point in the narrative. Luke's scope seems more panoramic in nature. He indicates that his narrative (διήγησιν) will focus upon events (πραγμάτων). Luke provides an account that relates a body of tradition as it was handed down from the beginning (ἀπ' ἀρχῆς) by certain eyewitnesses. This seems slightly reminiscent of the tendencies of the universal historians such as Herodotus, Dionysius, Diodorus Siculus, who recount the events of their histories from the beginning of time (or at least as far back as their sources go). It connects even more deeply with historians like Thucydides who open their preface by indicating that they will document a set of events (i.e. the Peloponnesian War) from the 'beginning' (ἀρξάμενος) (Thucydides, 1.1). Biographers often discuss beginnings as well but these tend to be the focalized genealogical beginnings of their subjects not the panoramic beginnings of large activity sequences or sets of events. Luke's scope is more wide-reaching, setting out to clarify for Theopholis the 'things' (λόγων) he had been instructed in, 'from the beginning'. All of this points to a quite panoramic scope for the Lukan preface.

Mark, Matthew, and John, by contrast, all share in common the lack of a formal preface, discussing methodology or other preliminary matters. As in the

14 G.A. Kennedy, *New Testament Interpretation through Rhetorical Criticism* (Chapel Hill: University of North Carolina Press, 1984), 107–08; Alexander, *Preface*, 204–05; Burridge, *What are the Gospels?*, 188–89.

15 Adams, 'Luke's Preface', 183.

Greco-Roman biographical tradition, the other canonical Gospels all begin by introducing their subject. So, unlike Luke, Mark, Matthew, and John all mention Jesus in the first line of the work. In this respect, the initiations of the non-Lukan Gospels are more *focalized* than the Third Gospel. Mark has the shortest introduction, a single verse, potentially introducing Jesus as the Son of God (depending on the textual variant). John's statement of the 'Word' and his role in cosmological origins occupies five verses and Matthew's Gospel contains the longest piece of family tradition at 17 verses. Luke's Gospel is, therefore, distinct not only in its inclusion of a formal preface but one that meets the length conventions for historiography but falls outside of the biographical ranges. That Luke's preface fits within the length range and scope parameters for ancient history helps agnate his Gospel toward history.

1.2 *The Initiation in Acts*

Luke's recapitulatory link in Acts 1:1–2 ties Acts to Luke's Gospel and so—whatever the genre for either or both volumes—(assuming unity) the preface for the entire work is found in Luke 1:1–4 with Acts 1:1–2 serving as a book-level transition. We have already made the case that the preface in Luke is quite panoramic, not mentioning Jesus, rather than focalized, as in the Greek βίοι. Further, I showed that histories often recruit anaphoric individualized participant identification strategies as book-level transitions. *They just fail to identify participants in the preface in this way.* And when they do introduce such participants at high levels of the discourse, as Craig Keener notes, it is through a focus on the words and deeds of the participant, just as Jesus is described in Acts 1:1.[16] So the individualized anaphoric character of Acts 1:1–2 with a focus on Jesus' words and deeds fits nicely with historical literary models but only works relative to biographical literature if the recapitulation functions as the preface for a self-standing work, which most recognize that it does not.

One might object, as Adams and Richard Pervo do, that ὧν ἤρξατο ὁ Ἰησοῦς ποιεῖν τε καὶ διδάσκειν links back to and defines the Third Gospel as a biographical writing.[17] But this concentration on deeds/words (teachings) was by no means limited to biographical texts. As Craig Keener observes: 'Histories focused on words, that is speeches (λόγοι), and deeds, or actions (e.g. Polyb. 2.56.11; deeds in Arist. *Rhet.* 1, 1360a35; Val. Max. 1 pref. first sentence; Quint. *Inst.* 2.4.2). Therefore, Valerius Maximus often links words and deeds to reinforce the title

16 C. Keener, *Acts: An Exegetical Commentary* (4 vols.; Grand Rapids, Mich.: Baker Academic, 2012–2015), 653.

17 R.I. Pervo, *Acts: A Commentary on the Book of Acts* (Hermeneia; Minneapolis: Fortress, 2009), 33; Adams, *Genre*, 174.

of his work'.[18] And they often summarize prior narratives accordingly. As with Acts, Appian (*Bel. civ.* 3.1.1) provides this kind of recapitulation as he transitions away from the large portion of his narrative that focused upon Caesar.[19] So does Thucydides (8.1).[20] Josephus (*Ant.* 14.68) refers to several historical authors who wrote on the 'acts of Pompey' (τὰς κατὰ Πομπήιον πράξεις), including Strabo, Nicolaus of Damascus, and 'Titus Livius, the writer of the Roman History', indicating a perception of the historical tradition—in part—in terms of the acts of a historically significant individual.

2 Commencement: Event- vs. Participant-Driven

Once an author has initiated their narrative with any necessary introductory remarks, they *commence* with the narrative body of the work. Such transitions provide another macrostructural frame, this time at the episode level. The narrative frame, marked by the transition from the preface into the narrative body, constitutes another somewhat underdeveloped criterion that has been suggested very briefly in Lukan genre studies, for example, by Loveday Alexander.[21] She does not propose that transitions mark a kind of agnation criterion but she does draw attention to the fact that historians, at least, tend to transition from the preface into the narrative in a somewhat consistent manner.

Lucian hints at the potential function of the transition from the preface into the body as distinctive of ancient history. He says: 'After the preface, long or short in proportion to the subject, should come an easy natural transition to the narrative' (Lucian, *Hist.* 55). Lucian argues that since history is essentially a 'long narrative' it must have all of the stylistic characteristics of a good narrative, but should also be characterized by the treatment of 'connected events'. It is the role of the transition or commencement into the narrative body, then, to *frame* these connected events.

Greek historical and biographical commencements tend to follow two opposing trajectories. They frame the subsequent discourse primarily in terms of

18 Keener, *Acts*, 653. See also Keener, *Acts*, 653 n56 for a massive assemblage of references to the 'words and deeds' of a significant figure in a wide range of nonbiographical genres.

19 **Οὕτω μὲν δὴ Γάιος Καῖσαρ πλείστου** Ῥωμαίοις ἄξιος ἐς τὴν ἡγεμονίαν γενόμενος ὑπὸ τῶν ἐχθρῶν ἀνῄρητο καὶ ὑπὸ τοῦ δήμου τέθαπτο· ἁπάντων δὲ αὐτοῦ τῶν σφαγέων δίκην δόντων, ὅπως οἱ περιφανέστατοι μάλιστα ἔδοσαν, ἥδε ἡ βίβλος καὶ ἡ μετὰ τήνδε ἐπιδείξουσιν, ἐπιλαμβάνουσαι καὶ ὅσα ἄλλα Ῥωμαίοις ἐμφύλια ἐς ἀλλήλους ἐγίγνετο ὁμοῦ.

20 ταῦτα μὲν τὰ περὶ Σικελίαν γενόμενα.

21 Alexander, *Preface*, 30–31.

events or *participants*, as Cicero's account of the beginnings of history seems to insinuate,

> For *historia* began as a mere compilation of annals, on which account, and in order to preserve the general traditions, from the earliest period of the City down to the pontificate of Publius Mucius, each High Priest used to commit to writing all the events of his year of office, and record them on a white surface, and post up the tablet at his house, that all men might have liberty to acquaint themselves therewith, and to this day those records are known as the Pontifical Chronicles.
>
> *De orat.* 2.52–53

This reflects a much different point of origin than the Greek βίος, which appears to have emerged as the result of collecting sayings, antidotes, and actions of an individual.[22] The basic narrative frame for history is organized around events and activities, from its very beginnings, rather than an individual, as with the βίος. Since histories tend to be activity focused emerging from chronicles of events, we might expect their narrative bodies to commence with an event or circumstance whereas we might expect βίοι to move directly into the life of the participant that constitutes the focus of the βίος.[23]

2.1 *Event-Driven Commencements in the Greek History*

Herodotus exemplifies the event orientation that he attests to in his preface at his commencement. He begins the body of his work with 'The Persian learned men say that the Phoenicians were the cause of the dispute' (the Persian war) (Herodotus 1.1). After introducing the origins Epidamnus (Thucydides 1.24.1–2), the Thucydidean preface (Thucydides 1.1–23) commences into the narrative body with the event of 'a war' fought by the city of Epidamnus 'with her neighbors the barbarians' (Thucydides 1.24.3). Xenophon's *Hellenica* lacks a proper preface, besides the formula indicating his continuation of Thucydides' work. After this formula, Xenophon also records a war as a significant opening event: 'not many days later, Thymochares came from Athens with a few ships; and thereupon the Lacedaemonians and the Athenians fought another naval battle, and the Lacedaemonians were victorious, under the leadership of Agesandridas' (*Hell.* 1.1). Polybius begins the body of his work by indicating that he 'shall adopt as the starting-point of this book', the event of 'the first occasion

22 D.S. Potter, *Literary Texts and the Roman Historian* (London: Routledge, 1999), 69.

23 Burridge, *What are the Gospels?*, 1.79, seems to grant this point in his response to my Achtemeier paper.

on which the Romans crossed the sea from Italy' (Polybius 1.5.1). Josephus opens the narrative body of his Jewish history with the Genesis creation event (*Ant.* 1.27) and continues to rewrite Israel's history from there. Diodorus transitions into a discussion about the origins of 'animal life' (1.9–10) 'since Egypt is the country where mythology places the origin of the gods' (1.9.6) and since 'animal life appeared first of all' there (1.10.2). His entire first book, therefore, covers a range of Egyptian customs and religious traditions. Dionysius transitions into a discussion about what can be known about the oldest inhabitants of a number of cities (*Ant.* 1.9). After its preface, Appian's *Civil Wars* begins with 'The Romans, as they subdued the Italian nations successively in war, seized a part of their lands and built towns there, or established their own colonies in those already existing, and used them in place of garrisons' (*Bel. civ.* 1.7). Each of the histories examined initiates its body, then, with mention of at least one of the events that the history will document.[24] Xenophon's *Anabasis* counts

---

24 Diodorus Siculus, for example, transitions into his history by giving an account of cosmic origins: 'Concerning the various conceptions of the gods formed by those who were the first to introduce the worship of the deity, and concerning the myths which are told about each of the immortals, although we shall refrain from setting forth the most part in detail, since such a procedure would require a long account, yet whatever on these subjects we may feel to be pertinent to the several parts of our proposed history we shall present in a summary fashion, that nothing which is worth hearing may be found missing. Concerning, however, every race of men, and all events that have taken place in the known parts of the inhabited world, we shall give an accurate account, so far as that is possible in the case of things that happened so long ago, beginning with the earliest times [περὶ δὲ τοῦ γένους τῶν ἁπάντων ἀνθρώπων καὶ τῶν πραχθέντων ἐν τοῖς γνωριζομένοις μέρεσι τῆς οἰκουμένης, ὡς ἂν ἐνδέχηται περὶ τῶν οὕτω παλαιῶν, ἀκριβῶς ἀναγράψομεν ἀπὸ τῶν ἀρχαιοτάτων χρόνων ἀρξάμενοι.]. Now as regards the first origin of mankind two opinions have arisen among the best authorities both on nature and on history. One group, which takes the position that the universe did not come into being and will not decay, has declared that the race of men also has existed from eternity, there having never been a time when men were first begotten; the other group, however, which hold that the universe came into being and will decay, has declared that, like it, men had their first origin at a definite time' (Diodorus Siculus 6.1–3). Dionysius of Halicarnassus clearly frames his narrative according to an event orientation. His opening line in the narrative body indicates that he will begin with a discussion of the origins of 'the city the Romans now inhabit': 'This city, mistress of the whole earth and sea, which the Romans now inhabit, is said to have had as its earliest occupants the barbarian Sicels, a native race. As to the condition of the place before their time, whether it was occupied by others or uninhabited, none can certainly say. But some time later the Aborigines gained possession of it, having taken it from the occupants after a long war' (Dionysius of Halicarnassus, *Rom. ant.* 9.1). Herodian constitutes a potential exception but the title of his history indicates that his event frame is the death of Marcus Aurelius and so this is where he begins (Herodian 2.1)—perhaps we note a bit of genre blending here. But again, the goal is to highlight highly persistent patterns across a large corpus of sample texts from a genre not to demonstrate a hard,

as a potential exception because it has no preface (which fits within historical convention, cf. Lucian, *Hist.* 52) and initiates with Cyrus in its opening line, who will become a major focus in his narrative; however, Cyrus later drops out of focus as other figures take the stage.

2.2 *Participant-Driven Commencements in the βίος*

After the formal preface, βίοι consistently initiate the body of their work with a mention of their subject (often in connection with their origins) in the first line of the narrative body. If the work does not have a preface, this is how the opening of the work itself begins. This seems to be the case in at least Philo, among the antecedents to the biographical tradition (Philo, *Mos.* 1.5) and Isocrates' *Evagoras* to a lesser degree (cf. *Eva.* 6–9). The feature seems much more strongly codified,[25] however, in the later collected βίοι (see Plutarch, *Alex.* 2.1; *Cae.* 1.1; *Dem.* 4. 1; *Cic.* 1.1; *Thes.* 3.1; *Rom.* 4.1; *Artex.* 2.1; *Oth.* 2.1; e.g. Diogenes Laërtius, *Vit. Phil.* 1.22)[26] as well as the two samples chosen to represent the individual Greek βίος (Lucian, *Dem.* 3; Philostratus, *Vit. Apol.* 1.5).

2.3 *The Commencement in the Gospels with Special Reference to Luke*

After the preface, Luke begins the body of his narrative with a time-frame, connected with a participant (King Herod) who will not be the primary focus of the Gospel: Ἐγένετο ἐν ταῖς ἡμέραις Ἡρῴδου βασιλέως τῆς Ἰουδαίας (Luke 1:5). Historians tended to follow this pattern.[27] In βίοι, it was shown, after the preface, the biographer moves immediately into a focus upon the biographical subject in all cases within the comparative corpus. Luke instead follows the event-driven pattern of the historians. He continues to move his narrative

---

inflexible boundary. This allows us to avoid reductionism while also accounting for potential genre blending, literary innovation, and lack of literary awareness.

25 On this language, see P.H. Matthews, *Syntax* (CTL. Cambridge: Cambridge University Press, 1981), 20–21.

26 See also Plutarch, *Lyc.* 1.1; *Num.* 1.1; *Pub.* 1.1. Suetonius seems to pick up the referent of his major bibliographical participant from the work's title rather than using a full noun phrase in the body of the work itself. See, for example, *Cea.* 1.1; *Aug.* 1.1; *Tib.* 1.1; *Cal.* 1.1; *Cla.* 1.1.1; *Ner.* 1.1; *Gal.* 1.1; *Oth.* 1.1; *Vit.* 1.1; *Ves.* 1.1; *Tit.* 1.1; *Dom.* 1.1. See also, on this feature, Nepos, *Mel.* 1.1; *Them.* 1.1; *Aris.* 1.1; *Paus.* 1; *Cim.* 1.1; *Alc.* 1.1; *Thr.* 1.1; *Dio.* 1.1; Jerome, *Vir. ill.* 1.1; 2.1; 4.1; 5.1; 7.1; 8.1.

27 See Dionysius of Halicarnassus, *Rom. ant.* 1.9.1, who after his preface immediately moves into the narrative to begin discussion of a city the Romans now possess but which at a latter time 'the Aborigines gained possession of it'. Diodorus Siculus 1.6.1–2 transitions out of the preface and claims that he will now document 'the events that have taken place in the known parts of the inhabited world'. He begins this discussion (1.7.1) by use of a temporal transition formula κατὰ γὰρ τὴν ἐξ ἀρχῆς and discusses an account of creation.

forward through temporal deictic markers. He initiates the next small paragraph with Μετὰ δὲ ταύτας τὰς ἡμέρας (1:24) and then moves into the prophecy of the birth of Jesus with another temporal transition: Ἐν δὲ τῷ μηνὶ τῷ ἕκτῳ (1:26). This paragraph mentions Jesus for the first time but the angel Gabriel, not Jesus, figures as the central participant on the stage (i.e. the first clause/clause complex) of the paragraph. Then the focus moves to Mary, with another temporal transitional device: Ἀναστᾶσα δὲ Μαριὰμ ἐν ταῖς ἡμέραις ταύταις (1:39). Luke recruits a final temporal marker to shift the narrative to Elizabeth's birth of John: Τῇ δὲ Ἐλισάβετ ἐπλήσθη ὁ χρόνος (1:57). The next paragraph centers upon Zachariah, introduced by a full noun phrase (1:67), before finally coming to the second chapter of the Third Gospel, detailing the birth of Jesus (introduced by a temporal formula: Τῇ δὲ Ἐλισάβετ ἐπλήσθη ὁ χρόνος [2:1]). Luke, as with the historians, then includes several events leading up to one of the participants that will take center stage within a large portion of his narrative.

We may compare Luke with Appian, a biographically oriented historian. Appian tends to move his narrative along according to several events, using a variety of temporal formulas in book 1 (e.g. *Bel. civ.* 1.2.14,[28] 4.28,[29] 12.103,[30] 13.110[31]) before Gaius Caesar becomes the central participant in focus for book 2. So Appian transitions out of his preface into the narrative body (often shifting his frame of reference and beginning new paragraphs through temporal markers) through documenting a series of events. Though Caesar plays a central role in his history, Appian still writes history and thus events set the orientation for the narrative directly after the preface, not Caesar's life and character—though this subject occupies a significant portion of the coming narrative (book 2). Book 3 even includes a book-level transition, recapitulating the focus on Caesar in book 2, including a death narrative, before finalizing Caesar's story and moving on to other participants in book 3, as we find in Acts 1:1–2.

2.4 *The Commencement in Acts*

In chapter 3, I sought to demonstrate that the kind of book-level transition we find in Acts 1:1–2 (with the material that follows in 1:2–11) seems quite at home with the book-level episode transitions in ancient histories, including those that deploy a recapitulatory link and/or dedication. It differs, however, from

28 Θέρος δ' ἦν ἤδη.
29 Τῷ δ' αὐτῷ χρόνῳ.
30 Τοῦ δ' ἐπιόντος ἔτους.
31 Καὶ τότε μὲν χειμῶνος ἐπιόντος.

collected biographies in that after the recapitulation, the author does not use an origins or genealogical formula to introduce its first or subsequent subjects.

The two most likely options for the commencement of the narrative body are Acts 1:6 or 1:12. If we take 1:6 as the beginning of the narrative body, the event of the disciples gathering to inquire of Jesus marks the transition. But in collected biographies, groups of individuals (i.e. the disciples) are never introduced as the topical focus of a life in a larger set of lives. And since the narrative immediately introduces multiple characters onto the stage—the apostles (cf. 1:2) and Jesus (1:7)—it is likely the event of gathering (Οἱ μὲν οὖν συνελθόντες ἠρώτων) that the author wishes to emphasize rather than any singular participant. Further, the finite verb that governs the transitional clause encodes the action of the group inquiring not details related to a specific biographical subject, as in the narrative commencements for lives in ancient biographies. If 1:12 marks the first line of the narrative body, the event of the apostles returning to Jerusalem (ὑπέστρεψαν εἰς Ἰερουσαλὴμ) drives the transition not a singular participant. Keener, for example, notes that 1:1–11 provides the first major structural unit, providing a transition from the promise of the Spirit to the church's ministry.[32] If Luke-Acts is a set of early Christian lives, we would expect it to transition into the narrative body with the introduction of the first life that it will relate (Peter). But this is not how things go in Acts.

Collected biographies invariably introduce the structural units (usually books) that deal with each of their subjects by means of an origins or genealogical formula. If some kind of preface or recapitulation is involved, the narrative body commences with these features. If not, the formal marking of the name of the subject in the opening line (typically coupled with a preceding title) followed by an origins or genealogical formula together mark definitive boundaries for the beginnings and ends of lives in the collected biographies. This is not at all what we discover in Acts. The only option for a participant-oriented transition, and attendant family tradition, into the narrative body is Acts 1:15, which seems unlikely since 1:12–14 appears to function as a transition of some kind into this unit (leaving 1:12 again, as the narrative commencement). But even though Peter is introduced here for the first time as the central

32 Keener, *Acts*, 646, 733. For those who see 1:12 marking the second or third major structural unit, see also Fitzmyer, *Acts*, 213; H. Conzelmann, *Acts of the Apostles: A Commentary on the Acts of the Apostles* (Hermeneia; Philadelphia: Fortress, 1987), 39; F.F. Bruce, *The Book of the Acts* (NCNT; Grand Rapids, Mich.: Eerdmans, 1988), 39; J.B. Polhill, *Acts* (NAC 26; Nashville: Broadman & Holman Publishers, 1992), 88; M.C. Parsons, *Acts* (PCNT; Grand Rapids: Baker Academic, 2008), 29; Pervo, *Acts*, 45. D.G. Peterson, *The Acts of the Apostles* (PNTC; Grand Rapids: Eerdmans, 2009), 113, divides the text at 1:9 but provides no basis (other than a loose topical connection) for doing so.

participant, we find no clear indication that the author is moving into a 'life of Peter' at this point in that it lacks an origins or genealogical formula, among other things. In fact, none of the top three major characters in Acts are introduced in this way. Consider the five character introductions for the top three subjects in Acts provided by Adams.[33] These can be compared with ten that we find in the collected biographies of Plutarch (5 lives) and Diogenes (5 lives).

TABLE 4.2 Narrative character introductions in Acts, Plutarch, and Diogenes

Acts	Plutarch, *Parallel Lives*	Diogenes Laërtius, *Lives*
Peter w/ Disciples (1:15): Καὶ ἐν ταῖς ἡμέραις ταύταις ἀναστὰς *Πέτρος* ἐν μέσῳ τῶν ἀδελφῶν εἶπεν·	**Alexander** (*Alex.* 2.1): *Ἀλέξανδρος* ὅτι τῷ γένει πρὸς **πατρὸς** μὲν ἦν Ἡρακλείδης ἀπὸ Καράνου πρὸς δὲ **μητρὸς** Αἰακίδης ἀπὸ Νεοπτολέμου, τῶν πάνυ πεπιστευμένων ἐστί.	**Pittacus** (*Vit. Phil.* 1.74): *Πιττακὸς* **Ὑρραδίου Μυτιληναῖος**. φησὶ δὲ Δοῦρις τὸν **πατέρα** αὐτοῦ Θρᾷκα εἶναι. οὗτος μετὰ τῶν Ἀλκαίου γενόμενος **ἀδελφῶν** Μέλαγχρον
Barnabas (Acts 4:36): *Ἰωσὴφ* δὲ ὁ ἐπικληθεὶς *Βαρναβᾶς* ἀπὸ τῶν ἀποστόλων ὅ ἐστιν μεθερμηνευόμενον υἱὸς παρακλήσεως, Λευίτης, Κύπριος τῷ **γένει**	**Theseus** (*Thes.* 3.1): *Θησέως* τὸ μὲν **πατρῷον** γένος εἰς Ἐρεχθέα καὶ τοὺς **πρώτους** αὐτόχθονας ἀνήκει, τῷ δὲ **μητρῴῳ** Πελοπίδης ἦν.	**Cleobulus** (*Vit. Phil.* 1.89): *Κλεόβουλος* **Εὐαγόρου Λίνδιος,** ὡς δὲ Δοῦρις, Κάρ· ἔνιοι δὲ εἰς Ἡρακλέα ἀναφέρειν τὸ **γένος** αὐτόν·
Saul/Paul alone (Acts 9:1): Ὁ δὲ *Σαῦλος* ἔτι ἐμπνέων ἀπειλῆς καὶ φόνου εἰς τοὺς μαθητὰς τοῦ κυρίου, προσελθὼν τῷ ἀρχιερεῖ	**Cato Minor** (*Cat. Min.* 1.1): *Κάτωνι* δὲ τὸ μὲν γένος ἀρχὴν ἐπιφανείας ἔλαβε καὶ δόξης ἀπὸ τοῦ **προπάππου** Κάτωνος…	**Periander** (*Vit. Phil.* 1.94) *Περίανδρος* **Κυψέλου Κορίνθιος** ἀπὸ τοῦ τῶν **Ἡρακλειδῶν** γένους.

33 Adams, *Genre*, 130–31.

TABLE 4.2 Narrative character introductions in Acts, Plutarch, and Diogenes (*cont.*)

Acts	Plutarch, *Parallel Lives*	Diogenes Laërtius, *Lives*
Peter alone (Acts 9:32): Ἐγένετο δὲ *Πέτρον* διερχόμενον διὰ πάντων κατελθεῖν καὶ πρὸς τοὺς ἁγίους τοὺς κατοικοῦντας Λύδδα.	**Cato Major** (*Cat. Maj.* 1.1): *Μάρκῳ* δὲ *Κάτωνί* φασιν ἀπὸ Τούσκλου τὸ γένος εἶναι…	**Anacharsis** (*Vit. Phil.* 1.101) *Ἀνάχαρσις* ὁ **Σκύθης Γνούρου** μὲν ἦν **υἱός, ἀδελφὸς** δὲ Καδουΐδα τοῦ Σκυθῶν βασιλέως, **μητρὸς** δὲ Ἑλληνίδος· διὸ καὶ δίγλωττος ἦν.
Paul and Barnabas (Acts 11:27): Ἐν ταύταις δὲ ταῖς ἡμέραις κατῆλθον ἀπὸ Ἱεροσολύμων προφῆται εἰς Ἀντιόχειαν …	**Brutus** (*Brut.* 1.1): *Μάρκου* δὲ *Βρούτου* πρόγονος ἦν Ἰούνιος Βροῦτος…	**Phaedo** (*Vit. Phil.* 2.105) **Φαίδων** Ἠλεῖος, τῶν **εὐπατριδῶν**, συνεάλω τῇ πατρίδι καὶ ἠναγκάσθη στῆναι ἐπ' οἰκήματος·

The genealogical or origins formulas at the transitions into a new life tend to involve at the very least the subject of the biography as a head term, followed by a genitive indicating origins—usually the first word of the narrative body. As we noted in chapter 3, Diogenes consistently employs this form. Take, for example, the biography of Solon, son of Execestides: Σόλων Ἐξηκεστίδου (Diogenes Laërtius, *Vit. Phil.* 1.45). Or the life of Myson: Μύσων Στρύμωνος (Diogenes Laërtius, *Vit. Phil.* 1.106) or Arcesilaus: Ἀρκεσίλαος Σεύθου (Diogenes Laërtius, *Vit. Phil.* 4.28). This structure often indicates a son-father relation but can indicate where person is from or their connection to a particular philosophical school or political movement. For example, Chilon's life opens not only with the name of his father but also with his place of origins in the appositional chain (Laodicea): Χίλων Δαμαγήτου Λακεδαιμόνοις (Diogenes Laërtius, *Vit. Phil.* 1.106; see also Diogenes Laërtius, *Vit. Phil.* 1.74, 82; 2.60; *passim*). In addition, we often discover clusters of words for family or kinship terms, as Louw and Nida label it.[34] Variations of γένος are most frequent, but we also find μητρὸς, πατρὸς, υἱός, ἀδελφὸς, and so on, tightly clustered at the openings (but after the preface/prologue) of a life. Temporal deictic markers also seem frequent, helping locate the subject in a prior time (i.e., in relation to his origins).

34 L&N, 1:110.

Even small texts like *Phaedo* employ this highly standardized transition. *Cebes*, the smallest life, opens with an origins formula, with almost no additional information beyond this. The entire life—in full—is as follows:

> *Κέβης* ὁ **Θηβαῖος**· καὶ τούτου φέρονται διάλογοι τρεῖς·
> Πίναξ.
> Ἑβδόμη.
> Φρύνιχος.
>
> DIOGENES LAËRTIUS, *Vit. Phil.* 2.125

Luke-Acts, by contrast, never introduces characters in this way, even though it contains genealogical information in other places (see Chapter 5). Though it may use proper names at some of the potential transitions into the narrative body, it does not introduce the subjects in the distinctively familial way of the collected biographies. And even in some instances of continuous (i.e. non-segmented) narrative, when disciples of a major teacher are introduced, an origins formula is still employed. We see this, for example, in Diogenes' life of *Epictetus*:

> Ἦν καὶ *Πολύαινος* **Ἀθηνοδώρου Λαμψακηνός**, ἐπιεικὴς καὶ φιλικός, ὥς οἱ περὶ Φιλόδημόν φασι. καὶ ὁ διαδεξάμενος αὐτὸν *Ἕρμαρχος* **Ἀγεμόρτου Μυτιληναῖος, ἀνὴρ πατρὸς μὲν πένητος, τὰς δ' ἀρχὰς προσέχων ῥητορικοῖς.**
>
> *Vit. Phil.* 8.24

Adams proposes that the opening of Acts, while resembling many of the collected biographies in important ways, is most like the biographical succession history of Diogenes Laërtius. He points to the transition from book 3 to book 4 as indicative of this similarity, in particular:

> Of particular interest is Diogenes Laertius' opening of book 4, which connects the lives of Plato's disciples with the previous work on Plato (book 3) ... Diogenes Laertius dedicated book 3 entirely to discussion of Plato's life, career, and teaching and is now stating that book 4 will trace Plato's disciples. Furthermore, the first two disciples discussed in book 4 have already been introduced by heading a disciple list in 3.46, bringing further continuity to this transition, and providing another parallel to Luke and Acts ... The prompt shift from Jesus to the disciples, moreover, is paralleled in the collected biographies and suggests further genre specification.[35]

35 Adams, *Genre*, 125.

But are these transitions as similar as Adams insists? I take Adam's first point to be claim about structural similarity. He seeks to establish that both Luke-Acts and Diogenes devote a single book to the founding member of a sect (Plato/Jesus) and then a subsequent book to the succession of their followers (Platonic philosophers/early Christian disciples). Here, Adams rightly emphasizes the recapitulation in both Acts 1:1–2 and in *Vit. Phil.* 4.1. But while

TABLE 4.3 Narrative initiations and commencements in Acts 1 and Diogenes Laërtius *Vit. Phil.* 4.1 and 8.1

Acts 1		**Diogenes Laërtius, *Lives***	
		***Vit. Phil.* 4.1**	***Vit. Phil.* 8.1**
Initiation (RECAPITULATORY)	Τὸν μὲν πρῶτον λόγον ἐποιησάμην περὶ πάντων, ὦ Θεόφιλε, ὧν ἤρξατο °ὁ Ἰησοῦς ποιεῖν τε καὶ διδάσκειν, ἄχρι ἧς ἡμέρας ἐντειλάμενος τοῖς ἀποστόλοις διὰ πνεύματος ἁγίου οὓς ἐξελέξατο ἀνελήμφθη (1:1–2)	τὰ μὲν περὶ Πλάτωνος τοσαῦτα ἦν ἐς τὸ δυνατὸν ἡμῖν συναγαγεῖν, φιλοπόνως διειλήσασι τὰ λεγόμενα περὶ τἀνδρός.	Ἐπειδὴ δὲ τὴν Ἰωνικὴν φιλοσοφίαν τὴν ἀπὸ Θαλοῦ καὶ τοὺς ἐν ταύτῃ διαγενομένους ἄνδρας ἀξιολόγους διεληλύθαμεν, φέρε καὶ περὶ τῆς Ἰταλικῆς διαλάβωμεν
Commencement	Οἱ μὲν οὖν συνελθόντες ἠρώτων αὐτὸν λέγοντες (1:6) **OR** Τότε ὑπέστρεψαν εἰς Ἰερουσαλὴμ ἀπὸ ὄρους τοῦ καλουμένου Ἐλαιῶνος (1:12) **OR** Καὶ ἐν ταῖς ἡμέραις ταύταις ἀναστὰς *Πέτρος* ἐν μέσῳ τῶν ἀδελφῶν εἶπεν· ἦν τε ὄχλος ὀνομάτων ἐπὶ τὸ αὐτὸ ὡσεὶ ἑκατὸν εἴκοσι (1:15)	διεδέξατο δ' αὐτὸν *Σπεύσιππος* **Εὐρυμέδοντος Ἀθηναῖος**, τῶν μὲν **δήμων** Μυρρινούσιος, **υἱὸς** δὲ τῆς **ἀδελφῆς** αὐτοῦ Πωτώνης.	ἧς ἦρξε *Πυθαγόρας* **Μνησάρχου** δακτυλιογλύφου, ὥς φησιν Ἕρμιππος, Σάμιος ἤ, ὡς Ἀριστόξενος, **Τυρρηνὸς ἀπὸ μιᾶς τῶν νήσων ἃς ἔσχον Ἀθηναῖοι Τυρρηνοὺς ἐκβαλόντες.**

the book-level transitions are similar (as noted in Chapter 3, histories and biographies use similar book-level transitions at times), the commencements (i.e. transitions into the narrative body) are quite distinctive.

The transition from book 7 to 8 in Diogenes is interesting in connection with Acts since—as Adams observes—both deploy a recapitulation referring back to the subject of the prior book. Diogenes' transition into the treatment of his next subject with a genealogical formula and Acts does not is perhaps more significant, however. The fact that it is unclear where (on the collected biography theory) the author of Acts marks the introduction of the first major narrative character (or begins the narrative body) provides an initial point of variation between Acts and Diogenes. The narrative boundaries are quite clear in the latter. And it is not just that the collected biographers, such as Diogenes, formally segmented their works (often through the use of very hard boundaries, such as titles) but that they invariably introduce their characters onto the narrative stage at major transitions through the use of a genealogical or origins formula (including the transition into the narrative body from a recapitulation or preface). As Patricia Cox notes regarding Diogenes:

> [Many] of the individual biographies follow a very standard format: an account of the philosopher's ancestry; his education, training, and travels; his founding of a school; his character, mannerisms, temperament, and habits, usually illustrated with antidotes and pithy sayings; important events of his life; description of his death; details of chronology; works and doctrines; documents like letters; and addenda.[36]

Of course, this is not at all how Acts lays out. None of the three possible transitions, including the introduction of Peter in 1:15, into the narrative body of Acts utilize anything like this nor do the other character introductions.[37]

For his character introduction, the author of Acts emphases Peter's speech, not his lineage. While historians often introduce central narrative figures in connection with a speech (Brasidas: Thucydides 1.39–40; Pericles:

36 P.M. Cox, 'Strategies of Representation in Collected Biography: Constructing the Subject as Holy', in T. Hägg, P. Rousseau, and C. Høgel (eds.), *Greek Biography and Panegyric in Late Antiquity* (Berkeley: University of California, 2000), 209–54 (218).

37 But I think Adams wishes to make a second claim as well: the discipleship list in Diogenes 3.46 of his *Lives* anticipates the new life introduced in 4.1 in a way that potentially parallels the mention of Peter in Acts 1:13 as anticipatory of a 'life of Peter', beginning in 1:15. But a few key differences should be stressed here. First, 3.46 is quite some distance from 4.1 with book 3 ending at 3.108, not, as in Acts, right at the transition. Second, the anticipatory link in Diogenes occurs in the prior book (book 3, at the episode level) and in Luke-Acts (at the paragraph or even clauses complex level) within the same book and likely the same paragraph, as it sets the scene for the unit that begins with Peter as the speaker (1:15).

Thucydides 4:11.2–4; Roman ambassadors: Polybius 2.8), this does not seem to be the pattern of the Greco-Roman biographers which prefer a genealogical or origins formula. The author does not clearly segment the text according to individual lives or sets of lives. The transitions from the initiation to the narrative body in ancient biographies could not differ more from what we find in Acts.

Adams concedes that Acts deviates 'from the typical form of contemporary collected biography',[38] due to a range of influences[39] resulting (among other things) in the adoption of the narrative structure of the Greek history. But without the formal segmentation of collected biographical narrative, can we really identify a text as a collected biography? Susan Stuart and Patricia Cox insist that *by definition*, the collected biography differs from other narratives (e.g. histories) that merely accumulate lives, since the collection, 'is not constructed by its elements; rather it comes to exist by means of its principle of organization'.[40] Although Adams endorses this definition,[41] he still aligns Acts with the collected biography *on the basis of its accumulated elements* (i.e. life sketches of Peter, Stephen, Paul, etc.) *not the principle of its organization* (narrative segmentation), since Adams grants that the latter is much different. In this way, Acts fails to meet the formal criteria for defining the collected biography that Adams' analysis seems to require.

3 Conclusions

This chapter explored two frames significant for genre agnation between the Greek history and the βίος—narrative initiations and commencements. Histories adopt more concise, panoramic narrative initiations while the βίος implements more detailed, focalized initiations. These can be measured by both the length (relative to the size of the work) and scope of the initiations, usually realized by a formal preface. Luke and Acts (especially if connected to Luke) align most closely with the history relative to this cline. Narrative commencements provide another agnation cline for Luke and Acts. Does the narrative body initiate as in histories with an event or as in the βίοι with a participant? This chapter has argued that the commencements in both Luke and Acts exhibit event- rather than a participant-oriented transitions into their narrative bodies.

38 Adams, *Genre*, 212.

39 Adams, *Genre*, 211–12.

40 Cox, 'Strategies', 215 citing S. Stewart, *On Longing: Narratives of the Miniature, the Gigantic, the Souvenir, the Collection* (Baltimore, MD: Johns Hopkins University Press, 1984), 155.

41 Adams, *Genre*, 109, quotes this same passage from Stewart.

CHAPTER 5

Frames II: Self-Identification and Genealogies

Literary self-identification and genealogies function as two further frames relevant for genre agnation and Luke-Acts. Many ancient works identify themselves with a particular genre, including most βίοι and a limited number of histories. These meta-level comments point at the very least to the author's intention to connect their work with a particular literary tradition, even if one goes on to argue that they have done so unsuccessfully (e.g. Philo, *Life of Moses*). Genealogies seem to serve divergent roles in Greek historical and biographical narrative, occurring at distinct structural positions in the discourse. Examining the position of these genealogical traditions in Luke-Acts, then, may help further clarify its literary context.

1 Self-Identification: Biographical vs. Nonbiographical

Edwards makes the observation that especially in the later periods, biographical literature tended to refer to itself as βίος.[1] However, he fails to recognize that this tends to occur mainly in writings that include a preface, being absent when they do not (e.g. Plutarch *Caesar; Cicero; Romulus*; Philostratus, *Life of Apollonius*). Several βίοι and even some histories lack a formal preface. Nevertheless, *when a preface does occur in a βίος*, it tends to include a genre attestation or *self-identification* through βίος-language. Historical prefaces, by contrast, lack such an indication, sometimes but not always attesting to writing history.

Historians typically begin their work with a discussion of theoretical concerns. These prologues tend to use very formalized, elevated Greek language,[2] often beginning with a third-person introduction of the historian and his

1 M.J. Edwards, 'Biography and Biographic', in M.J. Edwards and Simon Swain (eds.), *Portraits: Biographical Representation in the Greek and Latin Literature of the Roman Empire* (Oxford: Clarendon Press, 1997), 228–34 (230).

2 H.J. Cadbury, 'Commentary on the Preface of Luke', in F.J. Foakes-Jackson and K. Lake (eds.), *The Beginnings of Christianity* (5 vols.; London: Macmillan, 1922–1933), 1:489–510; W.C. van Unnik, 'Remarks on the Purpose of Luke's Historical Writing (Luke 1.1–4)', in W.C. van Unnik, *Sparsa Collecta: The Collected Essays of W.C. van Unnik* (Leiden: Brill, 1973), 6–15 (7); I.H. Marshall, *Luke: Historian and Theologian* (Exeter: Paternoster, 1970), 37–38.

 DOI:10.1163/9789004406544_006

origins (Herodotus 1.1; Thucydides 1.1).[3] They regularly include a discussion of various sources and prior histories (Thucydides 1.21–22; Josephus, *Ant.* 1.15–26). Often, there is a statement of the intention for why the historian composes the specific history (Herodotus 1.1; Thucydides 1.1–3; Josephus, *Ant.* 1.1–4) or an outline of the various events and persons that the history will document (Xenophon, *Hell.* 1.1; Appian, *Bell. Civ.* 1.6; Josephus, *Ant.* 1.1–14). And biographical prefaces actually share many of these features in common. One structure, however, that does seem to clearly distinguish a biographical from a historical preface involves the tendency of the former to describe the ensuing work as a βίος or collection of βίοι. Histories will often (but not invariably, e.g. Xenophon, *Anab.* 1.1; *Hell.* 1.1) indicate that they write ἱστορία (e.g. Herodotus 1.1; Arrian, *Anab.* 1.5; Appian, *Hist. rom.* 1.1; Josephus *Ant.* 1.1) but they certainly lack any indication that they are writing a biographical account. So, although some histories contain the Greek word βίος ('life') within their prefaces (e.g. Xenophon, *Anab.* 1.1; Diodorus Siculus 1.1), they do not designate themselves as such.

Many βίοι do not have a preface, but begin immediately with an origins or genealogical statement (see below). Of those that do have a preface, however, βίος language is typically used to indicate the type of work that the author composes. The feature is not strongly codified in the biographical predecessors. Xenophon's *Cyropaedia* does not contain it. Isocrates uses τοῦ βίου in *Evag.* 3 but not as a self-designation for the work. Philo adopts it for his *Life of Moses* (1.1). Plutarch's *Caesar, Cicero*, and *Romulus* do not employ the language, but each of these books share in common being the second volume of one of Plutarch's *Parallel Lives*. Each of these sets includes a preface for the set located at the beginning of the first life Plutarch documents and describe their work with βίος language, in the case of all three pairs: *Alexander* (3x), *Demosthenes* (1x), and *Theseus* (1x). Plutarch follows this pattern in several other of his βίοι as well (e.g. Plutarch, *Aem.* 1.1–3; *Ara.* 1.2–3; *Cim.* 2.3). Diogenes describes his work in terms of βίος within the preface to his *Lives* and Lucian's βίοι likewise continue this pattern (e.g. Lucian, *Alex.* 1–2; *Dem.* 1).

1.1 *Self-Identification in the Gospels with Special Reference to Luke*

Many histories indicated their genre in the preface but this was by no means consistent. The Greek βίοι, by contrast, do tend to self-identify in this way.

3 Cf. L. Alexander, *The Preface to Luke's Gospel* (SNTSMS 79; Cambridge: Cambridge University Press, 1993), 26–27. However, cf. the preface in Josephus, *Ag. Ap.* 1.1–2, which uses the first person. It also includes a dedication, another of Alexander's features that historical prefaces apparently lack. Cf. J.R. Martin and D. Rose, *Genre Relations: Mapping Culture* (London: Equinox, 2008), 103–105, for the typical third-person orientation of historical discourse.

Edwards emphasizes the self-attestation of a piece of literature to being a biographical work as a significant factor in determining whether a work is indeed a βίος, but this only applies to the preface. His exclusion of the non-canonical Gospels on this basis, therefore, seems unwarranted.[4] Many individual βίοι do not have a preface, which is where this self-attestation typically occurs, and often in the case of a Plutarchian pair of βίοι, for example, only the first βίος has a preface and the second generally commences with a genealogical statement, and only rarely includes a self-attestation (indicating that the document is a βίος) (but see Plutarch, *Cic.* 1.3). Therefore, since βίοι that lacked a formal preface often did not include a literary self-identification, this should not—on its own—be used to distance the non-Lukan Gospels from the βίος.

But what about Luke? In contrast to the other canonical Gospels, Luke *does* include a preface, as with many ancient βίοι. And this is precisely where self-identification so persistently occurs within the biographical tradition. Therefore, if Luke's Gospel is a βίος, we should expect him to mention this in his preface. So that Luke's Gospel *does include a preface but does not employ biographical language* within the preface as a literary self-designation further distinguishes Luke's Gospel from the βίοι of the ancient world.[5]

1.2 *Self-Identification in Acts*

The criterion of self-identification applies only to the preface of historical and biographical works. If Acts continues a two-volume set, Luke's failure to self-identify as βίος in Luke 1:1–4 has implications not only for the genre of the Gospel but for Acts as well. Biographical recapitulations do not tend to include βίος language (e.g. Diogenes Laërtius, *Vit. Phil.* 4.1; 8.1) but as noted above, biographical prefaces do. So, if the preface of Luke provides the preface for both volumes, with Acts 1:1–2 serving as the recapitulation, then the lack of biographical language in Luke 1:1–4 counts as evidence against the biographical nature of Acts as well.[6]

---

4 Edwards, 'Biography', 230.

5 Burridge, *What are the Gospels?*, 1.79, responds to my use of this criterion in my Achtemeier paper by stating that Luke's failure to use biographical language allows for it to be any other genre, including tragedy, arguing on this basis that the criterion is useless for affirming that Luke is a history. The point, however, is not that the criterion establishes Luke as a history but that it differentiates it from the βίοι in the ancient world that employed a preface.

6 On further parallels between the recapitulation and the historical tradition, see C. Keener, *Acts: An Exegetical Commentary* (4 vols.; Grand Rapids: Baker Academic, 2012–2015), 646–50.

2 Genealogies: Staged vs. Embedded

Genealogies have a storied history in the composition of the encomium, one of the principle genres from which the Greek βίος develops. Many of the ancient rhetorical exercises discuss the guidelines for stating a 'person's origins'. Aphthonius says that the encomiumist must 'construct a *prooimion* appropriate to the subject; then [they] will state a person's origins, which you will divide into nation, homeland, ancestors, parents; then upbringing, which [they] will divide into habits and acquired skill' (*Progymn.* 8; trans. Kennedy; see also, for the same idea: Aelius Theon, *Progymn.* 9; Hermogenes, *Progymn.* 7; Nicolaus, *Progymn.* 57–58; Libanius, *Encom.* 1–5). So in the rhetorical handbooks, not only is the genealogy seemingly regulated but so is its position in the macrostructure of the discourse—it occurs directly after the *prooimion* (which would become the preface in the biographical tradition) at the transition into the narrative body.

Since βίοι tend to focus on individuals or entities, we discover family tradition for the subject of their work among the first information in the body of their narrative. Since histories are more activity or event focused, they too contain family traditions, but these are usually introduced later in the discourse with the introduction of a significant participant. In this sense family tradition or genealogies can be *embedded* (history) or *staged* (the βίος) within the narrative. As Aimable Twagilimana notes,

> 'Staging' is the property of the whole text, a macro-structuring phenomenon that assumes coherence and continuity of senses over text. Staging supposes a continuous process towards an end, but different steps must corroborate the ultimate goal. Clements defines it as 'a dimension of prose structure which identifies the relative prominence given to various segments of prose discourse'.[7]

George Brown and Gillian Yule extend this to include rhetorical devices of prose discourse as well.[8] In this way, the biographical positioning of genealogical information at the beginning of the narrative provides a *staging* device relative to ancient histories, which *embed* this information more deeply in the narrative.[9]

---

7 A. Twagilimana, *Race and Gender in the Making of an African American Literary Tradition* (Oxford: Taylor and Francis, 2016), 70.

8 G. Brown and G. Yule, *Discourse Analysis* (CTL; Cambridge: Cambridge University Press, 1983), 134.

9 Burridge, *What are the Gospels?*, 1.79 seems to grant this criterion, noting that it results from the biographical focus of ancient histories. But Burridge's remarks say nothing about the fact that βίοι and history differ in their narrative placements of family tradition.

2.1 *Embedded Genealogies in the Greek History*

Histories contain genealogical information[10] about the participants in their histories[11] but in light of their activity focus and generic participant structure, they do not tend to occur in the programmatic narrative frame (in this sense, family tradition is not *staged* in the narrative).[12] Dionysius of Halicarnassus views

10 They also often competed with the prior genealogists that went before them, e.g. Herodotus, 2.143.1–4; 5.36.2; 6.137.1; Josephus, *Ant.* 1.108, 159.

11 Greek history emerged in close relationship with the transmission of family tradition, especially in ancient Athens. Family tradition appears to have originally been transmitted in the form of speeches, which then provided tradition for later historians to draw upon. We discover family tradition, especially from the elite, preserved in fifth- and fourth-century rhetoric as family members (usually from the aristocracy) would deliver addresses to the people (the *demos*) through defense speeches in an attempt to move the hearers in favorable direction toward a particular family and/or its ancestry when it had been called into question. These defenses would often function as a response to the accusations of other orators about themselves or their families and can sometimes embody both polis and family tradition. For example, Lysias (26.21) responds to the criticisms of Thrasybulus by reckoning the role of his ancestors in the city, insisting that 'concerning myself or my father or my ancestors he will have nothing to allege that points to hatred of the people ... or that my father did either, since he died while holding command in Sicily, long before those seditions'. Beyond these kinds of defense orations, family traditions remain limited to a small amount of poetry about various aristocratic families and the—even less helpful—tombstone inscriptions but these written traditions often contain legendary elements reaching far into the mythic past and by no means seem to be considered the primary vehicles for transmitting the tradition. On this, see R. Thomas, *Literacy and Orality in Ancient Greece* (Cambridge: Cambridge University Press, 1992), *passim.* Family tradition transmitted orally could include a number of elements. An account of a family's origins was not uncommon (e.g. Herodotus 5.57). Speeches often refer to accomplishments in the games by particular members of a family's ancestry that brought honor to a city. Demosthenes, for example, calls for the jury to 'remember' (ἀναμνησθέντες) his grandfather Epichares who 'was victor in the foot-race for boys at Olympia and won a crown for the city, and enjoyed good report among your ancestors as long as he lived' (Demosthenes 58.66; cf. also Isocrates 16.25). A memory then embedded within the Athenian society is called to mind and transmitted here in the form of oration before the jury, assuming a knowledge of such tradition on the part of the hearers. Other speeches highlight the embassy services of particular families. Xenophon (*Hell.* 7.3.4), for instance, records a speech of Callias, elevating the glory of his ancestors who were chosen by the Athenians to bring peace (see also Plato, *Charm.* 158a). Victories in war were also featured as a significant element of tradition transmitted in Athenian oratory (e.g. Isocrates 5.41; Demosthenes 40.25; 44.9). Lists of lack of family achievements also work their way into Athenian oratory when criticizing a family. Demosthenes (14.282), for example, asks (rhetorically) of Aeschines his family: 'Has the state ever had to thank any one of them in the whole course of his life for so much as a horse, or a war-galley, or a military expedition, or a chorus, or any public service, assessed contribution, or free gift, or for any deed of valor or any benefit whatsoever?'

12 On this terminology, see J.E. Grimes, *The Thread of Discourse* (JLSM 207; The Hague: Mouton, 1975), 323; Brown and Yule, *Discourse*, 134.

the insertion of a genealogy as something that 'interpret[s] the narration that follows' (βούλομαι … ἐπιστήσας τὸν ἑξῆς λόγον) (*Rom. ant.* 4.6.1)—nevertheless, he sees this material as useful for historical purposes and therefore includes a genealogy of Tarquinius in his *Roman Antiquities*. Genealogies in the historians were, therefore, typically *embedded* somewhere within the interior structure of the narrative rather than *staged*[13] in the programmatic introductory material for the entire work (i.e. the preface) or for the body of the narrative (i.e. the commencement). They were viewed as parenthetical information rather than a literary structure that helped develop the narrative. For example, Herodotus's first piece of family tradition outside of merely specifying the father-relation for the purpose of identification (e.g. Alexandrus, son of Priam, Herodotus 1.3.1) is found in his record of the genealogy of Cambyses at the introduction of book 2 (cf. also Herodotus 3.2.1 for a conflicting genealogy), who will become a significant figure throughout his history. He also includes family tradition for the Gephyraioi (Herodotus 5.57), and then refutes their version of their origins. Thucydides only use the father-relation to identify a person, for the most part avoiding full genealogies. Similarly, in Polybius, genealogical information appears for the most part limited to identification of a figure through the naming of his father. Xenophon's *Hellenica* includes a very brief genealogical (two generations) description of Autoboesaces and Mitraeus, although not until *Hell.* 2.1.8, but a much fuller genealogy occurs in *Hell.* 6.3.2, indicating the lineage of Callias. Likewise, Josephus rewrites the genealogy from Jared to Adam, but locates it well after the transition into the narrative body (*Ant.* 1.63). In *Civil Wars*, Appian's first piece of family tradition occurs at the end of chapter 2 of his first book with a brief genealogy of Gracchus (*Bel. civ.* 1.17).[14] The only exception to this I have found is in Xenophon, *Anabasis*, which leads with a brief genealogy for Cyrus (*Anab.* 1.1).[15] Histories, then, often include

13 Polybius 9.1 seems to relegate discussion of genealogies to an older style of historical writing (ὁ γενεαλογικὸς τρόπος; Polybius 9.1.4), suited for the 'curious reader' and he tends away from this style so that he can maintain a focus on 'actions' (τὰς πράξεις) (Polybius 9.1.6). This further lends itself to the view that historians, by Polybius's time, tended to understand genealogies as somewhat of an interruption to their style. This may be due to the ancient perception that genealogies frequently contained much legendary traditions—thus Polybius groups it with mythologies (Polybius 9.1.1–4; on this suspicion, see Sextus Empiricus, *Adv. gramm.* 1.25; Plato, *Thea.* 155d, 174e–175b).

14 Diodorus Siculus 4.57, after recording the 'deeds of Heracles' then details the deeds of his sons.

15 *Anabasis* begins with details regarding the lineage of Cyrus, though it is not quite as formalized as what we find in Plutarch or Diogenes Laërtius: 'Darius and Parysatis had two sons born to them, of whom the elder was Artaxerxes and the younger Cyrus' (*Anab.* 1.1).

genealogies[16] but they do not tend to initiate the body of their narrative with a genealogical formula or piece of family tradition but rather embed it deeply within the narrative.[17] Such embedding likely results from the generalized rather than specified orientation of the narrative. Since histories are broadly concerned with activity rather than entity based topical sequences, they tend to avoid bringing family tradition onto the *stage* of the narrative body.

2.2 *Staged Genealogies in the βίος*

Many of the βίοι in the ancient world constitute part of a set of βίοι. Ancient biographers tended to think of their βίοι in relation to the lives of other significant figures, leading to various groupings. Often, a group of βίοι will contain a preface but after the preface, the individual βίος usually begins with a genealogical formula or a statement of origins of some other type (e.g. citizenship, philosophical school, etc.). Individual βίοι follow the same pattern (e.g. Tacitus, *Agr.* 1.4; Lucian, *Dem.* 3; Philostratus, *Vit. Apoll.* 1.1).

Certain predecessors of the Greco-Roman βίος share in common the lack of a formal preface, including a statement of genealogical origins. Since Isocrates' *Evagoras* functions as a praise speech rather than a formal biography, it fails to exhibit many formal features of the βίος genre. Although it certainly entails literary innovation in departing from the then popular poetic encomium (cf. Isocrates, *Evag.* 8), using a prose form encomium, in praising King Evagoras for his deeds, it is still far from constituting an ancient βίος, in the formal sense of that description. One of the significant formal elements that it lacks is the biographical preface.[18] Nevertheless, after a preamble on the nature of his task, Isocrates does begin the body of his eulogy with genealogical informa-

16 As discussed in chapter 2, 'genealogy' was one of the earliest forms of ancient Greek history. Thomas, *Literacy*, 155, *passim*, marks the establishment of genealogies as the 'intrusion of writing' into oral history. Hecataeus's *Genealogies* is of course the most well-known, but we have evidence of other genealogies as well (e.g. Pherecydes *FGH* 3 F 2, F 59; Hellanicus *FGH* 223a F24). Thomas, *Literacy*, 161, argues that these genealogical traditions were shared by Herodotus but were preserved with major discrepancies.

17 We see this in the fragmentary historians as well. We do not have the introductory material for these histories so we do not know where the family tradition included in their works occurred in the body of the history. Ephorus records family traditions about the Nomad Scythians (Strabo 7.3.9 = F 42). Ephorus in fact represents the 'genealogical style' (ὁ γενεαλογικὸς τρόπος), according to Polybius (9.1.4). Theopompus relates the family tradition of Dionysius the Younger, indicating a lineage of drunkenness and tyranny (Athenaeus, 10.435d = F 283a; Aelian, *Var. hist.* 6.12 = F 283b).

18 R.A. Burridge, *What are the Gospels? A Comparison with Graeco-Roman Biography* (2nd ed.; Grand Rapids: Eerdmans, 2004; org. 1992), 130, attempts to sidestep this difficulty by noting that the speech includes a statement of intentionality but this hardly aligns it with later biographical prefaces.

tion regarding the King (Isocrates, *Evag.* 12). Satyrus' *Euripides* is fragmentary, so we do not possess the beginning of this work. Xenophon's *Cyropaedia*, although it contains a preface, begins a bit differently than later βίοι. He opens with a description of the instability that occurs in political structures as a natural consequence of ruling, but insists that Cyrus was nevertheless up to the task (*Cyr.* 1.1–6). In *Cyr.* 2.1, however, we arrive at what would later become standardized ways of beginning a biography, with a genealogical statement. In Philo's *Life of Moses*, we may notice the beginnings of a crystallization of the form (though again, Philo is not posited as a major influence in the biographical tradition, just a reflection of it). After the preface Philo states: 'Moses was by birth a Hebrew, but he was born, and brought up, and educated in Egypt' (Philo, *Mos.* 1.5). So in Isocrates, Xenophon, and especially Philo, we can begin to see the codification of this feature.

Plutarch's *Parallel Lives* are among the collected βίοι of the ancient world so that each collection of parallel Greek and Roman βίοι often has its own preface, preceding the individual βίοι contained within the collection. So, we will want to examine the individual βίοι themselves and how these texts initiate in order to draw proper comparisons with Gospel prologues. When we examine the introductions in Plutarch, we find a very distinct pattern in each βίος. They begin tracing of the lineage (γένος) of their biographical subject. Alexander's biography first traces his father's ancestry back to Heracles through Caranus and then locates his mother as a descendant of Aeacus through Neoptolemus (Plutarch, *Alex.* 2.1). Plutarch's *Caesar* starts with a discussion of Caesar's family, but traces Caesar's wife's lineage and provides details about Caesar's father's sister as well as his cousin. *Demosthenes* begins the collection of parallel lives devoted to Demosthenes and Cicero. The first three chapters introduce the collection and *Dem.* 4 begins the portion on Demosthenes himself. As with *Alexander*, Plutarch begins his βίος of Demosthenes with an account first of his father's ancestry and then of his mother's (Plutarch, *Dem.* 4.1). Similarly, *Cicero* begins with the biographical subject's mother and then proceeds to his father's lineage (Plutarch, *Cic.* 1.1). After introducing the *Theseus-Romulus* set of lives, Plutarch's *Theseus* begins with the heritage of Theseus' father and mother and then goes on to provide information regarding his grandfather and daughters (*Thes.* 3.1). *Romulus* provides the only exception to this pattern. Instead of going straight into Romulus's genealogy, Plutarch begins with the debate over the naming of Rome and its relation to Roma who turns out to be relevant to Romulus's lineage, a topic Plutarch turns to directly in chapter 2.

Diogenes Laërtius opens his collection with a preface regarding other sources on his topic and various other methodological concerns. However, his lives of the individual philosophers themselves share in common a persistent feature:

initiation of the βίος with genealogical remarks or a statement of origins. These take on a more formulaic expression than what we discover even in Plutarch's *Lives*, with each βίος essentially beginning with an identification of the philosopher's father in the form of a genitive modifier for the biographical subject in the head term slot.[19] So for the biography of Solon, son of Execestides: Σόλων Ἐξηκεστίδου (Diogenes Laërtius, *Vit. Phil.* 1.45). Similarly, the biography of Myson: Μύσων Στρύμωνος (Diogenes Laërtius, *Vit. Phil.* 1.106); the biography of Arcesilaus: Ἀρκεσίλαος Σεύθου (Diogenes Laërtius, *Vit. Phil.* 4.28). In both the case of Plutarch and Diogenes Laërtius, biographical openings tend to follow a very formalized pattern, beginning with genealogical remarks about their subjects as the very first topic addressed in the body of the βίος. By the first century, this seems to be one of the most pervasive (i.e. strongly codified) features of the genre, both in the Greek and Roman traditions of biography writing.[20]

Typically, the narrative structure of a βίος after the genealogy is quite consistent and straightforward. *If the biographer includes a birth narrative for the biographical subject that it reports*, it consistently follows the genealogy, positioned on the *stage* of the narrative body (see Plutarch, *Alex.* 3.2; *Cic.* 2.1; *Rom.* 3.3; *Thes.* 3.3–4.1; Tacitus, *Agr.* 4.1; Suetonius, *Aug.* 5.1; *Tib.* 5.1; *Cal.* 8.1; *Ner.* 6.1; *Gal.* 4.1; *Art.* 1.1; *Oth.* 2.1[21]). Nevertheless, several βίοι do not include a birth narrative, often picking up the story somewhere in the subject's youth

19 The main set of exceptions to this revolve around the account of various Peripatetics and those from other schools in Diogenes Laërtius, *Vit. Phil.* 2.65–125; 4.1–6. When Diogenes, in general, takes special interest in the development of the various philosophical schools he tends away from genealogical formulas to initiate the biography and focuses on the citizenship of the philosopher instead. Or in other cases, he will combine the two types of preface formulas, incorporating both ancestral information and national or philosophical heritage. Cf. *Life of Secundus the Philosopher* 1.1, which begins by stating Secundus's philosophical heritage as a Pythagorean. Apparently, he was separated from his mother at birth and reunited later, a fact that may have led the author to begin with philosophical rather than genetic origins.

20 See also, for example, *Vit. Aes.* 1; *Vit. Arist.* 1; *Vit. Eur.* 1–2; *Vit. Pind.* 1; *Vit. Soph.* 1; Athanasius, *Vit. Ant.* 1; Diogenes Laërtius, *Vit. Phil.* 1.22, 68, 74, 82, 89, 94, 101, 106, 109, 116; 2.1, 3, 6, 16, 18, 48, 60, 65, 105, 125; 3.1; 4.1, 6, 16, 21, 28, 46, 62; 5.1, 36, 58, 65, 75, 86; 6.1, 20, 85, 94; 7.1, 167, 168, 179; 8.1, 51–53, 78, 79, 86; 9.1, 18, 21, 24, 25, 34, 50, 57, 61; 10.1; Iamblichus, *Pyth.* 2.1; Plutarch, *Lyc.* 1.1–2.1; *Num.* 1.1–4; *Pub.* 1.1–3; Ps.-Herodotus, *Vit. Hom.* 1; Porphyry, *Vit. Pyth.* 1–2; Soranus, *Vit. Hip.* 1; Tacitus, *Agr.* 4; Suetonius, *Aug.* 1–5; *Tib.* 1–5; *Cal.* 1–7; *Cla.* 1.1–6; *Ner.* 1–5; *Gal.* 1–3; *Oth.* 1.1–3; *Vit.* 1.1–3.1; *Ves.* 1.1–4; *Tit.* 1.1; *Dom.* 1.1; Nepos, *Mel.* 1.1; *Them.* 1.1; *Aris.* 1.1; *Paus.* 1; *Cim.* 1.1; *Alc.* 1.1; *Thr.* 1.1; *Dio.* 1.1, and so on; Jerome, *Vir. ill.* 1.1; 2.1; 4.1; 5.1; 7.1; 8.1; and so on—Jerome, in general, tends to include genealogical tradition at the beginning of his life, but clearly in many cases this information was not available to him.

21 As can be seen from this list of Suetonius's lives, the birth narrative after the genealogy was a persistent literary feature for him. See also Suetonius, *Ver.* 3.2; *Ves.* 2.1; *Tit.* 1.1.

(e.g. Plutarch, *Cea.* 1.2; *Dem.* 4.1–2;[22] Diogenes Laërtius, *Vit. Phil.*[23] 1.22–23, 45–46; 5.1–2; Lucian, *Dem.* 3[24]).

2.3 *Genealogies in the Gospels with Special Reference to Luke*

The location of Jesus' family tradition in Luke's narrative facilities genre identification in some fairly significant ways, while also resolving interpretive enigmas involving Luke's genealogy with historiographic evidence overlooked by prior scholarship. Unlike Matthew (1:1–17), Mark (1:1), and John (1:1–4) (see below), who begin their narratives with a genealogy or statement of Jesus' origins, Luke does not introduce Jesus' family tradition until 3:23–38.

The distinction between staged/embedded family tradition represents a persistent and fundamental difference between the Greek history and the βίος.[25] The historians distinguish themselves from the biographers of antiquity in deploying genealogies that interrupt the narrative. As Dionysius locates the genealogy of Tarquinius at an intrusive point within his history (Dionysius of Halicarnassus, *Ant.* 4.6.1), several commentators read Luke's genealogy of

22 Here, after the genealogical formula, Plutarch picks up the story with Demosthenes at age 7: 'Demosthenes, the father of Demosthenes, belonged to the better class of citizens, as Theopompus tells us, and was surnamed Cutler, because he had a large factory and slaves who were skilled workmen in this business. But as for what Aeschines the orator says of the mother of Demosthenes, namely, that she was a daughter of one Gylon, who was banished from the city on a charge of treason, and of a barbarian woman, I cannot say whether he speaks truly, or is uttering slander and lies. However, at the age of seven, Demosthenes was left by his father in affluence, since the total value of his estate fell little short of fifteen talents; but he was wronged by his guardians, who appropriated some of his property to their own uses and neglected the rest, so that even his teachers were deprived of their pay'.

23 Diogenes Laërtius, in general, seems more concerned with a citizen's and a philosopher's early education and so does not include birth narratives in his βίοι.

24 As with several of the philosophers that Diogenes Laërtius write a βίος for, Lucian picks up Demonax's story with his education rather than his birth.

25 Burridge, *What are the Gospels?*, 141, recognizes this feature: 'Most βίοι begin with a mention of the subject's ancestry and heritage, his family, or his land or city. Isocrates has a long section on the nobility of Evagoras' ancestry, tracing it back to Zeus and down through the Trojan War hero, Teucer (chapters 12–20). Xenophon also praises Agesilaus' ancestry (back to Heracles), his royal family and the greatness of his country, Sparta (1.2–4). Nepos' opening sentence tells us that Atticus was born of the most ancient Roman stock ("ab origine ultima stirpis Romanae generates"), whereas Philo comments that Moses was a Chaldean by ancestry (Μωυσῆς γένος μέν ἐστι Χαλδαῖος), but born and raised in Egypt (*Moses* 1.5)'. However, he fails to note that Luke's Gospel does not begin this way and this feature aligns it more closely with ancient historical conventions. While Burridge, *What are the Gospels?*, 201, recognizes that 'Matthew and Luke include genealogies tracing Jesus' descent back to Abraham (Matt. 1:2–17) or to Adam (Luke 3:23–38)', but he overlooks the literary impact of the differing placement of the two genealogies.

Jesus as a narrative 'interruption'.[26] According to Mark Strauss, the reason Matthew stages and Luke embeds his genealogy so deeply within the narrative 'is uncertain'.[27] Scholars typically account for this apparent imposition of genealogical tradition through Lukan redaction of Mark's narrative structure. Joseph Fitzmyer represents this view when he says, 'it is clear that Luke is inserting a genealogy of Jesus into the otherwise Marcan framework—between the Marcan episodes of Jesus' baptism and temptation in the desert'.[28] But this really does not solve the problem of placing the genealogy so late in the narrative. Scholars remain perplexed as to why Luke would choose to insert the genealogy[29] so far along in the story.[30]

---

26 E.g. F. Schleiermacher, *A Critical Essay on the Gospel of St. Luke* (London: John Taylor, 1825), 54–55; I.H. Marshall, *The Gospel of Luke: A Commentary on the Greek Text* (NIGTC; Exeter: Paternoster, 1978), 156; J.B. Green, *The Gospel of Luke* (NICNT; Grand Rapids: Eerdmans, 1997), 188.

27 M.L. Strauss, *The Davidic Messiah in Luke-Acts: Promise and Its Fulfillment in Lukan Christology* (JSNTSup 110; Sheffield: Sheffield Academic Press, 1995), 209.

28 J.A. Fitzmyer, *Gospel according to Luke I–IX* (AB 28; Garden City: Doubleday, 1981), 488. Surprisingly, R.E. Brown, *The Birth of the Messiah: A Commentary on the Infancy Narratives in the Gospels of Matthew and Luke* (ABRL; New York: Doubleday, 1993), 84–95, does not address this issue though he seeks to compare the genealogies of Matthew and Luke, respectively.

29 A. Plummer, *A Critical and Exegetical Commentary on the Gospel According to St. Luke* (ICC 42; New York: C. Scribner's Sons, 1910), 101–102, asks and answers the question this way: 'Why does Lk. insert the genealogy here instead of at the beginning of his Gospel? It would be only a slight exaggeration to say that this is the beginning of his Gospel, for the first three chapters are only introductory. The use of ἀρχόμενος here implies that the Evangelist is now making a fresh start. Two of the three introductory chapters are the history of the Forerunner, which Lk. completes in the third chapter before beginning his account of the work of the Messiah. Not until Jesus has been anointed by the Spirit does the history of the Messiah, i.e. the Anointed One, begin; and His genealogy then becomes of importance. In a similar way, the pedigree of Moses is placed, not just before or just after the account of his birth (Exod. 2:1, 2), where not even the names of his parents are given, but just after his public appearance before Pharaoh as the spokesman of Jehovah and the leader of Israel (Exod. 6:14–27)'. Plummer's solution here begins to get at the event-driven framework of the Lukan narrative. As Plummer states, the first three chapters of the Third Gospel lay out the several key events significant to understanding not only the life of Jesus, but earliest Christian history. This results in the later placement of genealogy on my view, but can also, therefore, account for some of the observations made by Plummer.

30 F.B. Craddock, *Luke* (Interpretation; Louisville: John Knox, 1990), 52–53, picks up on this when he says, 'While it is evident that Luke is now following the outlines of Mark, he does insert a genealogy between the baptism and the temptation of Jesus. Luke's intention in giving the genealogy is not clear, nor is his reason for placing it here'. He suggests as one possible solution that 'that Luke's pattern was suggested by the fact that Moses' call and ministry are separated by a genealogy in Ex. 6:14–25 (53) and that it brings chapters 1–3 to

Our discussion so far seems to suggest a potential literary motivation for Luke's placement of the genealogy. Luke locates his genealogical material much later in his account of Jesus' deeds, as something of an interruption to the narrative.[31] In embedding rather than staging the genealogy of Jesus, Luke's Gospel defies strongly codified biographical conventions for outlining the of the life of the subject. The inclusion of embedded genealogical information for Jesus, then, aligns the Third Gospel more closely with the historical than the biographical tradition.

In addition to the placement of the genealogy in relation to the preface, Luke distinguishes himself from the other Gospels and from ancient βίοι in the way he relates Jesus' birth to his genealogy within the wider structure of his discourse.[32] βίοι either begin with a genealogy or place it directly after the preface (if a preface is included) and then narrate the birth account directly after the genealogy, if a birth account is included. Luke, by contrast, provides his account of the birth of Jesus *prior to* the genealogy, another biographical convention related to the genealogy that Luke's Gospel resists. There was no consistently formalized location for the genealogy and birth narratives in the Greek history, and a genealogy could appear after the birth narrative, as it does in the birth/genealogy of Tarquinius in Dionysius of Halicarnassus, *Ant.* 3.46.5 (birth narrative) and 4.6.1–6 (genealogy).

In the use and placement of family tradition, Matthew's Gospel seems to take the most explicitly biographical form, with a detailed genealogy

a close by offering several pieces of valuable information: (1) Jesus' age; (2) Jesus' link to God through Adam; (3) Jesus' heritage as a true son of Israel (53–54).

31 Similar to Plummer, *Gospel according to St. Luke*, 101–02 (see fn 237), F. Bovon, *Luke 1: A Commentary on the Gospel of Luke 1:1–9:50* (Hermeneia; Minneapolis: Fortress Press, 2002), 135, sees the motivation for placement stemming from literary strategies in the Hebrew Bible: 'In the Hebrew Bible, genealogies are placed either at the beginning of an account (Abraham, Gen 11:10–16*), or after a few initial episodes (Moses, Exod 6:14–20*). The same liberty in composition is evident in Matthew and Luke'. However, this seems to impose an otherwise artificial literary framework upon Luke. What other evidence do we have that Luke has organized his Gospel according to the literary conventions of the Torah? Perhaps we can account for certain mimetic elements here, but the historical explanation seems to have more to commend it.

32 D.E. Aune, 'Greco-Roman Biography', in D.E. Aune (ed.), *Greco-Roman Literature and the New Testament: Selected Forms and Genres* (Atlanta, Geo.: Scholars Press, 1988), 107–26 (122), groups Matthew and Luke together as exhibiting biographical tendencies in documenting Jesus' family tradition. He says: 'The authors of Matthew and Luke, who have more consciously literary concerns than Mark, follow accepted biographical practice by prefacing the career of Jesus with accounts of his birth and genealogy'. However, as the above analysis shows, Luke exhibits specifically non-biographical tendencies in his placement of Jesus' genealogy and birth.

introducing the narrative. As with the βίος, Matthew begins with a γένεσις of Jesus Christ who is the υἱοῦ Δαυὶδ υἱοῦ Ἀβραάμ (Matt 1:1).[33] Then we come to Jesus' genealogy. A parallel here may be found in Plutarch's *Antonius* (1.1, 2): 'Antonius, grandfather was that famous orator whom Marius slew because he took Sylla's part. His father was another Antonius surnamed Cretan ... His wife was Julia, of the noble house and family of Julius Caesar....' As with several βίοι, Matthew places his birth narrative directly after his genealogy of Jesus. John provides an account of Jesus' cosmic origins rather than a genealogical description (John 1:1–5),[34] but the statement of divine origins was not outside the purview of Greco-Roman biographical prologues (e.g. Plutarch, *Rom.* 2.4–6; *Alex.* 2.5–3.1).[35] Some manuscripts of Mark include Jesus as υἱοῦ θεοῦ (א[1] B D L W) while others do not (א* Θ 28. l 2211 pc sams) and so this may be either a scribal attempt to conform Mark to biographical genealogical standards or an attempt by Mark to reorient the genealogical formula to display Jesus' supernatural origins.[36] The external evidence is slightly in favor of υἱοῦ θεοῦ so that we can likely trace υἱοῦ θεοῦ back to the evangelist, which means there is a possibility of at the very least the use of kinship language in the opening line of the Gospel and/or perhaps a statement of divine ancestry (cf. Iamblichus, *Pyth.* 2.1, for similar usage). While it is true that a birth account, when it is included, always follows the genealogy in βίοι, not all ancient βίοι included a birth account. So, on its own, lack of a birth narrative does not rule decidedly against a biographical orientation for John and Mark. Returning to the example of

33 Cf. Plutarch's tendency to use a γένος-formula to introduce family tradition (e.g. Plutarch, *Alex.* 2.1; *Thes.* 3.1).

34 Cf. Burridge, *What are the Gospels?*, 216; A. Köstenberger, 'The Genre of the Fourth Gospel and Greco-Roman Literary Conventions', in S.E. Porter and A.W. Pitts (eds.), *Christian Origins and Greco-Roman Culture: Social and Literary Contexts for the New Testament* (TENTS 8; ECHC 1; Leiden: Brill, 2013), 435–62 (245–46).

35 We may note here especially Philostratus, *Vit. Apoll.* 1, where the divine origins of Apollonius, to the degree that he was said to be god, is documented in the prologue: 'in his own case he said that Apollo had come to him acknowledging that he was the god in person; and that Athena and the Muses and other gods, whose forms and names men did not yet know, had also consorted with him though without making such acknowledgment'. Many, especially in the older form-critical era, made a great deal of the many parallels with the life of Jesus and the life of Apollonius of Tyana. See M. Dibelius, *From Tradition to Gospel* (trans. B.E. Woolf; New York: Scribner, 1965; orig. 1919), 83; R. Bultmann, *The History of the Synoptic Tradition* (New York: Harper & Row, 1968), 218–44; M. Smith, *Jesus the Magician* (San Francisco: Harper & Row, 1978), 84–91.

36 Depending upon how we weigh the evidence, this may soften the point in A. Collins, *Is Mark's Gospel a Life of Jesus? The Question of Genre* (Père Marquette Lecture in Theology; Milwaukee: Marquette University, 1990), 28, that most βίοι begin with the ancestry, followed by a birth account, whereas Mark begins his narrative with John the Baptist.

Plutarch's *Antonius*, after the genealogy, Plutarch moves right into the early years of Antonius without providing a birth account at all (Plutarch, *Anton.* 1.2; see also Plutarch, *Dem.* 4.1–2; Diogenes Laërtius, *Vit. Phil.* 5.1–2; Lucian, *Dem.* 3). Matthew's Gospel aligns with biographical conventions in locating Jesus' birth directly after his genealogy.

2.4 *Genealogies in Acts*

In his discussion of the genre of Acts, Stanley Porter notes the significance of the genealogy as 'one of the important precursors of biography'.[37] He emphasizes the use of speeches, typological descriptions of character, sources, and genealogies as features that 'push us to see the Gospels as forms of ancient biography, but the book of Acts as well'.[38] But as we have seen, *that ancient biographies employ genealogies* is not nearly as significant as *how* or *where* they situate them.

Acts embeds rather than stages its genealogies. The paucity of staged genealogical information at 1:6, 1:12, and 1:15 (three possibilities for the narrative commencement) has already been noted. Further, none of the five proposed character introductions for the three most frequent narrative subjects in Adam's biographical theory (Paul [56.4%], Peter [23.4%], Barnabas [10.3%]) follow the very standardized staging of the genealogies for their subjects at the opening of the life. As a potential exception to this, one might point to Acts 4:36, which deals briefly with Barnabas: Ἰωσὴφ δὲ ὁ ἐπικληθεὶς Βαρναβᾶς ἀπὸ τῶν ἀποστόλων, ὅ ἐστιν μεθερμηνευόμενον υἱὸς παρακλήσεως, Λευίτης, Κύπριος τῷ γένει. But though Barnabas is introduced here with a genealogical statement, the clause complex occurs in a fairly embedded location in the syntax (not in a staged location). It mentions Barnabas as an example of a Christian who contributed financially to the community. The statement does not seem to occur on the stage of a book or episode that begins a life of Barnabas. Acts includes other genealogies as well. It records the most family information for Timothy: Τιμόθεος, υἱὸς γυναικὸς Ἰουδαίας πιστῆς, πατρὸς δὲ Ἕλληνος, ὃς ἐμαρτυρεῖτο ὑπὸ τῶν ἐν Λύστροις καὶ Ἰκονίῳ ἀδελφῶν (Acts 16:1–2). However, Paul seems to clearly function as the subject of this unit and Timothy does not make the list of Adam's of narrative subjects, according to which Acts divides.[39] Adams sees Acts 16:1–17:5 marking the unit devoted to the narrative subjects 'Paul and

37 S.E. Porter, 'The Genre of Acts and the Ethics of Discourse', in Thomas E. Phillips (ed.), *Acts and Ethics* (NTM 9; Sheffield: Sheffield Phoenix Press, 2005), 1–15 (12).

38 Porter, "Genre," 12–13.

39 S.A. Adams, *The Genre of Acts and Collected Biography* (SNTSMS 156; Cambridge: Cambridge University Press, 2013), 130–31.

Silas/"we", not Timothy or even Paul with Timothy.[40] This, then, marks another embedded origins formula (i.e. not staged with the introduction of a biographical subject at the beginning of a major book or episode devoted to that subject). We also find an embedded genealogy for Sopater in Acts 20:4 (Σώπατρος Πύρρου Βεροιαῖος), clearly not a major character in Acts. Paul includes information concerning his own family and origins in Acts 22:3–4 but this material embeds in his speech rather than being staged with his narrative subject introduction in Acts 9 (or even Acts 8, his first mention), for example.

As with the Third Gospel, Acts uses genealogies but does so in distinctively non-biographical ways. The use of genealogies in Acts reflects instead the historiographic use of embedded genealogies for its narrative characters.

3 Conclusions

Literary self-identification and genealogies offer two formal diagnostics for agnating the Greek history and the βίος. The failure of Luke or Acts, especially in the preface of the Gospel, to identify with the biographical tradition distinguishes Luke-Acts from prevailing tendencies among the βίοι. The consistent macrostructural position of family tradition functions as one of the most strongly codified features of the βίος. By the first century, genealogies occur in the opening lines of the work or the narrative body in virtually all cases. In the collected biographies of the ancient world, genealogical formulas help support formal segmentation, as shown in chapter 3. Not so with Luke or Acts. They both deploy genealogies but do so in embedded locations, as in the Greek history. Relative to these two frames, then, Luke's literary context seems to align more closely with the Greek history than the βίος.

40 Adams, *Genre*, 131.

CHAPTER 6

Time Management and Authentication Strategies

Two further clines address the rhetorical structure of historical and biographical narratives: time management and authentication strategies. Time management deals with the interior organization of the discourse. How does the author arrange his or her timeline? Do they structure it according to large, sweeping scenes or around the life-story of an individual (or set of individuals)? Authentication strategy refers to ways an author establishes authority for their claims. Ancient authors frequently recruit source citation as one such method of authorization but this technique surfaces in distinct ways relative to considerations of genre.

1 Time Management: Episodic Time vs. Field Time

Martin and Rose drew the important distinction between episodic time, where historical narratives tend to be organized around episodic features (geography/nations, events, political regimes, etc.)—moving more quickly from activity sequence to activity sequence—and field time, where biographical narratives seem more driven by a portrayal of the life experience of their subject, developing slower, more focused narrative.[1] In other words, biographical (field) timelines unfold along the axis of the life of their subjects while historical (episodic) timelines unfold along the axis of some much wider organizational paradigm (e.g. a war or series of wars, the world's history, etc.). This raises another possible cline, then, to consider for ancient histories and biographies.

1.1 *Episodic Time in the Greek History*

The historians consistently arrange their narratives according to episodic time in a variety of ways. This includes macrostructural organization around the histories of wars or civilizations[2] origins of cities,[3] the causes of war(s),[4] acts

1 J.R. Martin and D. Rose, *Genre Relations: Mapping Culture* (London: Equinox, 2008), 130–133.
2 Herodotus 1.1; Thucydides 1.1; Polybius 1.1; Dionysius of Halicarnassus, *Rom. Ant.* 1.4.1; Diodorus, *Lib.* 1.1–5.
3 Dionysius of Halicarnassus, *Rom. Ant.* 1.9.1; 1.45.1; 2.1.1.
4 Herodotus 1.1.2; 3.1.1; 7.1.1; 9.1.1; Thucydides 8.1.1; Xenophon, *Hell.* 3.1.1–2.

 | DOI:10.1163/9789004406544_007

of war(s),[5] famines,[6] temporal sequences,[7] the death of a significant narrative figure,[8] occurrences,[9] and great military strategies and/or achievements.[10]

Polybius' structural reflections on the organizing principles driving the construction of his narrative in book 1 are telling:

> In the previous book, I have described how the Romans, having subdued all Italy, began to aim at foreign dominion; how they crossed to Sicily, and the reasons of the war which they entered into against the Carthaginians for the possession of that island. Next, I stated at what period they began the formation of a navy; and what befell both the one side and the other up to the end of the war; the consequence of which was that the Carthaginians entirely evacuated Sicily, and the Romans took possession of the whole island, except such parts as were still under the rule of Hiero. Following these events, I endeavored to describe how the mutiny of the mercenaries against Carthage, in what is called the Libyan War, burst out; the lengths to which the shocking outrages in it went; its surprises and extraordinary incidents, until its conclusion, and the final triumph of Carthage. I must now relate the events which immediately succeeded these, touching summarily upon each in accordance with my original plan.
>
> POLYBIUS 2.1.1–4

Note the rapid pace Polybius sets for his narrative, quickly summarizing each activity sequence in large sweeps before moving on to the next. He organizes his narrative from major scene (e.g. causes of wars, formation of navies, mutinies) to major scene (e.g. ends of wars, beginnings of wars). Polybius says he writes summaries that 'lightly touch upon'[11] (κεφαλαιωδῶς ἑκάστων ἐπιψαύοντες) the events, as he narrates them in successive order. This is exactly what Martin and Rose mean by episodic time. We may compare this with the field time that often drives Greek biographical texts, dealing in much more detail with the

5 Herodotus 4.1.1; 5.1.1; 8.1.1–2; Thucydides 7.1.1–4; Xenophon, *Hell.* 1.1.1; 5.1.1–2; 6.1.1.
6 Dionysius of Halicarnassus, *Rom. Ant.* 7.1.1.
7 Sunrises: Xenophon, *Anab.* 2.2.1; 4.1.5; days: Herodotus 1.3.1; winters and summers: Thucydides 2.1.1; 3.1.1; 4.1.1; 5.1.1; 6.1.1; 8.1.2; Xenophon, *Hell.* 2.1.1; autumns: Xenophon, *Hell.* 4.1.1; years: Thucydides 2.1.2; Xenophon, *Hell.* 7.1.1; Dionysius of Halicarnassus, *Rom. Ant.* 5.1.1; 6.1.1; 8.1.1; 9.1.1; 10.1.1; 11.1.1.
8 Herodotus 2.1.1; 6.1; Dionysius of Halicarnassus, *Rom. Ant.* 3.1.1; 4.1.1.
9 Dionysius of Halicarnassus, *Pomp.* 3.771.
10 Thucydides 1.1.23; Xenophon, *Anab.* 3.2; 5.1.2; 6.1.1; 7.1.2.
11 Cf. LSJ, 674.

life experience of their subjects, creating a slower narrative momentum. And Dionysius of Halicarnassus renders the organizational paradigm driving both Herodotus and Thucydides as what we might refer to as different modes of episodic time—Herodotus arranges his material through the 'grouping of events' while Thucydides seeks to maintain the 'chronological order' (*Pomp.* 3.773). Biographies may follow chronological order too but the order is driven by a participant rather than broader paradigms.

Another formal consideration for issues of episodic time involves the termination or ending of the narrative. Histories tend to have *open* endings, terminating with an event but leaving open the task of continuing the history for later historians. They often begin where another historian ends and they tend to end abruptly, ambiguously, or anticlimactically. We observe this ambiguity in the final lines of Herodotus' *Histories*: 'The Persians now realized that Cyrus reasoned better than they, and they departed, choosing rather to be rulers on a barren mountain side than dwelling in tilled valleys to be slaves to others' (9.122.4). As Tory Troftgruben demonstrates, 'The final three scenes of [Herodotus' *Histories*] generate not closure but ambiguity',[12] concluding 'without any terminal markers'.[13] The liberty the historians felt to compose their works as continuations of prior histories reveals something significant about ancient perceptions of the historical tradition. This lack of finality affords future historians the latitude to continue their task. Conversely, the beginnings of several histories reveal how they perceived the endings of prior histories. Polybius states, for example, that 'My work thus begins where that of Aratus of Sicyon leaves off' (ταῦτα δ' ἔστι συνεχῆ τοῖς τελευταίοις τῆς παρ' Ἀράτου Σικυωνίου συντάξεως) (1.3.2). Similarly, Xenophon picks up where Thucydides left off (*Hell.* 1.1.1).

The ending of Thucydides was a point of discussion among the ancients. His narrative closing was left so open-ended that it led Dionysius of Halicarnassus to describe it in the following way:

> The conclusion of [Thucydides] is tainted by a more serious error. Although he states that he watched the entire course of the war and promises a complete account of it, yet he ends with the sea-flight which took place off Cynossema between the Athenians and the Peloponnesians in the twenty-second year of the war. It would have been better off, after he described all of the details of the war, to end his history with a most

12 T.M. Troftgruben, *A Conclusion Unhindered: A Study of the Ending of Acts Within Its Literary Environment* (WUNT 2.280; Tübingen: Mohr Siebeck, 2010), 96.

13 Troftgruben, *Conclusion*, 97.

> remarkable incident and one pleasing to his hearers, the return of the exiles of Phyle, from which event dates the recovery of freedom by Athens.
> *Pomp.* 3.371

So, we may agree with both Dionysius and Troftgruben, that 'Thucydides' *Peloponnesian War* ends with no closure at all'.[14] Both of Xenophon's histories that we have been considering (*Hellenica* and *Anabasis*) continue from prior historical tradition and leave open their endings as if to promote the future continuation of their historical trajectories. Similarly, in Sallust's Roman history, *The War with Jugurtha*, 'the ending is anti-climatic'.[15] One exception, however, is Josephus, who does provide a fairly decisive ending to his narrative: 'With this, I conclude my Antiquities' (20.259), he says. Nevertheless, the persistent pattern in ancient histories to leave their endings open seems to assume a basic episodic time framework.

1.2 *Field Time in the βίος*

In contrast to the Greek history, ancient biographies tend to revolve around field time. As one formal realization of a field time framework for the βίος, we may point to the persistent pattern in these texts of *closed* endings, where the narrative terminates with the death of its subject or some other climactic event. In the rare number of lives without a death scene, the narrative still seems to resolve in some climatic way (e.g. the deification of the subject; the death of the subject's greatest enemy, etc.). There does not seem to be any straightforward intention of a future biographer taking up the task of documenting that subject's life as some kind of continuation of the story, since the subject dies or is perhaps deified or the story of the subject's life is resolved in some other conclusive way.[16] But several other field time features drive the organization of biographical narratives as well.

Not much can be concluded about major structural divisions in Satyrus' *Life of Euripides* due to its fragmentary state and Isocrates' speech praising King Evagoras is rather short to be making episode-level assessments about its macrostructure. Nevertheless, the ancestry and activities of the King do seem to provide the major transitions between the parts of the speech, beginning in Isocrates, *Evag.* 12 (see 19, 21, 22, 33, etc.). Once it turns its full attention to Cyrus

---

14 Troftgruben, *Conclusion*, 98.

15 Troftgruben, *Conclusion*, 101.

16 But see S.A. Adams, *The Genre of Acts and Collected Biography* (SNTSMS 156; Cambridge: Cambridge University Press, 2013), 237–42, who argues for a limited number of collected biographies that may have more open endings, as we find in Acts. See below, for discussion.

in 2.1.1, Xenophon's *Cyropaedia* consistently organizes its narrative around the life experience of its subject—Cyrus—moving slowly through his life and achievements. Every book transitions by introducing a new chapter in Cyrus' life and each of these life-chapters is treated in some detail (see *Cry.* 2.1.1; 3.1.1; 4.1.1; 5.1.1; 6.1.1; 7.1.1; 8.1.1). Cyrus provides the episode-level frame of reference for the narrative not a sequence, event, or set of events. The same is true of Philo's *Life of Moses*. Beginning with the transition into the narrative body (Philo, *Mos.* 1.5), Moses tends to drive the major episode-level transitions (e.g. 1.9, 18, 46; 2.25; etc.). And notice the sense of finality that Philo imputes to the closing lines of the narrative: 'Such was the life and such was the death of the king, and lawgiver, and high priest, and prophet, Moses, as it is recorded in the sacred scriptures' (*Mos.* 2.292). Philo clearly deploys a closed narrative ending—his story ends with the death of his subject and is not likely to be resumed by a later biographer. Together, these reveal a field time organizational paradigm for the narrative.

The collected βίοι continue this pattern. After a digression on Alexander's linage (*Alex.* 2.1–3.5), Plutarch picks up with a detailed discussion of his outward appearance (4.1). The verbal form carries the transition with Alexander as the verbal subject in 5.1. For a time, Alexander will fall briefly into the background, even at the episode level (e.g. when a new key figure comes onto the stage, relevant to Alexander story; cf. *Alex.* 6.1; 7.1), but he is quickly brought back to the foreground of the discourse as things progress (*Alex.* 8.1; 43.1; 58.1; 71.1; 72.1). From the specifics of his birth to the details of his appearance to his many military and political successes, and finally to his death (*Alex.* 77–78), Plutarch structures his *Life of Alexander* around the singular field of his subject. In *Caesar*, Plutarch organizes the narrative in the same way, around the life of Caesar and his experiences, from—for example—his ransom (2.1), his friends (3.1), his return to Rome (4.1), the people's good will toward him (5.1), his journey back to Rome from Africa (55.1) up to Caesar's death (68.4–69.2).

Plutarch's *Life of Romulus* works a bit differently since much of the story is framed around the various mythological traditions surrounding Romulus. For example, Plutarch expends considerable energy recounting the traditions regarding the origins of Romulus' name (*Rom.* 4). Even here, however, the organizing principle remains his subject, Romulus—his origins, and all that this involved. And once Plutarch gets into the core of his story, he consistently structures it around Romulus' life experience (*Rom.* 8.1–9.4; 10.1; 11.1; 12.1; 13.1; 14.1; etc.) all the way to the detailed account of his deification (*Rom.* 27.4–28.5) or, in other words, through field time. After an in-depth account of Theseus' lineage (*Thes.* 3.1–4.1), the *Life of Theseus* consistently unfolds at the macrostructural level around Theseus' experiences (e.g. *Thes.* 5.1; 6.1;14.1), up to a very thorough account of his death, including the various mythological details connected with Theseus' tomb, where the narrative ends (*Thes.* 35–36). A range of mythological traditions are introduced along the way, sometimes causing digressions but these repeatedly relate back to the life-experiences and mythological traditions connected to Theseus (e.g. *Thes.* 7.1–13.2).

We find similar organizing principles in the *Demosthenes-Cicero* set of lives. Plutarch makes it explicit: 'Therefore, in this fifth book of my *Parallel Lives*, where I write about Demosthenes and Cicero, I shall examine their actions and their political careers to see how their natures and dispositions compare with one another' (*Dem.* 3.1). Plutarch organizes each life around the revelation of the nature and disposition of the subject and both begin with the birth (Plutarch, *Dem.* 4.1; *Cic.* 1.1) and end with the deaths (Plutarch, *Dem.* 30.1–4; *Cic.* 48.1–49.2) of their subjects, creating a temporal frame that essentially requires field time narration.

The death narrative or funeral scene is a highly persistent, but not invariable feature in Plutarch's *Parallel Lives*. Following Christopher Pelling's lead, Troftgruben cautions, 'more than one quarter of the parallel lives conclude not with the death of the main character but deaths of other characters (e.g. *Caesar* [Brutus]; *Crassus* [King Odes])'.[17] But in both cases noted by Troftgruben, a death narrative for the main subject occupies the last major structural unit (Plutarch, *Cae.* 68.4–69.2; *Cra.* 31.7–33.5). And the narrative in each case still ends with a death scene—even if subservient to the broader death narrative of the main character.[18] Pelling suggests that these narratives, in fact, provide more closure as they often connect to wider themes of vengeance (e.g. the death of a king's enemy) or other terminal devices for bringing closure to the narrative.[19] So even when a death scene is lacking, the narratives still exhibit a high degree of closure, functioning to resolve the story of the biographical subject.

The unpaired and individual Greek lives seem to follow the same organizing principles. Plutarch's *Artaxerxes* begins the narrative body with a comparison

17 Troftgruben, *Conclusion*, 73.

18 Adams, *Genre*, 239, notes certain exceptions to this tendency toward narrative closure through a death scene in the Latin tradition of collected biographies: 'Jerome's *On Illustrious Men* only mentions the deaths of 31 of his 134 subjects, and Eunapius speaks of a person's death in only 17 out of a possible 34 opportunities'. We will examine Adams' examples in more detail in our discussion of Acts below.

19 C.B.R. Pelling, 'Is Death the End? Closure in Plutarch's Lives', in Deborah H. Roberts (ed.), *Classical Closure: Reading the End in Greek and Latin Literature* (Princeton: Princeton University Press, 1997), 228–50; rep. in C.B.R. Pelling, *Plutarch and History: Eighteen Studies* (Swansea: Classical Press of Wales, 2011), 365–86 (365).

between the temperaments of Artaxerxes and Cyrus (*Art.* 2.1). Then Artaxerxes' political actions and relations (to the degree that they reveal his character) provide the major organizational paradigm for the subsequent narrative, right up to his death (*Art.* 30.5). The same is true of Plutarch's *Otho*, and Diogenes Laërtius' *Democrates*. In the case of the latter, for example, Diogenes begins with the character of *Democrates*, as revealed through his education (*Vit. Phil.* 9.35–37). He then transitions by noting that 'his character is also revealed through his writings' (before embarking on narrative outlining his philosophical commitments), again indicating the field time orientation of the narrative (*Vit. Phil.* 9.38), especially since the subject's death punctuates its termination (*Vit. Phil.* 9.43). Lucian's *Demonax*, likewise, arranges its major movements around the life experiences of Demonax. One of the consistent features of field time narratives that Martin and Rose propose involves the tendency for the story to be told from experience. And Lucian claims to do precisely this, since Demonax was his long-time mentor (*Dem.* 1–2). But in any case, the basic organization seems framed by Demonax in Lucian's brief work, from his Cypriote birth (*Dem.* 3–4) to his self-imposed death as the conclusion to the narrative (*Dem.* 65–67). The same is true of Philostratus' *Apollonius*. Apollonius' life provides the basic template for the story, beginning with his origins (1.5) and ending with his death (8.29–31).

We notice, then, in histories a tendency to organize the narrative in episodic time, often leaving their endings very open, and even abrupt or ambiguous but frequently assuming a future continuation of their topic by another historian. This is strongly suggested by the fact that many historians took it upon themselves to do just this. The narrative is also organized around events or sequences and characters are grouped into these broader episodic frameworks. Biographical texts follow the opposite pattern. A single participant drives the macrostructural organization of the narrative, usually from the subject's birth to their death or some other terminal narrative device. In this respect, βίοι deploy closed narrative endings.

1.3 *Time Management in Luke*

Already, since Luke narrates 'events' (πραγμάτων) (1.1) and 'matters' (λόγων) (1.4) rather than a specific life, we have a clue into the organizational structure of the Gospel. When Luke describes his narrative, he uses episodic language to describe his purpose for writing. If we assume unity with Acts, two further features of episodic time may be noted. First, despite the Gospel's introduction of the birth of Jesus somewhat early on, its ending with Paul on trial (rather than the death/resurrection of Jesus) would seem to suggest episodic time as the basic organizational framework—beginning with a number of events leading up to Jesus' birth and ending with events leading up to Paul's trial. And second, Luke's first volume ends with the death of a significant figure, one common way of transitioning to the next temporal phase in more episodically structured discourse (see Herodotus 2.1.1; 6.1; Dionysius of Halicarnassus, *Rom. Ant.* 3.1.1; 4.1.1). In these ways, the Third Gospel is at least more episodic than the other canonical Gospels, all of which organize their narratives around Jesus from the opening line to his death/resurrection, where their narratives end. So, we see episodic time as an organizational paradigm at the discourse level of Luke-Acts, both in the narrative initiation and termination (assuming unity with Acts), especially in relation to the other Gospels.

But Luke's narrative appears episodically driven at lower levels of the discourse, as well, especially in the earlier L material (specifically, chaps. 1–3), where the narrative is still being framed. In Luke 1:5, the evangelist deploys the temporal formula (ἐν ταῖς ἡμέραις Ἡρῴδου βασιλέως τῆς Ἰουδαίας) to shift out of the preface into the narrative body in connection with the prophecy regarding Elizabeth's pregnancy. Matthew employs the same temporal formula much later in his narrative but uses it to introduce Jesus (Matt 2:1), not an event that will provide a larger context for the coming narrative. We find another temporal formula used to move the narrative at 1:26 (Ἐν δὲ τῷ μηνὶ τῷ ἕκτῳ), transitioning into the revelatory encounter of Mary with Gabriel. Even after Jesus comes onto the scene in the birth narrative, Luke still creates major transitions around events like the Passover festival (2:41), the census during the time of Quirinius (Luke 2:1–2), and the imperial calendar (3:1)—the latter two being unique to the Third Gospel. And the evangelist carries his narrative in this episodic fashion all the way up to the end of chapter 3 (besides those mentioned above, see e.g. Luke 1:39, 46, 57), after which Jesus is tempted and begins his public ministry. There is a long stretch of text in the teaching and healing ministry of Jesus (4:16–19:44) that tracks Jesus' deeds and sayings very closely, followed by the temple incident and passion/resurrection narrative, so this must be configured as well. But certainly, at the wider macrostructural levels (and in much of the L material) of the discourse, the evangelist seems to structure his material more episodically.

1.4 *Time Management in Acts*

Turning to Acts, the narrative seems to move quickly from activity sequence to activity sequence, introducing and situating participants in light of larger episodic events, not in field time through a cradle-to-grave(-or other climactic ending) plot. We have already discussed the interlaced nature of the Lukan narrative. Participants are introduced, then as Luke narrates new events, he presents new participants and then later previous participants are resumed again in new activity sequences. This seems to suggest a more episodic mode of organization than what we find in the collected biographies. The narrative of Luke-Acts runs more quickly along activity sequences where participants are introduced in light of their relevance to the larger event-lines along which the discourse progresses.

One such larger activity sequence, for example, may be 'the spread of God's word', as suggested by William Kurz, when he says that the

> 'events that have come to fulfillment among us' (Luke 1:1) include the stage-by-stage spread of God's word from Jerusalem to Judea and Samaria (Acts 8:1, 5, 26), to Caesarea Maritima (8:40), and Galilee (9:31), to Damascus (9:2), to Phoenicia, Cyprus, and Antioch in Syria (11:19), to the Roman providences of Cilicia, Galatia, Asia, Macedonia, and Achaia, and finally to Rome (Acts 1:8; 23:11; 28:14).[20]

If something like this movement reflects the narrative momentum of Acts (feasibly suggested by Acts 1:8) then Luke-Acts' geographical organization around the larger activity sequence of the spread of the Word of God seems to reflect the work of the more ethnographically oriented histories than the individualized lives of the collected biographies. As Gary Gilbert notes, in Luke-Acts, 'Geographical elements not only provide the narrative backdrop in which the action unfolds but also take center stage in expressing some of the fundamental themes of the work'.[21] Luke-Acts at least seems *more likely organized* through geographical movements than segmented according to individual or parallel lives. Recall the many historians who organize their discourse around such geographical or ethnological paradigms. Herodotus drives his narrative with his visits to various nations as the author of Acts seems to imply (*via* a we-source, or otherwise), at least in the travel narrative (Acts 16–28). Similarly, both Dionysius of Halicarnassus and Diodorus Siculus organize their histories around the various nations they document. Josephus, likewise, documents the history of a religious-political group (Israel) in relation to several nations, especially Rome. Luke-Acts constructs its narrative along a similar axis, with a movement of its key groups or participants along the trajectory of their history in many different nations as part of the Way (see Acts 16:17; 18:25–26; 25:3; 26:13).

20 W.S. Kurz, 'Promise and Fulfillment in Hellenistic Jewish Narratives and in Luke-Acts', in David P. Moessner (ed.), *Jesus and the Heritage of Israel: Luke's Narrative Claim Upon Israel's Legacy* (Harrisburg: Trinity International, 1999), 147–70 (151).

21 G. Gilbert, 'The List of Nations in Acts 2: Roman Propaganda and the Lukan Response', *JBL* 121 (2002): 497–529 (497).

Just as Luke's opening has implications for Acts, the ending of Acts has implications for Luke's Gospel in terms of time management. Throughout this study, I have sustained the emphasis (popular in linguistic studies of genre) upon macrostructure as the most significant level of analysis for genre agnation. At the discourse level, we considered two macrostructural elements with potential implications for genre agnation in terms of time management—discourse initiations and terminations. The most significant discourse-level element to consider in Acts, then, will be its termination or ending. I argued earlier in this chapter that Greek histories tend to have *open* endings whereas the βίοι more often deploy *closed* endings. Histories avoid terminating their narratives with a sense of finality, preferring to leave matters more open, usually anticipating further developments beyond their own historical contribution.

In contrast, Adams argues that certain collected biographies (and Acts) use opened rather than closed endings. Adams and I can agree with much modern scholarship that Acts ends in a rather open-ended way[22] with Paul in prison, preaching and spreading the gospel. There is no mention of his death or a succession of followers to come after him or even the result of his trial.[23] Though scholars are in general agreement that the ending of Acts seems somewhat abrupt or open, they still debate its significance or potential motivation, ranging from an apologetic strategy[24] to a technique to avoid embracement[25] to a rhetorical-literary device.[26] My contention is that the level of openness we discover in the ending of Luke-Acts reflects Greek historiographic conventions.

22 In a recent survey of the scholarship, Adams, *Genre*, 229–33 identifies two groups of readings for the abrupt ending of Acts: (1) those who think it was unintentional and (2) those who think it was intentional. Adams' survey reveals that one thing that often unites these two groups in recent scholarship is their agreement that Acts ends in an open-ended way. Adams highlights especially the literary-rhetorical view, where Acts ends the way it does intentionally in order to leave the reader 'thirsty' (Chrysostom, *Hom. Act.* 15) for more. For the view that Acts concludes in a more finalized and fitting way, see E. Zeller and J. Dare, *The Contents and Origin of the Acts of the Apostles, Critically Investigated* (Whitefish, Mon.: Kessinger, 2009; org. 1875), 2:161–84.

23 The most recent monograph-level treatment of the ending of Luke-Acts, Troftgruben, *Conclusion*, 144–78, comes to similar conclusions but sees a mixture of open and closed elements.

24 K. Schrader, *Der Apostel Paulus* (Leipzig: Kollmann, 1836), 5:573–74; E. Haenchen, *The Acts of the Apostles: A Commentary* (Oxford: Basil Blackwell, 1982), 732; cf. also C.J. Hemer, *The Book of Acts in the Setting of Hellenistic History* (ed. C.H. Gempf; WUNT 49; Tübingen: Mohr Siebeck, 1989), 408.

25 Hemer, *Acts*, 406–407.

26 Adams, *Genre*, 232. I derived the references in this sentence from Adams' excellent survey (*Genre*, 229–33).

But Adams points to a small selection of evidence that may provide counterexamples to this observation.

He begins by noting the criticism of Damis by Philostratus for not including a death narrative in his life of Apollonius, implying a broad expectation of a closing death scene in the biographical tradition. He also acknowledges Brosend's view as 'common knowledge' that 'a biography which fails to narrate the death of its subject was either written before that death occurred, or is incomplete'.[27] But Adams seeks to elucidate a few key exceptions to this trend among the collected biographies. He says: 'Although this is undoubtedly true for biographies of individuals, it is clearly not the case for all types of collected biographies'.[28] Adams insists that this observation extends to the ends of some individual lives among the collected biographies, as in Jerome's *On Illustrious Men* which only 'mentions the deaths of 31 of his 134 subjects, and Eunapius speaks of a person's death in only 17 out of a possible 34 opportunities'.[29] Perhaps this arose as a feature of some four-century Latin biographies (which still contain death scenes for many more than just one of their primary subjects, as in Luke-Acts) but in the earlier Greek collected biographies of Plutarch (more contemporary with Luke-Acts) this feature is extremely persistent. And failure to close a narrative with the death of a subject on its own may not always indicate a closed narrative ending (see below on Pelling's contribution to this discussion).

Adams insists further that some sets of lives close their entire collections in open-ended ways. Among the Greek collected βίοι, he points to Diogenes Laërtius. After the death account of Epicurus, Diogenes indicates that he will conclude with Epictetus' maxims (Diogenes Laërtius, *Vit. phil.* 10.139–54). Though Adams notes that, 'This recounting of the philosopher's maxims is unique within the work and forms a puzzling ending',[30] the 'statement itself does provide a conclusion for the reader'.[31] Nevertheless, he insists 'the endings of the particular books are open and unresolved', which seems to at least refer

27 Brosend in Adams, *Genre*, 238. See also the much larger but less recent survey in Troftgruben, *Conclusion*, 7–28.

28 Adams, *Genre*, 238.

29 Adams, *Genre*, 239.

30 T. Soderqvist, *History and Poetics of Scientific Biography* (New York: Routledge, 2017), 23, speculates that Diogenes may have been an Epicurean, which motivated the ending with Epicurean maxims. J. Mejer, *Diogenes Laertius and His Hellenistic Background* (Wiesbaden: Steiner, 1978), 15–16, likewise argues for the appropriateness of Diogenes' ending.

31 Adams, *Genre*, 241.

to their failure to record the subjects' 'deaths'. Additionally, both Eunapius' and Philostratus' *Lives* 'lack a formal conclusion and so leave their narratives open'.[32]

We may treat these in reverse order. Philostratus decidedly closes the main the narrative of his *Lives* with Τοσαῦτα περὶ Ἀσπασίου, bringing to an end the final life (Aspasius) of his collection (Philostratus, *Lives* 2.628). This is followed by a very brief epilogue of sorts, indicating the few lives he excluded based on friendship, and—of course—his own life (2.628).

> But of Philostratus of Lemnos and his ability in the law courts, in political harangues, in writing treatises, in declamation, and lastly of his talent for speaking extempore, it is not for me to write. Nay nor must I write about Xicagoras 1 of Athens, who was appointed herald of the temple at Eleusis; nor of Apsines the Phoenician and his great achievements of memory and precision. For I should be distrusted as favoring them unduly, since they were connected with me by the tie of friendship.

But, at least according to Thomas Schmitz, Philostratus' conclusion in his *Lives*, with its 'reference to friendship should be seen as climactic'. 'It demonstrates how closely our author is connected to the stars of the second sophistic: he is actually one of those great performers himself, and when he writes about them, he does so on a par'.[33] Though the ending seems abrupt, at least to Adams, it has at least two things in common with the Diogenes ending: (1) a decisive closing for the last life of the collection, including a death narrative, followed by (2) a closing for the entire project, in both cases offering a meta-level comment on the broader collection. Acts by contrast does not conclude with the death of a subject or offer such comments. Therefore, the conclusions to Diogenes and Philostratus' *Lives* remain at least more closed than Acts which ends with one of its subjects (Paul) preaching, not dying, and then offers no meta-level comment on the two-volume project as a whole.

As with Diogenes and Philostratus, Eunapius' *Lives of the Philosophers* clearly brings to an end the life of Chrysanthius with his death by illness in 505.[34] He then closes with a succession of his followers:

---

32 Adams, *Genre*, 241.

33 T. Schmitz, 'Narrator and Audience in Philostratus' *Lives of the Sophists*', in E. Bowie and J. Elsner (eds.), *Philostratus* (Cambridge: Cambridge University Press, 2009), 49–68 (57).

34 LCL p. 563, 65.

> The successors of Chrysanthius in the profession of philosophy are Epigonus of Lacedaemon and Beronicianus of Sardis, men well worthy of the title of philosopher. But Beronicianus has sacrificed more generously to the Graces and has a peculiar talent for associating with his fellows. Long may he live to do so!

Although there is mention of disciples elsewhere in his lives (e.g. Eunapius, *Lives* 31–32, 33), the closing disciple list may very well have been appropriate for a succession history—ending with the last succession. Most of the lives, however, tend to close with the death of the subject, not a succession list (e.g. Iamblichus: 33; Sopater: 38; Ablabius: 40–41; Acacius: 146; Nymphidianus: 149 and so on).[35] I grant that this ending does not seem to punctuate the closing of the collection with the same sense of finality as Diogenes or Philostratus. It does seem to function as a formal ending of some kind, however—directly subsequent to the death of the last subject, as in other collected biographies. So, the succession list may function as a kind of conclusion to the entire work or may just provide the conclusion for the last book. Regardless, the narrative ends as *most* other Greco-Roman biographies, with the death of its last subject then an additional comment (as is sometimes the case in Eunapius), this time regarding the followers of the last subject. So, while the ending may be sudden, it does seem to offer a rather closed account (at least, more closed than most histories), ending with the death of Chrysanthius, and then quickly mentioning his two leading pupils, Epigonus and Beronicianus. Acts functions differently, mentioning neither Paul's death nor his disciples. On a typological scale, the ending of Acts seems far more open than any of the collected biographies Adams considers.

Two recent studies further demonstrate the sense of closure maintained by Plutarch's many lives. First, Christopher Pelling's study of endings in Plutarch's *Lives* entertains the question: 'Is Death the End?' of the Plutarchian life? He concludes: 'Often it is, but it is striking how often a Life ends with someone else's death, not the principal's'.[36] But, according to Pelling, 'Death is a prime example of a motif that conveys a closure feel', no matter whose death is being narrated. And the closing narrations of the non-principle subject's deaths in Plutarch seem to provide a pronounced sense of finality for the closing in ways

35 When the subject is still alive, he indicates this specifically, since it breaks the pattern of the death narrative. For example, Eunapius says of Magnus, 'He himself, at this time of writing, is alive; long life to him' (153).

36 Pelling, 'Is Death the End?' 365.

perhaps not accommodated by the narration of the death of the biographical subject alone. For example, in some cases, Pelling argues, the subject's death is tied up in the destiny of another person's death so that the two deaths together provide the greatest sense of closure for the life.[37] Second, Troftgruben echoes Pelling's point regarding the several Plutarchian lives that end with someone other than the biographical subject's death, and insists that 'when the Lives deviate from a 'cradle-to-grave' plot, they often demonstrate literary circularity'.[38] He notes that, 'The death of a central figure (an expected event) often begins the closing scenes, but closure in Plutarch does not hinge on a single event'.[39] Plutarch enlists a range of 'terminal devices' (e.g. list of a character's descendants, funeral/burial instructions) that help bring narrative resolution. *Synkrisis* provides one such device in the comparisons between the lives. As Adams notes, in Plutarch's *Parallel Lives*, 'the synkrisis forms an important structural component of the Lives by providing a clear ending to each pair'.[40] So though many lives do not include a death (though by far, most do, and almost always at the end of an entire collection), they still seem to conclude climactically or with finality through a number of other terminal devices—many of which, Troftgruben shows, are not present in the ending of Acts.[41]

We can agree then with the contemporary tendency of scholarship to view the ending of Luke-Acts as *opened* rather than *closed*,[42] or at least certainly far more open than the vast majority of collected biographies, including those proposed by Adams as potential exceptions to this prevailing tendency. Luke-Acts simply lacks the terminal devices that so often characterize the closings of the collected biographies. This agnates Luke-Acts again toward history rather than collected biography relative to the *closed* termination as an episodic feature.

37 Pelling, "Is Death the End?" 365.

38 Troftgruben, *Conclusion*, 73.

39 Troftgruben, *Conclusion*, 80.

40 S.A. Adams, 'Luke and the *Progymnasmata*: Rhetorical Handbooks, Rhetorical Sophistication, and Genre Selection', in M.R. Hauge and A.W. Pitts (eds.), *Ancient Education and Early Christianity* (LNTS 533; London: T&T Clark, 2016), 137–154 (151). See also, e.g., C.B.R. Pelling, 'Synkrisis in *Plutarch's Lives*', in Frederick E. Brenk and I. Gallo, (eds.), *Miscellanea Plutarchea: atti del I convegno di studi su Plutarco* (Ferrara: International Plutarch Society, sezione italiana, 1986), 83–96; H. Beck, 'Interne 'synkrisis' bei Plutarch', *Hermes* 130 (2002): 467–489.

41 Troftgruben, *Conclusion*.

42 E.g. Troftgruben, *Conclusion*, 166–67; Adams, *Genre*, 239–41.

2 Authentication Strategy: Bounded vs. Unbounded[43]

The classicist David Potter suggests that,

> In terms of form, perhaps the most important point is that [the βίος] allowed for direct quotation of documents in a way that the generic rules for narrative history did not. It is not altogether clear why this should be so, but it may be that the tradition of the eyewitness memorialist influenced the later practitioners in such a way that they too wished to include first-hand statements about their subject.[44]

Similarly, James Luce discovers that, 'History ... was to be written in the language of its creator: quotation of documents and direct transcriptions had little place. Only rarely would a historian admit into his text the verbatim language of others'.[45] This is not to say that historical writings did not employ direct citations—they just did so less frequently, and for differing purposes. According to Potter, we find a distributional distinction between the Greek history and the βίος in terms of what is acceptable regarding direct citation of sources. Unfortunately, Potter does not provide us with quantifiable data by which we can assess his claim empirically. To test Potter's intuition, we may compare authoritative citation density in our two respective genres. Interestingly, Potter fails to notice differences in source-citation density distribution within the New Testament Gospel tradition, treating them all as βίος on the basis that they frequently cite prophetic sources.[46] Potter's equation of the Gospel writer's use of Israel's Scriptures with the Greek's citation of sources nonetheless seems significant.

One challenge with citation related criteria involves defining and quantifying citations. First, what is an authoritative citation? A very minimalist definition of a citation can be proposed for the purpose of this study. Authoritative citation should be understood in the context of this study as *the use of source material (i.e. reference to an external authority) within a narrative marked by a citation formula of some kind*. It thus refers to any mention of source material, whether a direct quote from the source is included or not. This is not meant

43 Burridge, *What are the Gospels?*, 1.79–81, argues that this criterion is determinative in my model but I deny this. Authentication Strategies function along with the 8 other criteria to make the case that Luke-Acts seems more similar to history than ancient biographical narratives.

44 D.S. Potter, *Literary Texts and the Roman Historian* (London: Routledge, 1999), 67.

45 T.J. Luce, *The Greek Historians* (London: Routledge, 1997), 3.

46 Potter, *Literary Texts*, 145–46.

to minimize the vast amount of source material brought into narratives without a formula. Assessment of these traditions is valuable, but citations with a formula seem to function more explicitly in terms of *authentication strategies*.

An authoritative citation, then, as technically defined in this study, does not merely refer to the use of a source but to the formal marking of source material through a formula. This raises a second question. How big is a typical citation formula? The average source citation formula consists of roughly three words (e.g. οἱ πολλοὶ λέγουσιν, Plutarch, *Alex.* 46.1), whether we are dealing with the βίος or the Greek history—this does not, of course, include the amount of text cited, only the citation formula. Citation formulas can constitute a clause either as a single verb (e.g. λέγονται, Diogenes Laërtius, *Vit. Phil.* 6.76) or with an explicit subject (e.g. καθά φησι Σωσικράτης, Diogenes Laërtius, *Vit. Phil.* 1.62). While these distinct citation formulas can take on varying lengths based on these considerations (e.g. whether explicit subjects are employed), they tend on average to use around three words. But I employ a three-word average density not as a scientific or reductionistic heuristic but simply because it will be important to determine a quantifiable word density space that can then be measured against the total word count of a book in order to gage citation (formula) density in the βίος as opposed to the Greek history.

In order to fit all of the data onto a single display and in order to not increase work beyond necessity, I have slightly limited the corpus to represent literature along the chronological trajectory of the biographical and historical samples identified above. This subsample includes 7 of the 9 histories and 8 biographical texts, including Diogenes, *Thales*. Though the corpus has been modestly limited in order to conduct these extensive manual investigations, I think the data presented will be more than enough to sufficiently establish the argument of this section.

Classicists tend to agree that one of the major functions for the citation of sources was to authenticate the narrative in some way. What we will discover is that the biographical samples tend to deploy *unbounded* authentication strategies whereas history tends to reflect more *bounded* environments for citation. As John Marincola suggests, 'Presumably, when the reader sees a continuous citation of historians, he is meant to conclude that the present historian is consistently basing his work on the authoritative historians he names'.[47]

47 J. Marincola, *Authority and Tradition in Ancient Historiography* (Cambridge: Cambridge University Press, 1997), 243. Similarly, D. Fehling, *Herodotus and His "Sources": Citation, Invention and Narrative Art* (trans. J.G. Howie; ARCA 21; Wiltshire: Francis Cairns, 1989), 143, asserts, that one of Herodotus's primary reasons for citing a source was to establish credibility and he employs sources most frequently when events are most fantastic, especially for 'astounding stories' involving the miraculous. For a summary of this

Biographical discourses, by contrast, make frequent and free use of authoritative citations, indicating *bounded* authentication environments for the Greek history and *unbounded* authentication environments for βίος.

2.1 *Bounded Authentication Strategies in the Greek History*

With the exception of the biographical predecessor *Cyropaedia*,[48] ancient histories tended to introduce their source material with a citation formula far less frequently than did ancient βίοι (see Tab. 6.2, for comparison). This likely results from the fluid state and early shaping of a literary form with some components only beginning to slowly solidify. Further evidence of this extends from the fact that the two histories with the highest citation densities—Xenophon's *Anabasis* and Appian's *Civil Wars*—also contain the highest number of biographical portraits within the flow of the historical narrative. For this reason, Arnaldo Momigliano positions Xenophon's *Anabasis* as an important precedent for Xenophon's later biographical developments in *Cyropaedia*.[49]

The historians recruit a wide range of citation forms. Herodotus employs a fairly standardized set of formulas that will be adopted by later historians. He uses only 93 anonymous citations and 188 explicit citations (i.e. where the

TABLE 6.1 Citation density in Greek historiography

	Herodotus	**Thucydides**	**Xenophon, *Hellenica***	**Xenophon, *Anabasis***	**Polybius**	**Josephus, *Ant.***	**Appian, *Bell Civ.***
Citations	281	43	29	45	187	120	85
Word Count	184,947	150,173	66,514	57,174	311,667	305,870	116,927
Density	0.45%	0.08%	0.13%	0.23%	0.17%	0.11%	0.21%

position in classics and application to Luke's Gospel, see A.W. Pitts, 'Source Citation in Greek Historiography and in Luke(-Acts)', in S.E. Porter and A.W. Pitts (eds.), *Christian Origins and Greco-Roman Culture: Social and Literary Contexts for the New Testament* (TENTS 8; ECHC 1; Leiden: Brill, 2013), 349–88. Cf. also V. Gray, 'Interventions and Citations in Xenophon's Hellenica and Anabasis', *CQ* 53 (2003): 111–23.

48 Although *Cyropaedia* exhibits a higher citation density than the histories examined, it does so only slightly more than Xenophon's *Anabasis* and Appian's *Civil Wars* but does significantly exceed the other histories.

49 A. Momigliano, *The Development of Greek Biography* (Carl Newell Jackson Lectures 143; Cambridge, Mass.: Harvard University Press, 1993), 50.

source is named).[50] He primarily cites oral sources in these instances, and only rarely documents, inscriptions, or literary sources.[51] Many of his formulas are based on λέγω, including the imperfective (e.g. λέγεται, 1.75.4, 87.1, 153.1; 202.1; 6.61.4, 74.2; 7.56.2; λέγουσι, 1.1.4, 2.1, 3.1, 5.1, 21.1, 23.1, 65.4 2x, 70.2, 70.3; 2.2.5; λέγοντες, 1.78.3; 2.15.1; 3.30.1) and, less frequently, the perfective (e.g. εἰπόντα, 1.27.2; ἔλεξαν, 2.20.1) aspects. Herodotus also employs at times various forms of φημί (e.g. φασί[ν], 1.33.2, 37.2, 38.2, 51.3; 3.105.2). Thucydides deploys citations with proper names 17x. The remaining 26 anonymous source citations tend to use forms of λέγω in imperfective aspect, both in the present (esp. λέγεται [with ὡς: 1.24.4, 32.5, 38.1, 118.3; 2.18.5, 93.4, 102.5; 3.24.5, 79.3, 94.5; 6.2.4; 7.2.4; without ὡς: 1.34.1, 138.6; 2.20.1, 98.3, 77.6; 4.24.5; 4.103.5]; λέγονται, 1.13.2) and imperfect (ἐλέγοντο, 5.74.3; ἐλέχθη, 2.57.1) tense forms. Westlake insists on the 'undoubtedly oral' character of the tradition introduced by a citation formula grammaticalzing perfective aspect (aorist tense-form) in Thucydides.[52] As for Xenophon, *Hellenica* contains a total of 29 citations.[53] These are built off of forms for φημί or λέγω. By far the most common usage in *Hellenica* is ἔφασαν (e.g. with ὡς: *Hell.* 5.4.57; 6.4.30 and without ὡς: *Hell.* 2.3.56; 3.5.21 [καὶ πολλὴν ἔφασαν]; 6.2.6, 4.7, 4.12, 4.29; 6.5.26, 5.29, 5,49; 7.1.30, 32; 7.4.40), a formula fairly distinct to *Hellenica* (but cf. Xenophon, *Cyr.* 3.3.38; *Anab.* 5.4.27; 7.4.21). Xenophon also employs φασὶν when using anonymous citation at *Hell.* 7.1.31. *Hellenica* marks anonymous sources through the use of λέγω-formulas as well (with ὡς: 5.4.57; 6.2.16; 6.4.30; and without: 3.1.14, 2.10, 27; 4.2.22, 4.10, 8.36; 5.3.2, 4.7; 6.4.7). *Anabasis* exhibits the same kind of scenario. We could go on, but it is not necessary. But we do need to give some attention to the exact formal realizations being discussed so that when we move between histories, biographies,

50 G.S. Shrimpton and K.M. Gillis, 'Herodotus' Source Citations', in G.S. Shrimpton, *History and Memory in Ancient Greece* (Montreal: McGill-Queen's University, 1997), 237–242—this essay significantly contributes to the data on Herodotus below. According to Shrimpton and Gillis, Herodotus' books 1 and 5–8, have less frequency of direct citations (a ratio of 0.8720) and one and a half times this much in books 2 to 4. And they are least frequent in book 9 (0.9513).

51 The estimate is typically that Herodotus relied on oral sources for roughly 80% of the entire stock of his source material. See D.A. Aune, 'Prolegomena to the Study of Oral Tradition in the Hellenistic World', in H. Wansbrough (ed.), *Jesus and the Oral Gospel Tradition* (JSNTSup 64; London: T&T Clark, 2004), 77; K.H. Waters, *Herodotus the Historian: His Problems, Methods and Originality* (Norman, Oak.: University of Oklahoma Press, 1985), 75.

52 H.D. Westlake, 'ΛΕΓΕΤΑΙ in Thucydides', *Mnemosyne* 30 (1977): 345–62.

53 Cf. C. Tuplin, *The Failings of Empire: A Reading of Xenophon Hellenica 2.3.11–7.5.27* (HE 76; Stuttgart: Steiner, 1993), 39–40, counts 33 of these citations but he does not provide a comprehensive list nor does he make his methodology for determining a citation clear.

and Luke-Acts, we can have assurances that we are counting the same kinds of forms.

As with Xenophon's *Cyropaedia* for Greco-Roman biographical literature, Herodotus (484–425 BCE) seems to function as a kind of entry point into the historiographic tradition that represents a transitional link into universal history rather than a prototypical sample. Developing out of epic poetry and largely influenced by the Homeric tradition, Herodotus' narrative exhibits a range of poetic dimensions, representing a kind of epic history.[54] While acknowledging the origins of Greek historiography in ethnography, Dionysius of Halicarnassus, for example, in his essay *On Thucydides*, considered the tradition of universal history writing to have been initiated with Herodotus and then to have congealed with Thucydides.[55] Felix Jacoby, by contrast, although he recognizes Herodotus's history as having strong universal tendencies, situates it at least partially in relation to ethnographic practice since it still embodies the more descriptive elements of this tradition, especially in books 7–9.[56] For Jacoby, Herodotus functions as an important transitional writer, incorporating geography, ethnography, and war monograph. While many have subjected Jacoby's model to extensive criticism,[57] the basic insight that in Herodotus we find a still fluid state of ancient history seems valid.[58] So while Herodotus certainly represents a milestone in the development of the Greek historical tradition, its transitional status may account for its slightly higher densities than the histories that came after him.

Not until Thucydides do we see the most complete expression of early contemporary Greek history. His history strongly codifies this form, exhibiting the lowest density for authoritative citation in the corpus. Thucydides, then,

54 Cf. A. Momigliano, *Studies in Historiography* (New York: Harper & Row, 1966), 79, summarizes the evolution of the stages as follows: '(1) Homeric poems; (2) epic cycle; (3) "logographoi"; (4) Herodotus'.

55 J. Marincola, 'Introduction', in John Marincola (ed.), *A Companion to Greek and Roman Historiography* (BCAW; LC; Malden, Mass.: Blackwell, 2007), 1–9 (5), suggests that this developmental view goes back originally to Aristotle's *On History*.

56 F. Jacoby, 'Über die Entwicklung der griechischen Historiographie und den Plan einer neuen Sammlung der griechischen Historikerfragmente', *Klio* 9 (1909): 80–123.

57 See J. Marincola, 'Genre, Convention, and Innovation in Greco-Roman Historiography', in C.S. Kraus (ed.), *The Limits of Historiography: Genre and Narrative in Ancient Texts* (MBCB 191; Leiden: Brill, 1999), 281–324.

58 In reference to the historian's citation of sources, J. Marincola, *Greek Historians* (GR 31; Oxford: Oxford University Press, 2001), 40, observes how atypical the first-person intrusions of source-citation that we find in Herodotus are when set against the backdrop of the development of later history: 'The Herodotean narrator is, in fact, unique amongst ancient historical texts, and even later writers who consciously imitate him have nothing like the number of authorial intrusions that we find in Herodotus'.

represents the low end (0.08%) and Herodotus the high end (0.45%) of the range. Just under Xenophon's *Anabasis* (0.23%), we find Appian's *Civil Wars* (0.21%), another more biographically oriented history (with a significant emphasis upon Caesar's military achievements in the early parts of the work), occupying the middle portions of the range. This is not to say some histories may not be higher or even somewhat lower than these density ranges, but the contrast is nevertheless stark when compared with Greco-Roman βίοι.

2.2 *Unbounded Authentication Strategies in the βίος*

As Potter suspected, βίοι tend to cite their sources far more frequently than the Greek histories.

If authentication strategies seem to most strongly codify from Thucydides on in the Greek history, then in the biographical tradition it already seems highly formalized in the βίος by Satyrus on Euripides.[59] Satyrus' *Life of Euripides* (third century BCE) is one of the most important texts in the corpus developmentally. We know of the document not only from the citations of ancient scholars but also through its partial preservation in the manuscript P.Oxy. 1176.[60] Many have ignored P.Oxy. 1176 in their treatments of ancient biography precisely because the text of Satyrus' biography is so fragmentary but a substantial amount of the original remains (at the least the part that dealt with the life of Euripides) and since the history of ancient biography remains so patchy prior to Plutarch, P.Oxy. 1176 deserves serious consideration in our reconstruction. We first begin to see here, for example, the massive spike in citation density relative to ancient history. According to an appendix provided by Burridge, 17.5 % of the

TABLE 6.2 Citation density in Greek biographical writings

	Xenophon, ***Cyrop.***	**Satyrus,** ***Euripides***	**Plutarch,** ***Alexander***	**Plutarch,** ***Caesar***	**Plutarch,** ***Dem.***	**Plutarch,** ***Cicero***	**Plutarch,** ***Romulus***	**Diogenes,** ***Thales***
Citations	64	12	114	56	47	28	78	67
Word Count	79,283	1,321	20,118	16,119	6,959	12,197	9,440	1,866
Density	0.24%	2.7%	1.70%	1.04%	2.02%	0.68%	2.47%	10.77%

59 Isocrates' *Evagoras* contains only a few authoritative citations (3x), perhaps due to its origins in rhetoric rather than the (at his time) impending biographical tradition.

60 On this text, see S.E. Porter, 'The Use of Authoritative Citations in Mark's Gospel and Ancient Biography: A Study of P.Oxy. 1176', in Thomas R. Hatina (ed.), *Biblical Interpretation in Early Christian Gospels.* Volume 1: *The Gospel of Mark* (LNTS 304; London: T&T Clark, 2006), 79–96.

total text that we possess consists of quoted material.[61] Gilbert Murray summarizes the content as 'a mass of quotations, antidotes, bits of literary criticism, all run together with an air of culture and pleasantness …'.[62]

When we measure the length of the small portion that we have of this work, we arrive at somewhere around 1,321 words (depending on how the *lacuna* are reconstructed) and likely 12 citation formulas, indicating a density of 2.7% according to the scale used in this chapter. Now for any kind of definitive analysis, we would want to be able to examine a more extended (complete) text, but this assessment does yield some indication that βίοι in the third century BCE were beginning to stabilize toward more frequent usage of citation formulas than we find in ancient history, at least in some sectors.[63]

Plutarch's voluminous collection of βίοι, *Parallel Lives*, represents not only an excellent specimen of the βίος but a potentially prototypical one. Quantitative examination of several of Plutarch's βίοι confirms that βίοι tend to have a much greater density of authoritative citations than ancient histories. Plutarch's citations usually consist of λέγεται formulas (e.g. *Alex.* 2.1; 6.5; 9.2; 13.2; 14.3; 39.6; *Thes.* 29.1), often with ὡς but sometimes with γάρ (e.g. *Alex.* 10.4). Plutarch also uses other forms of λέγω. At times, for example, he will introduce his subject (e.g. Alexander) (or someone else) as a narrative figure and then use him as a source with the formula ὡς αὐτὸς ἔλεγε (e.g. *Alex.* 8.3), other times merely adjusting the tense form to suit his narrative (e.g. λέγουσι, *Alex.* 3.1; *Thes.* 4.1; 30.1) or sometimes using a nominal form with a copulative verb (e.g. ἐστὶ λόγος, *Alex.* 2.5).

Plutarch also frequently uses φημί to construct source citations (e.g. *Alex.* 2.3; 3.2; 27.1; 63.1; *Thes.* 30.4). But sometimes he prefers a verb of cognition rather than speech (e.g. ὡς οἴεται Θεόφραστος, *Alex.* 4.3; Ἡρόδωρος μὲν οὐδενὸς οἴεται τὸν Θησέα μετασχεῖν, *Thes.* 29.3). Plutarch also shows knowledge of documents written by his subjects and cites them verbatim (e.g. ὡς ἐκ τῶν ἐπιστολῶν λαβεῖν ἔστιν, *Alex.* 8.1; cf. also *Alex.* 7.4). He cites various historians and other

61 R.A. Burridge, *What are the Gospels? A Comparison with Graeco-Roman Biography* (2nd ed.; Grand Rapids: Eerdmans, 2004; org. 1992), 312.

62 G. Murray, *Euripides and His Age* (2nd ed. Oxford: Oxford University Press, 1946), 13.

63 As M.R. Lefkowitz, *The Lives of the Greek Poets* (Baltimore: Johns Hopkins University Press, 2012), 99–100, puts it: 'As a biographer, however, Satyrus is distinguished by his learning and his understanding of the biographer's art. Like other writers, Satyrus continued to use quotations as the building blocks for his biography and has his interlocutors use whatever the poet wrote as evidence of his own personal views, although none of Euripides's dramas (by their very nature) could have contained explicit biographical materials'. Similarly, T. Hägg, *The Art of Biography in Antiquity* (Cambridge: Cambridge University Press, 2012), 78, asserts that the basic structure of Euripides' biography is between 'paraphrase and quotation'.

literary texts (e.g. τοῦτο μὲν οὖν καὶ Ἀριστοτέλης ὁ φιλόσοφος εἴρηκεν, *Thes.* 3.2; τοῦτο μὲν οὖν καὶ Ἀριστοτέλης ὁ φιλόσοφος εἴρηκεν, *Thes.* 5.1; see also *Thes.* 23.3; 24.4) as well as representatives from various nations he apparently interviewed (*Thes.* 26.2). He cites coins and various inscriptions (e.g. *Thes.* 25.3). At times, he draws attention to a narrative figure reading or reciting a passage from a source (ἐντυχόντος, *Alex.* 10.4). Plutarch also often alludes to the consensus view of 'writers' as a body of source material (e.g. οἱ πλεῖστοι γράφουσιν αὐτός, *Alex.* 27.1).[64] We may observe the densities of these formulas in several of his biographical writings.

If we compare Plutarch's *Alexander* (see Tab. 6.2) with our seven ancient histories (see Tab. 6.1), we will notice that Plutarch exhibits more than a 200% increase in citation (formula) density relative to Herodotus and much more to the Greco-Roman historians on the lower end of the density spectrum. This marks a distinct quantifiable, formal difference between the two genres. Featuring the highest density of citation formulas within the βίοι of Plutarch examined, the *Life of Theseus* yields in most cases more than a 400% increase in citation density relative to the Greek histories. Again, this confirms formally Potter's intuition that βίοι tend to cite their sources more frequently than ancient Greek histories. Although the *Life of Caesar* evidences less citation density relative to some of Plutarch's other βίοι, when compared to works of history, Plutarch still consists of between 0.81% (relative to Xenophon, *Anabasis*) and 0.96% (relative to Thucydides) greater citation density than what we find in six of the seven Greek histories analyzed above, and still significantly above Herodotus.

Diogenes Laërtius offers one of the most thorough collections of Greek βίοι from the ancient world. By the time that Diogenes writes, we have a highly formalized genre, although his numerous βίοι are a bit shorter than earlier works. As Thucydides moves radically beyond Herodotus in formalizing the trends that Herodotus had set in motion, so in Diogenes we find an overwhelming response to the Plutarchian emphasis on authoritative citation where almost every portion of the narrative derives from explicitly cited source material. Mimesis (borrowing source material without a citation formula) is virtually lacking, at least on a surface reading. Diogenes Laërtius' *Plato* certainly exhibits a lower density than his *Thales*, but his *Thales* provides an important

64 N.G.L. Hammond, *Sources for Alexander the Great: An Analysis of Plutarch's 'Life' and Arrian's Anabasis* (Cambridge: Cambridge University Press, 2007), 6, thinks that in these cases, Plutarch calls attention to his source material to indicate that the events he documents were in doubt.

sample since it shows how strongly codified this formal feature became in the later development of the biographical tradition.

Having examined three significant predecessors to the ancient βίος, six of Plutarch's βίοι and Diogenes Laërtius' *Thales*, the following picture emerges. Beginning with the extant formal beginnings of the genre in Plutarch, the density of citation formulas range from 0.68% to 10.77%, and these by far exceed the normal densities for the histories examined. Even Satyrus' *Life of Euripides* exhibits a fairly high citation density, substantially earlier than Plutarch. Historians, by contrast, seldom deploy authoritative citations. They apparently reserve their citations. The constraints of the genre seem to have developed in such a way that frequent citation, as we find in later Greco-Roman βίοι, became suddenly inappropriate with Herodotus. It is not entirely clear why this is the case, but it may be that as the writers of contemporary history began their attempt to move beyond the legends that so often infiltrated the early mythographies and ethnographies they had less need for authorization. And many view mythography as a deep and abiding influence well into the development of the Greek biographical tradition.[65]

We also notice a scale within this criterion (from *more* or *less bounded* citation strategies), confirming that a hard boundary between these two genres cannot be drawn in most cases, accentuating the need for topological analysis. In histories with biographical material (e.g. Xenophon, Appian), we discover a higher density of citations but still not at the level of any of the βίοι we examined. But even in βίοι, where the citation densities are lower, they still are not as low as even the highest density histories (Herodotus) examined. So while we do observe a degree of flexibility for this feature, the trends easily seem persistent (i.e. highly codified) enough to support genre agnation.

2.3 *Authentication Strategy in the Gospels with Special Reference to Luke*

Luke-Acts, history, and βίος share in common the use of authoritative citation within their narratives. In Luke-Acts (and the Gospels), we do not have citation of 'sources' as such, but we do observe the use of numerous authoritative citation formulas. These introduce Israel's Scriptures, often cited in order to lend prophetic authority to their narratives. This may at first seem foreign to the kinds of sources used by the ancient histories and βίοι until we realize that the kinds of sources cited by these texts were not only sources that provided the content for their narratives but also the normative literary texts

65 See the several essays on this theme in K. Temmerman and K. Demoen (eds.), *Writing Biography in Greece and Rome: Narrative Technique and Fictionalization* (Cambridge: Cambridge University Press, 2016).

of the Greco-Roman world. Thucydides, for example, cites Homer more than any other single source (see 1.3.2–3; 1.9.4; 1.10.3–4; cf. also 2.41.4; 3.104.4 for references to Homer).[66] And these citations seem to function in quite the same ways as the other sources Thucydides cites.[67]

One reason why the Gospels may share many of the features of the Greek βίος and history but lack their citation of Greco-Roman sources could be that the standard Greco-Roman texts not only had nothing to say about Jesus but were also not largely normative for the Jewish communities that the Gospels (at least partially) addressed. Jewish education in the diaspora in fact followed the Hellenistic paradigm but, instead of Homer and other Greco-Roman literature functioning as the normative texts, Jews learned the LXX.[68] We also have precedent for this in Josephus. Josephus cites the Old Testament in ways that often parallel the Greek histories that he refers to, quoting as authoritative normative bodies of writings not only for the Jews, but also for the Roman audience that he addresses.[69] Many studies of the Gospels thus rightly understand that the evangelists employ authoritative citation of the Old Testament in functionally similar ways to the historians and biographers when they cite normative texts as authoritative—even if the content of these two sets of texts

66 L. Kallet, *Money and the Corrosion of Power in Thucydides: The Sicilian Expedition and Its Aftermath*. Berkeley: University of California Press, 2001), 97–110, proposes that the entire Troy exhibition in Thucydides is mapped on the Homer account. See also Richard B. Rutherford, 'Structure and Meaning in Epic and Historiography', in Edith Foster and Donald Lateiner (eds.), *Thucydides and Herodotus* (Oxford: Oxford University Press, 2012), 13–38. N. Luraghi, *The Historian's Craft in the Age of Herodotus* (Oxford: Oxford University Press, 2001), 271, thinks that Thucydides used Homer's epic poetry, in spite of its genre, because it was viewed as a political source for the ship catalogues. On the rhetorical use of Homer in Thucydides, see V.J. Hunter, 'Thucydides and the Uses of the Past', *Kilo* 62 (1980): 191–218 (197) and G. Crane, *Thucydides and the Ancient Simplicity: The Limits of Political Realism* (Berkeley: University of California Press, 1998), 127–34.

67 E.g. Thucydides uses Homer as proof (τεκμηριοῖ δὲ μάλιστα Ὅμηρος) for the gradual application of the name Hellene (Ἕλλην) to Hellen and his sons only after they grew mighty in Phthiotis and were invited to ally with other cities in 1.3.2–3.

68 See A.W. Pitts, 'Paul in Tarsus: Historical Factors in Assessing Paul's Early Education', in S.E. Porter and B. Dyer (eds.), *Paul and Ancient Rhetoric: Theory and Practice in the Hellenistic Context* (Cambridge: Cambridge University Press, 2016), 43–67 (44–49).

69 See A.W. Pitts, 'The Use and Non-Use of Prophetic Literature in Hellenistic Jewish Historiography', in M.J. Boda and L.W. Beal (eds.), *Prophets and Prophecy in Ancient Israelite Historiography* (BCP; Winona Lake, Ind.: Eisenbrauns, 2012), 229–52, for further analysis. He also tends to prefer prophetic sources for his citations rather historical or legal Old Testament material: Jonah (*Ant.* 9.205–208), Isaiah (*Ant.* 9.276), Jeremiah (*Ant.* 10.104, 106, 112, 114–20, 124, 141; cf. *Ant.* 10.176–80; so also *J.W.* 5.391–92), and Daniel (*Ant.* 10.264–68; cf. *Ant.* 10.272–80; 11.337; 12.332).

remains radically different.[70] Others have argued that early Christians were so certain that Israel's Scriptures spoke of Jesus that they felt warranted in using them *as historical sources for the life of Jesus*.[71] Citation of Scripture also fits the criteria for authoritative citation used his this chapter to assess historical and biographical material as *the use of source material (i.e. reference to an external authority) within the narrative marked by a citation formula of some kind.*

From here we may formulate a genre agnation criterion based on density of authoritative citations. Our empirical study confirmed Potter's suspicion that histories exhibit a drastically lower citation density than do ancient βίοι. The lowest density for the βίοι examined was 0.68%, which is still a stark contrast to the highest density levels for ancient history at 0.45%, and the extremes on both ends remain incredibly accentuated with Thucydides at 0.08% and Diogenes Laërtius at 10.77%. And the higher and lower end spectrums are explicable in terms of literary evolution (Herodotus) or greater biographical influence (Appian's *Civil Wars* and Xenophon's *Anabasis*) and deeper formalization of the genre in the case of Diogenes Laërtius. So where do Luke and the other Gospels fit within these ranges of authoritative citation density?

Many observe that in comparison to the other Gospels in the synoptic tradition, the Third Gospel is far more selective in its authoritative citations than Mark or Matthew. Luke only contains 15 authoritative citations, defined above as source material marked by a citation formula, about 75% less than Matthew (54) and only slightly less than Mark (16). But as Steve Moyise notes, 'Bearing in mind that Luke is nearly twice as long as Mark, we can say that quotations in Luke are about half as frequent as in Matthew and Mark'.[72] We will see below

70 E.g. P.L. Shuler, *A Genre for the Gospels: The Biographical Character of Matthew* (Philadelphia: Fortress, 1982), 99; G.E. Sterling, *Historiography and Self-Definition: Josephos, Luke-Acts, and Apologetic History* (NovTSup 64; Leiden: Brill, 1992), *passim*; Potter, *Literary Texts*, 145–46; Porter, 'Authoritative Citation', 79–96. Cf. also C.D. Stanley, 'Paul and Homer: Greco-Roman Citation Practice in the First Century CE', *NovT* 32 (1990): 48–78, who makes this equation for Paul.

71 E.g. T. Brodie, *The Birthing of the New Testament: The Intertextual Development of the New Testament Writings* NTM 1; Sheffield: Sheffield Phoenix Press, 2006), *passim*. Similarly, A.T. Hanson, *The Prophetic Gospel: A Study of John and the Old Testament* (Edinburgh: T&T Clark, 1991), 251–414 (242), claims that in John's Gospel, 'theophanies under the old dispensation afford [John] the opportunity of claiming that the appearance of the Word in Jesus Christ was no bolt from the blue, but was the culmination of a series of appearances of the Word in Israel's history'.

72 Cf. S. Moyise, The Old Testament in the New: An Introduction (TTCABS; London: T&T Clark, 2001), 45. A feature also noticed but explained away by D. Pao and E. Schnabel, 'Luke', in G.K. Beale and D.A. Carson (eds.), *Commentary on the New Testament Use of the Old Testament* (Grand Rapids: Baker Academic, 2007), 251–414 (251): 'The fact that Luke uses fewer explicit quotations in his Gospel (twenty-five [(according to) Fitzmyer ...])

that Moyise's appraisal here is not quite as precise as we would hope, but this basic distributional phenomenon is interesting in light of its densities for the Greek history and the βίος.

All four Gospels and their density levels in comparison to the ranges and averages for both the Greek history and the βίος break down as follows:

TABLE 6.3 Citation density in the βίος, the Greek history, and the gospels

	Luke	Mark	Matthew	John	Range for βίος	Average βίος	Range for history	Average history
Citations	15	17	54	25	28–114	71	29–187	131.66
Word Count	19,482	11,304	18,346	15,335*	6,959–20,118	10,614	57,174–311,667	170,467
Density	0.23%	0.45%	0.88%	0.48%	0.68–10.77%	3.6%	0.08–0.45%	0.15%

* This number excludes John 7:53–8:11.

Luke hits right in the upper mid-portions of the range (with Xenophon's *Anabasis* and just below it Appian's *Civil Wars*) of citation densities for Greek history (with the more biographically oriented histories) and Matthew fits nicely within the lower range of the βίος, right between Plutarch's *Cicero* (0.68%) and Plutarch's *Caesar* (1.04%). This data is what we would expect to find if Luke composed a history with significant biographical interest (as with

than Matthew does in his (thirty-eight) must not be misread to suggest that Luke was less interested in intertextual links with Israel's Scriptures. Luke's allusions to OT material need to be taken into account as well: C. A. Kimball ... finds 439 OT allusions in the Gospel of Luke (note that Kimball ... finds thirty-three OT quotations in Luke). It is not helpful to argue that "Jesus rarely appropriates scripture to talk about himself specifically", interpreting Luke's use of explicit quotations as 'a conservative portrayal' on the basis of eliminating allusions to and echoes of OT passages.... In the first-century Jewish context it does not seem to have made much difference whether a passage of Scripture is explicitly quoted or alluded to. Luke's references to the law of Moses, the prophets, and the psalms clearly express his conviction that the person and ministry of Jesus, as well as the Christian communities and their message, are based on the Jewish Scriptures'. As we shall see, recourse to Luke's allusions or mimetic references remains unnecessary to account for his less frequent usage of authoritative citations while still allowing the evangelist to hold the LXX in high regards. Luke has plenty of respect for his normative texts but the genre of ancient historiography, in which he writes, potentially constrains him toward selective citation of these sources.

Xenophon, *Anabasis*, and Appian, *Civil Wars*), and if Matthew is a βίος. Mark and John fall around the very top end of the historical ranges, close to the position of Herodotus. At least with respect to this scale, Mark (and John) tend to be more historically oriented, confirming at least relative to this feature the thesis of Adela Collins that Mark resembles the historical monograph more than the Greco-Roman biography.[73] The data from Mark and John may also be less conclusive due to the relatively lessened 'literary level' of these Gospels.[74]

2.4 *Authentication Strategy in Acts*

Stanley Porter notices, 'Explicit quotations of the Old Testament in Luke and Acts are plentiful, though not as frequent or as numerous as those in Matthew or Mark'.[75] Acts employs a range of citation formulas. Several of these utilize the γέγραπται formula (1:20; 7:42; 13:33; 13:29; 17:2, 11; 18:24, 28; 23:5; 24:14). More frequently, however, the author uses the 'saying' formulas so abundant in the historians and biographers, including εἶπον (2:16, 25, 34; 3:22, 25; 7:7; 13:22, 40), λέγω (3:25; 7:48; 13:35; 15:17), λαλέω (2:31; 26:22; 28:25), and ἐντέταλται (13:47). There are roughly 26[76] authoritative citations in Acts, making the total between Luke and Acts, 41. This yields a percentage of 0.42, which is less than any of the Gospels but at the high end of the range for histories, along with Herodotus (0.45). However, when we treat Luke-Acts together, we get a percentage of 0.32.

---

73 A.Y. Collins, *Is Mark's Gospel a Life of Jesus? The Question of Genre* (Père Marquette Lecture in Theology; Milwaukee: Marquette University Press, 1990); A.Y. Collins, 'Genre and the Gospels', *JR* 75 (1995): 239–46; A.Y. Collins, *Mark: A Commentary on the Gospel of Mark* (Hermeneia; Minneapolis: Fortress Press, 2007), 15–43.

74 Cf. D.A. Aune, *The New Testament in its Literary Environment* (LEC 8; Philadelphia: Westminster, 1987), 63–65.

75 S.E. Porter, 'Scripture Justifies the Mission: The Use of the Old Testament in Luke-Acts', in S.E. Porter (ed.), *Hearing the Old Testament in the New* (Grand Rapids: Eerdmans, 2006), 104–26 (104).

76 Cf. Porter, 'Scripture', 104, who notes 27. Some of this depends on whether tightly clustered citation formulas referring to the same text count as two citations or one. For example, in Acts 7:47–48, we find two tightly clustered formulas, referring to the same passage: προφήτης λέγει· ὁ οὐρανός μοι θρόνος, ἡ δὲ γῆ ὑποπόδιον τῶν ποδῶν μου· ποῖον οἶκον οἰκοδομήσετέ μοι, λέγει κύριος. I have counted this as one citation but you could see how it could be counted as two—see, e.g., I.H. Marshall, 'Acts', in G.K. Beale and D.A. Carson (eds.), *Commentary on the New Testament Use of the Old Testament* (Grand Rapids: Baker Academic, 2007), 513–605 (522). This seems to be how J.A. Fitzmyer, *The Acts of the Apostles: A New Translation with Introduction and Commentary* (AB 31; New Haven: Yale University Press, 2008; orig. 1998), 90–91 comes up with 33 quotations. Or perhaps how J.A. Meek, *The Gentile Mission in the Old Testament Citations in Acts: Text, Hermeneutic, and Purpose* (LNTS 385; London: T&T Clark, 2008), 19, came up with his number.

TABLE 6.4 Authoritative citation densities in Acts, Luke-Acts, the Greek history, and the βίος

	Acts	Luke-Acts	Range for βίος	Average βίος	Range for history	Average history
Citations	26	41	28–114	71	29–187	131.66
Word Count	18,454	37,936	6,959–20,118	10,614	57,174–311,667	170,467
Density	0.42%	0.32%	0.68–10.77%	3.6%	0.08–0.45%	0.15%

Luke-Acts, then, exhibits a citation density a good deal lower than Herodotus (0.45), among the upper-mid-range densities of the Greek histories, just higher than the biographically oriented histories of Xenophon and Appian. And Luke's citations reflect much lower densities (often many times lower) than all of the individual and collected biographies or Gospels examined. Further, the spike in citations in the Book of Acts, ultimately balanced out by the Gospel of Luke, was not atypical among the historians. They tend to cluster their citations in certain books or sections, but their ratios even out due to low or null distributions in other books.[77]

We can refer back both to our topological scale as well as our typological or binary criteria (see chapter 1). We said that authoritative citations may be *bounded* (restricted in use and density) as in histories or *unbounded* (unrestricted in use and density) as in the βίοι. In other words, more bounded environments for authoritative citation will reflect lower densities and less bounded environments will involve higher densities. Typologically, Luke-Acts certainly seems *more bounded* than the collected biographies or the non-Lukan Gospels, even if not *as bounded as some other histories*.[78]

77 Thucydides' *Peloponnesian War*, for example, includes spikes in books 1 (13x) and 2 (11x) but these drop off in books 3 (4x), 4 (2x), 5 (1x), 6 (4x), 7 (3x), and 8 (5x). Similarly, in Xenophon's *Hellenica*, book 6 includes a drastic spike (13x) relative to the citation distributions of books 1 (0x), 2 (1x), 3 (5x), 4 (4x), 5 (3x), and 7 (3x). Likewise, in Xenophon's *Anabasis*, book 1 features the most dramatic spike (26x) with books 2 (7x) and 7 (5x) providing the next closest runners up. The pattern is perhaps most accentuated in Polybius. 58 of the citations in his *Histories* occur in books 12, 16 citations in book 9, 11 in book 10, 10 in book 8 and nothing over 8 after that, with many of the books coming in at zero (e.g. books 11, 13, 17, 19–21, 23–26, etc.).

78 This may potentially still raise the question for some, as to why Luke-Acts tends toward the upper-mid ranges for the Greek history rather than closer to the middle, where many of the histories tend to fall. See, for example, Burridge, *What are the Gospels?*, 1.79–81. It should be noted that *historians and biographers tended to cite their sources outside of the speech margins*. All of Thucydides' citations occur outside of the speech margins, as do

3 Conclusions

This chapter considered two final genre agnation clines connected with the rhetorical structure of Greek historical and biographical discourse. The first of these draws from Martin and Rose's time management cline. Histories organize their narratives around *episodic time* whereas biographies tend to utilize *field time*. Especially when considered together, Luke-Acts seems to arrange its narrative most frequently through episodic rather than field time, situating it closer to the Greek history relative to this cline. We also noted differences in the authentication strategies employed in both genres, as reflected by densities of

the ones in Herodotus and Xenophon's *Hellenica*. So, it could be that the form of the tradition in Luke's sources influenced citation densities in that the author seems to limit his citations—especially in Acts—to the speech material. And as Pao and Schnabel 'Luke', 251, observe regarding the Third Gospel, 'In contrast to the *Reflexionszitate* in Matthew, in Luke's Gospel all except the first three quotations (2:23, 24; 3:4–6) are found in the narration of direct speech—that of Jesus (4:4, 8, 12, 18–19; 7:27; 18:20; 19:46; 20:17, 37, 42–43; 22:37), of the devil (4:10–11), of a scribe (10:27), and of the Sadducees (20:28)'. Similarly, as Marshall, 'Acts', 513, notes that in Acts: 'The so-called speeches are naturally the main location for scriptural material in Acts, and all the quotations introduced by formulas occur in speeches addressed to Jewish (or Jewish-Christian) audiences (Steyn 1995: 230); contrast the lack of direct citation in the speeches in Lystra and Athens'. Marshall overstates the situation here a bit. In Acts 1:20, for example, the citation of Psalms falls outside of the speech margins but for the most part, authoritative citations do seem limited to speech material, with few exceptions. If we use the number of citations deployed only outside of speech margins (as is typical in ancient histories and biographies) in Luke-Acts (37,936 words), we get a citation density percentage below even Thucydides, at 0.03%. Most of the citations within the speeches in Acts occur in the early portions, especially the sections most crucial to the development of what C.H. Dodd calls the Jerusalem kerygma. As B.T. Arnold, 'Luke's Characterizing use of the Old Testament in the Book of Acts', in B. Witherington (ed.), *History, Literature, and Society in the Book of Acts* (Cambridge: Cambridge University Press, 1996), 300–323 (306), observes, 'Luke's quotations of the Old Testament in Acts occur in concentration in the speeches of Peter in chapters 1–4, the speech of Stephen in chapter 7, and the speech of Paul in chapter 13'. So it could be the case, as Dodd thought, that specific scriptural passages attached to the apostolic kerygma through consistent proclamation, congealing the merger of certain Old Testament traditions with the messianic interpretations of the early Jesus movement. Thus, much of Luke's scriptural tradition may have come packaged with (or 'attached to') his traditions about Jesus and the early church—especially if Luke used apostolic speeches as a major source in the composition of Luke-Acts. This would allow us to explain the slightly higher than normal historical (but still very far from standard biographical) citation density ranges in Luke-Acts. And when we readjust the numbers to reflect only authoritative citations outside of the speech margins of Luke-Acts (0.03%), the two-volume set sharply distinguishes itself from its biographical contemporaries which exhibit much higher densities for authoritative citation in the main narrative, ranging from 0.68% (Plutarch, *Cicero*) to 2.47% (Plutarch, *Romulus*) to 2.7% (Satyrus) to 10.77% (Diogenes, *Thales*).

authoritative citation of sources. Histories tend to reflect *bounded* citation environments where citation seems highly restricted. Correspondingly, the much higher citation densities exhibited by the Greek biographies seem to suggest an *unbounded* environment for authoritative citation—biographers feel the liberty (necessity?) to cite sources freely and frequently. When compared to the βίος and the other canonical Gospels, Luke tends to fall on the more bounded end of the scale among the Greek histories. When combined with Acts, the densities spike some but still leave Luke-Acts much closer to the densities of the Greek history than the βίος.

CHAPTER 7

The Genre of Luke-Acts

1 The Enigma

We began this study by isolating a particular enigma in Lukan studies. How do we study the genre of Luke-Acts? Several recent proposals commend themselves. Collectively, this research reveals shared features between Luke-Acts and at least the Greco-Roman history, the biography, and the epic/novel. Though they arrive at differing conclusions, these studies tend to capitalize on genre similarities while methodologically minimizing genre differences. We traced the theoretical underpinnings of this tendency to Richard Burridge's use of Alistair Fowler's family resemblance model. Though many scholars before him had correlated formal features of the βίος with literary structures in the canonical Gospels (e.g. Votaw, Talbert, Schuler, Aune), Burridge's study sought for the first time to justify this practice *via* the canons of literary theory. Unfortunately, Fowler's model was no canon. It passed from the scene almost as quickly as it emerged since it failed to assess genre differences—a shortcoming eventually conceded by Fowler himself. Burridge's analysis succumbs to the same weakness. His many criteria only assess genre proximity, not genre divergence.

Though many New Testament scholars claim to borrow from 'the best' of literary theory, most of the models currently used date back to the problematic paradigms of the structuralist era. When Burridge published his monograph in 1992, a new consensus had already arisen in contemporary genre studies that sought to restore the role of context in genre study that prior models had displaced. Beginning with the work of M.A.K. Halliday (sociolinguistics) and Carolyn Miller (rhetorical theory) in the 1970s and 1980s, genre studies has become increasingly interdisciplinary with a distinct focus on the sociological dimensions of genre. Although New Testament scholars have typically neglected these developments, I have sought to show that contemporary genre theory still has much to offer the interpreter of Luke-Acts.

2 Bringing Lukan Genre Studies Up-to-Date

Following in the stream of Halliday, J.R. Martin represents one of the most well-developed recent accounts of genre. This model offers a number of advantages for a study of the genre of Luke-Acts. To begin with, it proceeds from

 | DOI:10.1163/9789004406544_008

the most up-to-date linguistic and literary methodologies, seeking to attend to the criticisms and developments that have led to substantial advancements in the contemporary study of genre. Most importantly, it emphasizes genre agnation, focusing on a specific kind of family relation. In contrast to the family resemblance model that Burridge deploys—focusing on genre proximity—J.R. Martin's topological and typological analysis of genre navigates both genre proximity *and* genre divergence *via* his genre agnation analysis.

Finally, Martin and Rose have constructed genre agnation scales designed specifically for the differentiation of *historical* and *biographical* genres. These scales and a few others inspired by them can be assessed within the macrostructures of a discourse, where M.A.K. Halliday, Ruqaiya Hasan, and Martin insist some of the most significant generic encoding recurs. This analysis assumes a layered or hierarchical view of language, as advocated originally by Halliday, in which the most distinctive features of a genre tend to surface in the higher-level structures of a discourse (e.g. in a formal preface, at the transition to the narrative body, the closing of a narrative, etc.) while *topoi* are shared by many genres, often occurring at lower levels. This is not an invariable rule but does guide our analysis toward the consideration of higher-level structures in genre agnation.

3 Agnating the Greek History and the βίος

The SFL scales provided by Martin and Rose supply the theoretical foundations for the genre agnation study undertaken in Chapters 3–6. Proceeding from recent work integrating genre study and corpus linguistics, we began by establishing representative corpora for the Greek history and the βίος genres (Chapter 2). Each chapter then argued that our genre agnation scales consistently agnate the Greek history and the βίος in differing directions relative to eight scales. We discovered that these texts tend to topicalize either activity- or entity-focused discourse. Participants may be identified through generic or individualized structures. Initiations (including prefaces) can be either panoramic or focalized. Commencements or transitions into the narrative body may be either event- or participant-driven. While some works inconsistently self-identify with their literary tradition, others do so more frequently. Some texts embed their genealogies, others stage them. Discourses may also be organized around episodic or field time and may employ bounded or unbounded authentication strategies. Selection between each of these choices tends to correlate with the genres we established in our sample corpora. Histories tend to group according to the first set of scales and biographies according to the second—not absolutely or invariably, but quite consistently. For this reason, each of these typological criteria (binary; +/-) can be recast as topological scales. This allows us then to talk about some works as *more* historical or biographical than others relative to these specific scales while also accounting for phenomena like genre blurring and elasticity.

4 What Genre is Luke-Acts? Micro and Macrogenre Reconsidered

When we turn to Luke-Acts, we notice a distinct literary orientation toward the Greek history genre *relative to* the βίος genre. One could also consider the Greek novel or epic through genre agnation but as Burridge notes, 'The only serious alternative to historiography for the genre of Acts is ancient biography'.[1] And this certainly applies to Luke's Gospel as well. The study of ancient genre is complex and requires sustained genre agnation analysis in order to make convincing evaluations. In order to establish more secure and stable conclusions, genre agnation scales need to be developed not only for the Greek history and the βίος, but likely for the Greek novel and epic as well (as both genres have been proposed for Luke-Acts). Nevertheless, this study seeks to advance the discussion relative to the two largest contenders for the genre of Luke-Acts—history and biography—by establishing the claim that *Luke-Acts is ostensibly more like the Greek history than the βίος*. I sought to establish this for both Luke and Acts through a consideration of the same genre agnation scales that seem to consistently differentiate widely agreed upon historical and biographical texts and the result was—consistently—that Luke-Acts gravitates more in the direction of the historical side of the spectrum of Greek prose discourse than the biographical side.

This still leaves open the question of Luke's relationship to the other Gospels, which our analysis seemed to show reflect the biographical genre much more strongly than the historical genre. If Luke is the first volume of a two-scroll history, why does it seem so akin, especially to the other two Synoptics. To begin with, Luke probably uses the other Gospels (or at least Mark and perhaps Q, if such a document existed) as sources for his first volume. This almost certainly impacted the shape of his Gospel.

Second, we may treat the problem in terms of the difference between micro and macrogenre. For example, Herodotus has a very generic opening, as with other histories, but then in book 2, he transitions with 'After the death

1 R.A. Burridge, 'The Genre of Acts Revisited', in Steve Walton (ed.), *Reading Acts Today: Essays in Honour of Loveday C.A. Alexander* (LNTS 472; London: T&T Clark, 2011), 3–28 (15).

of Cyrus ...' (τελευτήσαντος δὲ Κύρου) (2.1.1), a more individualized structure. We note here too the anaphoric function of the individualized transition, referring back to the prior book's narrative (as in Acts) of Cyrus, including his death. The long portion of narrative that Herodotus devotes to Cyrus could be considered, at the microgeneric level, a kind of biographical discourse, even though Herodotus clearly employs historiographic features that define his work's macrogenre.

Similarly, Diodorus Siculus marks the major episode-level transition at *Lib.* 17.118 into book 18 (and vol. 9) with Alexander's death. And as in Luke-Acts, Diodorus includes a recapitulatory link that sets up his intention to chronicle Alexander's successors after his death: 'The preceding Book included all the acts of Alexander up to his death; this one, containing the deeds of those who succeeded to his kingdom, ends with the year before the tyranny of Agathocles and includes seven years' (*Lib.* 18.1.6). The individualized episode-level transitions Diodorus' history again seem to reflect biographical conventions for the prior narrative but only at the level of microgenre.

Likewise, Appian's second book on Cyrus has a distinct biographical orientation, which is reflected strongly at the transition from book 2 into book 3 of his *Civil Wars*, where Appian refers to the prior narrative *via* an individualized transition by stating, 'Thus was Gaius Caesar, who had been foremost in extending the Roman sway, slain by his enemies and buried by the people' (Appian, *Bel. Civ.* 3.1.1). Again, as in Acts, we have an anaphoric individualized book-level transition referring back to the prior book's narrative of Caesar, including his deeds and death, reflecting biographical microgenre but without forsaking the wider historiographic macrogenre. Or take Josephus' transition into book 2 of *Against Apian*. After reference to book 1, Josephus transitions with individualized reference to Apian in book 2 (Josephus, *Ag. Ap.* 2.1–7). Again, the biographical microgenre is helpful for understanding how a large portion of Josephus' historical work could be devoted a singular individual.

Luke-Acts deploys similar literary features. After Jesus' genealogy, Luke's Gospel takes on a very individualized focus, with Jesus' deeds, death, and resurrection occupying a major focus, as in ancient biography. Then, in Acts, we find a transition back into more generic discourse, reminiscent of historiography. Luke 3–24 then takes the shape of a biography at the microgeneric level. This use of the biographical microgenre does not undermine Luke's wider historiographic macro genre. As Keener contends,

> Ancient historians such as Livy might follow the lives of a famous general or other hero (often interspersing other information where relevant

> chronologically), but such biographic elements did not change the genre from history to biography. Dionysius of Halicarnassus has biographic sections in his larger history, such as that about Tarquin (*Ant. rom.* 4.41–85), but his work remains a multivolume history.[2]

Thus, Luke's biographical emphasis in his first volume does not undermine the historiographic character of his wider two-volume work in Luke-Acts. In Acts, Luke then transitions back into the historical tenure that defines the wider macrogenre of Luke-Acts. In doing so, Luke follows the lead of several other histories from the ancient world.

Luke's use of the biographical microgenre likely impacts its reception history with the other Gospels, however. Though Luke intended his work to be a two-volume history, the first volume was read along with the other canonical Gospels as a life of Jesus. So, in terms of canonical history, the Third Gospel seems to function with the other three canonical Gospels as a life of Jesus, but in terms of its literary history, the Third Gospel functions with Acts as a two-volume history of the Early Church.

5 The Literary Unity of Luke-Acts

The paradigm-shifting work of Henry Cadbury has convinced most of the literary unity of Luke-Acts.[3] Though some still resist the unity thesis,[4] many leverage it in one of two directions in contemporary discussions of genre. If one reads Acts as history, then an argument can be formulated for a historiographic

---

2 Keener, *Acts*, 60.

3 H.J. Cadbury, *Making of Luke-Acts*. For recent surveys of the issues involved, see I.H. Marshall, 'Acts and the "Former Treatise"', in Bruce W. Winter and Andrew D. Clarke (eds.), *The Book of Acts in its First Century Setting*. 1. *The Book of Acts in its Literary Setting* (Grand Rapids: Eerdmans, 1993), 163–82; L. Alexander, 'The Preface to Acts and the Historians', in B. Witherington (ed.), *History, Literature and Society in the Book of Acts* (Cambridge: Cambridge University Press, 1996), 23–27; J. Verheyden, 'The Unity of Luke-Acts: What are we up to?', in J. Verheyden (ed.), *The Unity of Luke-Acts* (Leuven: Leuven University Press, 1999), 3–56 (esp. 27–50); and various essays in A.F. Gregory and C.K. Rowe (eds.), *Rethinking the Unity and Reception of Luke and Acts* (Columbia, S.C.: University of South Carolina Press, 2010). Cf. also P. Walters, *The Assumed Authorial Unity of Luke and Acts: A Reassessment of the Evidence* (CSNTMS 145; Cambridge: Cambridge University Press, 2009), 3–24, who eventually advocates for authorial disunity against the consensus view.

4 E.g. R.I. Pervo, 'Must Luke and Acts Belong to the Same Genre?', in D. Lull (ed.), *SBLSP* 28 (Atlanta: Scholars, Press, 1989), 309–16.

reading of the Gospel as well.[5] If, however, the Gospel is a βίος then together Luke-Acts reflects the tradition of collected biography writing.[6] Smith and Kostoplouos think that such arguments are misguided, however, since they attempt to force both documents into a single genre, wrongly assuming that authorial unity requires literary unity.[7]

Keener's position is interesting in this connection:

> Luke's Gospel is indeed biography, but it is part of a two-volume work (Luke-Acts) that when taken together cannot easily be defined as biography. Although the two volumes may differ somewhat in genre, the narrative unity of the two works would invite any attentive auditors to hear them together. Many scholars suggest that Luke may combine elements of two genres, especially in this case the related genres of history and biography. While taken by itself the Gospel is biography, as part of Luke's two-volume work the Gospel becomes a biographic component in a larger history. Ancient auditors would not find such a combination difficult to comprehend; authors of multivolume histories could devote an entire volume or section to a particularly prominent character. Luke's biography of Jesus is thus inseparable from his larger historical work.[8]

5 E.g. D.E. Aune, *The New Testament in its Literary Environment* (LEC 8; Philadelphia: Westminster Press, 1987), 77; B. Shellard, *New Light on Luke: Its Purpose, Sources, and Literary Context* (JSNTSup 215; London: Sheffield Academic, 2002), 18–23; C.K. Rothschild, *Luke-Acts and the Rhetoric of History: An Investigation of Early Christian Historiography* (WUNT 2.175; Tübingen: Mohr Siebeck, 2004), 16–23.

6 E.g. C.H. Talbert, *Literary Patterns, Theological Themes, and the Genre of Luke-Acts* (Missoula: Scholars Press, 1987); L. Alexander, 'Acts and Ancient Intellectual Biography', in L. Alexander, *Acts in its Ancient Literary Context: A Classicist Looks at the Acts of the Apostles* (ECC; LNTS 289; New York: T&T Clark, 2005; orig. 1993), 43–68; S.E. Porter, 'The Genre of Acts and the Ethics of Discourse', in T.E. Phillips (ed.), *Acts and Ethics* (NTM 9; Sheffield: Sheffield Phoenix Press, 2005), 1–15; S.A. Adams, *The Genre of Acts and Collected Biography* (SNTSMS 156; Cambridge: Cambridge University Press, 2013).

7 D.L. Smith and Z.L. Kostopoulos, 'Biography, History, and the Genre of Luke-Acts', *NTS* 63 (2017): 390–410. Similarly. D.W. Palmer, 'Acts and the Ancient Historical Monograph', in B.W. Winter and A.D. Clarke (eds.), *The Book of Acts in its First Century Setting*. I. *The Book of Acts in its Literary Setting* (Grand Rapids: Eerdmans, 1993), 1–29 (25), claims that some collections in antiquity were understood as a unit, but did not employ the same genre throughout the entire collection, as with Josephus' three major works: *Jewish War*, the *Antiquities*, and *Against Apion*. Those books do not constitute a kind of collection as is proposed in the case of Luke-Acts, however—even if *Antiquities* and *Against Appian* may be related. And as Alexander, 'Preface', 27 points out, 'in these cases the changed subject matter and genre of the new work are indicated clearly in the preface'. This is not the case in Acts. There are no obvious indicators that a shift in genre is occurring.

8 C. Keener, *The Historical Jesus of the Gospels* (Grand Rapids: Eerdmans, 2009), 85–86.

I do not find this solution compelling, and not only because the research developed within this study disconfirms it based solely on observations connected with Luke's Gospel (independent of Acts), but also because we certainly have biographic portions (i.e. microgenres) represented as parts of histories (e.g. Appian's *Bell. Civ.* 2; portions of Xenophon's *Anab.* 1), but this does not mean that those parts of the history are some kind of independent biography when taken on their own—if anyone did in fact take them on their own. Historians may document the life of a person but it is always in the context of how that life relates to surrounding (e.g. political) events. βίοι, by contrast, focus on the acts or deeds of people, not mainly nations/wars and the relation of participants to these wider event frames. However, since Luke does use other Gospels as sources, much biographical material ends up within his Gospel. Furthermore, as a Gospel, Luke was likely read in the context of the other Gospels as something of a biography, when read (as Keener puts it) on its own. It seems plausible that when read with the other Gospels, much of Luke's text functions within a kind of biographical microgenre that allows the document to be read very much like the other Gospels, in a biographical kind of way, but it's original intention was to function along with Acts as a two-volume history, or so the evidence would seem to indicate.

We return to the problem of literary divergence. Smith and Kostoplouos only give up hope for literary unity because their criteria are not able to isolate formal divergences between the Greek history and the βίος. The generic features are too blended and the boundaries too blurred to confine Luke-Acts to a single literary genre, Smith and Kostoplouos claim. But with the appropriate genre agnation scales in place, a historical reading of Luke-Acts does not seem forced at all.

The argument of this study is not dependent upon the unity of Luke-Acts, but this assumption does greatly strengthen its case. It explains, for example, minor anomalies in topicalization and participant structure that surface when either document is considered independently. With its plural participant references and failure to mention Jesus, the preface leaves little doubt that groups/activities not individuals will be in view in the coming narrative. Yet after much of the L material in chapters 1–3, Jesus becomes the central topic/participant for the majority of the remaining discourse. Reading Acts as the sequel volume to Luke makes sense of this tension, widening the participant range so that Jesus becomes one of many individuals discussed in the two-volume project rather than the subject of a βίος. When read together, Luke-Acts exhibits the structure of several histories, where one figure takes center stage early on in the form of a biographical portrait (e.g. Jesus in book 1 of Luke-Acts; Caesar in Appian, *Bel. civ.* 2; Xenophon, *Anab.* 1; Diodorus 16–17) but the historian transitions into a wider event-frame later in the narrative (e.g. book 2 of Luke-Acts; books 2–7 in Xenophon's *Anabasis* and books 3–6 in Appian's *Civil Wars*; Diodorus 18).

Our analysis of literary framing also intersects with discussions of unity, especially in relation to the preface. Even those who doubt unity acknowledge that Acts 1:1 functions as a 'secondary preface' of some kind due to its reference to 'the former treatise'.[9] Although the possibility that Luke is composing an (literarily) independent sequel to some other previous composition cannot be ruled out,[10] this possibility remains difficult to assess since the underlying claim is non-falsifiable. Even if we read Acts on its own and treat its recapitulation as the sequel to a non-extent work, it was shown that the recapitulation in Acts aligns comfortably with both the historical *and* biographical conventions for recapitulation. So, the preface in Acts would not resist historiographic convention, even if considered independently. But when read as the transition from book 1 into book 2 of a two-volume set, the preface works with the recapitulation in Acts to agnate the collection decidedly in the direction of ancient history.

Similar observations apply to the commencement into the narrative body. Nothing about the potential transitions into the narrative body of Acts defy historical literary canons. The failure to use genealogical formulas at these transitions does, however, distinguish it from the collected biographies. Considered independently, Acts agnates toward history (event-oriented) and away from the collected biography (participant-oriented) relative to the commencement. When we add the Third Gospel to the equation, this position is only strengthened. Luke's Gospel includes a clear, event-oriented commencement into the narrative body (the transition is not a point of debate, as in Acts). On a unified reading, this counts as the commencement for the entire work, supplying further evidence for reading Acts, along with Luke, as history.

The other two frames we considered were literary self-identification and the function of the genealogy. Literary self-identification occurs in the prefaces of historical and biographical writings. By the first century, the vast majority of βίοι self-identify with their literary tradition, *when they include a preface*. Histories sometimes identify as ἱστορία in their prefaces but not consistently. Luke's Gospel includes a preface but lacks biographical attestation, as does Acts. Independently considered, both texts agnate toward history with respect

9 Cf. R.I. Pervo, *Acts: A Commentary on the Book of Acts* (Hermeneia. Minneapolis: Fortress, 2009), 33.

10 Cf. Alexander, 'Preface', 27.

to this cline. Obviously, the Gospel is on surer footing here with a full formal preface rather than a recapitulation. It seems odd to leverage too much on the recapitulation as an episode-level preface form since all known instances of these formulas occur in the context of unified multi-volume works. If Luke's recapitulation functions as others we find in the ancient world, then it pushes the reader back to the preface of the entire work, in this case Luke 1:1–4, which again lacks the kind of self-identification we would expect in a biographical preface. Unity may have implications for the function of the genealogy as well. None of the major character introductions in Acts use a genealogy and Jesus' genealogy in the Third Gospel is not used to introduce his character but instead occurs after the birth narrative. Together, these strategies seem to reflect a unified movement away from the Greek collected biographical tradition toward the Greek history.

Two final scales address the rhetorical structure of Luke and Acts: time management and authentication strategy. Time management dealt with a number of features but most significantly for the question of unity, it addresses narrative endings as part of a wider discussion involving differing generic timelines (episodic vs. field time; see Chapter 6). If the preface in Luke has implications for the genre of Acts; the ending of Acts has implications for the genre of Luke. When read with Luke, the open rather than closed ending of Acts strongly implies a episodic time axis for the entire narrative, beginning with the circumstances leading up to Jesus' birth and concluding unresolved with Paul on trial.

The authentication strategies of both Luke and Acts (grounded in source-citation densities) also reflect those of the historians (ranging from 0.08–0.45%). The densities for both documents fall well below (often multiple times) any of the biographical documents considered (ranging from 0.68–10.77%). The Third Gospel's citation densities fall comfortably within the historical range (0.23%) while Acts is high but also in range (0.42%), nearly reviling Herodotus (who marks the top end of the range at 0.45%). However, when considered together, Luke's ratios balance out those in Acts so that Luke-Acts is positioned more comfortably within the historical range, just beyond its midpoint (0.32%).

6 Conclusion

Based upon the SFL genre agnation scales applied in this study, an independent case can be made for either Luke or Acts as a closer proximate to the Greek history than the βίος. These SFL scales also expose a range of further complementary elements when the two volumes are read together. Against the current consensus (at least for Luke's Gospel),[11] we may draw the following conclusion: Luke-Acts reflects the literary tradition of the historians far more frequently than that of the individual or collected biographies of the Greco-Roman world.

11 S. Walton, 'What Are the Gospels? Richard Burridge's Impact on Scholarly Understanding of the Genre of the Gospels', *CBR* 14 (2015): 81–93, argues that this is the case for the Gospels, including Luke, and biographical readings are slowly gaining more momentum in Acts research as well.

Bibliography

Primary Sources and Critical Editions

Appian: The Civil Wars, with an English translation by Horace White. Medford, Mass.: MacMillan, 1899.

Aristotle: Ars rhetorica, with an English translation by J.H. Freese, LCL. London: Heinemann, 1921.

Aristotle: Ars rhetorica, ed. W.D. Ross, OCT. Oxford: Oxford University, 1959.

Arrian: Anabasis, with an English translation by P.A. Brunt, 2 vols., LCL. London: Heinemann, 1983.

Cicero: De inventione, De optimo genere oratum, Topica, with an English translation by H.M. Hubbell, LCL. London: Heinemann, 1949.

Cicero: On the Orator: Books 1–2, with an English translation by E.W. Sutton. Cambridge, Mass.: Harvard University, 1968.

Demetrius, On Style, with an English translation by D. Innes, 2nd ed., LCL. London: Harvard University Press, 1995.

Diodorus Siculus: Bibliotheca historica, with an English translation by C.H. Oldfather, 12 vols., LCL. London: Heinemann, 1933–1967.

Diogenis Laertii: Vitae philosophorum, ed. M. Miroslav, 3 vols., Stuttgart: Teubner, 1999–2003.

Diogenes Laertius: Lives of Eminent Philosophers, with an English translation by R.D. Hicks, 2 vols., LCL. London: Heinemann, 1925.

Dionysius of Halicarnassus: The Three Literary Letters (*Ep. ad Ammaeum I, Ep. ad Pompeium, Ep. ad Ammaeum II*), ed. W. Rhys Roberts. Cambridge: University, 1901.

Herodotus: Historiae, with an English translation by A.D. Godley, 4 vols., LCL. London: Heinemann, 1926.

Homer: Iliad: Greek Text, ed. G.P. Goold. 2 vols. LCL. Cambridge, Mass.: Harvard University, 1924.

Homer: "The Iliad in Greek," with a translation by A.T. Murray. Logos Bible Software, 2008.

Homer: Odyssey, with an English translation by G.E. Dimock and A.T. Murray, 2nd ed., 2 vols. LCL. London: Harvard University, 1995.

Horace: Satires, Epistles, Ars poetica, with an English translation by H.R. Fairclough, LCL. London: Heinemann, 1929.

Horace on Poetry II: The Ars poetica, ed. C.O. Brink. Cambridge: Cambridge University, 1971.

Iamblichus: De vita Pythagorica, ed. M. von Albrecht, Darmstadt: Wissenschaftliche Buchgesellschaft, 2002.

Iamblichus: On the Pythagorean Life, trans. G. Clark, TTH. Liverpool: Liverpool University, 1989.

Isocrates, with an English translation by G. Norlin vols. 1–2, and L. Van Hook vol. 3, LCL. London: Heinemann, 1928, 1945.

Jerome: De viris illustribus, with an Italian translation and commentary, A. Ceresa-Gastaldo, Florence, 1988.

Josephus, with an English translation by H. St J. Thackeray vols. 1–5, R. Marcus vols. 5–8, and L.H. Feldman, 10 vols., LCL. London: Heinemann, 1926–1981.

Flavius Josephus: The Works of Josephus: Complete and Unabridged, translated by William Whiston. Peabody: Hendrickson, 1987.

Longinus: On the Sublime, with an English translation by W.H. Fyfe, revised by D.A. Russell, 2nd ed., LCL. London: Harvard University, 1995.

Lucian, with an English translation by A.M. Harmon, 8 vols., LCL. London: Heinemann, 1913.

Cornelius Nepos, ed. E.O. Winstedt, OCT. Oxford: Oxford University Press, 1904.

Cornelius Nepos, with an English translation by J.C. Rolfe, LCL. London: Heinemann, 1984.

Philo, with an English translation by F.H. Colson, 11 vols., LCL. London: Heinemann, 1950.

Philostratus: Life of Apollonius of Tyana, with an English translation by F.C. Coneybeare, 2 vols., LCL. London: Heinemann, 1917.

Philostratus: Lives of the Sophists, with an English translation by W.C. Wright, 2 vols., LCL. London: Heinemann, 1921.

Philostratus and Eunapius: the lives of the sophists with an English translation by Wilmer Cave Wright, 2 vols., LCL. London: W. Heinemann, 1922.

Plato: Republic, with an English translation by P. Shorey, 2 vols., LCL. London: Heinemann, 1937.

Plutarch: Lives, with an English translation by B. Perrin, 11 vols., LCL. London: Heinemann, 1919.

Polybius: Historiae, with an English translation by W.R. Paton, 6 vols., LCL. London: Heinemann, 1922–1927.

Polybius: The Histories of Polybius, with an English translation by E.S. Shuckburgh, 2 vols. London: Macmillan, 1889.

Porphyry: La vie de Plotin, ed. L. Brisson, M.-O. Goulet-Cazé, R. Goulet, and D. O'Brien, 2 vols., Paris, Vrin, 1982–1992.

Quintilian: Institutio oratoria, with an English translation by H.E. Butler, 4 vols., LCL. London: Heinemann, 1921–1922.

Suetonius, with an English translation by J.C. Rolfe, 2 vols., LCL. London: Heinemann, 1914.

Suetonius Claudius, ed. J. Mottershead, Bristol: Classical Press, 1982. Suetonius: Nero, ed. B.H. Warmington, Bristol: Classical, 1977.

Cornelii Taciti: De vita Agricolae, ed. R.M. Ogilvie and I.A. Richmond, Oxford: Oxford University, 1967.

Aelius Theon: Progymnasmata, trans. G.A. Kennedy, Atlanta: SBL Press, 2003.

Aelius Théon: Progymnasmata, ed. M. Patillon and G. Bolognesi, Budé. Paris: Les Belles Lettres, 1997.

Thucydides: History of the Peloponnesian War, with an English translation by C.F. Smith, 4 vols., LCL. London: Heinemann, 1928–1935.

Thucydides: The Peloponnesian War, with an English translation by J.M. Dent. London: E.P. Dutton, 1910.

Xenophon, with an English translation by E.C. Marchant, 4 vols., LCL. London: Heinemann, 1923.

Xenophon: Cyropaedia, with an English translation by W. Miller, 2 vols., LCL. London: Heinemann, 1943–1947.

Xenophon: Scripta minora, ed. E.C. Marchant, LCL. Cambridge, MA: Harvard University, 1925.

Xenophon: Xenophon in Seven Volumes, with an English translation by Carleton L. Brownson, 7 vols., LCL. London: Heinemann, 1918–1968.

Secondary Sources

Aaron, David H. *Etched in Stone: The Emergence of the Decalogue*. New York: T&T Clark, 2006.

Adams, Edward. *Parallel Lives of Jesus: A Guide to the Four Gospels*. Louisville, Ken.: Westminster John Knox, 2011.

Adams, Sean A. "Luke's Preface and its Relationship to Greek Historiography: A Response to Loveday Alexander." *JGRChJ* 3 (2006): 177–191.

Adams, Sean A. "The Genre of Luke and Acts: The State of the Question." In *Issues in Luke-Acts: Selected Essays*, edited by Sean A. Adams and Michael W. Pahl, 97–120. Piscataway, N.J.: Gorgias, 2012.

Adams, Sean A. "Atticism, Classicism, and Luke-Acts: Discussions with Albert Wifstrand and Loveday Alexander." In *The Language of the New Testament Context, History, and Development*, edited by Stanley E. Porter and Andrew W. Pitts, 91–111. ECHC 3. LBS 6. Leiden: Brill, 2013.

Adams, Sean A. *The Genre of Acts and Collected Biography*. SNTSMS 156. Cambridge: Cambridge University, 2013.

Adams, Sean A. "Luke and the Progymnasmata: Rhetorical Handbooks, Rhetorical Sophistication, and Genre Selection." In *Ancient Education and Early Christianity*, edited by Matthew Ryan Haugen and Andrew W. Pitts, 137–154. LNTS 533. T&T Clark, 2016.

Aijmer, Karin, and Diana Lewis. *Contrastive Analysis of Discourse-Pragmatic Aspects of Linguistic Genres*. Yearbook of Corpus Linguistics and Pragmatics. Cham, Switzerland: Springer, 2017.

Alexander, Philipp. "Retelling the Old Testament." In *It is Written: Scripture Citing Scripture*, edited by D.A. Carson and H.G.M. Williamson, 99–121. Cambridge: Cambridge University, 1988.

Alexandre, Manuel. "Rhetorical Hermeneutics in Philo's Commentary of Scripture." *RRTCA* 1 (2001) 29–41.

Alexander, Loveday. *The Preface to Luke's Gospel*. SNTSMS 79. Cambridge: Cambridge University, 1993.

Alexander, Loveday. "The Preface to Acts and the Historians." In *History, Literature and Society in the Book of Acts*, edited by Ben Witherington, 73–103. Cambridge: Cambridge University, 1996.

Alexander, Loveday. "Acts and Ancient Intellectual Biography." In *Acts in its Ancient Literary Context: A Classicist Looks at the Acts of the Apostles*, by Loveday Alexander, 43–68. ECC. LNTS 289. New York: T&T Clark, 2005 (orig. 1993).

Allison, Dale C. *The New Moses: A Matthean Typology*. Minneapolis: Fortress, 1993.

Alonso-Nuñez, José Miguel. *The Idea of Universal History in Greece: From Herodotus to the Age of Augustus*. Amsterdam: Gieben, 2002.

Andersen, Jack. "The Concept of Genre in Information Studies." *Annual Review of Information Science and Technology* 42 (2008) 339–67.

Anderson, Hugh. "Broadening Horizons: The Rejection of the Nazareth Pericope in Light of Recent Critical Trends." *Interp* 18 (1964) 259–75.

Anderson, Robert John, John A. Hughes, and W.W. Sharrock. *Philosophy and the Human Sciences*. London: Routledge, 1988.

Applegarth, Risa. *Rhetoric in American Anthropology: Gender, Genre, and Science*. Pittsburgh Series in Composition, Literacy, and Culture. Pittsburg, PA: Pittsburg University Press, 2014.

Argyle, A.W. "The Accounts of the Temptations of Jesus in Relation to the Q Hypothesis." *ExpTim* 64 (1952–53) 382.

Artemeva, Natasha, and Aviva Freedman, eds. *Genre Studies Around the Globe: Beyond the Three Traditions*. Bloomington: Trafford Publishing, 2016.

Ash, Rhiannon. "Appian, c. AD 95–160s." In *Encyclopedia of Ancient Greece*, edited by N.G. Wilson, 67–68. New York: Routledge, 2006.

Ashton, John. *The Gospel of John and Christian Origins*. Minneapolis: Fortress, 2014.

Atkinson, Kenneth R. "On the Use of Scripture in the Development of Militant Davidic Messianism at Qumran: New Light from Psalm of Solomon 17." In *The Interpretation of Scripture in Early Judaism and Christianity: Studies in Language and Tradition*, edited by Craig A. Evans, 106–23. JSPSS 33. SSEJC 7. Sheffield: Sheffield Academic, 2000.

Attridge, Harold W. "Historiography." In *Jewish Writings of the Second Temple Period Apocrypha, Pseudepigrapha, Qumran Sectarian Writings, Philo, Josephus*, edited by M.E. Stone, 157–83. Assen: Van Gorcum, 1984.

Auken, Sune. "Utterance and Function in Genre Studies: A Literary Perspective." In *Genre Theory in Information Studies*, edited by Jack Andersen, 155–78. Bingley, UK: Emerald, 2015.

Aune, David E. "The Problem of the Genre of the Gospels: A Critique of C.H. Talbert's What is a Gospel?" In *Gospel Perspectives: Studies of History and Tradition in the Four Gospels*. Vol. 2, edited by R.T. France and David Wenham, 9–60. Sheffield: JSOT, 1981.

Aune, David E. *The New Testament in its Literary Environment*. LEC 8. Philadelphia: Westminster, 1987.

Aune, David E. "Greco-Roman Biography." In *Greco-Roman Literature and the New Testament: Selected Forms and Genres*, edited by David E. Aune, 107–26. Atlanta, Geo.: Scholars, 1988.

Aune, David E. "Luke 1.1–4: Historical or Scientific Prooimon?." In *Paul, Luke and the Graeco-Roman World: Essays in Honour of Alexander J.M. Wedderburn*, edited by Alf Christophersen, et al., 138–48. JSNTSup 217. London: T&T Clark, 2002.

Aune, David E. "Prolegomena to the Study of Oral Tradition in the Hellenistic World." In *Jesus and the Oral Gospel Tradition*, edited by H. Wansbrough, 59–106. JSNTSup 64. London: T&T Clark, 2004.

Bakker, Egbert J. "Verbal Aspect and Mimetic Description in Thucydides." In *Grammar as Interpretation: Greek Literature in Its Linguistic Contexts*, edited by Egbert J. Bakker, 7–54. MBCB 171. Leiden: Brill, 1997.

Bal, Mieke. *Narratology: Introduction to the Theory of Narrative*. Toronto: University of Toronto, 1997.

Balch, David L. "The Genre of Luke-Acts: Individual Biography, Adventure Novel, or Political History?" *SwJT* 33 (1990) 5–19.

Balch, David L. "Comments on the Genre and a Political Theme of Luke-Acts: A Preliminary Comparison of Two Hellenistic Historians." In *SBLSP 1989*, edited by David J. Lull, 343–61. Atlanta: Scholars, 1991.

Balch, David L. "ἀκριβῶς ... γράψαι (Luke 1:3): To Write the Full History of God's Receiving All Nations." In *Jesus and the Heritage of Israel*, edited by David P. Moessner, 229–50. Philadelphia: Trinity, 1999.

Balch, David L. "ΜΕΤΑΒΟΛΗ ΠΟΛΙΤΕΙΩΝ—Jesus as Founder of the Church in Luke-Acts: Form and Function." In *Contextualizing Acts*, edited by Todd Penner and C.V. Stichele, 139–88. Atlanta: Society of Biblical Literature, 2003.

Balch, David L. *Contested Ethnicities and Images Studies in Acts and Arts*. WUNT 345. Tübingen: Mohr Siebeck, 2015.

Balch, David L. *Luke the Historian of Israel's Legacy, Theologian of Israel's 'Christ' A New Reading of the 'Gospel Acts' of Luke*. BZNW 182. Berlin: De Gruyter, 2016.

Bale, Alan J. *Genre and Narrative Coherence in the Acts of the Apostles*. LNTS 514. London: Bloomsbury T&T Clark, 2015.

Baragwanath, Emily, and Mathieu de Bakker. *Herodotus: Oxford Bibliographies*. New York: Oxford University, 2009.

Barber, Godfrey Louis. *The Historian Ephorus*. Cambridge: Cambridge University, 1935.

Barr, David, and Judith Wentling. "The Conventions of Classical Biography and the Genre of Luke-Acts: A Preliminary Study." In *Perspectives on Luke-Acts*, edited by Charles H. Talbert, 63–88. Danville, Vir.: Association of Baptist Professors of Religion, 1978.

Barrett, C.K. "Luke/Acts." In *It Is Written—Scripture Citing Scripture: Essays in Honour of Barnabas Lindars, SSF*, edited by D.A. Carson and H.G.M. Williamson, 231–44. Cambridge: Cambridge University, 1988.

Barrett, C.K. *A Critical and Exegetical Commentary on the Acts of the Apostles. International Critical Commentary*. ICC. 2 vols. Edinburgh: T&T Clark, 2004.

Bateman, John A. *Multimodality and Genre: A Foundation for the Systematic Analysis of Multimodal Documents*. Basingstoke, Eng.: Palgrave Macmillan, 2008.

Batten, L.W. *A Critical and Exegetical Commentary on the Books of Ezra and Nehemiah*. ICC. New York: Scribner, 1913.

Bawarshi, Anis S., and Mary Jo Reiff. *Genre: An Introduction to History, Theory, Research, and Pedagogy*. Reference Guides to Rhetoric and Composition. West Lafayette, Ind.: Parlor Press, 2010.

Beale, G.K., and D.A. Carson, eds. *Commentary on the New Testament Use of the Old Testament*. Grand Rapids: Baker Academic, 2007.

Beck, Hans. "Interne 'synkrisis' bei Plutarch." *Hermes* 130 (2002) 467–489.

Beck, Mark. "Lucian's Life of Demonax: The Socratic Paradigm, Individuality, and Personality." In *Writing Biography in Greece and Rome: Narrative Technique and Fictionalization*, edited by Koen de Temmerman and Kristoffel Demoen, 80–96. Cambridge: Cambridge University, 2016.

Begg, Christopher. "The 'Classical Prophets' in Josephus' *Antiquities*." *LS* 13 (1988) 341–57. Reprinted in *"The Place is too Small for Us": The Israelite Prophets in Recent Scholarship*, edited by R.P. Gordon, 547–62. SBTS 5. Winona Lake, Ind.: Eisenbrauns, 1995.

Begg, Christopher. *Josephus' Story of the Later Monarchy (AJ 9,1–10,185)*. BETL 145. Leuven: Peeters, 2000.

Beran, David. *Early British Romanticism, the Frankfurt School, and French Post-Structuralism: In the Wake of Failed Revolution*. New York: Peter Lang, 2001.

Berger, Klaus. "Hellenistische Gattungen im Neuen Testament." In *ANRW* II.25.2 (1984) 1031–432 and 1831–85.

Berry, Margaret H. *An Introduction to Systemic Linguistics*. 2 vols. New York: St. Martin's Press, 1975.

Betz, Otto. *Offenbarung und Schriftforschung in der Qumransekte*. WUNT 6. Tübingen: Mohr, 1960.

Bhatia, Vijay Kumar. "Genres in Conflict." In *Analysing Professional Genres*, edited by Anna Trosborg, 147–161. PBNS 74. Amsterdam: John Benjamins, 2000.

Bhatia, Vijay Kumar. *Critical Genre Analysis: Investigating Interdiscursive Performance in Professional Practice*. London: Routledge, 2017.

Biber, Douglas. *Variation Across Speech and Writing*. Cambridge: Cambridge University, 1988.

Biber, Douglas. "Representativeness in Corpus Design." *LLC* 8 (1993) 243–57.

Biber, Douglas. *Dimensions of Register Variation: A Cross-Linguistic Comparison*. Cambridge: Cambridge University Press, 1995.

Biber, Douglas, and Susan Conrad. *Register, Genre, and Style*. CTL. Cambridge: Cambridge, 2012.

Binder, Guyora, and Robert Weisberg. *Literary Criticisms of Law*. Princeton, N.J.: Princeton University, 2000.

Bird, Michael F. *1 Esdras: Introduction and Commentary on the Greek Text in Codex Vaticanus*. SPS. Leiden: Brill, 2012.

Black, Stephanie L. *Sentence Conjunction in the Gospel of Matthew: Kai, De, Tote, Gar, Syn and Asyndeton in Narrative Discourse*. JSNTSup 216. Sheffield: Sheffield Academic, 2002.

Blenkinsopp, Joseph. "Prophecy and Priesthood in Josephus." *JJS* 25 (1974) 239–62.

Bloch, Heinrich. *Die Quellen des Flavius Josephus in seiner Archäologie*. Leipzig: B.G. Teubner, 1879.

Blomberg, Craig E. "Matthew." In *Commentary on the New Testament Use of the Old Testament*, edited by G.K. Beale and D.A. Carson, 1–109. Grand Rapids: Baker Academic, 2007.

Bock, Darrell L. *Proclamation From Prophecy and Pattern: Lukan Old Testament Christology*. JSNTSup 12l. Sheffield: Sheffield Academic, 1987.

Bock, Darrell L. *Luke Volume 1: 1:1–9:50*. BECNT. Grand Rapids: Baker Academic, 1994.

Bock, Darrell L. *Luke Volume 2: 9:51–24:53*. BECNT. Grand Rapids: Baker Academic, 1996.

Boedeker, Deborah. "Herodotus's Genre(s)." In *Matrices of Genre: Authors, Canons, and Society*, edited by Mary Depew and Dirk Obbink, 97–114. Cambridge, Mass.: Harvard University, 2000.

Boedeker, Deborah. "Ethical Heritage and Mythical Patterns in Herodotus." In *Brill's Companion to Herodotus*, edited by Egbert Bakker, Irene J.F. de Jong, and Hans van Wees, 97–116. Leiden: Brill, 2012.

Boje, D.M. *Narrative Methods for Organizational and Communication Research*. London: SAGE, 2001.

Bollansée, Jan. "Historians of Agathocles of Samus: Polybius on Writers of Historical Monographs." In *The Shadow of Polybius: Intertextuality as a Research Tool in Greek Historiography: Proceedings of the International Colloquium, Leuven, 21–22 September 2001*, edited by Guido Schepens and Jan Bollansée, 237–53. SH 42. Leuven: Peeters, 2005.

Bolin, Thomas M. *Freedom Beyond Forgiveness: The Book of Jonah Re-examined*. JSOTSup 236. Sheffield: Sheffield Academic, 1997.

Bond, John. *The Gospel According to St. Luke*. London: Macmillan, 1890.

Bonz, Marianne Palmer. *The Past As Legacy: Luke-Acts and Ancient Epic*. Minneapolis: Fortress, 2000.

Borg, Marcus J. *Jesus, a New Vision: Spirit, Culture, and the Life of Discipleship*. San Francisco: HarperSanFrancisco, 1991.

Borgen, Peder. *Philo of Alexandria: An Exegete for His Time*. NovTSup 86. Leiden: Brill, 1997.

Boring, M. Eugene. *The Continuing Voice of Jesus: Christian Prophecy and the Gospel Tradition*. Louisville: Westminster / John Knox Press, 1991.

Bovon, François. "The Interpretation of the Old Testament." In *Luke the Theologian: Thirty-Three Years of Research (1950–1983)*, edited by François Bovon and Ken McKinney, 78–108. Allison Park, Penn.: Pickwick, 1987.

Bovon, François. "The Role of the Scriptures in the Composition of the Gospel Accounts: The Temptations of Jesus (Lk 4.1–13 par.) and the Multiplication of the Loaves (Lk 9.10–17 par.)." In *Luke and Acts*, edited by Gerald O'Collins and Gilberto Marconi, 26–31. New York: Paulist, 1991.

Bovon, François. *Luke 1, 2, 3: A Commentary on the Gospel of Luke 1:1–24:53. Hermeneia*. Minneapolis: Fortress, 2002–2012.

Bovon, François. *Luke the Theologian: Fifty-Five Years of Research (1950–2005)*. Waco, Tex.: Baylor University, 2006.

Bowie, Ewen Lyall. "Apollonius of Tyana: Tradition and Reality." In *ANRW* II.16.2 (1978) 1652–99.

Brawley, Robert L. *Luke-Acts and the Jews: Conflict, Apology, and Conciliation*. SBLMS 33. Atlanta: Scholars, 1987.

Brawley, Robert L. *Text to Text Pours Forth Speech: Voices of Scripture in Luke-Acts*. ISBL. Bloomington, Ind.: Indiana University, 1995.

Brodie, Thomas L. "Greco-Roman Imitation of Texts as a Partial Guide to Luke's Use of Sources." In *Luke-Acts: New Perspectives from the Society of Biblical Literature Seminar*, edited by Charles H. Talbert, 17–46. New York: Crossroad, 1984.

Brodie, Thomas L. "Towards Unraveling Luke's Use of the Old Testament: Luke 7.11–17 as an Imitation of 1 Kings 17.17–24." *NTS* 32 (1986) 247–67.

Brodie, Thomas L. *Luke the Literary Interpreter: Luke-Acts as a Systematic Rewriting and Updating of the Elijah-Elisha Narrative in 1 and 2 Kings*. Rome: Pontifica Studiorum Universitas A.S. Thoma Aq. in Urbe, 1987.

Brodie, Thomas L. "Luke 9.57–62: A Systematic Adaptation of the Divine Challenge to Elijah (1 Kings 19)." In *SBLSP 1989*, edited by David J. Lull, 237–45. Atlanta: Scholars, 1990.

Brodie, Thomas L. "Luke-Acts as an Imitation and Emulation of Elijah-Elisha Narrative." In *New Views on Luke and Acts*, edited by Earl Richard, 78–85. Collegeville, Min.: Michael Glazier, 1990.

Brodie, Thomas L. *The Crucial Bridge: The Elijah-Elisha Narrative as an Interpretive Synthesis of Genesis-Kings and a Literary Model for the Gospels*. Collegeville, Minn.: Liturgical Press, 2000.

Brodie, Thomas L. *The Birthing of the New Testament: The Intertextual Development of the New Testament Writings*. NTM 1. Sheffield: Sheffield Phoenix, 2006.

Brooke, George J. "Isaiah 40:3 and the Wilderness Community." In *New Qumran Texts and Studies: Proceedings of the First Meeting of the International Organization for Qumran Studies, Paris 1992*, edited by George J. Brooke, 117–32. STDJ 15. Leiden: Brill, 1994.

Brooke, George J. "Luke-Acts and the Qumran Scrolls: The Case of MMT." In *Luke's Literary Achievement*, edited by Christopher M. Tuckett, 186–94. JSNTSup 116. Sheffield: Sheffield Academic, 1995.

Brooke, George J. "Rewritten Bible." In *Encyclopedia of the Dead Sea Scrolls*, edited by Lawrence H. Schiffman and James C. VanderKam, 2:777–81. New York: Oxford University, 2000.

Brooke, George J. "The Rewritten Law, Prophets and Psalms: Issues for Understanding the Text of the Bible." In *The Bible as Book: The Hebrew Bible and the Judaean Desert Discoveries*, edited by Edward D. Herbert and Emanuel Tov, 31–40. London: British Library, 2002.

Brown, Gillian, and George Yule. *Discourse Analysis*. CTL. Cambridge: Cambridge University, 1983.

Brown, Raymond E. *The Birth of the Messiah: A Commentary on the Infancy Narratives in the Gospels of Matthew and Luke*. ABRL. New York: Doubleday, 1993.

Bruce, F.F. "Josephus and Daniel." *ASTI* 4 (1965) 148–62. Reprinted in *A Mind for What Matters: Collected Essays of F.F. Bruce*, by F.F. Bruce, 19–31. Grand Rapids: Eerdmans, 1990.

Bruce, F.F. *The Book of the Acts*. NCNT. Grand Rapids, MI: Wm. B. Eerdmans Publishing Co., 1988.

Bucher, Gregory S. "The Origins, Program, and Composition of Appian's Roman History." *TAPA* (2000) 411–458.

Bucher, Gregory S. "Toward a Literary Evaluation of Appian's Civil Wars, Book 1." In *A Companion to Greek and Roman Historiography*, edited by John Marincola, 454–60. Malden, Mass.: Blackwell, 2007.

Buckwalter, Douglas. *The Character and Purpose of Luke's Christology*. SNTSMS 89. Cambridge: Cambridge University, 1996.

Bultmann, Rudolf. *Theology of the New Testament*. New York: Scribner, 1951.

Bultmann, Rudolf. *The History of the Synoptic Tradition*. New York: Harper & Row, 1968.

Burton, Anne. *Diodorus Siculus: Book I: A Commentary*. Études préliminaires aux religions orientales dans l'empire romain 29. Leiden: Brill, 1972.

Burridge, Richard A. *What are the Gospels? A Comparison with Graeco-Roman Biography*. SNTSMS 70. Cambridge: Cambridge University, 1992.

Burridge, Richard A. *What are the Gospels? A Comparison with Graeco-Roman Biography*. 2nd ed. Grand Rapids: Eerdmans, 2004 (org. 1992).

Burridge, Richard A. "Reading the Gospels as Biographies." In *The Limits of Ancient Biography*, edited by Brian C. McGing and Judith Mossman, 31–50. Swansea: Classical Press of Wales, 2006.

Burridge, Richard A. 'The Genre of Acts Revisited'. In *Reading Acts Today: Essays in Honour of Loveday C.A. Alexander*, edited by Steve Walton, 3–28. LNTS 472. London: T&T Clark, 2011.

Burney, C.F. *The Aramaic Origin of the Fourth Gospel*. Oxford: Oxford University, 1922.

Bury, J.B. *The Ancient Greek Historians (Harvard Lectures)*. New York: Macmillan, 1909.

Butler, Christopher S. *Systemic Linguistics: Theory and Applications*. London: Batsford Academic and Educational, 1985.

Byrskog, Samuel. *Story as History—History as Story: The Gospel Tradition in the Context of Ancient Oral History*. WUNT 123. Tübingen: Mohr Siebeck, 2000.

Cadbury, H.J. "Commentary on the Preface of Luke." In *The Beginnings of Christianity*, edited by F.J. Foakes-Jackson and Kirsopp Lake, 1:489–510. 5 vols. London: Macmillan, 1922–1933.

Cadbury, H.J. *The Making of Luke-Acts*. New York: Macmillan, 1927.

Callan, Terrance. "The Preface of Luke-Acts and Historiography." *NTS* 31 (1985) 576–81.

Camiciottoli, Belinda Crawford. *Rhetoric in Financial Discourse: A Linguistic Analysis of ICT-Mediated Disclosure Genres*. Utrecht Studies in Language and Communication 26. Amsterdam: Rodopi, 2013.

Campbell, Constantine R. *Advances in the Study of Greek: New Insights for Reading the New Testament*. Grand Rapids: Zondervan, 2015.

Cancik, Hubert. "The History of Culture, Religion, and Institutions in Ancient Historiography: Philological Observations Concerning Luke's History." *JBL* 116 (1997) 673–94.

Carroll, John T. *Luke: A Commentary*. Louisville, Ken.: Westminster John Knox, 2012.

Cawkwell, G.L. "Epaminondas and Thebes." *CQ* 22 (1972) 254–78.

Cawkwell, G.L. "Agesilaus and Sparta." *CQ* 26 (1976) 62–84.

Cawkwell, G.L. "Introduction." In *Xenophon: "A History of My Times" ("Hellenica")*. Translated by Rex Warner, 7–46. London: Penguin, 1966.

Cawkwell, G.L. "Between Athens, Sparta, and Persia: The Historical Significance of the Libertatin of Thebes in 379." In *On the Daimonion of Socrates: Human Liberation, Divine Guidance and Philosophy*, edited by Heinz-Günther Nesselrath, 101–109. Sapere Bd. 16. Tübingen: Mohr Siebeck, 2010.

Champion, Craige Brian. *Cultural Politics in Polybius's Histories*. HCS 41. Berkeley: University of California, 2004.

Chance, J. Bradley. *Jerusalem, the Temple, and the New Age in Luke-Acts*. Macon, Geo.: Mercer/Peeters, 1988.

Charles, R.H. *The Apocrypha and Pseudepigrapha of the Old Testament in English: With Introductions and Critical and Explanatory Notes to the Several Books*. 2 vols. Oxford: Clarendon Press, 1976 (orig. 1913).

Charles, R.H. *The Book of Jubilees or The Little Genesis*. London: A. and C. Black, 1902.

Charlesworth, James H. "Documents: Expansions of the 'Old Testament' and Legends: Introduction." In *The Old Testament Pseudepigrapha and the New Testament. Vol. 2: Expansions of the "Old Testament" and Legends, Wisdom, and Philosophical Literature, Prayers, Psalms and Odes, Fragments of Lost Judeo-Hellenistic Works*, edited by James H. Charlesworth, 3–7. New Haven: Yale University, 1985.

Chester, Andrew. *Messiah and Exaltation: Jewish Messianic and Visionary Traditions and New Testament Christology*. WUNT 207. Tübingen: Mohr Siebeck, 2007.

Chitwood, Ava. *Death by Philosophy: The Biographical Tradition in the Life and Death of the Archaic Philosophers Empedocles, Heraclitus, and Democritus*. Ann Arbor, Mich.: University of Michigan, 2004.

Cirafesi, Wally V. *Verbal Aspect in Synoptic Parallels: On the Method and Meaning of Divergent Tense-Form Usage in the Synoptic Passion Narratives*. LBS 7. Leiden: Brill, 2013.

Clark, Elizabeth A. *History, Theory, Text: Historians and the Linguistic Turn*. Cambridge, Mass.: Harvard University, 2004.

Clarke, Simon. *The Foundations of Structuralism: A Critique of Lévi-Strauss and the Structuralist Movement*. Totowa, N.J: Barnes & Noble, 1981.

Clayton, Jay, and Eric Rothstein. *Influence and Intertextuality in Literary History*. Madison, Wis.: University of Wisconsin, 1991.

Coggins, R.J., and Michael A. Knibb. *The First and Second Books of Esdras*. CBC. Cambridge: Cambridge University, 1979.

Cohen, S.J.D. "Josephus, Jeremiah and Polybius." *HT* 21 (1982) 366–81.

Cohen, S.J.D. *Josephus in Galilee and Rome: His Vita and Development as a Historian*. Leiden: Brill, 2002.

Cohn-Sherbok, Rabbi D.M. "Jesus' Defense of the Resurrection from the Dead." *JSNT* 11 (1981) 64–73. Rep. in *The Historical Jesus: A Sheffield Reader*, edited by Craig A. Evans and Stanley E. Porter, 157–66. BS 33. Sheffield: Sheffield Academic, 2001.

Coleridge, Mark. *The Birth of the Lukan Narrative: Narrative As Christology in Luke 1–2*. JSNTSup 88. Sheffield: JSOT, 1993.

Collins, Adela Yarbro. *Is Mark's Gospel a Life of Jesus? The Question of Genre*. Père Marquette Lecture in Theology. Milwaukee: Marquette University, 1990.

Collins, Adela Yarbro. "Genre and the Gospels." *JR* 75 (1995) 239–46.

Collins, Adela Yarbro. *Mark: A Commentary on the Gospel of Mark*. Hermeneia. Minneapolis: Fortress, 2007.

Collins, John J. "The Genre of Jubilees." In *A Teacher for All Generations: Essays in Honor of James C. VanderKam*, edited by Eric F. Mason, 737–55. SJSJSup 153. Leiden: Brill, 2011.

Conley, Thomas M. "Ancient Rhetoric and Modern Genre Criticism." *Communication Quarterly* 7 (1979) 47–53.

Conzelmann, Hans. *Die Mitte der Zeit; Studien zur Theologie des Lukas*. BHT 17. Tübingen: Mohr, 1954. ET: *The Theology of St. Luke*. New York: Harper, 1961.

Conzelmann, Hans. *Acts of the Apostles: A Commentary on the Acts of the Apostles*. Hermeneia. Philadelphia: Fortress, 1987.

Coot, Robert B., and Mary P. Coot. "Homer and Scripture in the Gospel of Mark." In *Distant Voices Drawing Near: Essays in Honor of Antoinette Clark Wire*, edited by Marvin L. Chaney and Holly E. Hearon, 189–202. Collegeville, Minn.: Liturgical, 2004.

Corona, Isabel. "The Management of Conflict: Arbitration in Corporate E-releases." In *Interpersonality in Legal Genres*, edited by Ruth Breeze, Maurizio Gotti, and Carmen Sancho Guinda, 355–84. Legal Insights: Studies in Language and Communication. New York: Peter Lang, 2014.

Craddock, Fred B. *Luke*. Interpretation. Louisville: John Knox, 1990.

Crane, G. *Thucydides and the Ancient Simplicity: The Limits of Political Realism*. Berkeley: University of California, 1998.

Crawford, S.W. *Rewriting Scripture in Second Temple Times*. Grand Rapids: Eerdmans, 2008.

Creed, J.M. *The Gospel according to St. Luke*. London: Macmillan, 1930.

Crockett, L.C. "The Old Testament in the Gospel of Luke with Emphasis on the Interpretation of Isaiah 61, 1–2." Unpublished Ph.D. diss.: Brown University, 1966.

Cross, Frank Moore. "A Reconstruction of the Judean Restoration." *JBL* 94 (1975) 4–18.

Crowston, Kevin, Barbara Kwaśinik, and Joseph Rubleske. In "Problems in the Use-Centered Development of a Taxonomy of Web Genres." In *Genres on the Web: Computational Models and Empirical Studies*, edited by Alexander Mehler, Serge Sharoff, and Marina Santini, 69–84. TSLT 42. Dordrecht: Springer, 2010.

Culler, Jonathan D. *Structuralist Poetics: Structuralism, Linguistics and the Study of Literature*. London: Routledge, 1975 (rep. 2008).

Culler, Jonathan D. *On Deconstruction: Theory and Criticism After Structuralism*. Ithaca, NY: Cornell University, 1982 (rep. 2014).

Culler, Jonathan D. *The Pursuit of Signs: Semiotics, Literature, Deconstruction*. London: Routledge, 2002 (rep. 2011).

Culler, Jonathan D. *Structuralism: Critical Concepts in Literary and Cultural Studies*. Critical Concepts in Literary and Cultural Studies. London: Routledge, 2006.

Culler, Jonathan D. *Literary Theory: A Very Short Introduction*. Oxford: Oxford University, 2011.

Daly-Denton, Margret. *David in the Fourth Gospel: The Johannine Reception of the Psalms*. AGAJU 47. Leiden: Brill, 2000.

Daly-Denton, Margret. "Review of The Birthing of the New Testament." *RBL* 8 (2006).

Dahl, Nils. "The Story of Abraham in Luke-Acts." In *Studies in Luke-Acts; Essays Presented in Honor of Paul Schubert*, edited by Leander E. Keck and J. Louis Martyn, 139–58. Nashville: Abingdon, 1966.

Damgaard, Finn. "Philo's Life of Moses as Rewritten Bible." In *Rewritten Bible After Fifty Years: A Last Dialogue with Geza Vermes*. JSJSup 166. Edited by József Zsengellér, 233–48. Leiden: Brill, 2014.

Danker, Frederick W. *Jesus and the New Age: A Commentary on St. Luke's Gospel*. Philadelphia: Fortress, 1988.

Danove, Paul L. *Grammatical and Exegetical Study of New Testament Verbs of Transference: A Case Frame Guide to Interpretation and Translation*. LNTS 329. SNTG 13. London: T&T Clark, 2009.

Danove, Paul L. "A Comparison of ΔΙΔΩΜΙ and ΔΙΔΩΜΙ Compounds in the Septuagint and in the New Testament." In *The Language of the New Testament: Context, History and Development*, edited by Stanley E. Porter and Andrew W. Pitts, 365–99. ECHC 3. LBS 6. Leiden: Brill, 2013.

Darr, John A. *Herod the Fox: Audience Criticism and Lukan Characterization*. JSNTSup 163. Sheffield: Sheffield Academic, 1998.

Daube, David. "Typology in Josephus." *JJS* 31 (1980) 18–36.

Davidson, Scott, and Marc-Antoine Vallée. *Hermeneutics and Phenomenology in Paul Ricoeur: Between Text and Phenomenon*. Switzerland: Springer, 2016.

Davis, C.J. *The Name and Way of the Lord: Old Testament Themes, New Testament Christology*. JSNTSup 129. Sheffield: Sheffield Academic, 1996.

DeJong, I.J.F. "Homer and Herodotus." In *A New Companion to Homer*, edited by Ian Morris and Barry B. Powell, 305–25. MBCB 163. Leiden: Brill, 1997.

Denova, Rebecca I. *The Things Accomplished among us Prophetic Tradition in the Structural Pattern of Luke-Acts*. JSNTSup 141. Sheffield: Sheffield Academic, 1997.

Depew, Mary, and Dirk Obbink, eds. *Matrices of Genre: Authors, Canons, and Society*. Cambridge, Mass.: Harvard University, 2000.

Destinon, Justus. *Die Quellen des Flavius Josephus 1, Die Quellen des Flavius Josephus in der Jüd. Arch. Buch XII–XVII = Jüd. Krieg Buch I.* Kiel: Lipsius & Tischer, 1882.

Devitt, Amy J. *Writing Genres.* Rhetorical Philosophy and Theory. Carbondale, Ill.: Southern Illinois University, 2004.

Devitt, Amy J. "Re-fusing Form in Genre Study." In *Genres in the Internet: Issues in the Theory of Genre,* edited by Janet Giltrow and Dieter Stein, 27–47. Amsterdam: John Benjamins, 2009.

De Wette, W.M.L. *Kurze Erklärung der Evangelien des Lukas und Markus.* 3rd ed. KEHNT 1/2. Leipzig: Weidmann, 1846.

Dibelius, Martin. *From Tradition to Gospel.* Translated by B.E. Woolf. New York: Scribner, 1965 (orig. 1919).

Dihle, Albrecht. *Studien zur Griechischen Biographie.* Abhandlungen der Akademie der Wissenschaften in Göttingen. Philologische-Historische Klasse 37. Göttingen: Vandenhoeck & Ruprecht, 1970.

Dihle, Albrecht. "Die Evangelien und die biographischen Traditionen der Antike." *ZTK* 80 (1983) 33–49.

Dihle, Albrecht. "The Gospels and Greek Biography." In *The Gospel and the Gospels,* edited by Peter Stuhlmacher, 361–86. Grand Rapids: Eerdmans, 1991.

van Dijk, Teun A. *Discourse and Literature: New Approaches to the Analysis of Literary Genres.* Critical Theory 3. Amsterdam: John Benjamins, 1989.

Dillery, John. "Greek Sacred History." *AJP* 126 (2005) 505–26.

Dillery, John. *Xenophon and the History of His Times.* London: Routledge, 2012.

Dimant, Devorah. "Use and Interpretation of Mikra in the Apocrypha and Pseudepigrapha." In *Mikra: Text, Translation, Reading and Interpretation of the Hebrew Bible in Ancient Judaism and Early Christianity,* edited by M.J. Mulder, 379–19. CRINT: Section 2: The Literature of the Jewish People in the Period of the Second Temple and the Talmud. Minneapolis: Fortress, 1990.

Doble, Peter. "The Psalms in Luke-Acts." In *The Psalms in the New Testament,* edited by Steve Moyise and M.J.J. Menken, 83–117. NTSI. London: T&T Clark, 2004.

Dodd, C.H. *According to the Scriptures: The Sub-Structure of New Testament Theology.* London: Nisbet, 1952.

Dodd, C.H. *The Apostolic Preaching and its Developments.* New York: Harper & Row, 1964.

Dosse, François, and Deborah Glassman. *History of Structuralism.* Minneapolis, Minn.: University of Minnesota, 1998.

Dowd, Sharyn. "Review of Homeric Epics." *CBQ* 63 (2001) 155–56.

Dubrow, Heather. *Genre.* London: Routledge, 2014 (orig. 1982).

Duff, David. "Introduction." In *Modern Genre Theory,* edited by David Duff, 1–24. Edinburgh: Longman, 2000.

Duff, Tim. *Plutarch's Lives: Exploring Virtue and Vice.* Oxford: Oxford University, 2005.

Dupont, J. "L'arrière-fond biblique du récit des tentations de Jesus." *NTS* 3 (1956–57) 287–88.

Dupont, J. *Les tentations de Jésus au desert*. StudNeot 4. Paris: Desclée de Brouwer, 1968.

Earl, Donald. "Prologue-Form in Ancient Historiography." In *ANRW* I.2 (1972) 842–56.

Earle, B. "Plato, Aristotle, and the Imitation of Reason." *PL* 27 (2003) 382–401.

Eckman, Fred R., et al., eds. *Markedness*. New York: Plenum, 1986.

Edwards, M.J. "Biography and Biographic." In *Portraits: Biographical Representation in the Greek and Latin Literature of the Roman Empire*, edited by M.J. Edwards and Simon Swain, 228–34. Oxford: Clarendon, 1997.

Eggins, Suzanne. *An Introduction to Systemic Functional Linguistics*. New York: Continuum, 2004.

Eggins, Suzanne, and J.R. Martin. "Genres and Registers in Discourse." In *Discourse As Structure and Process*, edited by Teun A. van Dijk, 230–256. London: SAGE, 1998.

Ego, Beate. "The Repentance of Nineveh in the Story of Jonah and Nahum's Prophecy of the City's Destruction—A Coherent Reading of the Book of the Twelve as Reflected in the Aggada." In *Thematic Threads in the Book of the Twelve*, edited by P.L. Redditt and A. Schart, 155–64. BZAW 325. Berlin: Walter de Gruyter, 2003.

Eissfeld, O. *The Old Testament, An Introduction*. Oxford: Blackwell, 1966.

Ejxenbaum, B.M. 'Literary Environment'. In L. Matejka and K. Pomorska (eds.), *Readings in Russian Poetics: Formalist and Structuralist Views*. Cambridge, MA: MIT Press, 1971. 56–65.

Ellis, E.E. *The Old Testament in Early Christianity: Canon and Interpretation in the Light of Modern Research*. WUNT 54. Tübingen: Mohr Siebeck, 1991.

Ellis, E.E. *The Gospel of Luke*. Grand Rapids: Eerdmans, 1987.

Engels, John. "Geography and History." *A Companion to Greek and Roman Historiography*, edited by John Marincola, 541–52. BCAW. Malden, Mass.: Blackwell, 2007.

Erlich, Victor. *Russian Formalism: History, Doctrine*. The Hague: Mouton, 1965.

Eskenazi, Tamara Cohn. "The Chronicler and the Composition of 1 Esdras." *CBQ* 48 (1986) 39–61.

Eskenazi, Tamara Cohn. *In an Age of Prose: A Literary Approach to Ezra-Nehemiah*. SBLMS 36. Atlanta: Scholars, 1988.

Eskola, Timo. *Messiah and the Throne: Jewish Merkabah Mysticism and Early Christian Exaltation Discourse*. WUNT 2.142. Tübingen: Mohr Siebeck, 2001.

Espelosín, Francisco Javier Gómez. "'Appian's Iberiké'. Aims and Attitudes of a Greek Historian." *ANRW* II.34.1 (1993) 403–27.

Evans, Craig A. *Luke*. UBCS. Grand Rapids: Baker, 1990.

Evans, Craig A. "Luke and the Rewritten Bible: Aspects of Lukan Hagiography." In *The Pseudepigrapha and Early Biblical Interpretation*, edited by James H. Charlesworth and Craig A. Evans, 170–201. JSPSup 14. SSEJC 2. Sheffield: Sheffield Academic, 1993.

Evans, Craig A. "Prophecy and Polemic: Jews in Luke's Scriptural Apologetic." In *Luke and Scripture: The Function of Sacred Tradition in Luke-Acts*, by Craig A. Evans and James A. Sanders, 171–211. Philadelphia: Fortress, 1993.

Evans, Craig A. "The Prophetic Setting of the Pentecost Sermon." In *Luke and Scripture: The Function of Sacred Tradition in Luke-Acts*, by Craig A. Evans and James A. Sanders, 212–24. Philadelphia: Fortress, 1993.

Evans, Craig A. *Mark 8:27–16:20*. WBC 34B. Dallas: Word, 2001.

Evans, C.F. *Saint Luke*. London: SCM Press, 1990.

Eve, Eric. *The Jewish Context of Jesus' Miracles*. JSNTSup 231. Sheffield: Sheffield Academic, 2002.

Falk, Daniel K. *The Parabiblical Texts Strategies for Extending the Scriptures in the Dead Sea Scrolls*. London: T&T Clark, 2007.

Fang, Chengyu, and Jing Cao. *Text Genres and Registers: The Computation of Linguistic Features*. Berlin: Springer, 2015.

Farrar, F.W. *The Gospel According to St Luke, with Maps, Notes and Introduction*. CBSC. Cambridge: Cambridge University, 1891.

Farrar, F.W. *The Gospel According to St Luke*. CGTSC. Cambridge: Cambridge University, 1893.

Farrington, Scott T. "Action and Reason: Polybius and the Gap between Encomium and History." *CP* 106 (2011) 324–42.

Farris, Stephen. *The Hymns of Luke's Infancy Narratives: Their Origin, Meaning and Significance*. JSNTSup 9. Sheffield: JSOT, 1985.

Fawcett, R.P. "The English Personal Pronouns: An Exercise in Linguistic Theory." In *Linguistics in a Systemic Perspective*, edited by J.D. Benson, M.J. Cummings and W.S. Greaves, 185–220. CILT 39. Amsterdam: John Benjamins, 1988.

Fehling, Detlev. *Herodotus and His "Sources": Citation, Invention and Narrative Art*. Translated by J.G. Howie. ARCA 21. Wiltshire: Francis Cairns, 1989.

Feldman, L.H. "Hellenizations in Josephus' Version of Esther." *TAPA* 101 (1970) 143–70.

Feldman, L.H. "Josephus' Interpretation of Jonah." *AJSR* 17 (1992) 1–29.

Feldman, L.H. "Josephus' Portrait of Isaiah." In *Writing and Reading the Scroll of Isaiah: Studies of an Interpretive Tradition*, edited by Craig C. Broyles and Craig A. Evans, 583–608. Leiden: Brill, 1997.

Feldman, L.H. *Josephus's Interpretation of the Bible*. HCS 27. Berkeley: University of California, 1998.

Feldman, L.H. *Studies in Josephus' Rewritten Bible*. JSJSup 58. Leiden: Brill, 1998.

Feldman, L.H. "Restoration in Josephus." In *Restoration: Old Testament, Jewish and Christian Perspectives*, edited by J.M. Scott, 223–61. JSJSup 72. Leiden: Brill, 2001.

Feldman, L.H. "Prophets and Prophecy in Josephus." In *Prophets, Prophecy, and Prophetic Texts in Second Temple Judaism*, edited by Michael H. Floyd and Robert D. Haak, 210–39. LHBS 427. New York: T&T Clark, 2006.

Feldman, L.H. *Christianity and Judaism in Antiquity: Philo's Portrayal of Moses in the Context of Ancient Judaism*. Notre Dame: University of Notre Dame, 2008.

Ferrario, Sarah Brown. *Historical Agency and the 'Great man' in Classical Greece*. Cambridge: Cambridge University, 2014.

Finley, M.I. *The Greek Historians: The Essence of Herodotus, Thucydides, Xenophon, Polybius*. Harmondsworth, Eng.: Penguin, 1977.

Finley, M.I. *Ancient History: Evidence and Models*. New York: Viking, 1986.

Fisk, Bruce Norman. "Rewritten Bible in Pseudepigrapha and Qumran." In *Dictionary of New Testament Background*, edited by Craig A. Evans and Stanley E. Porter, 947–53. Downers Grove, Ill.: InterVarsity, 2000.

Fisk, Bruce Norman. *Do You Not Remember? Scripture, Story and Exegesis in the Rewritten Bible of Pseudo-Philo*. JSPSup 37. Sheffield: Sheffield Academic, 2001.

Fitzmyer, Joseph A. *The Gospel according to Luke*. AB 28. Garden City: Doubleday, 1981.

Fitzmyer, Joseph A. "The Use of the Old Testament in Luke-Acts." In *To Advance the Gospel: New Testament Studies*, by Joseph A. Fitzmyer, 295–313. 2nd ed. Grand Rapids: Eerdmans, 1995.

Fitzmyer, Joseph A. *The Acts of the Apostles: A New Translation with Introduction and Commentary*. AB 31. New Haven; London: Yale University Press, 2008 [1998].

Fleischman, Suzanne. *Tense and Narrativity: From Medieval Performance to Modern Fiction*. London: Routledge, 1992.

Fludernik, Monika. *Towards a 'Natural' Narratology*. London: Routledge, 1996.

Fornara, Charles W. *The Nature of History in Ancient Greece and Rome*. Berkeley: University of California Press, 1983.

Fowler, Alastair. *Kinds of Literature: An Introduction to the Theory of Genres and Modes*. Cambridge: Harvard University, 1982.

Fowler, Alastair. "Genre." In *Encyclopedia of Literature and Criticism*, edited by Martin Coyle, Peter Garside, M.M. Kelsall, and John Peck, 151–63. Routledge Companion Encyclopedias. New York: Routledge, 1993.

Fowler, Robert L. "Herodotus and his Contemporaries." *JHS* 116 (1996) 62–87.

Fowler, Robert L. *Early Greek Mythography*. 2 vols. Oxford: Oxford University Press, 2000–2013.

France, R.T. *Jesus and the Old Testament: His Application of Old Testament Passages to Himself and His Mission*. Downers Grove, Ill.: InterVarsity, 1971.

Franklin, Eric. *Christ the Lord: A Study in the Purpose and Theology of Luke-Acts*. Philadelphia: Westminster, 1975.

Franxman, Thomas W. *Genesis and the "Jewish Antiquities" of Flavius Josephus*. BO 35. Rome: Biblical Institute, 1979.

Freedman, Aviva and Peter Medway. "Locating Genre Studies: Antecedents and Prospects." In *Genre in The New Rhetoric*, edited by Aviva Freedman and Peter Medway, 2–18. London: Taylor & Francis, 1994.

Frein, Brigid Curtin. "Genre and Point of View in Luke's Gospel." *BTB* 38 (2008) 4–13.

Fröhlich, Ida. *Time and Times and Half a Time: Historical Consciousness in the Jewish Literature of the Persian and Hellenistic Eras*. JSPSup 19. Sheffield: Sheffield Academic, 1996.

Frow, John. *Genre*. New Critical Idiom. London: Routledge, 2015.

Fuller, Michael F. *The Restoration of Israel: Israel's Re-gathering and the Fate of the Nations in Early Jewish Literature and Luke-Acts*. BZNW 138. Berlin: De Gruyter, 2006.

Gabba, Emilio. *Appiano e la storia delle guerre civili*. Florence: La Nuova Italia, 1956.

Gair, J.W. "Kinds of Markedness." In *Linguistic Theory and Second Language Acquisition*, edited by Suzanne Flynn and Wayne A. O'Neil, 225–50. STP. Dordrecht: Kluwer, 1988.

Gallagher, David. *Metamorphosis: Transformations of the Body and the Influence of Ovid's Metamorphoses on Germanic Literature of the Nineteenth and Twentieth Centuries*. Amsterdam: Rodopi, 2009.

Gardner, Anne E. "The Purpose and Date of 1 Esdras." *JJS* 37 (1986) 18–27.

Garland, David E. *Luke*. ZECNT 3. Grand Rapids, Mich.: Zondervan, 2011.

Geiger, Joseph. *Cornelius Nepos and Ancient Political Biography*. Stuttgart: Franz Steiner, 1985.

Gentili, Bruno, and Giovanni Cerri. *History and Biography in Ancient Thought*. Amsterdam: J.C. Gieben, 1988.

George, Augustine. *Etudes sur l'œuvre de Luc*. SB. Paris: Gabalda, 1978.

Gera, Deborah Levine. *Xenophon's "Cyropaedia": Style, Genre and Literary Technique*. OCM. Oxford: Clarendon, 1993.

Ghadessy, Mohsen, ed. *Text and Context in Functional Linguistics*. Amsterdam: John Benjamins, 1998.

Gibson, Jeffrey B. *The Temptations of Jesus in Early Christianity*. JSNTSup 112. London: T&T Clark, 2004.

Gilbert, Gary. "The List of Nations in Acts 2: Roman Propaganda and the Lukan Response." *JBL* 121 (2002) 497–529.

Gildersleeve, Basil L. *Syntax of Classical Greek from Homer to Demosthenes*. Medford, Mass.: American Book Company, 1900.

Gill, Christopher. "The Question of Character-Development: Plutarch and Tacitus." *CQ* 33 (1983) 476–87.

Giltrow, Janet. "Genre as Difference: The Sociality of Linguistic Variation." In *Syntactic Variation and Genre*, edited by Heidrun Dorgeloh and Anja Wanner, 29–51. Topics in English Linguistics 70. Berlin: De Gruyter Mouton, 2010.

Ginsberg, H.L. "Review of Joseph A. Fitzmyer, The Genesis Apocryphon of Qumran Cave I: A Commentary (Rome: Pontifical Biblical Institute, 1966)." *TS* 28 (1967) 574–77.

Givón, Talmy. "Topic, Pronoun, and Grammatical Agreement." In *Subject and Topic*, edited by Charles N. Li, 149–88. New York: Academic Press, 1976.

Givón, Talmy. *Functionalism and Grammar*. Amsterdam: J. Benjamins, 1995.

Gnuse, Robert Karl. *Dreams and Dream Reports in the Writings of Josephus: A Traditio-Historical Analysis*. AGAJU 36. Leiden: Brill, 1996.

Godet, Frédéric Louis. *A Commentary on the Gospel of St. Luke*. 2 vols. Translated by Edward William Shalders and M.D. Cusin. New York: I.K. Funk, 1881.

Golden, Leon. *Aristotle on Tragic and Comic Mimesis*. Oxford: Oxford University, 1992.

Goldstein, J.A. "How the Authors of 1 and 2 Maccabees Treated the 'Messianic Prophecies.'" In *Judaisms and Their Messiahs at the Turn of the Christian Era*, edited by Jacob Neusner, et al., 69–96. Cambridge: Cambridge University, 1987.

Goldstein, J.A. *II Maccabees*. AB 41A. Garden City: Doubleday, 1983.

Gordley, Matthew E. *Teaching Through Song in Antiquity: Didactic Hymnody Among Greeks, Romans, Jews, and Christians*. WUNT 2.302. Tübingen: Mohr Siebeck, 2011.

Goud, Thomas E. "The Sources of Josephus 'Antiquities' 19." *Historia* 45 (1996) 472–82.

Goulder, Michael D. *Luke: A New Paradigm*. JSNTSup 20. Sheffield: JSOT Press, 1989.

Goulet, Richard. *La philosophie de Moïse: essai de reconstitution d'un commentaire philosophique préphilonien du Pentateuque*. HDAC 11. Paris: J. Vrin, 1987.

Guelich, Robert. "The Gospel Genre." In *The Gospel and the Gospels*, edited by Peter Stuhlmacher, 173–208. Grand Rapids: Eerdmans, 1991.

Gutbrod, Walter. "νόμος." *TDNT* 4:1022–91.

Gray, Rebecca. *Prophetic Figures in Late Second Temple Jewish Palestine: The Evidence from Josephus*. Oxford: Oxford University, 1993.

Gray, Vivienne. "Mimesis in Greek Historical Theory." *AJP* 8 (1987) 467–86.

Gray, Vivienne. *The Character of Xenophon's Hellenica*. Baltimore: Johns Hopkins University, 1989.

Gray, Vivienne. "Interventions and Citations in Xenophon's Hellenica and Anabasis." *CQ* 53 (2003) 111–23.

Grabbe, Lester L. "Jewish Historiography and Scripture in the Hellenistic Period." In *Did Moses Speak Attic? Jewish Historiography and Scripture in the Hellenistic Period*, edited by Lester L. Grabbe, 130–55. JSOTSup 317. ESHM 3. Sheffield: Sheffield Academic, 2001.

Green, Joel B. *The Gospel of Luke*. NICNT. Grand Rapids: Eerdmans, 1997.

Greenberg, Joseph H. *Language Universals, with Special Reference to Feature Hierarchies*. The Hague: Mouton, 1966.

Greimas, Algirdas Julien, and J. Courtès. *Semiotics and Language: An Analytical Dictionary*. Translated by Larry Christ. Advances in Semiotics. Bloomington, Ind.: Indiana University, 1982.

Greimas, Algirdas Julien, and J. Courtès. *Structural Semantics: An Attempt at a Method*. Lincoln: University of Nebraska Press, 1984.

Grethlein, Jonas. *The Greeks and Their Past: Poetry, Oratory and History in the Fifth Century BCE*. Cambridge: Cambridge University, 2010.

Grethlein, Jonas. *Experience and Teleology in Ancient Historiography Futures Past from Herodotus to Augustine*. Cambridge: Cambridge University, 2016.

Gribble, David. "Narrator Interventions in Thucydides." *JHS* (1998) 41–67.

Grieve, Jack, Douglas Biber, Eric Friginal, and Tatiana Nekrasova. "Variation Among Blogs: A Multi-Dimensional Analysis." In *Genres on the Web: Computational Models and Empirical Studies*, edited by Alexander Mehler, Serge Sharoff, and Marina Santini, 303–322. Text, Speech, and Language Technology 42. Dordrecht: Springer, 2010.

Griffin, Miriam T. *A Companion to Julius Caesar*. Chichester: Wiley-Blackwell, 2009.

Grimes, Joseph E. *The Thread of Discourse*. JLSM 207. The Hague: Mouton, 1975.

Grundmann, Walter. *Das Evangelium nach Lukas*. Berlin: Evangelische Verlagsanstalt, 1966.

Hägg, Tomas. *The Art of Biography in Antiquity*. Cambridge: Cambridge University, 2012.

Hägg, Tomas, Philip Rousseau, and Christian Høgel, eds. *Greek Biography and Panegyric in Late Antiquity*. Berkeley: University of California, 2000.

Haenchen, Ernst. *The Acts of the Apostles: A Commentary*. Oxford: Basil Blackwell, 1982.

Haenchen, Ernst. *John 1: A Commentary on the Gospel of John, Chapters 1–6*. Philadelphia: Fortress, 1984.

Halliday, M.A.K. "Linguistic Function and Literary Style: An Inquiry into the Language of William Golding's *The Inheritors*." In *Literary Style: A Symposium*, edited by Seymour Chatman, 330–65. London: Oxford University, 1971.

Halliday, M.A.K. *Explorations in the Function of Language*. New York: Edward Arnold, 1973.

Halliday, M.A.K. *System and Function in Language: Selected Papers*. London: Oxford University, 1976.

Halliday, M.A.K. *Language as Social Semiotic: The Social Interpretation of Language and Meaning*. Baltimore: University Park, 1978.

Halliday, M.A.K. *An Introduction to Functional Grammar*. London: Edward Arnold, 1985.

Halliday, M.A.K. "Context of Situation." In *Language, Context, and Text: Aspects of Language in a Social-Semiotic Perspective*, by M.A.K. Halliday and Ruqaiya Hasan, 3–14. Oxford: Oxford University, 1989.

Halliday, M.A.K. "Functions of Language." In *Language, Context, and Text: Aspects of Language in a Social-Semiotic Perspective*, by M.A.K. Halliday and Ruqaiya Hasan, 15–28. Oxford: Oxford University, 1989.

Halliday, M.A.K. *Bloomsbury Companion to M. A. K. Halliday*, edited by Jonathan Webster. New York: Continuum, 2015.

Halliday, M.A.K., and Ruqaiya Hasan. *Cohesion in English*. London: Longman, 1976.

Halliday, M.A.K., and Ruqaiya Hasan. *Language, Context, and Text: Aspects of Language in a Social-Semiotic Perspective*. Oxford: Oxford University Press, 1989.

Halliday, M.A.K., and J.R. Martin, eds. *Readings in Systemic Linguistics*. London: Batsford, 1981.

Halliday, M.A.K., and Christian M.I.M. Matthiessen. *Construing Experience Through Meaning a Language-Based Approach to Cognition*. London: Continuum, 2006.

Halliday, M.A.K., and Jonathan Webster, eds. *Continuum Companion to Systemic Functional Linguistics*. London: Continuum, 2009.

Hamerton-Kelly, R.G. "Sources and Traditions in Philo Judaeus: Prolegomena to an Analysis of his Writings." *SPhilo* 1 (1972) 3–21.

Hammond, N.G.L. *Sources for Alexander the Great: An Analysis of Plutarch's 'life' and Arrian's Anabasis*. Cambridge: Cambridge University, 2007.

Hanson, Anthony Tyrrell. *The Prophetic Gospel: A Study of John and the Old Testament*. Edinburgh: T&T Clark, 1991.

Hardison, O.B. "Epigone: An Aristotelian Imitation." In *Aristotle's Poetics*, edited by Leon Golden and O.B. Hardison, 281–296. Englewood Cliffs: Prentice Hall, 1968.

Harrington, Daniel J. "Palestinian Adaptations of Biblical Narrative and Prophecies: Part I, Rewritten Bible (Narrative)." In *Early Judaism and its Modern Interpreters*, edited by Roger A. Kraft and George E.W. Nickelsburg, 239–46. Atlanta: Scholars, 1986.

Harington, Daniel J., and M.P. Horgan. "Palestinian Adaptations of Biblical Narratives and Prophecies." In *Early Judaism and its Modern Interpreters*, edited by Roger A. Kraft and George W.E. Nickelsburg, 239–58. BMI. Atlanta: Scholars, 1986.

Havránek, Bohuslav. "The Functional Differentiation of the Standard Language." In *A Prague School Reader on Esthetics, Literary Structure, and Style*, edited by Paul L. Garvin, 3–16. Washington, DC: Georgetown University, 1964.

Hay, David M. *Glory at the Right Hand: Psalm 110 in Early Christianity*. Nashville: Abingdon, 1973.

Hawkes, Terence. *Structuralism & Semiotics*. London: Methuen, 1977.

Heath, Malcolm. "Dionysius of Halicarnassus 'On Imitation.'" *Hermes* 117 (1989) 370–73.

Hedrick, Charles W. "The Meaning of Material Culture: Herodotus, Thucydides and their Sources." In *Nomodeiktes: Greek Studies in Honor of Martin Ostwald*, edited by Ralph Mark Rosen and Joseph Farrell, 17–37. Ann Arbor: University of Michigan, 1993.

Hemer, Collin J. *The Book of Acts in the Setting of Hellenistic History*, edited by C.H. Gempf. WUNT 49. Tübingen: Mohr Siebeck, 1989.

Hengel, Martin. *Acts and the History of Earliest Christianity*. Philadelphia: Fortress Press, 1980.

Hengel, Martin. *The Charismatic Leader and His Followers*. New York: Crossroad, 1981.

Hengel, Martin. "Literary, Theological, and Historical Problems in the Gospel of Mark." In *The Gospel and the Gospels*, edited by Peter Stuhlmacher, 209–51. Grand Rapids: Eerdmans, 1991.

Hengel, Martin. *Studies in Early Christology*. Edinburgh: T&T Clark, 1995.
Hendrickx, Herman. *The Infancy Narratives*. London: Chapman, 1984.
Heyvaert, Liesbet. *A Cognitive Functional Approach to Nominalization in English*. Cognitive Linguistics Research 26. Berlin: Mouton de Gruyter, 2003.
Hirsch, E.D. *Validity in Interpretation*. New Haven: Yale University, 1967.
Hock, Ronald F. "Review of *Homeric Epic and the Gospel of Mark*." *BIAC* 27 (2000) 12–15.
Holladay, Carl R. *Theios Aner in Hellenistic Judaism: A Critique of the Use of This Category in New Testament Christology*. SBLDS 40. Missoula: Scholars Press, 1977.
Hölscher, Gustav. "Josephus." *PWRE* 18 (1916) cols. 1966, 1981–1983, 1992–1993.
Holtz, Traugott. *Untersuchungen über die alttestamentlichen Zitate bei Lukas*. TUGAL 104. Berlin: Akademie-Verlag, 1968.
Hooker, Morna. "Review of *Homeric Epics*." *JTS* (2002) 196–98.
Hornblower, Simon. *A Commentary on Thucydides*. Oxford: Clarendon, 1991.
Hornblower, Simon. "Introduction." In *Greek Historiography*, edited by S. Hornblower, 1–54. Oxford: Clarendon, 1993.
Hornblower, Simon. "Narratology and Narrative Techniques in Thucydides." In *Greek Historiography*, edited by Simon Hornblower, 131–66. Oxford: Clarendon, 1993.
Howorth, H. "Some Unconventional Views on the Text of the Bible. I: The Apocryphal Book of Esdras A and the Septuagint." *Proceedings of the Society of Biblical Archaeology* 23 (1901) 147–59.
Howorth, H. "Some Unconventional Views on the Text of the Bible. II: The Chronology and Order of Events in Esdras A, Compared with and Preferred to those in the Canonical Ezra." *Proceedings of the Society of Biblical Archaeology* 24 (1902) 147–72.
Huber, Ludwig. "Herodots Homerverständnis." *Synusia. Intended for Wolfgang Schadewaldt on 15 March 1965*, edited by Wolfgang Schadewaldt, Hellmut Flashar, and Konrad Gaiser, 29–52. Pfullingen: Neske, 1965.
Hunter, R.L. *Encomium of Ptolemy Philadelphus: Text and Translation with Introduction and Commentary*. Berkeley: University of California, 2003.
Hunter, R.L. *Critical Moments in Classical Literature: Studies in the Ancient View of Literature and Its Uses*. Cambridge: Cambridge University, 2009.
Hunter, Virginia J. "Thucydides and the Uses of the Past." *Kilo* 62 (1980) 191–218.
Hurtado, Larry W. *Lord Jesus Christ: Devotion to Jesus in Earliest Christianity*. Grand Rapids: Eerdmans, 2003.
Hyde, Theresa. "A Model for Describing New and Old Properties of CMC Genres." In *Genres in the Internet: Issues in the Theory of Genre*, edited by Janet Giltrow and Dieter Stein, 239–61. PB 188. Amsterdam: John Benjamins, 2009.
Hyon, Sunny. "Genre in Three Traditions: Implications for ESP." TESOL Quarterly 30 (1996) 693–722.
Jackson, Leonard. *Poverty of Structuralism*. New York: Routledge, 2014.

Jackson, Leonard. *The Dematerialisation of Karl Marx: Literature and Marxist Theory*. Hoboken: Taylor and Francis, 2014.

Jacoby, Felix. “Über die Entwicklung der griechischen Historiographie und den Plan einer neuen Sammlung der griechischen Historikerfragmente.” *Klio* 9 (1909) 80–123.

Jakobson, Roman. “The Structure of the Russians Verb.” In *Russian and Slavic Grammar: Studies, 1931–81*, by Roman Jakobson, 1–14. JLrSM 106. Berlin: Mouton, 1984.

Jeremias, Joachim. *New Testament Theology*. Vol. 1: *The Proclamation of Jesus*. London: SCM, 1971.

Jervell, Jacob. *The Unknown Paul: Essays on Luke-Acts and Early Christian History*. Minneapolis: Augsburg, 1984.

Johnson, Garry Lance. “Josephus: Heir Apparent to the Prophetic Tradition.” In SBL Seminar Papers 1983, edited by Kent Richards, 337–46. Chico, Cal.: Scholars Press, 1983.

Johns, Ann M., ed. *Genre in the Classroom: Multiple Perspectives*. New York: Routledge, 2009.

Johns, Ann M. “Introduction: Genre in the Classroom.” In *Genre in the Classroom: Multiple Perspectives*, edited by Ann M. Johns, 1–13. New York: Routledge, 2009.

Johnson, Luke Timothy. “Review of *Imitating Homer*.” *CL* 54 (2005) 285.

Juel, Donald. *Messianic Exegesis: Christological Interpretation of the Old Testament in Early Christianity*. Philadelphia: Fortress, 1988.

Jung, Chang-Wook. *The Original Language of the Lukan Infancy Narrative*. JSNTSup 267. London: T&T Clark, 2004.

Kallet, Lisa. *Money and the Corrosion of Power in Thucydides: The Sicilian Expedition and Its Aftermath*. Berkeley: University of California, 2001.

Kasher, Aryeh. “Polemic and Apologetic Methods of Writing in *Contra Apion*.” In *Josephus’ Contra Apionem: Studies in its Character and Context with a Latin Concordance to the Portion Missing in Greek*, edited by Louis H. Feldman and John R. Levison, 143–86. AGJU 34. Leiden: Brill, 1996.

Kean, M.-L. “On a Theory of Markedness.” In *Theory of Markedness in Generative Grammar*, edited by Adriana Bel-letti et al., 559–604. Pisa: Scuola Normale Superiore Pisa, 1981.

Kee, Howard Clark. “Aretalogy and Gospel.” *JBL* 92 (1973) 402–33.

Keener, Craig. *The Historical Jesus of the Gospels*. Grand Rapids: Eerdmans, 2009.

Keener, Craig. *Acts: An Exegetical Commentary*. 4 vols. Grand Rapids: Baker Academic, 2012–2015.

Keener, Craig, and Edward T. Wright, eds. *Biographies and Jesus: What Does It Mean for the Gospels to Be Biographies?* Lexington: Emeth, 2016.

Kelly, Nicole. “The Cosmopolitan Expression of Josephus’s Prophetic Perspective in the ‘Jewish War.’” *HTR* 97 (2004) 257–74.

Kennedy, George A. *New Testament Interpretation through Rhetorical Criticism*. Chapel Hill: University of North Carolina, 1984.

Kennedy, Graeme D. *An Introduction to Corpus Linguistics*. New York: Routledge, 2016.

Kent, Thomas. *Interpretation and Genre: The Role of Generic Perception in the Study of Narrative Texts*. Lewisburg: Bucknell University, 1986.

Kim, Lawrence Young. *Homer between History and Fiction in Imperial Greek Literature*. Cambridge: Cambridge University, 2010.

Kimball, Charles A. "Jesus' Exposition of Scripture in Luke 20:9–19: An Inquiry in Light of Jewish Hermeneutics." *BBR* 3 (1993) 77–92.

Kimball, Charles A. *Jesus' Exposition of the Old Testament in Luke's Gospel*. JSNTSup 94. Sheffield: Sheffield Academic, 1994.

Klein, Ralph W. "I Esdras." In *The HarperCollins Bible Commentary*, edited by James Luther Mays and John Blenkinsopp, 698–704. San Francisco: HarperSanFrancisco, 2000.

Klutz, Todd. *The Exorcism Stories in Luke-Acts: A Sociostylistic Reading*. SNTMS 129. Cambridge: Cambridge University, 2004.

Knights, Chris H. "Towards a Critical Introduction to 'The History of the Rechabites.'" *JSJ* 26 (1995) 234–42.

Knowles, Michael. *Jeremiah in Matthew's Gospel: The Rejected Prophet Motif in Matthaean Redaction*. JSNTSup 63. Sheffield: JSOT, 1993.

Koester, Helmut. "Überlieferung und Geschichte der frühchristlichen Evangelienliteratur." *ANRW* II.25.2 (1984) 1543–704.

Koester, Helmut. *Introduction to the New Testament*. Vol. 1: *History, Culture, and Religion of the Hellenistic Age*. Berlin: De Gruyter, 1995.

Koester, Helmut. *Introduction to the New Testament*. Vol. 2: *History and literature of Early Christianity*. Berlin: de Gruyter, 2000.

Koet, B.J. *Dreams and Scripture in Luke-Acts: Collected Essays*. Leuven: Peeters, 2006.

Kosso, Peter. "Historical Evidence and Epistemic Justification: Thucydides as a Case Study." *HT* 32 (1993) 1–13.

Kosso, Peter. "John." In *Commentary on the New Testament Use of the Old Testament*, edited by G.K. Beale and D.A. Carson, 411–512. Grand Rapids: Baker Academic, 2007.

Köstenberger, Andreas. "The Genre of the Fourth Gospel and Greco-Roman Literary Conventions." In *Christian Origins and Greco-Roman Culture: Social and Literary Contexts for the New Testament*, edited by Stanley E. Porter and Andrew W. Pitts, 435–62. TENTS 8. ECHC 1. Leiden: Brill, 2013.

Kovacs, B.W. "Philosophical Foundations for Structuralism." *Semeia* 10 (1978) 85–103.

Kraemer, C.J. "Imitation and Originality." *CW* 20 (1927) 135–36.

Krischer, Tilman. "Herodotus Prooimion." *Hermes* 93 (1965) 159–67.

Kristeva, Julia. *Desire in Language: A Semiotic Approach to Literature and Art*. New York: Columbia University, 1980.

Kuhn, Thomas S., and Ian Hacking. *The Structure of Scientific Revolutions*. Chicago, IL: The University of Chicago Press, 2012.

Kümmel, Werner Georg. *Introduction to the New Testament*. Translated by Howard Clark Kee. Nashville: Abingdon, 1975.

Kuester, Martin. *Framing Truths: Parodic Structures in Contemporary English-Canadian Historical Novels*. Toronto: University of Toronto, 1992.

Kurz, William S. "Intertextual Use of Sirach 48.1–16 in Plotting Luke-Acts." In *The Gospels and the Scriptures of Israel*, edited by Craig A. Evans and William Richard Stegner, 308–24. JSNTSup 104. SSEJC 3. Sheffield: Sheffield Academic, 1994.

Kurz, William S. "Promise and Fulfillment in Hellenistic Jewish Narratives and in Luke-Acts." In *Jesus and the Heritage of Israel: Luke's Narrative Claim Upon Israel's Legacy*, edited by David P. Moessner, 147–70. Harrisburg: Trinity International, 1999.

Kurzweil, Edith. *The Age of Structuralism: From Lévi-Strauss to Foucault*. New Brunswick, N.J.: Transaction, 2004.

Lakoff, George. *Women, Fire, and Dangerous Things*. Chicago: University of Chicago, 1987.

Land, Christopher D. *The Integrity of 2 Corinthians and Paul's Aggravating Absence*. NTM 36. Sheffield: Sheffield Phoenix, 2015.

Laqueur, Richard. *The Jewish Historian Flavius Josephus: A Biographical Investigation based on New Critical Sources*. Translated by Caroline Disler and edited by Steve Mason. Toronto: York University, 2005 (orig. 1920).

Laurentin, R. *Structure et théologie de Luc I–II*. EBib. Paris: Gabalda, 1964.

Leach, E.R. "Levi-Strauss in the Garden of Eden." *Transactions of the New York Academy of Sciences* 23 (1961) 386–396.

Lee, Jae Hyun. *Paul's Gospel in Romans A Discourse Analysis of Rom. 1:16–8:39*. LBS 3. Leiden: Brill, 2010.

Lee, John A.L. "The Atticist Grammarians." In *The Language of the New Testament Context, History, and Development*, edited by Stanley E. Porter and Andrew W. Pitts, 283–310. ECHC 3. LBS 6. Leiden: Brill, 2013.

Lefkowitz, Mary R. *The Lives of the Greek Poets*. Baltimore: Johns Hopkins University, 2012.

Lemke, J.L. "Typology, Topology, Topography: Genre Semantics." Unpublished Paper (1987, rev. 1999), last accessed August, 5, 2017: http://academic.brooklyn.cuny.edu/education/jlemke/papers/Genre-topology-revised.htm

Lentricchia, Frank. *After the New Criticism*. Chicago, Ill.: University of Chicago, 1981.

Leo, Friedrich. *Die griechisch-römische Biographie nach ihrer litterarischen Form*. Leipzig: B.G. Teubner, 1901.

Licona, Michael R. *Why Are There Differences in the Gospels?: What We Can Learn from Ancient Biography*. New York: Oxford, 2017.

Lieb, Hans-Heinrich. "Introduction." In *Prospects for a New Structuralism*, edited by Hans-Heinrich Lieb, 1–13. Current Issues in Linguistic Theory 96. Amsterdam: John Benjamins, 1992.

Liebert, Hugh. *Plutarch's Politics: Between City and Empire*. New York: Cambridge University, 2017.

Lightfoot, John. *A Commentary on the New Testament from the Talmud and Hebraica, Matthew-I Corinthians*. Grand Rapids: Baker, 1979 (orig. 1733).

Lindars, Barnabas. *New Testament Apologetic*. Philadelphia: Westminster Press, 1961.

Linhares-Dias, Rui. *How to Show Things with Words: A Study on Logic, Language and Literature*. TL. SM 155. Berlin: Mouton de Gruyter, 2006.

Litwak, Kenneth Duncan. *Echoes of Scripture in Luke-Acts: Telling the History of God's People Intertextually*. JSNTSup 282. London: T&T Clark, 2005.

Lohse, Eduard. "Lukas als Theologe der Heilsgeschichte." *EvT* 14 (1954) 256–75.

Longacre, Robert E. *The Grammar of Discourse*. New York: Plenum, 1983.

Longacre, Robert E. "Discourse Peak as a Zone of Turbulence." In *Beyond the Sentence: Discourse and Sentential Form*, edited by J.R. Wirth, 435–50. Ann Arbor, Mich.: Karoma, 1985.

Loraux, Nicole. *The Invention of Athens: The Funeral Oration in the Classical City*. Cambridge, Mass.: Harvard University Press, 1986.

Louw, J.P. *Semantics of New Testament Greek*. SS. Philadelphia: Fortress Press, 1982.

Lu, Houliang. *Xenophon's Theory of Moral Education*. Newcastle upon Tyne, UK: Cambridge Scholars, 2015.

Luce, T. James. *The Greek Historians*. London: Routledge, 1997.

Luraghi, Nino. *The Historian's Craft in the Age of Herodotus*. Oxford: Oxford University, 2001.

Lyons, John. *Introduction to Theoretical Linguistics*. Cambridge: Cambridge University, 1968.

Lyons, John. *Semantics*. 2 Vols. Cambridge: Cambridge University, 1977.

MacDonald, Dennis R. "Introduction." In *Mimesis and Intertextuality in Antiquity and Christianity*, edited by Dennis R. MacDonald, 1–9. SAC. Harrisburg: Trinity, 2003.

MacDonald, Dennis R. *Does the New Testament Imitate Homer? Four Case from the Acts of the Apostles*. New Haven: Yale University, 2003.

MacDonald, Dennis R. "The Breasts of Hecuba and Those of the Daughters of Jerusalem: Luke's Transvaluation of a Famous Iliadic Scene." In *Ancient Fiction: The Matrix of Early Christian and Jewish Narrative*, edited by J.A.A. Brant et al., 239–54. SymSBL 32. Atlanta: Society of Biblical Literature, 2005.

Maier, Paul. "Luke as Hellenistic Historian." In *Christian Origins and Greco-Roman Culture: Social and Literary Contexts for the New Testament*, edited by Stanley E. Porter and Andrew W. Pitts, 413–34. ECHC 1. TENTS 9. Leiden: Brill, 2013.

Mallen, Peter. *The Reading and Transformation of Isaiah in Luke-Acts.* LNTS 367. London: T&T Clark, 2008.

Mansfeld, Jaap. *Studies in the Historiography of Greek Philosophy.* Assen: Van Gorcum, 1990.

Marincola, John. *Authority and Tradition in Ancient Historiography.* Cambridge: Cambridge University, 1997.

Marincola, John. "Genre, Convention, and Innovation in Greco-Roman Historiography." In *The Limits of Historiography: Genre and Narrative in Ancient Texts*, edited by Christina Shuttleworth Kraus, 281–324. MBCB 191. Leiden: Brill, 1999.

Marincola, John. *Greek Historians.* GR 31. Oxford: Oxford University, 2001.

Marincola, John. "Odysseus and the Historians." *Syllecta Classica* 18 (2007) 1–79.

Marincola, John. "Introduction." In *A Companion to Greek and Roman Historiography*, edited by John Marincola, 1–9. BCAW. LC. Malden, Mass.: Blackwell, 2007.

Markham, Ian. "Richard Burridge's Achievement." *First Things* (2014) 22–24.

Marshall, I. Howard. *Luke: Historian and Theologian.* Exeter: Paternoster, 1970.

Marshall, I. Howard. *The Gospel of Luke: A Commentary on the Greek Text.* NIGTC. Exeter: Paternoster, 1978.

Marshall, I. Howard. *Acts: An Introduction and Commentary.* TNTC 5. Downers Grove, Ill.: InterVarsity, 1980.

Marshall, I. Howard. "Acts and the 'Former Treatise.'" In *The Book of Acts in its First Century Setting. I. The Book of Acts in its Literary Setting*, edited by Bruce W. Winter and Andrew D. Clarke, 163–82. Grand Rapids: Eerdmans, 1993.

Marshall, I. "Acts." In *Commentary on the New Testament Use of the Old Testament*, edited by G.K. Beale and D.A. Carson, 513–605. Grand Rapids: Baker Academic, 2007.

Martín-Asensio, Gustavo. *Transitivity-Based Foregrounding in the Acts of the Apostles: A Functional-Grammatical Approach to the Lukan Perspective.* JSNTSup 202. Sheffield: Sheffield Academic, 2000.

Martin, J.R. *English Text: System and Structure.* Philadelphia: John Benjamins, 1992.

Martin, J.R. "A Contextual Theory of Language." In *The Powers of Literacy: A Genre Approach to Teaching Writing*, edited by Bill Cope and Mary Kalantzis, 116–36. Pittsburgh: University of Pittsburgh, 1993.

Martin, J.R. "Analysing Genre: Functional Parameters." In *Genre and Institutions: Social Processes in the Workplace and School*, edited by Frances Christie and J.R. Martin, 3–39. London: Cassell, 1997.

Martin, J.R., and David Rose. *Genre Relations: Mapping Culture.* London: Equinox, 2008.

Martin, Michael. "Progymnastic Topic Lists: A Compositional Template for Luke and Other Bioi?" *NTS* 54 (2008) 18–41.

Martín-Martín, Pedro. *The Rhetoric of the Abstract in English and Spanish Scientific Discourse: A Cross-Cultural Genre-Analytic Approach.* Europäische Hochschulschriften 21. Linguistik 279. New York: Peter Lang, 2005.

Martin, Raymond A. *Syntactical Evidence of Semitic Sources in Greek Documents*. SCSt 3. Cambridge, Mass.: Society of Biblical Literature, 1974.

Martin, Raymond A. *Syntax Criticism of the Synoptic Gospels*. Lewiston, N.Y.: Mellen, 1987.

Mary-Louise, Kean. "On a Theory of Markedness: Some General Considerations and a Case in Point." In *Theory of Markedness in Core Grammar*, edited by A. Belletti et al., 559–604. Pisa: Scuola Normale Superiore Pisa, 1981.

Mason, Steve. "Josephus, Daniel, and the Flavian House." In *Josephus and the History of the Greco-Roman Period: Essays in Memory of Morton Smith*, edited by Fausto Parente and Joseph Sievers, 161–91. StPB 41. Leiden: Brill, 1994.

Mason, Steve. "Should Any Wish To Inquire Further (Ant. 1.25): The Aim and Audience of Josephus's Judean Antiquities/Life." In *Understanding Josephus: Seven Perspectives*, edited by Steve Mason, 64–103. JSPS 32. Sheffield: Sheffield Academic, 1998.

Mason, Steve. *Flavius Josephus on the Pharisees: A Composition-Critical Study*. Leiden: Brill, 2001.

Mason, Steve. "Contradiction or Counterpoint? Josephus and Historical Method." *RRJ* 6 (2003) 145–48.

Matthews, Peter H. *Syntax*. Cambridge: Cambridge, 1981.

Maurer, Bernard. "The Book of Ecclesiastes As a Derash of Genesis 1–4: A Study in Old Testament Literary Dependency." Unpublished Ph.D. diss.: Southeastern Baptist Theological Seminary, 2007.

Mauser, Ulrich. *Christ and the Wilderness: The Wilderness Theme in the Second Gospel and its Basis in the Biblical Tradition*. SBT 39. London: SCM, 1963.

Mays, James Luther. *The Lord Reigns: A Theological Handbook to the Psalms*. Louisville: Westminster John Knox, 1994.

Mccarthy, Michael. *Language As Discourse: Perspectives for Language Teaching*. Oxford: Taylor & Francis, 2016.

McGing, B.C. "Appian's 'Mithridatios.'" *ANRW* II.34.1 (1993) 496–522.

McGing, B.C. "Philo's Adaptation of the Bible in his Life of Moses." In *The Limits of Ancient Biography*, edited by B.C. McGing and Judith Mossman, 113–40. Swansea: Classical Press of Wales, 2006.

McGing, B.C. *Polybius' Histories*. OACL. New York: Oxford University, 2010.

McQueen, E.I. "Quintus Curtius Rufus." In *Latin Biography*, edited by T.A. Dorey, 17–43. London: Routledge & Kegan Paul, 1967.

Meek, James A. *The Gentile Mission in the Old Testament Citations in Acts: Text, Hermeneutic, and Purpose*. LNTS 385. London: T&T Clark, 2008.

Mehl, Andreas. *Roman Historiography: An Introduction to Its Basic Aspects and Development*. Malden, Mass.: Wiley-Blackwell, 2011.

Mehler, Alexander, Serge Sharoff, and Marina Santini, eds. *Genres on the Web: Computational Models and Empirical Studies*. Text, Speech, and Language Technology 42. Dordrecht: Springer, 2010.

Mellor, Ronald. *The Roman Historians*. London: Routledge, 2003.

Menzies, Robert P. *Empowered for Witness: The Spirit in Luke-Acts*. JPTSup 6. London: T&T Clark, 2004.

Miller, Carolyn R. "Genre as Social Action." *Quarterly Journal of Speech* 70 (1984) 151–67.

Miller, Carolyn R. "Rhetorical Community: The Cultural Basis of Genre." In *Genre and the New Rhetoric*, edited by Aviva Freedman and Peter Medway, 67–78. London: Taylor & Francis, 1994.

Miller, Patricia Cox. "Strategies of Representation in Collected Biography: Constructing the Subject as Holy." In *Greek Biography and Panegyric in Late Antiquity*, edited by Tomas Hägg, Philip Rousseau, and Christian Høgel, 209–54. Berkeley: University of California, 2000.

Minear, P.S. "Luke's Use of the Birth Stories." In *Studies in Luke-Acts*, edited by Leander E. Keck and J. Louis Martyn, 111–30. Philadelphia: Fortress, 1980.

Miner, Earl. "Some Issues of 'Literary Species, or Distinct Kind.'" In *Renaissance Genres: Essays on Theory, History, and Interpretation*, edited by Barbara Kiefer Lewalski, 15–34. HES 14. Cambridge, Mass.: Harvard University, 1986.

Mirhady, David C., and Yun Lee Too. "Introduction to 9. Evagoras." In *Isocrates I*, edited by David C. Mirhady, and Yun Lee Too, 139–40. Austin: University of Texas, 2000.

Mitchell, Margret. "Homer in the New Testament?" *JR* 83 (2003) 244–58.

Miura, Yuzuru. *David in Luke-Acts: His Portrayal in the Light of Early Judaism*. WUNT 2.232. Tübingen: Mohr Siebeck, 2007.

Moessner, David P. "The Appeal and Power of Poetics (Luke 1:1–4)." In *Jesus and the Heritage of Israel*, edited by David P. Moessner, 84–123. Philadelphia: Trinity, 1999.

Moessner, David P. "The Lukan Prologues in the Light of Ancient Narrative Hermeneutics." In *The Unity of Luke-Acts*, edited by J. Verheyden, 399–417. Leuven: Leuven University, 1999.

Moessner, David P. *Luke the Historian of Israel's Legacy, Theologian of Israel's 'Christ'*. BZNW 182. Berlin: De Gruyter, 2016.

Moisl, Hermann. *Cluster Analysis for Corpus Linguistics*. QL 66. Berlin: De Gruyter Mouton, 2015.

Momigliano, Arnaldo. *Studies in Historiography*. New York: Harper & Row, 1966.

Momigliano, Arnaldo. "Greek Historiography." *HT* 17 (1978) 1–28.

Momigliano, Arnaldo. *The Classical Foundations of Modern Historiography*. Berkeley: University of California, 1990.

Momigliano, Arnaldo. *The Development of Greek Biography*. Carl Newell Jackson Lectures 143. Cambridge, Mass.: Harvard University, 1993.

Momigliano, Arnaldo. "What Josephus Did Not See." In *Essays on Ancient and Modern Judaism*, edited by Arnaldo Momigliano, 67–78. Chicago: University of Chicago, 1994.

Morley, David. *Syntax in Functional Grammar: An Introduction to Lexicogrammar in Systemic Linguistics*. London: Continuum, 2000.

Morris, Leon. *Luke: An Introduction and Commentary*. TNTC 3. Downers Grove: IVP, 1988.

Morrison, James V. "Preface to Thucydides: Rereading the Corcyrean Conflict (1.24–55)." *CA* (1999) 94–131.

Most, Glen. "Generating Genres: The Idea of the Tragic." In *Matrices of Genre: Authors, Canons, and Society*, edited by Mary Depew and Dirk Obbink, 15–36. Cambridge, Mass.: Harvard University, 2000.

Moyise, Steve. *The Old Testament in the New: An Introduction*. TTCABS. London: T&T Clark, 2001.

Muckelbauer, John. "Imitation and Invention in Antiquity: An Historical-Theoretical Revision." *Rhetorica* 21 (2003) 61–88.

Muntz, Charles Edward. *Diodorus Siculus and the World of the Late Roman Republic*. Oxford: Oxford University, 2017.

Murphy, Fredrick J. "Retelling the Bible: Idolatry in Pseudo-Philo." *JBL* 107 (1988) 275–87.

Murphy, Fredrick J. *Rewriting the Bible*. New York: Oxford University, 1993.

Murray, Gilbert. *Euripides and His Age*. 2nd ed. Oxford: Oxford University, 1946.

Myers, Jacob M. *I and II Esdras: A Translation with Introduction and Notes*. AB 43. New York: Doubleday, 1974.

Nagy, Gregory. "Herodotus the Logios." *Arethusa* 20 (1987) 175–84.

Nevin, Sonya. *Military Leaders and Sacred Space in Classical Greek Warfare: Temples, Sanctuaries and Conflict in Antiquity*. Library of Classical Studies. London: Tauris, 2017.

Newsome, Carl A. "Spying out the Land: A Report from a Genealogy." In *Bakhtin and Genre Theory in Biblical Studies*, edited by Roland Boer, 19–30. SS 63. Atlanta: Society of Biblical Literature, 2010.

Nickelsburg, G.E.W. "The Bible Rewritten and Expanded." In *Jewish Writings of the Second Temple Period: Apocrypha, Pseudepigrapha, Qumran Sectarian Writings, Philo, Josephus*, edited by M.E. Stone, 33–156. CRINT. Philadelphia: Fortress, 1984.

Nolland, John. *Luke 1–9:20*. WBC 35A. Dallas: Word, 1989.

Nolland, John. *Luke 18:35–24:53*. WBC 35C. Dallas: Word, 1998.

Norden, Eduard. *Die germanische Urgeschichte in Tacitus Germania*. Leipzig: B.G. Teubner, 1920.

O'Brien, Peter T. *Introductory Thanksgivings in the Letters of Paul*. NovTSup 4. Leiden: Brill, 1977.

O'Donnell, Matthew Brook. *Corpus Linguistics and the Greek of the New Testament*. NTM 6. Sheffield: Sheffield Phoenix, 2005.

Oesterley, W.O.E. *An Introduction to the Books of the Apocrypha*. London: SPCK, 1935.

Ó Fearghail, Fearghus. *The Introduction to Luke-Acts: A Study of the Role of Lk 1,1–4,44 in the Composition of Luke's Two-volume Work*. AnBib 126. Rome: Pontifical Biblical Institute, 1991.

O'Leary, Anne M. *Matthew's Judaization of Mark: Examined in the Context of the Use of Sources in Graeco-Roman Antiquity*. LNTS 323. London: T&T Clark, 2006.

Oliver, H.H. "The Lucan Birth Stories and the Purpose of Luke-Acts." *NTS* 10 (1964) 202–26.

Ong, Hughson T. *The Multilingual Jesus and the Sociolinguistic World of the New Testament*. LBS 12. Leiden: Brill, 2016.

Osborne, Robin. "Archaic Greek History." In *Brill's Companion to Herodotus*, edited by I.J.F. de Jong and H. van Wees, 497–520. Leiden: Brill, 2002.

Osley, A.S. "Greek Biography before Plutarch." *GR* 43 (1946) 7–20.

Overbeck, Franz. "Über die Anfänge der patristischen Literatur." *HZ* 12 (1882) 417–72.

Paffenroth, Kim. *The Story of Jesus According to L*. JSNTSup 147. Sheffield: Sheffield Academic, 1997.

Palmer, David W. "Acts and the Ancient Historical Monograph." In *The Book of Acts in its First Century Setting. I. The Book of Acts in its Literary Setting*, edited by Bruce W. Winter and Andrew D. Clarke, 1–29. Grand Rapids: Eerdmans, 1993.

Paltridge, Brian. *Genre, Frames and Writing in Research Settings*. Amsterdam: John Benjamins, 1997.

Pang, Francis G.H. *Revisiting Aspect and Aktionsart A Corpus Approach to Koine Greek Event Typology*. LBS 14. Leiden: Brill, 2016.

Pao, David W. *Acts and the Isaianic New Exodus*. Grand Rapids: Baker Academic, 2002.

Pao, David W. *Thanksgiving: An Investigation of a Pauline Theme*. NSBT 13. Downers Grove, Ill.: InterVarsity, 2003.

Pao, David, and Eckhard Schnabel. "Luke." In *Commentary on the New Testament Use of the Old Testament*, edited by G.K. Beale and D.A. Carson, 251–414. Grand Rapids: Baker Academic, 2007.

Paolillo, John C., Jonathan Warren, and Breanne Kunz. "Genre Emergence in Amateur Flash." In *Genres on the Web: Computational Models and Empirical Studies*, edited by Alexander Mehler, Serge Sharoff, and Marina Santini, 277–302. TSLT 42. Dordrecht: Springer, 2010.

Parsons, Mikeal C. *Acts*. PCNT. Grand Rapids: Baker Academic, 2008.

Parsons, M.C., and R.I. Pervo. *Rethinking the Unity of Luke and Acts*. Minneapolis: Fortress, 1993.

Patron, Sylvie. "Enunciative Narratology: A French Specialty." In *Current Trends in Narratology*, edited by Greta Olson, 313–35. Narratologia 27. Berlin: de Gruyter, 2011.

Patton, John H. "Generic Criticism: Typology at an Inflated Price." *RSQ* 6 (1976): 4–8.

Pearson, Lionel. *The Local Historians of Attica*. APAMS 11. Chico, Cal.: Scholars, 1981.

Pedech, Paul. *Histories French & Greek 1961–95*. Paris: Belles, 1961.

Pedech, Paul. *La méthode historique de Polybe*. Collection d'études anciennes. Paris: Société d'édition Les Belles, 1964.

van Peer, Willie. *Stylistics and Psychology: Investigations of Foregrounding*. London: Croom Helm, 1986.

Pellicia, H. "Sappho, Gorgias' Helen, and the Preface to Herodotus' Histories." *YCS* 29 (1992) 63–84.

Pelling, C.B.R. "Plutarch's Method of Work in the Roman Lives." *JHS* 99 (1979) 74–96.

Pelling, C.B.R. "Plutarch's Adaptation of His Source Material." *JHS* 100 (1980) 127–40.

Pelling, C.B.R. "Synkrisis in Plutarch's Lives." In *Miscellanea Plutarchea: atti del I convegno di studi su Plutarco*, edited by Frederick E. Brenk ed., Italo Gallo, 83–96. Ferrara: International Plutarch Society, sezione italiana, 1986.

Pelling, C.B.R. *Characterization and Individuality in Greek Literature*. Oxford: Clarendon Press, 1990.

Pelling, C.B.R. "Is Death the End? Closure in Plutarch's Lives." In *Classical Closure: Reading the End in Greek and Latin Literature*, edited by Deborah H. Roberts, 228–50. Princeton, N.J.: Princeton, 1997. Reprinted in *Plutarch and History: Eighteen Studies*, by C.B.R. Pelling, 365–86. Swansea: Classical Press of Wales, 2011.

Pelling, C.B.R. *Literary Texts and the Greek Historian*. London: Routledge, 2000.

Pelling, C.B.R. *Tragedy and the Historian*. Oxford: Clarendon, 2001.

Pelling, C.B.R. "Homer and Herodotus." In *Epic Interactions: Perspectives on Homer, Virgil, and the Epic Tradition; Presented to Jasper Griffin by Former Pupils*, edited by M.J. Clarke, 75–104. Oxford: Oxford, 2009.

Pelling, C.B.R. *Plutarch and History: Eighteen Studies*. Swansea: Classical Press of Wales, 2011.

Pelling, C.B.R. *Plutarch* Caesar*: Translated with an Introduction and Commentary*. Clarendon Ancient History Series. Oxford: Oxford University, 2011.

Pelling, C.B.R., and Maria Wyke. *Twelve Voices from Greece and Rome: Ancient Ideas for Modern Times*. Oxford: Oxford University, 2016 (orig. 2014).

Penner, Todd. *In Praise of Christian Origins: Stephen and the Hellenists in Lukan Apologetic Historiography*. ESTEC. London: T&T Clark, 2004.

Perrin, Nicholas. *Jesus the Temple*. Grand Rapids: Baker, 2010.

Perrin, Norman. *Rediscovering the Teaching of Jesus*. New York: Harper & Row, 1967.

Perrot, Charles, and Pierre Bogaert. *Les antiquités bibliques. Tome II*. Sch 230. Paris: Éditions du Cerf, 1976.

Perry, Ellen. "Rhetoric, Literary Criticism, and the Roman Aesthetics of Imitation." In *The Ancient Art of Emulation: Studies in Artistic Originality and Tradition from the Present to Classical Antiquity*, edited by Elaine K. Gazda, 153–71. MAARSup 1. Ann Arbor: University of Michigan, 2002.

Pervo, Richard I. *Profit with Delight*. Philadelphia, Penn.: Fortress, 1987.

Pervo, Richard I. *Acts: A Commentary on the Book of Acts*. Hermeneia. Minneapolis: Fortress, 2009.

Petersen, Norman. "So-called Gnostic Type Gospels and the Question of the Genre 'Gospel.'" Unpublished SBL Paper (1970) cited in *What is a Gospel? The Genre of the Canonical Gospels*, by Charles H. Talbert, 20. Philadelphia: Fortress, 1977.

Peterson, David G. *The Acts of the Apostles*. PNTC. Grand Rapids: Eerdmans, 2009.

Pfeiffer, Robert H. *History of New Testament Times with an Introduction to Apocrypha*. New York: Harper and Brothers, 1949.

Phillips, Thomas E. "The Genre of Acts: Moving toward a Consensus?" *CBR* 4 (2006) 365–96.

Pigon, Jakub. *The Children of Herodotus: Greek and Roman Historiography and Related Genres*. Newcastle: Cambridge Scholars, 2008.

Pitcher, Luke. "War Stories: The Use of the Plupast in Appian." In *Time and Narrative in Ancient Historiography: The 'plupast' from Herodotus to Appian*, edited by Jonas Grethlein and Christopher B. Krebs, 199–210. Cambridge: Cambridge University, 2012.

Pitcher, Luke. "Future's Bright? Looking Forward in Appian." In *Knowing Future Time in and Through Greek Historiography*, edited by Alexandra Lianeri, 281–92. Trends in Classics 32. Boston: De Gruyter, 2016.

Pitts, Andrew W. "Philosophical and Epistolary Contexts for Pauline Paraenesis." In *Paul and the Ancient Letter Form*, edited by Stanley E. Porter and Sean A. Adams, 269–306. PAST 6. Leiden: Brill, 2010.

Pitts, Andrew W. "The Use and Non-Use of Prophetic Literature in Hellenistic Jewish Historiography." In *Prophets and Prophecy in Ancient Israelite Historiography*, edited by Mark J. Boda and Lissa Wray Beal, 229–52. BCP. Winona Lake, Ind.: Eisenbrauns, 2012.

Pitts, Andrew W. "Source Citation in Greek Historiography and in Luke(-Acts)." In *Christian Origins and Greco-Roman Culture: Social and Literary Contexts for the New Testament*, edited by Stanley E. Porter and Andrew W. Pitts, 349–88. TENTS 8. ECHC 1. Leiden: Brill, 2013.

Pitts, Andrew W. "Greek Word Order and Clause Structure: A Comparative Study of Some New Testament Corpora." In *The Language of the New Testament: Context, History and Development*, edited by Stanley E. Porter and Andrew W. Pitts, 311–46. LBS 6. ECHC 3. Leiden: Brill, 2013.

Pitts, Andrew W. "Style and Pseudonymity in Pauline Scholarship: A Register Based Configuration." In *Paul and Pseudonymity*, edited by Stanley E. Porter and Gregory Fewster, 113–52. PAST 8. Leiden: Brill, 2013.

Pitts, Andrew W. "Paul in Tarsus: Historical Factors in Assessing Paul's Early Education." In *Paul and Ancient Rhetoric: Theory and Practice in the Hellenistic Context*, edited by Stanley E. Porter and Bryan Dyer, 43–67. Cambridge University, 2016.

Pitts, Andrew W. "Interdisciplinary New Testament Scholarship: An Introduction to the Research of Stanley E. Porter." In *The Language and Literature of the New Testament: Essays in Honor of Stanley E. Porter's 60th Birthday*, edited by Lois F. Dow, Craig A. Evans, and Andrew W. Pitts, 1–70. BINS 150. Leiden: Brill, 2016.

Pohlmann, K.-F. *Studien zum dritten Esra: Ein Beitrag zur Frage nach dem ursprünglichen Schluß des chronistischen Geschichtswerkes*. FRLANT 104. Göttingen: Vandenhoeck & Ruprecht, 1970.

Polhill, John B. *Acts*. NAC 26. Nashville: Broadman & Holman Publishers, 1992.

Pomorska, Krystyna. "The Segmentation of Narrative Prose." In *Jakobsonian Poetics and Slavic Narrative: From Pushkin to Solzhenitsyn*, edited by Henryk Baran, 13–33. Durham: Duke University, 1992.

Porter, Stanley E. *Verbal Aspect in the Greek of the New Testament: With Reference to Tense and Mood*. SBG 1. New York: Peter Lang, 1989.

Porter, Stanley E. "Thucydides 1.22.1 and Speeches in Acts: Is There a Thucydidean View." *NovT* 32 (1990) 121–42. Reprinted in *Studies in the Greek New Testament: Theory and Practice*, by Stanley E. Porter, 173–93. SBG 6. New York: Peter Lang, 1996.

Porter, Stanley E. *Idioms of the Greek New Testament*. 2nd ed. BL: Greek 2. Sheffield: Sheffield, 1994 (1992).

Porter, Stanley E. "The Use of the Old Testament in the New Testament: A Brief Comment on Method and Terminology." In *Early Christian Interpretation of the Scriptures of Israel: Investigations and Proposals*, edited by Craig A. Evans and James A. Sanders, 79–96. SSEJC 5. JSNTSup 148. Sheffield: Sheffield, 1997.

Porter, Stanley E. "Register in the Greek of the New Testament: Application with Reference to Mark's Gospel." In *Rethinking Contexts, Rereading Texts: Contributions from the Social Sciences to Biblical Interpretation*, edited by M. Daniel Carroll R., 209–29. JSOTSup 299. Sheffield: Sheffield Academic, 2000.

Porter, Stanley E. "The Genre of Acts and the Ethics of Discourse." In *Acts and Ethics*, edited by Thomas E. Phillips, 1–15. NTM 9. Sheffield: Sheffield Phoenix, 2005.

Porter, Stanley E. "Further Comments on the Use of the Old Testament in the New Testament." In *The Intertextuality of the Epistles: Explorations of Theory and Practice*, edited by Thomas L. Brodie et al., 98–110. NTM 16. Sheffield: Sheffield Phoenix, 2006.

Porter, Stanley E. "The Use of Authoritative Citations in Mark's Gospel and Ancient Biography: A Study of P.Oxy. 1176." In *Biblical Interpretation in Early Christian Gospels*. Volume 1: *The Gospel of Mark*, edited by Thomas R. Hatina, 79–96. LNTS 304. London: T&T Clark, 2006.

Porter, Stanley E. "Scripture Justifies the Mission: The Use of the Old Testament in Luke-Acts." In *Hearing the Old Testament in the New*, edited by Stanley E. Porter, 104–26. Grand Rapids: Eerdmans, 2006.

Porter, Stanley E. "Prominence: An Overview." In *The Linguist as Pedagogue: Trends in the Teaching and Linguistic Analysis of the Greek New Testament*, edited by Stanley E.

Porter and Matthew Brook O'Donnell, 45–74. NTM 11. Sheffield: Sheffield Phoenix, 2009.

Porter, Stanley E., and Sean A. Adams, eds. *Paul and the Ancient Letter Form*. PAST 6. Leiden: Brill, 2010.

Porter, Stanley E., and Matthew Brook O'Donnell, eds. *The Linguist as Pedagogue: Trends in the Teaching and Linguistic Analysis of the Greek New Testament*. NTM 11. Sheffield: Sheffield Phoenix, 2009.

Porter, Stanley E., and Andrew W. Pitts. "New Testament Greek Language and Linguistics in Recent Research." *CBR* 6 (2008) 214–55.

Porter, Stanley E., and Andrew W. Pitts. "Πίστις with a Preposition and Genitive Modifier: Lexical Semantic and Syntactic Considerations in the πίστις Χριστου/ Discussion." In *The Faith of Jesus Christ: Problems and Prospects*, edited by Michael F. Bird and Preston M. Sprinkle, 33–53. Peabody, Mass.: Hendrickson, 2009.

Porter, Stanley E., and Andrew W. Pitts. "The Disclosure Formula in the Epistolary Papyri and in the New Testament: Development, Form, Function and Syntax," In *The Language of the New Testament: Context, History, and Development*, edited by Stanley E. Porter and Andrew W. Pitts, 421–38. LBS 6. ECH 3. Leiden: Brill, 2013.

Potter, David S. *Literary Texts and the Roman Historian*. London: Routledge, 1999.

Powery, Emerson B. *Jesus Reads Scripture: The Function of Jesus' Use of Scripture in the Synoptics*. BIS 63. Leiden: Brill, 2003.

Poythress, Vern S. "Structuralism and Biblical Studies." *JETS* 21 (1978) 221–237.

Prevo, R.I. *Profit with Delight: The Literary Genre of the Acts of the Apostles*. Philadelphia: Fortress, 1987.

Prevo, R.I. *Acts: A Commentary on the Book of Acts*. Hermeneia. Minneapolis, Minn.: Fortress, 2009.

Prince, Gerald. *A Dictionary of Narratology*. Lincoln: University of Nebraska, 2003.

Prior, Michael. *Jesus the Liberator: Nazareth Liberation Theology (Luke 4.16–30)*. Sheffield: Sheffield Academic, 1995.

Propp, Vladimir. *Morfologia skaski*. Leningrad: Academia, 1928. ET: *The Morphology of Folktale*. Translated by Laurence Scott. 2nd ed. Revised and edited by Louis A. Wagner. American Folklore Society, Bibliographical and Special Series 9. Arlington, Tex.: University of Texas, 1968.

Rabatel, Alain. "A Brief Introduction to an Enunciative Approach to Point of View." In *Point of View, Perspective, and Focalization: Modeling Mediation in Narrative*, edited by Peter A. Hühn et al., 79–98. Narratologia 17. Berlin: Walter de Gruyter, 2009.

Race, W.H. "Pindaric Encomium and Isocrates' Evagoras." *TAPhA* 117 (1987) 131–155.

Rajak, Tessa. *Josephus: The Historian and His Society*. London: Duckworth, 2002.

Ravens, David. *Luke and the Restoration of Israel*. JSNTSup 119. Sheffield: Sheffield Academic, 1995.

Reed, Jeffery T. "Identifying Theme in the New Testament: Insights from Discourse Analysis." In *Discourse Analysis and Other Topics in Biblical Greek*, edited by Stanley E. Porter and D.A. Carson, 79–101. JSNTSup 113. Sheffield: Sheffield Academic, 1995.

Reed, Jeffery T. *A Discourse Analysis of Philippians: Method and Rhetoric in the Debate Over Literary Integrity*. JSNTSup 136. Sheffield: Sheffield Academic, 1997.

Rees, Roger. *Latin Panegyric*. New York: Oxford, 2012.

Renfrew, Alastair. *Towards a New Material Aesthetics: Bakhtin, Genre, and the Fates of Literary Theory*. London: Legenda, Modern Humanities Research Association and Maney, 2006.

Rengstorf, Karl Heinrich. *Das Evangelium nach Lukas*. NTD 3. 14th ed. Göttingen: Vandenhoeck und Ruprecht, 1969.

Rese, Martin. *Alttestamentliche Motive in der Christologie des Lukas*. SNT 1. Gütersloh: Gütersloher Verlagshaus G. Mohn, 1969 (orig. 1967).

Rhodes, P.J. "Documents and the Greek Historians." In *A Companion to Greek and Roman Historiography*, edited by John Marincola, 56–66. BCAW. Malden, Mass.: Blackwell, 2007.

Richards, E. Randolph. *Paul and First-Century Letter Writing: Secretaries, Composition and Collection*. Downers Grove: InterVarsity, 2004.

Rindoš, Jaroslav. *He of Whom It Is Written: John the Baptist and Elijah in Luke*. ÖBS 38. Frankfurt am Main: Peter Lang, 2010.

Ritchie, Matthew Jeremy. "Functional Context: Underlying Principles of Language Structures in Literary Interpretation." Unpublished Ph.D. diss.: University of California, Berkeley, 2008.

Rivara, R. *La langue du récit: Introduction à la narratologie énonciative*. Paris: L'Harmattan, 2001.

Romaine, Suzanne. *Language in Society: An Introduction to Sociolinguistics*. Oxford: Oxford University, 1994.

Rood, Tim. *Thucydides: Narrative and Explanation*. OCM. Oxford: Clarendon, 1998.

Rosch, Eleanor. "Human Categorization." In *Studies in Cross-cultural Psychology*, edited by Neil Warren, 1–49. London: Academic, 1977.

Roth, S. John. *The Blind, the Lame, and the Poor: Character Types in Luke-Acts*. JSNTSup 144. Sheffield: Sheffield Academic, 1997.

Rothschild, Clare K. *Luke-Acts and the Rhetoric of History: An Investigation of Early Christian Historiography*. WUNT 2.175. Tübingen: Mohr Siebeck, 2004.

Roughley, Alan. *James Joyce and Critical Theory: An Introduction*. Hemel Hempstead: Harvester Wheatsheaf, 1991.

Ruiten, J. van. *Abraham in the Book of Jubilees: The Rewriting of Genesis 11:26–25:10 in the Book of Jubilees 11:14–23:8*. JSJSup 161. Leiden: Brill, 2012.

Runge, Steven E. *Discourse Grammar of the Greek New Testament: A Practical Introduction for Teaching and Exegesis*. Peabody, Mass.: Hendrickson, 2013.

Rusam, Dietrich. *Das Alte Testament bei Lukas*. BZNW 112. Berlin: de Gruyter, 2003.

Russell, D.A. "De Imitatione." In *Creative Imitation and Latin Literature*, edited by David Alexander West and A.J. Woodman, 1–16. Cambridge: Cambridge University, 1979.

Rutherford, R.B. "Structure and Meaning in Epic and Historiography." In *Thucydides and Herodotus*, edited by Edith Foster and Donald Lateiner, 13–38. Oxford: Oxford University, 2012.

Sacks, Kenneth. *Diodorus Siculus and the First Century*. Princeton Legacy Library. Princeton: Princeton University, 1990.

Sadler, M.F. *The Gospel According to St. Luke, with Notes Critical and Practical*. 4th ed. London: George Bell and Sons, 1892.

Sahlin, Harald. *Der Messias und das Gottesvolk; Studien zur protolukanischen Theologie*. Uppsala: Almqvist & Wiksells, 1945.

Sanders, E.P. *Jesus and Judaism*. Philadelphia: Fortress, 1985.

Sanders, James T. "The Prophetic Use of Scripture in Luke-Acts." In *Early Jewish and Christian Exegesis: Studies in Memory of William Hugh Brownlee*, edited by Craig A. Evans and W.F. Stinespring, 191–98. SPHS 10. Atlanta: Scholars, 1987.

Sangster, Rodney B. *Reinventing Structuralism: What Sign Relations Reveal about Consciousness*. Trends in Linguistics: Studies and Monographs 264. Mouton: De Gruyter, 2013.

Santoro L'Hoir, Francesca. *Tragedy, Rhetoric, and the Historiography of Tacitus' "Annales."* Ann Arbor, Mich.: University of Michigan, 2006.

Satran, David. *Biblical Prophets in Byzantine Palestine: Reassessing the Lives of the Prophets*. SVTP 11. Leiden: Brill, 1995.

Saussure, Ferdinand. *Course in General Linguistics*. Edited by Charles Bally, Albert Sechehaye, and Albert Riedlinger. Translated by Roy Harris. London: McGraw Hill, 1959.

Sawaki, Tomoko. *Analysing Structure in Academic Writing*. Postdisciplinary Studies in Discourse. London: Palgrave Macmillan, 2016.

Scalon, T.F. "Echoes of Herodotus in Thucydides: Self-Sufficiency, Admiration and Law." *Historia* 43 (1994) 143–76.

Schepens, Guido, and John Bollansée, eds. *The Shadow of Polybius: Intertextuality as a Research Tool in Greek Historiography: Proceedings of the International Colloquium, Leuven, 21–22 September 2001*. SH 42. Leuven: Peeters, 2005.

Schiffner, Kerstin. *Lukas liest Exodus: Eine Untersuchung zur Aufnahme ersttestamentlicher Befreiungsgeschichte im lukanischen Werk als Schrift-Lektüre*. BWA(N)T 9. Stuttgart: Kohlhammer, 2008.

Schleiermacher, Friedrich. *A Critical Essay on the Gospel of St. Luke*. London: John Taylor, 1825.

Schmeling, Gareth L. *The Novel in the Ancient World*. MBCB 159. Leiden: E.J. Brill, 1996.

Schmid, Wolf. *Narratology: An Introduction*. New York: Walter de Gruyter, 2010.

Schmidt, Karl Ludwig. "Die Stellung der Evangelien in der allgemeinen Literaturgeschichte." *ΕΥΧΑΡΙΣΤΗΙΟΝ: Studien zur Religion und Literatur des Alten und Neuen Testaments*, 59–62. FRLANT 36. Göttingen: Vandenhoeck & Ruprecht, 1923.

Schmitz, Thomas. "Narrator and Audience in Philostratus' Lives of the Sophists." In *Philostratus*, edited by Ewen Bowie and Jaś Elsner, 49–68. Cambridge: Cambridge University, 2009.

Schrader, Karl. *Der Apostel Paulus*. Leipzig, 1836.

Schreck, Christopher J. "The Nazareth Pericope: Luke 4:16–30 in Recent Study." In *L'evangile de Luc*, edited by F. Neirynck, 399–471. Leuven: Leuven University, 1989.

Schrift, Alan D. "Introduction." In *The History of Continental Philosophy*, edited by Alan D. Schrift and David Ingram, 6:1–17. 8 Vols. Chicago: University of Chicago, 2010.

Schubert, Paul. "The Structure and Significance of Luke 24." In *Neutestamentliche Studien für Rudolf Bultmann zu seinem siebzigsten Gerburtstag am 20. August 1954*, edited by Walther Eltester, 165–86. BNZW 21. Berlin: A. Töpelmann, 1957.

Schürmann, Heinz. *Das Lukasevangelium: Erster Teil: Kommentar zu Kap. 1,1–9, 50*. HTKNT 3/1. Freiburg: Herder, 1969.

Schwankl, Otto. *Die Sadduzäerfrage (Mk 12, 18–27 parr): Eine exegetisch-theologische Studie zur Auferstehungserwartung*. BBB 66. Frankfurt am Main: Athenäum, 1987.

Schwartz, Daniel R. "The End of the ΓΗ (Acts 1:8): Beginning or End of the Christian Vision?" *JBL* 105 (1986) 669–76.

Schwartz, Daniel R. *Agrippa I: The Last King of Judaea*. TSAJ 23. Tübingen: J.C.B. Mohr, 1990.

Schwartz, Seth. *Josephus and Judean Politics*. CSCT 18. Leiden: Brill, 1990.

Schweitzer, Albert. *The Quest of the Historical Jesus*. Translated by John Bowden. Minneapolis: Fortress, 2001.

Scolnic, B.E. *Alcimus, Enemy of the Maccabees*. SJ. Lanham, Mar.: University Press of America, 2005.

Segal, Michael. *The Book of Jubilees: Rewritten Bible, Redaction, Ideology and Theology*. JSJSup 117. Leiden: Brill, 2007.

Shapiro, Michael. "Explorations into Markedness." *Language* 48 (1972) 343–64.

Shellard, Barbara. *New Light on Luke: Its Purpose, Sources, and Literary Context*. JSNTSup 215. London: Sheffield Academic, 2002.

Shin, Gabriel Kyo-Seon. *Die Ausrufung des endgültigen Jubeljahres durch Jesus in Nazaret: Eine historische-kritische Studie zu Lk 4,16–30*. Bern: Peter Lang, 1989.

Shrimpton, Gordon Spencer. *History and Memory in Ancient Greece*. Montreal: McGill-Queen's University Press, 1997.

Shrimpton, Gordon Spencer, and K.M. Gillis. "Herodotus' Source Citations." In *History and Memory in Ancient Greece*, by Gordon Spencer Shrimpton, 231–65. Montreal: McGill-Queen's University, 1997.

Shuler, Philip L. *A Genre for the Gospels: The Biographical Character of Matthew*. Philadelphia: Fortress, 1982.

Shultz, Siegfried. *Q: Die Spruchquelle der Evangelisten*. Zurich: Theologischer Verlag, 1972.

Silhanek, D.K. "Pylos Revisited: Thucydides' Primary Source." *CW* 64 (1970) 10–13.

Simpson, Peter. "Aristotle on Poetry and Imitation." *Hermes* 116 (1988) 279–91.

Sinding, Michael. "Foregrounding." In *Routledge Encyclopedia of Narrative Theory*, edited by David Herman, 18. London: Routledge, 2005.

Skinner, Joseph E. *Invention of Greek Ethnography*. Oxford: Oxford University Press, 2016.

Smarczyk, Bernhard. "Thucydides and Epigraphy." In *Brill's Companion to Thucydides*, edited by Antonios Rengakos and Antonis Tsakmakis, 495–522. Leiden: Brill, 2006.

Smith, Daniel Lynwood and Zachary Lundin Kostopoulos. "Biography, History, and the Genre of Luke-Acts." *NTS* 63 (2017): 390–410.

Smith, Justin Marc. "Genre, Sub-Genre, and Questions of Audience: A Proposed Typology for Greco-Roman Biography." *JGChJ* 4 (2007) 184–216.

Smith, Justin Marc. *Why βίος?: On the Relationship between Gospel Genre and Implied Audience*. LNTS 518. London: T&T Clark, 2015.

Smith, Morton. "Prolegomena to a Discussion of Aretalogies, Divine Men, the Gospels, and Jesus." *JBL* 90 (1971) 174–99.

Smith, Morton. *Jesus the Magician*. San Francisco: Harper & Row, 1978.

Smith, Morton, and Moses Hadas. *Heroes and Gods: Spiritual Biographies in Antiquity*. London: Routledge & Kegan Paul, 1965.

Sneen, Donald J. "An Exegesis of Luke 1:1–4 with Special Regard to Luke's Purpose as a Historician." *ExpTim* 83 (1971) 40–43.

Soderqvist, Thomas. *History and Poetics of Scientific Biography*. New York: Routledge, 2017.

Soliday, Mary. *Everyday Genres: Writing Assignments Across the Disciplines*. Carbondale, Ill.: Southern Illinois University, 2010.

Songer, H.S. "Luke's Portrayal of the Origins of Jesus." *RevExp* 64 (1967) 453–63.

Spencer, Patrick E. *Rhetorical Texture and Narrative Trajectories of the Lukan Galilean Ministry Speeches*. LNTS 341. London: T&T Clark, 2007.

Squires, J.T. *The Plan of God in Luke-Acts*. SNTSMS 76. Cambridge: Cambridge University, 1993.

Sreedharan, E. *A Textbook of Historiography, 500 B.C. to A.D. 2000*. New Delhi: Orient Blackswan, 2009.

Stadter, Philip. "Biography and History." *A Companion to Greek and Roman Historiography*, edited by John Marincola, 528–40. BCAW. Malden: Blackwell, 2007.

Stanley, Christopher D. "Paul and Homer: Greco-Roman Citation Practice in the First Century CE." *NovT* 32 (1990) 48–78.

Stanley, Christopher D. *Paul and the Language of Scripture: Citation Technique in the Pauline Epistles and Contemporary Literature.* SNTSMS 69. Cambridge: Cambridge University, 1992.

Stanley, Christopher D. "'Pearls before Swine': Did Paul's Audience Understand his Biblical Quotations?" *NovT* 41 (1999) 124–44.

Stegner, William Richard. *Narrative Theology in Early Jewish Christianity*. Westminster: John Knox, 1989.

Stein, Robert H. *Luke*. NAC 24. Nashville: Broadman & Holman, 1992.

Steiner, R.C. "Incomplete Circumcision in Egypt and Edom: Jeremiah (9:24–25) in the Light of Josephus and Jonckheere." *JBL* 118 (1999) 497–505.

Stem, Stephen Rex. *The Political Biographies of Cornelius Nepos*. Ann Arbor: University of Michigan, 2012.

Stendahl, Krister. *The School of St. Matthew, and Its Use of the Old Testament.* Philadelphia: Fortress, 1968.

Stenschke, Christopher W. *Luke's Portrait of Gentiles Prior to Their Coming to Faith.* WUNT 2.108. Tübingen: Mohr Siebeck, 1999.

Sterling, Gregory E. *Historiography and Self-Definition: Josephos, Luke-Acts, and Apologetic History*. NovTSup 64. Leiden: Brill, 1992.

Sterling, Gregory E. "The Jewish Appropriation of Hellenistic Historiography." In *A Companion to Greek and Roman Historiography*, edited by J. Marincola, 231–43. BCAW. Malden, Mass.: Blackwell, 2007.

Stevens, Bonnie Klomp, and Larry L. Stewart. *A Guide to Literary Criticism and Research.* Fort Worth, Tex.: Harcourt Brace College, 1996.

Steyn, Gert J. *Septuagint Quotations in the Context of the Petrine and Pauline Speeches of the Acta Apostolorum*. Kampen: Kok Pharos, 1995.

Steyn, Gert J. "Luke's Use of ΜΙΜΗΣΙΣ: Reopening the Debate." In *The Scriptures in the Gospels*, edited by Christopher M. Tuckett, 551–57. BETL 131. Leuven: Leuven University, 1997.

Stewart, Susan. *On Longing: Narratives of the Miniature, the Gigantic, the Souvenir, the Collection*. Baltimore: Johns Hopkins University, 1984.

Strasburger, Hermann. *Homer und die Geschichtsschreibung*. Sitzungsberichte der Heidelberger Akademie der Wissenschaften, Philosophisch-Historische Klasse, 1972/1. Heidelberg: Carl Winter Universitätsverlag, 1972.

Streeter, B.H. *The Four Gospels; A Study of Origins, Treating of the Manuscript Tradition, Sources, Authorship, & Dates*. London: Macmillan, 1930.

Stuart, D.R. *Epochs of Greek and Roman Biography*. New York: Biblo and Tannen, 1928.

Subramanian, J. Samuel. *The Synoptic Gospels and the Psalms as Prophecy*. LNTS 351. London: T&T Clark, 2007.

Swales, John. *Genre Analysis: English in Academic and Research Settings*. Cambridge: Cambridge University, 1991.

Swales, John. "Texts and its Commentaries: Toward a Reception History of 'Genre in Three Literary Traditions' (Hyon, 1996)." In *Genre Studies Around the Globe: Beyond the Three Traditions*, edited by Natasha Artemeva and Aviva Freedman, 1–15. Bloomington: Trafford, 2016.

Swanston, Hamish. "The Lukan Temptation Narrative." *JTS* 17 (1966) 71.

Swart, G.J. "Rahab and Esther in Josephus—An Intertextual Approach." *APB* 17 (2006) 50–65.

Syme, Ronald. "History or Biography. The Case of Tiberius Caesar." *Historia* 23 (1974) 481–96.

Talbert, Charles H. *What Is a Gospel?: The Genre of the Canonical Gospels*. London: S.P.C.K., 1978.

Talbert, Charles H. *Literary Patterns, Theological Themes, and the Genre of Luke-Acts*. Missoula: Scholars, 1987.

Talbert, Charles H. *Reading Luke: A Literary and Theological Commentary on the Third Gospel*. RNTS. Macon, Geo.: Smyth & Helwys, 2002.

Talbert, Charles H. *The Development of Christology During the First Hundred Years, and Other Essays on Early Christian Christology*. NovTSup 140. Leiden: Brill, 2011.

Talshir, Zipora. *I Esdras: From Origin to Translation*. Atlanta: Society of Biblical Literature, 1999.

Tamiolaki, Melina. "Xenophon's Cyropaedia: Tentative Answers to an Enigma." In *The Cambridge Companion to Xenophon*, edited by Michael A. Flower, 174–94. Cambridge Companions to Literature. Cambridge: Cambridge University, 2017.

Tannehill, Robert C. *The Narrative Unity of Luke-Acts: A Literary Interpretation*. FF. Philadelphia: Fortress, 1986.

Tatum, W.B. "The Epoch of Israel: Luke i–ii and the Theological Plan of Luke-Acts." *NTS* 13 (1966–67) 184–95.

Taylor, Joan E. *The Immerser: John the Baptist within Second Temple Judaism*. Grand Rapids: Eerdmans, 1997.

Taylor, Vincent. *Behind the Third Gospel: A Study of the Proto-Luke Hypothesis*. Oxford: Clarendon, 1926.

Taylor, Vincent. *The Passion Narrative of St. Luke: A Critical and Historical Investigation*, edited by Owen E. Evans. SNTSMS 19. Cambridge: Cambridge University, 1971.

Temmerman, Koen de, and Kristoffel Demoen, eds. *Writing Biography in Greece and Rome: Narrative Technique and Fictionalization*. Cambridge: Cambridge University, 2016.

Thackeray, Henry St.J. *Josephus, the Man and the Historian*. New York: Jewish Institute of Religion, 1929.

Theisohn, Johannes. *Der auserwählte Richter: Untersuchungen z. traditionsgeschichtl. Ort d. Menschensohngestalt d. Bilderreden d. Äthiopischen Henoch*. SUNT 12. Göttingen: Vandenhoeck und Ruprecht, 1975.

Thiselton, Anthony. "Semantics and New Testament Interpretation." In *New Testament Interpretation: Essays on Principles and Methods*, edited by I. Howard Marshal, 75–104. Grand Rapids, Mich.: Eerdmans, 1977.

Thiselton, Anthony. "Keeping up with Recent Studies: Structuralism and Biblical Studies: Method or Ideology?" *ExpTim* 89 (Oct 1977–Sep 1978) 331.

Thiselton, Anthony. *New Horizons in Hermeneutics*. Grand Rapids: Zondervan, 1992.

Thomas, David. "Introduction." In *The Landmark Xenophon's Hellenika*. Translated by John Marincola, ix–lxvi. New York: Anchor Books, 2009.

Thomas, K.J. "Liturgical Citations in the Synoptics." *NTS* 22 (1975–76) 205–14.

Thomas, Rosalind. *Literacy and Orality in Ancient Greece*. Cambridge: Cambridge University, 1992.

Thompson, Clive. "Bakhtin's 'Theory' of Genre." *Studies in 20th Century Literature* 9 (1984) 29–40.

Thompson, G.H.P. "Called—Proved—Obedient: A Study in the Baptism and Temptation Narratives of Matthew and Luke." *JTS* (1960) 1–12.

Thompson, Thomas L. *The Messiah Myth: The Near Eastern Roots of Jesus and David*. New York: Basic Books, 2005.

Tiede, David Lenz. *The Charismatic Figure as Miracle Works*. Missoula: Society of Biblical Literature, 1972.

Tiede, David Lenz. *Prophecy and History in Luke-Acts*. Philadelphia: Fortress, 1980.

Tiede, David Lenz. *Luke*. ACNT. Minneapolis: Augsburg, 1988.

Todorov, Tzvetan. "The Origins of Genre." In *Modern Genre Theory*, edited by Duff, David, 193–209. New York: Routledge, 2000. Rep. from Tzvetan Todorov, *Genres in Discourse*. Translated by Catherine Porter. Cambridge: Cambridge University, 1978, 13–76.

Todorov, Tzvetan. *Genres in Discourse*. Translated by Catherine Porter. Cambridge: Cambridge University, 1978.

Tomic, O.M., ed. *Markedness in Synchrony and Diachrony*. Berlin: Mouton, 1989.

Torrey, Charles Cutler. "The Nature and Origin of 'First Esdras.'" *AJSL* 23 (1907) 116–41.

Torrey, Charles Cutler. *Ezra Studies*. Chicago: University of Chicago, 1910.

Torrey, Charles Cutler. *Our Translated Gospels; Some of the Evidence*. London: Harper & Bros, 1936.

Tov, Emanuel. "Forward." In *Qumran Cave 4. VIII: Parabiblical Texts, Part 1*, edited by Harold W. Attridge and James C. VanderKam, ix. Oxford: Clarendon, 1994.

Troftgruben, Troy M. *A Conclusion Unhindered: A Study of the Ending of Acts Within Its Literary Environment*. WUNT 2.280. Tübingen: Mohr Siebeck, 2010.

Tsagalis, Christos C. "Names and Narrative Technique's in Xenophon's Anabasis." In *Narratology and Interpretation: The Content of Narrative Form in Ancient Literature*, edited by Jonas Grethlein and Antonios Rengakos, 451–80. TCSup 4. Berlin: Walter de Gruyter, 2009.

Tuckett, C.M. *The Revival of the Griesbach Hypothesis: An Analysis and Appraisal.* SNTSMS 44. Cambridge: Cambridge University, 1983.

Tuplin, Christopher. *The Failings of Empire: A Reading of Xenophon Hellenica 2.3.11–7.5.27*. HE 76. Stuttgart: Steiner, 1993.

Turner, Max. *Power from on High: The Spirit in Israel's Restoration and Witness in Luke-Acts*. Sheffield: Sheffield Academic, 1996.

Twagilimana, Aimable. *Race and Gender in the Making of an African American Literary Tradition*. Oxford: Taylor and Francis, 2016.

Tyson, Joseph B. "The Birth Narratives and the Beginning of Luke's Gospel." *Semeia* 52 (1991) 103–20.

Uytanlet, Samson. *Luke-Acts and Jewish Historiography. A Study on the Theology, Literature, and Ideology of Luke-Acts*. WUNT 2.366. Tübingen: Mohr Siebeck, 2014.

VanderKam, J.C. "The Origins and Purposes of the Book of Jubilees." In *Studies in the Book of Jubilees*, edited by Matthias Albani et al., 3–24. TSAJ 65. Tübingen: Mohr Siebeck, 1997.

Van Langendonck, Willy. "Markedness, Prototypes and Language Acquisition." *Cahiers de' l'institut de Linguistique de Louvain* 12 (1986) 39–76.

van Unnik, W.C. "Remarks on the Purpose of Luke's Historical Writing (Luke 1.1–4)." In *Sparsa Collecta: The Collected Essays of W.C. van Unnik*, by W.C. van Unnik, 6–15. Leiden: Brill, 1973.

van Unnik, W.C. "Once More St Luke's Prologue." *Neot* 7 (1973) 7–26.

Ventola, Eija, ed. *Functional and Systemic Linguistics: Approaches and Uses*. TL. SM 55. Berlin: Mouton de Gruyter, 1991.

Ventola, Eija. *Perspectives on Multimodality*. Amsterdam: Benjamins, 2004.

Vermes, Geza. *Scripture and Tradition in Judaism: Haggadic Studies*. StPB 4. Leiden: Brill, 1961.

Vermes, Geza. "Biblical Exegesis at Qumran." In *Yigael Yadin Memorial Volume, Eretz-Israel XX*. Jerusalem: Israel Exploration Society, 1989, 184–91. Rep. in *Scrolls, Scriptures, and Early Christianity*, edited by G. Vermes, 41–55. LSTS 56. London. New York: T&T Clark, 2005.

Vielhauer, Philipp. *Geschichte der urchristlichen Literatur*. Berlin: de Gruyter, 1975.

Virtanen, Tuija. "Variation across Texts and Discourses: Theoretical and Methodological Perspectives on Text Type and Genre." In *Syntactic Variation and Genre*, edited by Anja Wanner and Heidrun Dorgeloh, 53–84. TEL. Berlin: De Gruyter, 2010.

Votaw, C.W. "The Gospels and Contemporary Biographies." *AJT* 19 (1915) 45–73, 217–49.

Wacholder, Benjamin. *Eupolemus: A Study of Judaeo-Greek Literature*. MHUC 3. New York: Hebrew Union College-Jewish Institute of Religion, 1974.

Walbank, F.W. "Polemic in Polybius." *JRS* 52 (1962): 1–12. Reprinted in *Selected Papers: Studies in Greek and Roman History and Historiography*, edited by F.W. Walbank, 262–79. Cambridge: Cambridge University, 2010.

Walbank, F.W. *Polybius*. Sather Classical Lectures 42. Berkeley: University of California, 1990.

Walbank, F.W. *Polybius, Rome, and the Hellenistic World: Essays and Reflections*. New York: Cambridge University, 2002.

Wallace-Hadrill, Andrew. *Suetonius: The Scholar and His Caesars*. London: Duckworth, 1983.

Wallace, Stephen. "Figure and Ground: The Interrelationships of Linguistic Categories." In *Tense-Aspect: Between Semantics and Pragmatics*, edited by P.J. Hopper, 201–223. Amsterdam: John Benjamins, 1982.

Walton, Steve. "What Are the Gospels? Richard Burridge's Impact on Scholarly Understanding of the Genre of the Gospels." *CBR* 14 (2015) 81–93.

Ward, Bernard. *The Holy Gospel According to Saint Luke with Introduction and Notes*. ECSSH. London: Catholic Truth Society, 1897.

Warren, James. "Diogenes Laërtius, Biography of History." In *Ordering Knowledge in the Roman Empire*, edited by Jason König, 133–49. Cambridge: Cambridge University, 2011.

Waters, K.H. *Herodotus the Historian: His Problems, Methods and Originality*. Norman, Oak.: University of Oklahoma, 1985.

Watts, Joel L. *Mimetic Criticism and the Gospel of Mark: An Introduction and Commentary*. Eugene, Org.: Wipf & Stock, 2013.

Watts, Rikki E. *Isaiah's New Exodus and Mark*. WUNT 2.88. Tübingen: Mohr Siebeck, 1997.

Watts, Rikki E. "Mark." In *Commentary on the New Testament Use of the Old Testament*, edited by G.K. Beale and D.A. Carson, 111–249. Grand Rapids: Baker Academic, 2007.

Webb, Robert L. *John the Baptizer and Prophet: A Socio-Historical Study*. JSNTSup 62. Sheffield: Sheffield Academic, 1991.

Weber, Wilhelm. *Josephus und Vespasian: Untersuchungen zu dem juedischen Krieg des Flavius Josephus*. Stuttgart: W. Kohlhammer, 1921.

Webster, T.B.L. "The Architecture of Sentences." In *Studies in French Language and Mediaeval Literature: Presented to Prof. Mildred K. Pope*, edited by E.J. Arnould et al., 381–92. Manchester: Manchester University, 1939.

Wehrli, Fritz. "Gnome, Anecdote and Biography." *Museum Helveticum* 30 (1973) 193–208.

Weima, Jeffrey A.D. *Paul the Ancient Letter Writer: An Introduction to Epistolary Analysis*. Grand Rapids: Baker Academic, 2016.

Wellek, René, and Austin Warren. *Theory of Literature*. New York: Harcourt, Brace and Company, 1948.

Wendel, Susan J. *Scriptural Interpretation and Community Self-Definition in Luke-Acts and the Writings of Justin Martyr*. NovTSup 139. Leiden: Brill, 2011.

Wenk, Matthias. *Community-Forming Power: The Socio-Ethical Role of the Spirit in Luke-Acts*. London: T&T Clark, 2004.

van Wess, Hans. "Thucydides on Early Greek History." In *The Oxford Handbook of Thucydides*, edited by Sara Forsdyke, Edith Foster, and Ryan K. Balot, 39–62. Oxford: Oxford University, 2017.

West, Stephanie. "Herodotus' Epigraphical Interests." *CQ* 35 (1985) 278–305.

Westfall, Cynthia Long. *A Discourse Analysis of the Letter to the Hebrews: The Relationship between Form and Meaning*. LNTS 297. SNTG 11. London: T&T Clark, 2005.

Westlake, H.D. "ΛΕΓΕΤΑΙ in Thucydides." *Mnemosyne* 30 (1977) 345–62.

Westlake, H.D. "Thucydides on Pausanias and Themistocles—A Written Source?" *CQ* 110 (1977) 95–110.

Whidden, S.A. *Models of Collaboration in Nineteenth-Century French Literature: Several Authors, One Pen*. Farnham, Eng.: Ashgate, 2009.

Wifstrand, Albert. *Epochs and Styles: Selected Writings on the New Testament, Greek Language and Greek Culture in the Post-Classical Era*, edited by Lars Rydbeck and Stanley E. Porter. Translated by Denis Searby. WUNT 179. Tübingen: Mohr Siebeck, 2005.

Wilder, Laura. *Rhetorical Strategies and Genre Conventions in Literary Studies: Teaching and Writing in the Disciplines*. Carbondale, Ill.: Southern Illinois University, 2012.

Wilkens, Wilhelm. "Die Versuchungsgeschichte Luk. 4, 1–13 und die Komposition des Evangeliums." *ThZ* 30 (1974) 267–72.

Willamson, H.G.M. *Israel in the Books of Chronicles*. Cambridge: Cambridge University, 1977.

Willamson, H.G.M. *Ezra-Nehemiah*. WBC 16. Dallas: Word, 2002.

Willis, Lawrence M. *The Quest for the Historical Gospel: Mark, John and the Origins of the Gospel Genre*. London: Routledge, 1997.

Willoughby, Robert. "The Concept of Jubilee in Luke 4:18–30." In *Mission and Meaning: Essays Presented to Peter Cotterell*, edited by Antony Billington, et al., 41–55. Carlisle: Paternoster, 1995.

Winn, Adam. *Mark and the Elijah-Elisha Narrative: Considering the Practice of Greco-Roman Imitation in the Search for Markan Source Material*. Eugene, Org.: Pickwick, 2010.

Winters, Margaret E. "Toward a Theory of Syntactic Prototypes." In *Meanings and Prototypes: Studies in Linguistic Categorization*, edited by Savas L. Tsohatzidis, 285–307. London: Routledge, 1990.

Witherington, Ben. *History, Literature, and Society in the Book of Acts*. Cambridge: Cambridge, 1996.

Witherington, Ben. *The Acts of the Apostles: A Socio-Rhetorical Commentary*. Grand Rapids: Eerdmans, 1998.

Wright, N.T. *Jesus and the Victory of God*. COQG. Philadelphia: Fortress, 1996.

Yang, Bingjun, and Rui Wang. *Language Policy: A Systemic Functional Linguistic Approach*. China Perspectives Series. New York: Routledge, 2017.

Yoder, Joshua. *Representatives of Roman Rule Roman Provincial Governors in Luke-Acts.* BZNW 209. Berlin: Gruyter, 2014.

Zeller, Eduard, and Joseph Dare. *The Contents and Origin of the Acts of the Apostles, Critically Investigated.* Whitefish, Mon.: Kessinger, 2009 (org. 1875).

Ziem, Alexander, and Catherine Schwerin. *Frames of Understanding in Text and Discourse: Theoretical Foundations and Descriptive Applications.* Human Cognitive Processing 48. Amsterdam: John Benjamins, 2014.

Zimmermann, Frank. *The Aramaic Origin of the Four Gospels.* New York: Ktav, 1979.

Index of Ancient Authors

Index of Modern Authors

Printed in the United States
By Bookmasters